THE POLITICAL CULTURE OF THE ABBASID COURT (279–324 AH/892–936 CE)

RESOURCES IN ARABIC AND ISLAMIC STUDIES

Number 16
The Political Culture of the Abbasid Court (279–324 AH/892–936 CE)

THE POLITICAL CULTURE OF THE ABBASID COURT

(279–324 AH/892–936 CE)

DAVID MARMER

LOCKWOOD PRESS
Columbus, Georgia
2025

THE POLITICAL CULTURE OF THE ABBASID COURT

(279–324 AH/892–936 CE)

ISBN 978-1-957454-56-6 (hardcover)

Cover design by Susanne Wilhelm.

Cover image: Portrait of the Abbāsid Caliph al-Muqtadir (d. 932) from the genealogy Zübdet-üt Tevarih (1598). Wikimedia Commons, general domain.

Library of Congress Cataloging-in-Publication Data

Names: Marmer, David Bruce Jay, 1966- author
Title: The political culture of the Abbasid Court (279-324 AH/892-936 CE) / David Bruce Jay Marmer.
Description: Columbus : Lockwood Press, 2025. | Series: Resources in Arabic and Islamic studies ; 16 | Revised version of the author's Ph. D. dissertation, Princeton University, 1994. | Includes bibliographical references and index. | Summary: "This study is an analysis of the behavior of different individuals and groups at the Abbasid court-the center of the largest empire in the world in the eighth-ninth centuries CE-during a period of political turmoil and governmental collapse, between the years 892 and 932. The study explores how individuals viewed themselves relative to their peers and competitors both within and outside their social/professional groups and at the strategies different individuals employed to cope with the increasing social and political instability. The book, which proceeds both chronologically and thematically, beginning with a period of revival and superior leadership and concluding with one of incompetence and regicide, is also an attempt to uncover individual and group dynamics relevant to the study of other periods, contexts, and courts"— Provided by publisher.
Identifiers: LCCN 2025036585 (print) | LCCN 2025036586 (ebook) | ISBN 9781957454566 hardcover | ISBN 9781957454542 pdf
Subjects: LCSH: Abbasids | Political culture—Islamic Empire | Islamic Empire—History—750-1258 | Islamic Empire—Court and courtiers
Classification: LCC DS38.6 .M375 2025 (print) | LCC DS38.6 (ebook)
LC record available at https://lccn.loc.gov/2025036585
LC ebook record available at https://lccn.loc.gov/2025036586

Printed in the United States of America on acid-free paper.

Contents

Series Editors' Preface

In July 2022, at the Fifteenth Meeting of The School of 'Abbasid Studies (hosted at St John's College Oxford), David Marmer, someone we were meeting for the first time, presented the paper, "Greed is Good: A Look at the Mercantile World of Third/Ninth Century Baghdad." We were impressed with the research, the analysis, and the conclusions and urged him to submit it to the Journal of Abbasid Studies. While it was being refereed (and it has since appeared), Monique Bernards—a director of the school, managing editor of the Journal, and RAIS advisory board member—contacted us and suggested David Marmer's unpublished 1994 Princeton dissertation, "The Political Culture of the Abbasid Court, 279–324 A.H." for our series. We found it to be as compelling as the presentation we'd heard and asked David if he would be interested in having it published. To our delight, he agreed, and we decided that it would appear under the same title.

In the time since he undertook his research for the dissertation, one very significant work has been published about the period 279–324/892–936, namely, *Crisis and Continuity at the Abbasid Court: Formal and Informal Politics in the Caliphate of al-Muqtadir (295–320/908–32)*, coauthored by Maaike van Berkel, Nadia El Cheikh, Hugh Kennedy, and Letizia Osti (Leiden: Brill, 2013). Many of the conclusions they draw concur with the findings of David Marmer from twenty years earlier, a testament to his acumen when reading the sources, something on display also in his paper, "Financial Risk Assessment and Investment Management in Third/Ninth Century Baghdad," delivered at the Sixteenth Meeting of the School of Abbasid Studies (hosted at Università Cà Foscari, Venice) in July 2024, and soon to appear also in the *Journal of Abbasid Studies*. As these articles reveal, David knows about finance. A successful banker and financial consultant, he only recently decided to return to his research. We are very pleased indeed that it is through our series that his first major work will be broadly disseminated.

As always, we are grateful to the Lockwood and ISD team Billie Jean Collins, Ian Stevens, and Susanne Wilhelm—who are always a joy to work with.

Joseph E. Lowry
Devin J. Stewart
Shawkat M. Toorawa

Preface

This publication is a lightly edited version of the dissertation I wrote thirty years ago, under the supervision of Professor Michael Cook at Princeton University. I did not publish any version of that research until now, for multiple reasons: I was exhausted from the writing process and could not imagine undertaking any serious editing at the time; I also instinctively believed I needed distance from the material—and a little more intellectual maturity—before making necessary improvements. Most importantly: I wanted to explore a career in financial markets, which led to a twenty-five-year professional detour, and corresponding hiatus from academic research. I have finally rediscovered my love for research in Islamic history, and thankfully have been granted the opportunity—much delayed by my own decisions—to finally publish this research.

I should immediately address one obvious question: is this text still relevant? I was originally inspired by Roy Mottahedeh's *Loyalty and Leadership in an Early Islamic Society* (1980), which explores the structure of relationships in a premodern Islamic society: I was fascinated by the attempt to understand human connections and societal patterns, which would both humanize a society distant in time, and also illuminate mechanisms that facilitate comparisons with other societies. In my doctoral research, I endeavored to capture the variety of such relationships, in one specific location during a short period of significant stress, as a once-flourishing empire, the Abbasid Empire of the ninth–tenth centuries CE, centered in Baghdad, was in the process of collapse. At the time, my dissertation was one of the few pieces of research from early Islamic history to view and analyze the imperial court elite as a collection of individuals forming social groups and alliances, reacting to conditions of dramatic change. To the best of my knowledge, this remains one of the few pieces of research to look at one element of early Islamic society holistically—certainly for the Abbasid period.

I also endeavored to provide copious translations from a variety of original sources; my intention was to give a sense of texture to sociopolitical interactions and to reflect the individuality, personality, and character of historical figures. In reading the original sources, I always found the people of ninth-century Baghdad to be remarkable, and they were described as such by many eloquent and clever authors. I accordingly wanted to make a sampling of this material within its historical context available to a broader audience. I believe that this close interpretation of original texts—and the admiration for the people who appear and are memorialized in them—provides a strong sense of how the people of Baghdad thought, felt, and interacted.

For this publication, I decided to make a minimum of changes: I have cleaned up the language, such as removing unnecessary repetition and exaggeration, or sharpening word choice, and corrected several mistakes in the footnotes; but I have not altered the argumentation or evidence, as I want to be faithful to my thoughts at the time of original writing. Although a full-scale revision after such a long break was impractical, I did, importantly, want to make absolutely clear which ideas were my own—as they appeared in the original dissertation—before the subsequent research of other scholars in the intervening years.

One indication that my research was perhaps headed in the right direction is the fact that a handful of other scholars of Islamic history have taken up similar themes and perspectives, and from roughly the same period of the decline and collapse of the Abbasid state. Maaike van Berkel, Nadia El-Cheikh, Letizia Osti, and Hugh Kennedy have published articles over the past two decades that illuminate various aspects of the Abbasid court; indeed, in 2011 they collectively published *Crisis and Continuity at the Abbasid Court*, which—similar to my dissertation—analyzes the various elements of court society. Their research, however, also incorporates material from the courtier and historian al-Ṣūlī, based upon an Arabic text that had not yet been published at the time of my dissertation.

Given that scholars have pursued and published research from this era of Abbasid history, why read this text, based upon a dissertation from 1994? I believe that the analysis, perceptions, and conclusions remain unique and relevant, something that is especially true of the conclusion, which summarizes the various insights of the work.

Regarding the footnotes, these are largely in the original version, with only cosmetic changes. I have, however, added references from the past thirty years, indicated in the footnotes with an asterisk so that current readers know where to turn for the most recent research. I have also indicated briefly when scholars have either come to similar conclusions, or on minor points disagreed. I have not incorporated subsequent research into the body of the text: the writing thus remains faithful to my original thoughts from thirty years ago.

That said, looking at the material with the benefit of some maturity and a great deal of hindsight, what are my own impressions, and what might I do differently? First, I have learned an important lesson: to publish research as quickly as possible. Second, the research was originally intended to include the activity of judges, whom I view as an important link—socially and culturally—between court society and the general Baghdadi populace. That analysis will not appear here, but will be published separately. Most importantly, this research does not include a theoretical framework. My opinion, when I was a student—which has not significantly changed—is that we still have a huge amount of empirical evidence to collect for Abbasid history; I suspected that approaching the material within a theoretical framework might shift the focus and alter the questions I ask. In short, I wanted to let the evidence guide my observations and interpretations; once we have collected substantial empirical evidence, it will be vital to endeavor to make comparisons to other periods of Islamic history, and human history. Contributing to that ultimate goal remains the main objective of this research.

Acknowledgments

During the past thirty-five years, from the inception of this research to its final publication, many people have contributed to my intellectual and personal growth. Ze'ev Brinner inspired me to undertake academic research and encouraged me to pursue my fascination with Islamic history. Michael Cook was a patient and diligent mentor for a doubtful and often frustrated young scholar-in-training, and continues to be supportive even after an interlude of decades. David Ben-Zur accompanied me for much of this multidecade journey, from the ice storms in Princeton to anxiety attacks in Istanbul; he will always be a cherished part of my life. So many loyal friends have taught me about the joys in life: Dave, Eric, and Brian, Nurit, Nimrod, and Dina, Aaron and Natalie, NB, Alon and David, Daniel, Dror, Carine and Philip, and of course Eli. The Sheldons and Waldmans have always been caring supporters of my various endeavors. Thanks to all of you for sharing so much with me.

Avi has been a remarkable partner for these past years and has given me the peace of mind and freedom to complete this project. I would be lost without him.

I'd like to thank the editors of this series for giving me an opportunity to publish my research, and Monique Bernards for bringing my dissertation to their attention. Special thanks go to Shawkat Toorawa for his generous investment of time and wisdom in this project, and to David Wasserstein for extensive comments on the original dissertation. I'd also like to thank the staff at the Sourasky Library, who helped me digitize an old and faded photocopy of my dissertation.

Most importantly, I wish to thank—and honor—my entire family: Charlene, Melinda, and Alan: you have always wrapped me in love; I cannot be more grateful. My nieces and nephews are a constant source of pride. And most of all, Mom and Dad: thank you for raising me to become whatever person I wanted to be. Nobody could ever ask for more than that.

David Marmer
Tel Aviv, February 2025

Prominent Personages at the Abbasid Court

(dates in office; death date if died not in office)

Abbasids

al-Muʿtaḍid (279–289/892–902)
al-Muktafī (289–295/902–908)
al-Muqtadir (295–320/908–932)
Ibn al-Muʿtazz (d. 296/908)
al-Qāhir (320–322/932–934; d. 339/950)
Prince Abū al-ʿAbbās, later caliph al-Rāḍī (322–329/934–940)

Wazirs

ʿUbaydallāh b. Sulaymān (279–288/892–901)
al-Qāsim b. ʿUbaydallāh (288–291/901–904)
al-ʿAbbās b. al-Ḥasan (291–296/904–908)
Abū al-Ḥasan Ibn al-Furāt (296–299/908–911, 304–306/917–919, 311–312/923–924)
Muḥammad al-Khāqānī (299–301/911–913; d. 312/924)
ʿAlī b. ʿĪsā (301–304/913–917, 314–316/926–928; d.334/946)
Ḥāmid b. al-ʿAbbās (306–311/918–923)
ʿAbdallāh b. Muḥammad al-Khāqānī (312–313/924–925)
Abū al-ʿAbbās al-Khaṣībī (313–314/925–926)
Muḥammad b. ʿAlī, Ibn Muqla (316–318/928–930; d. 328/940)
al-Ḥusayn b. al-Qāsim (319–320/931–932)

Women

Sayyida, Shaghab Umm al-Muqtadir (d. 321/933)
Fāṭima (d. 300/913)
Umm Mūsā (300–310/913–923; d. 315/927)
Thumal (?)
Zaydān (?)

Military Figures

Badr (279–289/892–902)
Sawsan the chamberlain (d. 296/908–909)
Ṣāfī al-Ḥuramī the eunuch (d. 298/910–911)
Gharīb the uncle (295–305/908–917)

Muʾnis al-Khāzin (d. 301/914)
Muʾnis al-Khādim (296–321/908–933)
Naṣr the chamberlain (296–316/908–928)
Hārūn b. Gharīb (305–323/917–935)
Shafīʿ al-Luʾluʾī (d. 312/924–925)
Shafīʿ al-Muqtadirī (died sometime after 320/932)
Ibn Abī al-Sāj (d. 315/928)
Mufliḥ the eunuch (died sometime after 324/936)
Nāzūk (d. 317/929)
Abū al-Hayjāʾ (d. 317/929)
Yāqūt (d. 324/936)

Timeline

279/892
Caliph al-Muʿtaḍid enthroned
289/902
Caliph al-Muktafī enthroned
295/908
Caliph al-Muqtadir enthroned
296/908
Failed coup attempt
296-299/908-911
Ibn al-Furāt 1st wazirate
301-304/913-917
ʿAlī b. ʿĪsā 1st wazirate
305/917
Byzantine delegation
308-309/920-921
Food riots in Baghdad
312/924
Ibn al-Furāt executed
315/927
Qarmatians invade Iraq
317/929
Second failed coup attempt
320/932
Caliph al-Muqtadir murdered.
324/936
Caliph al-Rāḍī appts amīr al-umarāʾ

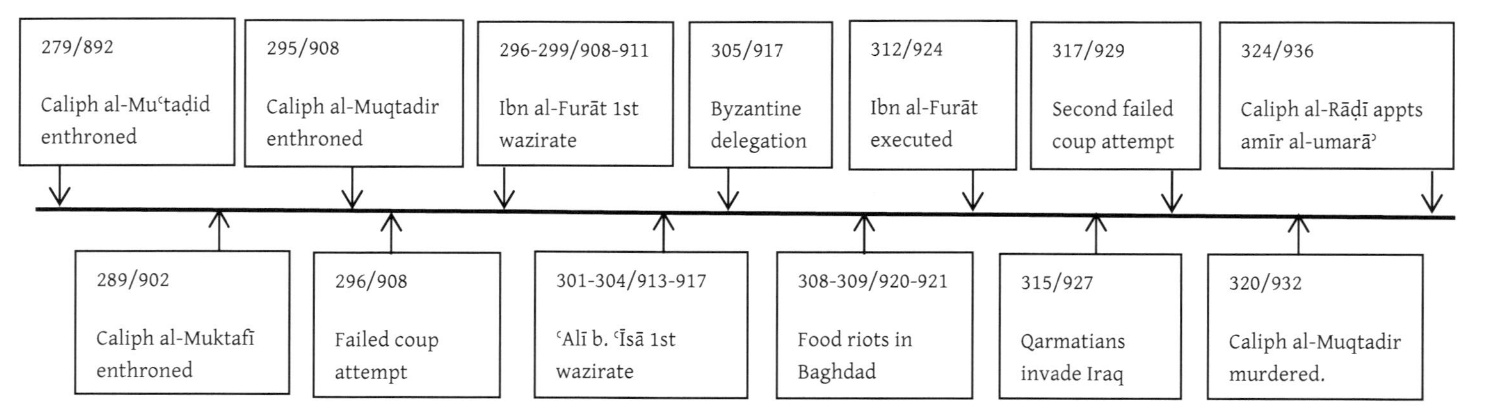

Introduction

The goal of this research is to understand the political culture of the Abbasid court, that is, the ways in which people at the center of the Abbasid Empire competed for power. The setting for this competition was the complex world of the imperial court in Baghdad, a system of social relations and staged events, ceremonial, and scheming. Each member of the court had a specific social position that entailed particular opportunities and limitations for acquiring and maintaining power. The main focus of this analysis will be to examine how individuals developed strategies for manipulating opportunities and maneuvering within restrictions in pursuit of their own interests and to show that these strategies formed patterns of behavior and interaction that made the Abbasid court a coherent sociopolitical system.

The time frame for this analysis is the latter part of the independent Abbasid caliphate, from the return of the capital to Baghdad (279 AH/892 CE) through the delegation of governmental authority to the *amīr al-umarāʾ* (324 AH/936 CE). I have chosen this period for several reasons. The period encompasses a resurgence of Abbasid power under one caliph and the subsequent decline of power under another, a contrast that facilitates insight into the nature of court society. Moreover, the later decades involved tremendous turmoil and competition, so that the mechanisms of sociopolitical behavior and competition are more apparent, enabling us to see how people reacted under conditions of extreme stress. This period also marks the break from centralized caliphal authority to predominantly decentralized military authority (in the form of the *amīr al-umarāʾ* and then the Būyids), which involved different forms of social relations and political culture. In addition, the end of the third Muslim century is blessed with an upsurge in the number, quality, and variety of primary sources available. Finally, this period has been relatively neglected by scholars, as the focus of research has been the "glory years" of the first Abbasid century.[1]

Any study of Abbasid social relations must begin with Roy Mottahedeh's groundbreaking work, *Loyalty and Leadership in an Early Islamic Society*. In this book, Mottahedeh

1. The secondary works that concentrate on this period are: Bowen, *ʿAlī b. ʿĪsā*, a very detailed, but also slightly tedious narrative; Sourdel, *Le Vizirat abbaside*; and Massignon, *The Passion of al-Ḥallāj*, also very detailed works that approach the material from very specific perspectives, and do not try to understand court relations in general; and al-Kabisi, *al-Muqtadir*, which organizes the material in the same way that I will (viz. by social groups), but does not investigate the social and political mechanisms of the court. The best summary of this period is Kennedy, *Prophet and the Age of the Caliphates*.

References to all secondary literature published after the original writing of this dissertation and undertaking of this research will appear with an asterisk (*). As I mention in the preface, the most comprehensive subsequent publication covering the Abbasid Empire of this era, is van Berkel et al, *Crisis and Continuity at the Abbasid Court*, published in 2013.

reconstructs the fundamental patterns of social relations in fourth/tenth century Iraq. He distinguishes between the formal ties that bound individuals, "acquired loyalties," which were generally very strong and expired only upon the death of one party; and the less formal ties within groups, "loyalties of category," which were less strong, acquired involuntarily through participation in preexisting groups (generally professions), and negative in the sense that they engendered cooperation primarily in self-defense. The lasting importance of Mottahedeh's work lies in his presentation of social relations in the terms and concepts of contemporaries, and in his argument that the stability of social relations was based upon bonds between individuals and not among members of a group.[2]

I expand upon Mottahedeh's work in several directions. First, by concentrating on a relatively short period of time (279–324/892–936), and on a small sector of society (the court elite), I undertake a more detailed analysis of personal relations and interactions. In other words, now that we have a cohesive view of how such relations were generated, it is worth taking a closer look at how they were maintained, manipulated, threatened, and defended. More importantly, because Mottahedeh sets out to explain the relations that bound people together, he necessarily emphasizes the stability of these relations. By concentrating on a period of great turmoil, we can problematize the relations outlined by Mottahedeh, and ask: under what conditions did such relations remain intact, or break down? Just how stable were these relations, both between individuals and groups?

I approach these issues by dividing the court into distinct social groups, and by identifying the patterns of social relations and political behavior that were typical for members of these groups. I begin with the caliph, and look at how his power is constructed and wielded, as the construction of this power established certain norms for the rest of court society. I then examine each of the prominent social groups—the royal family, the palace staff, the military, the bureaucracy, and the judiciary[3]—and focus on the dynamics within each social group, as well as the dynamics between members of different social groups. This structure is based upon two assumptions: first, that an individual's participation at court was shaped primarily by the opportunities and limitations of the social group with which he/she was affiliated; and second, that the caliph was the center of the social system, as he largely defined the roles and parameters of activity for everyone else. This presentation of court society is thus, to a great extent, about how the caliph set the rules of political culture, and how everyone else reacted within and against these guidelines. I then try to assess these two fundamental assumptions.[4]

2. Mottahedeh, *Loyalty and Leadership*, especially the introduction, pp. 3–7.

3. *As noted in the preface, I did not manage to include analysis of the judiciary in this research, as originally intended; this will hopefully appear in future publications.

4. *Osti has similar thoughts: "Looking into these troubled years ... can also unveil the inner workings of the different social groups involved and their particular methods for pursuing personal gain" ("ʿAbbāsid Intrigues," 6). So, too, do van Berkel et al: "Through a detailed and systematic examination of the working of the Abbasid institutions, as well as the court ... we shall uncover the formal and informal politics of the ruling family and the various power groups surrounding it" (*Crisis and Continuity*, 2).

In the conclusion, I use my findings to ask more abstract questions about court society. Regarding the assumption that social groups are the defining units of this society, I ask what degree of cohesiveness was achieved in these groups: Do colleagues pursue common goals and group unity? To what extent are people confined by group affiliation, and how important are cross-group alliances? In the relationship between an individual and social position, how much latitude was there for asserting personal uniqueness and individuality within any given social position, and how important were personal differences? The ultimate question here is the relevance of individuals in history, relative to the power of social mechanisms. And I consider the individual's relationship with society as a whole: to what extent could people change the rules or patterns of sociopolitical relations? Could they abandon court society, and live another kind of life? The answers to these questions will affect the way we conceive of power at the Abbasid court.[5]

Like Mottahedeh's book, this analysis does not follow a historical narrative, for two main reasons. First, one of the primary goals is to enable comparisons with other periods of Islamic history and other historical settings in general. A thematic structure, in this case based upon distinct social groups, facilitates such comparisons more than does a narrative.[6] Second, I am highly skeptical about our ability to derive a sequence of historical facts that constitute an accurate narrative. As a result, the basic question I am asking is not "what happened," but "how would it have happened"; my purpose is to look at the mechanisms of behavior rather than the progression of events. Unfortunately, this nonchronological approach can result in back-tracking, repetition, and general confusion. To alleviate such complications, I have added a brief chronological survey at the end of this introduction, along with a timeline and a list of prominent personages at the Abbasid court.

The Sources

For the period under investigation (279–324/892–936), especially the first two decades of the fourth/tenth century, the primary sources are numerous and varied.[7] The most

5. We can conceptualize these questions more compactly as follows: relations between groups; relations within groups; relations between the individual and his/her social position; and relations between an individual and court society. In the conceptualization of these questions, I am highly influenced by Elias, *Court Society*.

6. This preference for a structure that facilitates comparison is founded upon my underlying view regarding the methodology and purpose of Islamic history. I believe that our understanding of Islamic history will be enhanced by comparisons to the historical patterns of other societies. My research is only a first step in that direction, and unfortunately no meaningful comparisons are made here. Ultimately, I see the goal of research in Islamic history, like that of other societies, as contributing to a better understanding of the human condition, through comparisons and contrasts. For this reason, I express the structure of my analysis, and the questions that gradually emerge, in abstract, universal terms, to the extent possible.

7. Rosenthal points this out in the introduction of his translation of al-Ṭabarī (*History of al-Ṭabarī*, 38:xiv).

prominent genre is the historical chronicle. Works of this genre were written chronologically, usually divided by year, and generally purported to convey the most important political events of the time. The crucial work by al-Ṭabarī (d. 310/923), *Tārīkh al-rusul wa'l-mulūk*, runs through the year 302/915; it has been noted, however, that al-Ṭabarī was cautious in relating the events that took place in the later period of his life, and his chronicle is therefore of marginal value after 295/908.[8] Al-Masʿūdī's account in *Murūj al-dhahab* is also brief and unsystematic, yet his selection of anecdotes and poetry sometimes succeeds in capturing the political atmosphere without the narrative filler.[9] Unfortunately these two works are the most systematic accounts we have of the years 279–295/892–908; but this dearth of material is somewhat compensated for by the plethora of material in literary works (*adab*), discussed below. More important for this entire period, especially the fourth/tenth century, are the works of Abū Bakr al-Ṣūlī (d. 335/947),[10] ʿArīb b. Saʿd al-Qurṭubī (d. 370/980)[11], and Miskawayh (d. 421/1030).[12] All three authors follow al-Ṭabarī's general format, with information organized by year, and a general goal of surveying the most important occurrences of the time. A fourth crucial text is that of Hilāl al-Ṣābī (d. 448/1056); his *Kitāb al-Wuzarāʾ*, while focusing on the lives of individual bureaucrats, also incorporates material about the most important events at the Abbasid court during this era.[13]

---

*van Berkel et al have also made this point: "We are amazingly well informed about the politics and culture of the reign [of al-Muqtadir]. The writers who recorded the events of the reign were remarkable in their literary skill, the variety of their approaches and, perhaps most strikingly, their interest in the personalities who dominated the life of the court, with all their achievements" (*Crisis and Continuity*, 1).

8. Rosenthal, *History of al-Ṭabarī*, 38:xiii.

9. For example, al-Masʿūdī relates Ibn Bassām's poems that succinctly characterize the head of the bureaucracy of the wazirate (see ch. 5).

10. *The published edition of *Kitāb al-Awrāq* that was available to me at the time of the dissertation only covered the years 322–333/934–945. A longer edition has since been published, beginning with the year 295/908; I have not incorporated the new material, except for the rare instances when subsequent research by other scholars has led to different conclusion based on this newly available evidence, which I indicate in the footnotes. An excellent recent analysis of al-Ṣūlī's biography and writings is Osti, *History and Memory in the Abbasid Caliphate*.

11. ʿArīb was a courtier at the court in Andalusia (Ch. Pellat, "ʿArīb," *Enyclopaedia of Islam, New Edition* [hereafter *EI2*]). His chronicle is titled *Ṣilat Tārīkh al-Ṭabarī* ("A Continuation of the History of al-Ṭabarī").

12. Miskawayh was a secretary at the Būyid court in Iraq (M. Arkoun, "Miskawayh," *EI2*). His historical chronicle is titled *Tajārib al-umam* ("Experiences of the Nations"). The section of this chronicle for the caliphate of al-Muqtadir, was translated by H. F. Amedroz and D. S. Margoliouth, as *The Eclipse of the Abbasid Caliphate*. The page references here refer to the original Arabic text, edited by Amedroz and Margoliouth. Translations from the Arabic are my own; where my translation is either very similar or follows Amedroz/Margoliouth, I indicate the page numbers from *Eclipse*.

13. Like Miskawayh, Hilāl al-Ṣābī was a secretary at the Būyid court (D. Sourdel, "Hilāl al-Ṣābī," *EI2*). Unfortunately, most of this text is lost; the surviving parts encompass the lives of the wazirs Ibn al-Furāt, al-Khāqānī, and ʿAlī b. ʿĪsā, roughly covering the years 279–316/892–928. Hilāl al-Ṣābī also wrote *Rusūm dār al-khilāfa*, about Abbasid court protocol, which contains important information for this period.

ʿArīb, Miskawayh, and Hilāl al-Ṣābī are the most comprehensive sources for this period, and they complement one another due to their differences. In terms of methodology, Miskawayh and Hilāl al-Ṣābī, both of whom lived in Baghdad, received much of their information directly from the descendants of men who participated in the events about which they write. Moreover, as secretaries in government service with access to state archives, both Miskawayh and Hilāl al-Ṣābī enliven their accounts by reproducing original documents. Many of these documents—such as financial records, policy statements distributed to the provinces, and letters from the wazir to the caliph—focus on administration and the bureaucracy. However, a few documents—the budget of 279–280 (892–893) reproduced by Hilāl al-Ṣābī, and the caliph's written response to the rebellion of 317/929 found in Miskawayh—shed light on court life and politics beyond the world of the bureaucrats. In this regard, ʿArīb is clearly inferior. Writing from the distant Iberian Peninsula, ʿArīb had less access to either documents or informants, and his account is not the view of an insider.[14]

This difference in proximity is reflected in subtle stylistic differences. For the first ten years of al-Muqtadir's reign, that is, 295–305/908–918, ʿArīb relates many orders of the central government in the passive voice, suggesting that he did not quite know who was giving the orders at that time. For example, regarding the reconquest of Fārs in 297–298/910–911, he states on several occasions that generals "were dispatched," not indicating who actually dispatched them. Miskawayh, however, makes very clear that the wazir Ibn al-Furāt gave each of these orders.[15] Generally, Miskawayh and Hilāl al-Ṣābī name the source of a given report, while ʿArīb does not.[16] Because Miskawayh and Hilāl al-Ṣābī were closer to the sources of information, their language is more precise, and their accounts are generally more reliable.

The superiority of Miskawayh and Hilāl al-Ṣābī is somewhat qualified by their emphasis on, and even bias for, bureaucratic issues and personages. Hilāl al-Ṣābī's work is specifically about wazirs, and his interpretation of historical events based upon the bureaucratic perspective is sometimes obviously misplaced.[17] Miskawayh, while covering court politics as a whole, concentrates on bureaucratic intrigue. Fully one fourth of his text (60 of 240 pages, in the English translation) for the years 295–320/908–932 is devoted to the politicking of the wazir Ibn al-Furāt in 306/918–919 and 311–312/923–924; by con-

14. *One caveat regarding ʿArīb: he often quotes al-Ṣūlī, whose information is very much that of a participant at the Abbasid court.

15. ʿArīb, *Ṣilat*, 32 (when Muʾnis is dispatched), and 34 (when Waṣīf Kāmah is dispatched). Both are written in passive voice. Miskawayh clarifies that Ibn al-Furāt gave theses orders. Miskawayh, *Tajārib*, 18–19.

16. The absence of named sources in ʿArīb, relative to Miskawayh and Hilāl al-Ṣābī, undermines the credibility of his accounts, especially when they differ from those of the Iraqi authors.

17. For example, Hilāl al-Ṣābī reports an account that claims that the failure of the coup of 296/908 was due to the nonparticipation of one particular bureaucrat, which ignores the crucial role of military units in the failed coup, as is discussed below.

trast, the general Muʾnis's campaign against al-Muqtadir in 319–320/931–932, and the climactic battle in which the caliph is killed, are recounted in only 4 pages. In general, Miskawayh pays close attention to the vicissitudes of bureaucratic life at the expense of information regarding the military. This is not the case with ʿArīb, who presents a very detailed account of the battle between the forces of Muʾnis and al-Muqtadir; he is more diligent than Miskawayh in reporting military assignments and changes in posts; and he mentions the deaths of important generals, accompanied by interesting biographical material, all of which Miskawayh ignores.[18] ʿArīb also provides most of our information about the extended royal family and the princes. Thus, while Miskawayh and Hilāl al-Ṣābī preserve documents, give intricate bureaucratic details, and more frequently name their sources, ʿArīb provides a more balanced view of court life as a whole.

In addition to these three early sources, we have a variety of later works that contain information for this historical period. The anonymous *ʿUyūn al-ḥadāʾiq*, and the works of al-Hamadhānī (d. 521/1127),[19] Ibn al-Athīr (d. 620/1233),[20] Ibn Kathīr (d. 774/1373),[21] and Ibn Taghrībirdī (d. 874/1470),[22] follow the standard organization of chronicles; they generally paraphrase material found in earlier sources, though the first four occasionally preserve information that is not found elsewhere. Ibn al-Athīr is particularly useful in that he often collates material from multiple sources and rearranges it in a clearer style, though losing much detail in the process. Other sources—such as Ibn al-Jawzī (*al-Muntaẓam*) and al-Dhahabī, who combine chronicles with biographical listings, and the strictly biographical works of al-Khaṭīb al-Baghdādī (*Tārīkh Baghdād*), Yāqūt (*Muʿjam al-udabāʾ*), and Ibn Khallikān—contain limited information not found in early sources, and for the most part only summarize previously recorded material. Since most of these sources focus primarily on intellectuals and the religious sciences, their coverage of court personages is devoted almost exclusively to bureaucrats and judges (with the rare reference to a member of the Abbasid royal family) who participate in cultural activities. Even more than Miskawayh and Hilāl al-Ṣābī, these sources ignore military figures almost entirely.

The other main category of sources is *adab*, literary works typically produced for didactic and entertainment purposes.[23] For the late third/ninth and early fourth/tenth centuries, by far the most important author of this kind is al-Muḥassin b. ʿAlī al-Tanūkhī (d. 384/994).[24] A judge at the Būyid court, al-Tanūkhī could interview men who had wit-

18. For example, ʿArīb provides lengthier accounts of the deaths of military officers Gharīb, Yūnus al-Muwaffaqī, and Shafīʿ al-Luʾluʾī (described in ch. 4).

19. al-Hamadhānī, *Takmilat Tārīkh al-Ṭabarī*.

20. Ibn al-Athīr, *al-Kāmil fī al-tārīkh*.

21. Ibn Kathīr, *al-Bidāya wa-l-nihāya*.

22. Ibn Taghrībirdī, *al-Nujūm al-zāhira*.

23. For more varied definitions of *adab*, and the breadth of works encompassed in this branch of literature, see F. Gabrieli, "Adab," *EI2*; and S. A. Bonebakker, "Adab and the Concept of *belles-lettres*."

24. For the biography of al-Tanūkhī, see H. Fähndrich, "al-Tanūkhī," *EI2*.

nessed earlier events in Baghdad, especially members of his extended family who held senior positions in the Abbasid judiciary for generations; accordingly, he differs from the somewhat later Miskawayh and Hilāl al-Ṣābī in that he relies more on oral transmission than documentary evidence or books.[25] His two lengthy works, the *Nishwār al-muḥāḍara* (partially translated by D. Margoliouth as "The Table-talk of a Mesopotamian Judge"), and *al-Faraj ba*ᶜ*d al-shidda* ("Deliverance Following Adversity), collect anecdotes from the first two centuries of Abbasid rule. The *Nishwār* in particular concentrates on court life in the years after 279/892; in fact, it is the best source we have (in addition to al-Ṭabarī) for the years 279–289 (892–902), and Hilāl al-Ṣābī subsequently derived much of his information from al-Tanūkhī.[26]

The beauty of al-Tanūkhī's two compendia, for our purposes, is that most of the anecdotes convey a theme or moral related to court life; here we have colorful stories regarding the nature of court politics, detached from a narrative structure, which is precisely the focus of this research. Of course, one might object that al-Tanūkhī's stories are perhaps fictional, or at best embellished.[27] I would respond to this concern in two ways. First, as discussed above, I am not specifically interested in "who did what and when;" I am interested in social and political mechanisms: how people acted, or would have acted. From this perspective, the historicity of a given story is virtually irrelevant; the characters in these stories act in ways that are consistent with the current sociopolitical norms and expectations, whether or not the event in question actually took place. In other words, even if the anecdotes are embellished, the sociopolitical context surrounding them is accurate, or they would have had no relevance for the intended audience. Second, such a devaluation of literary anecdotes overvalues historical chronicles. One could make a strong case that the latter also misrepresent or distort historical events, since they include certain information and discard the rest, follow particular biases, and generally present one interpretation of an event that is open to myriad interpretations. We can never truly know "what happened;" but we can approximately know patterns of behavior.

After reading large amounts of source material for one particular period, I have come away with some general impressions. On the one hand I am struck that a limited number of writers can preserve a coherent view of their society for posterity; in reading al-Tanūkhī, ᶜArīb, Miskawayh, and Hilāl al-Ṣābī, we develop a solid sense of what life

---

*A more comprehensive biography of al-Tanūkhī now appears in the introduction to J. Bray's partial translation of al-Tanūkhī's *al-Faraj ba*ᶜ*d al-shidda*, entitled *Stories of Piety and Prayer.*

25. *For al-Tanūkhī's reliance upon family informants, see Bray, "Place and Self Image."

26. Only volumes 1, 2, and 8 survive of the *Nishwār*. However, the editor of this work (ᶜAbbūd Shāljī) has collected anecdotes from later sources that attribute their information to al-Tanūkhī; Shaljī assembled these additional anecdotes as volumes 3–7. Much of volume 5 consists of material that Hilāl al-Ṣābī quoted from al-Tanūkhī.

27. *C. Wickham states that "many of [al-Tanūkhī's] stories were doubtless also invented by himself, not told to him" ("Administrators' Time," 433).

was like at the Abbasid court. On the other hand, these writers often present different accounts of the same dialogue or event, and these differences are most prevalent for important (and hence controversial) events.[28] This reinforces my belief that a chronological narrative cannot be accurately reconstructed. How can we piece together the "facts" of a particular event, when scholars much closer to the event, with far better information, did not produce consistent narratives? In setting aside the reconstruction of a narrative, and concentrating on mechanisms of behavior and competition, my tactics for analyzing the source material are twofold: to look closely at the details of a specific narrative in order to understand how people interacted (not that they necessarily did so on the occasion described); and to look collectively at many reports and anecdotes for patterns of such sociopolitical behavior.

Another impression I derive from the sources is that the authors—al-Tanūkhī in particular—represent court life as a series of binary oppositions: the caliph al-Muʿtaḍid is contrasted with his son al-Muqtadir, the bureaucrat Ibn al-Furāt with his rival ʿAlī b. ʿĪsā, the judge Abū ʿUmar with his colleague Ibn al-Buhlūl. This presentation of contrasts might in fact follow reality, in that many of the interesting personalities and events of history emerge from clashes of opposites, or tend to foster opposition. These contrasts no doubt also serve a literary and didactic purpose: they create a moralizing drama, whereby lessons can be drawn from the past through description and evaluation of alternative approaches to life. I have found this system of oppositions informative and useful, and to a great extent I have incorporated this device in order to elucidate common patterns of behavior, and the flexibility and variabililty of these patterns.

The Abbasid Court

Before turning to an examination of social relations at the Abbasid court, I should first define what I mean by *court*. I understand the court to be a combination of a location, the geographic center of societal authority, usually where government is conducted; and a community of people, namely those who exercise authority over much of society, and manage government.[29] Neither element is independent: people invest particular spaces

28. For example, there is a great deal of contradiction and general confusion regarding the coups of 296/908 and 317/929, the Byzantine visit of 305/917, and the climactic battle in 320/932 that ended with the death of the caliph al-Muqtadir.

29. I concede that societies have more than one center of authority, which is not necessarily where government is conducted. One example might be a religious center, which also disseminates and manipulates social values. The society in question here certainly had an alternative locus of authority, the religious elite, commonly referred to as the *ʿulamāʾ*, who in this case were geographically scattered, albeit with a prominent presence in the imperial capital of Baghdad. The ever-changing relationship between these two centers of authority—the imperial court and the *ʿulamāʾ*—is one of the great questions of Islamic history, and is elusive in part because religious authority was quite diffuse. For the purposes of this research, suffice to say that the most important texts written by and for the court elite of the

and edifices with lasting value, and these spaces and edifices in turn endow changing generations of people with status. In the following discussion I will describe the physical setting of the court, identify the people who constituted it, and analyze the relationship between space and people, that is, how space was used for different social purposes and endowed with different values, and how the competition for power was shaped by understandings of space. Many of the themes that emerge from this discussion of the court will reappear throughout the subsequent analysis of Abbasid sociopolitics.

Political Geography

In 279/892, the energetic and reform-minded Abbasid caliph al-Muʿtaḍid succeeded to the throne. Following a decision apparently initiated by his predecessor, al-Muʿtaḍid abandoned Samarra, the relatively isolated Abbasid palatine capital of the previous half-century, and took up permanent residence in the original imperial capital of Baghdad, the thriving commercial metropolis founded nearly 150 years earlier by the caliph al-Manṣūr. Since the entire administrative structure of the empire moved with al-Muʿtaḍid, Baghdad was once again the capital of the empire. Al-Muʿtaḍid occupied the Ḥasanī palace on the southeast bank of the Tigris River.[30] This was an opportune location for the new royal residence: it was removed from the densely populated neighborhoods of northern and western Baghdad, which was in keeping with long-standing Abbasid policy to maintain a distance from civilians;[31] it was adjacent to primarily open land to the east, which allowed for expansion of the royal grounds and allocation of property to favorites; and it was situated along central waterways (the Tigris, and the Mūsā canal with its tributaries), which enabled easy communication with the rest of the city, and provided an escape route from the palace in case of emergency.[32]

late third/early fourth (late ninth/early tenth) centuries pay little attention to the noncourtly religious elite, just as the biographical works that focus on the religious elite generally ignore court officials.

30. The shift of the Abbasid capital back to Baghdad, and al-Muʿtaḍid's occupation of the Ḥasanī palace, are discussed only briefly in the sources. The Ḥasanī palace already had a long history: originally built by Jaʿfar the Barmakid, the property was subsequently granted to the caliph al-Maʾmūn (when he was actually still a prince), later transferred to the senior bureaucrat al-Ḥasan b. Sahl (hence the moniker "Ḥasanī"), and then inherited by al-Ḥasan's daughter Būrān. The transfer of ownership from Būrān to the caliph al-Muʿtaḍid, though described in some detail, is something of a mystery in that Būrān died before the beginning of al-Muʿtaḍid's reign, so she likely delivered the property to al-Muʿtaḍid's predecessor, al-Muʿtamid (see al-Khaṭīb, *Tārīkh Baghdād*, 1:99; Yāqūt, *Muʿjam al-udabāʾ*, 1:808). This is discussed by Lassner, *Topography*, 267n5; and Bowen, *ʿAlī b. ʿĪsā*, 21.

31. Lassner, *Shaping*, 194.

32. Much of the movement to and from the palace took place by boat; for example, we hear of judges arriving at the palace for official audiences and being forced to wait in their boats. Also, the caliph al-Muqtadir was initially brought to the palace by boat; and his protector Muʾnis attacked the conspirators of the coup of 296/908, by boat.

Al-Muʿtaḍid and his successors, al-Muktafī (289–295/902–908) and al-Muqtadir (295–320/908–932) undertook tremendous construction in the area surrounding the Ḥasanī palace, which became a huge complex known as the *Dār al-Khilāfa*. Al-Muʿtaḍid appropriated adjacent lands to the east, undertaking construction of three additional palaces spread over several kilometers: the Tāj, Firdaws, and Thurayyā; the latter was reportedly two miles from the Ḥasanī palace, and was connected to it by an underground passageway.[33] Al-Muktafī completed the Tāj palace—subsequently the primary residence of the caliphs for centuries—and added symbolic appropriation of authority by insisting that bricks from the palace of Khosroes at Ctesiphon be used for the most visible parts of his palace.[34] In between the main palaces, the royal complex was dotted with impressive and functional structures: a large square for military reviews, a hippodrome and polo field, reflecting pools, a wild animal park, and the residences of other prominent figures at court (such as the royal mother and chamberlain.) By 305/917, Byzantine envoys visiting al-Muqtadir were given an exhausting tour of the complex that included twenty-three palaces of various sizes.[35] This massive complex necessitated a large and varied staff, consisting of thousands of craftsmen, laborers, servants, eunuchs, and soldiers, with a yearly budget of millions of dinars.[36] By the end of the third/ninth century, the new palace complex of *Dār al-Khilāfa* had become the political center of the city, and a magnet for economic activity; al-Muʿtaḍid and his successors had created a powerful image of the caliphate's return to Baghdad.

The physical layout of the palace complex is unclear, and it is virtually impossible to know where different buildings were located in relation to one another.[37] Nevertheless, Heribert Busse has suggested a plausible reconstruction of the main features from the beginning of al-Muʿtaḍid's reign.[38] Busse argues that the heart of the *Dār al-Khilāfa* was the Ḥasanī (and later the Tāj) palace, where al-Muʿtaḍid and subsequent caliphs resided. The palace was surrounded by an area called the *Dār al-Khāṣṣa*, which was accessible only to elite officials and specially assigned eunuchs and soldiers. A gate, the *Bāb al-Khāṣṣa*, led to an outer section called the *Dār al-ʿĀmma*, where most of the palace staff worked and possibly resided. The *Dār al-ʿĀmma* was separated from the rest of the city by another gate, the *Bāb al-ʿĀmma*. According to this reconstruction, the palace complex, probably like most royal complexes, was a series of concentrically arranged areas, in which authority,

33. Le Strange, *Baghdad*, 251; Lassner, *Topography*, 267n4.

34. Yāqūt, *Muʿjam al-buldān*, 1:808–9. Al-Muktafī's architect makes an interesting comment about how rulers come and go and appropriate authority from one another, down to the bricks of their palace.

35. al-Khaṭīb, *Tārīkh*, 1:100–105; also described by Hilāl al-Ṣābī, *Rusūm*, 8–10. The Byzantine envoys arrived in late June of 917.

36. According to a budget found in Hilāl al-Ṣābī, *Wuzarāʾ*, 15–27, during the reign of al-Muʿtaḍid.

37. Lassner, *Topography*, 265–66n1. Le Strange reconstructs some of these features but does not differentiate well between different periods (spanning three centuries), and no coherent image emerges. See Le Strange, *Baghdad*, map VIII, and 263–78.

38. See Busse, "Hofbudget," 30–33.

and inaccessibility, increased the closer one approached to the geographic and symbolic center: the caliph's residence. The *Dār al-Khilāfa* thus established a political axis for Baghdad, and the entire Abbasid Empire, whereby proximity to the complex, and within the complex to the Ḥasanī palace, represented favor and obedience, while distance from the complex represented disfavor and rebellion. Thus, when generals entered Baghdad, they were expected to head straight for the palace in deference to the caliph, while all members of society came to the palace to receive special honors and distinction. By contrast, rebellious officers and troops distanced themselves from the palace and camped in the far northern outskirts of the city, while disgraced officials were usually forbidden from entering the palace complex or were expelled from Baghdad.[39]

Like most royal complexes, the *Dār al-Khilāfa* was both a residence and the center of government. At the outer part of the complex (alongside the *Bāb al-ʿĀmma*) was the chamber for public petitions or grievances (*maẓālim*), where leading officials in the state held audience for the resolution of specific problems. Deeper within the complex, and possibly inside the royal palace itself, the chief administrator (the wazir) had an office for conducting affairs of state. This was where the more formal aspects of administration—appointments, grants, and interrogations—were conducted, and the caliph apparently had representatives at such meetings, which gave him a measure of supervision.[40] In addition, any important governmental decision that involved the caliph and/or a number of court officials took place inside the palace.[41]

This dual function of the palace complex as royal residence and governmental center had important implications. First, the fact that government was conducted near the caliph's residence meant that access to the center of government was highly restricted. As a result, access became power; and the space within the palace that divided residence from government was a center of competition and intrigue. As we shall see, the chamberlain and eunuchs controlled this space, which gave them enormous potential for political influence. Second, the conjunction of functions within the palace established a sociopolitical theme that resonated throughout court life: the overlap of public and private space, the inseparability of professional and personal life.

Court life was not confined to the palace complex, however, but actually spread across Baghdad. The original founder of Baghdad, the caliph al-Manṣūr, had found it im-

---

39. Bernard Lewis summarized this standard feature of political culture: "Supreme sovereign power is at the center. The nearer to the center, the greater the power; the further from the center, the less the power" (*Political Language*, 13).

40. For example, when the wazir ʿUbaydallāh b. Sulaymān honored a merchant who had provided favors, the caliph immediately knew about it and promptly summoned the senior bureaucrat for a sharp rebuke (al-Tanūkhī, *Nishwār*, 1:78–81; translated by Margoliouth, *Table-talk*, 48–50).

*See now also Marmer, "Greed Is Good," 10–11.

41. For example, the wazir ʿAlī b. ʿĪsā discussed the reconquest of Egypt with military leaders, inside the royal palace (Hilāl al-Ṣābī, *Wuzarāʾ*, 380).

possible to create a single administrative center distanced from the civilian populace;[42] al-Muʿtaḍid, returning more than a century later to a city that boasted many palaces, in which most of the court elite already owned homes, and generally having little space for urban design, did not even try to establish a single center. Thus, the daily tasks of administration were conducted at the official residence of the wazir, located in the suburb of Mukharrim to the north of the palace complex. Bureaucrats regularly gathered at this location, and only came to the *Dār al-Khilāfa* on official audience days. This palace also became an alternative symbolic center of authority: the wazir Ibn al-Furāt refurbished it and made it the culminating point of grand processions,[43] and the conspirators in the failed coup of 296/908 gathered at this palace to take the oath of allegiance to a new caliph. As well, the homes of bureaucrats and other members of the court elite were scattered throughout the city, so that there was apparently not even a residential concentration of the court elite.[44]

The location of the military within Baghdad is more difficult to ascertain. Paul Forand has argued that one of al-Muʿtaḍid's innovations was to keep his military entirely within the walls of the palace complex.[45] Certainly the elite units were stationed near the royal palace, as protection for the caliph; yet it is doubtful that the entire military resided there. For one thing, the palace complex was probably not large enough to house the entire military; moreover, it would be strategically dangerous to house all of one's forces in a particular area, for this invited mutiny: al-Manṣūr had found it wise to separate military units in order to play one against another should the need arise, and subsequent caliphs likely followed this precedent.[46] This hypothesis is borne out by scant pieces of evidence. First, we know that important members of the military elite did not live in the royal complex: for example, the palace of Muʾnis al-Muẓaffar, al-Muqtadir's leading general, was located at the far end of the Shamsiyyah quarter, on the northern outskirts of the city. Indeed, this was the general area where military factions often congregated and began riots or rebellions. Lower-ranking soldiers seem to have lived all over Baghdad: for example, soldiers under the authority of Ibn al-Furāt reportedly lived in scattered parts of the city;[47] and the commander al-Ḥusayn b. Ḥamdān resided near agricultural fields on

42. Lassner, *Shaping*, 223–24.

43. Most notably, the procession honoring the Byzantine ambassadors in 305/917 (Miskawayh, *Tajārib*, 53–54). When wazirs were appointed, they were usually accompanied by the court elite in a procession, which ended at the official waziral palace. The wazir then held a reception there and received congratulations.

44. The secretary Zanjī lived in Mukharrim (on the east bank) but visited relatives on the west bank (Hilāl al-Ṣābī, *Wuzarāʾ*, 210), and visited a tax official who was also living in western Baghdad (Hilāl al-Ṣābī, *Wuzarāʾ*, 218–19). The poet and pretender to the throne, Ibn al-Muʿtazz, lived on the Ṣarāt canal in western Baghdad (Miskawayh, *Tajārib*, 5), and subsequently went into hiding at the home of the merchant Ibn al-Jaṣṣāṣ, on the bank of the Tigris River (ʿArīb, *Ṣilat*, 29–30; al-Tanūkhī, *Nishwār*, 1:26–28.)

45. Forand, "Development of Military Slavery," 55–56.

46. Lassner, *Shaping*, 208.

47. Miskawayh, *Tajārib*, 11; Hilāl al-Ṣābī, *Wuzarāʾ*, 30–31.

the outskirts of western Baghdad.[48] In addition, the primary office of the police chief was apparently across the river from the royal complex in the western part of town, and the intelligence bureau was also some distance from the caliphal complex.[49] Thus it would seem that while the royal complex was the main center of administration, there were additional focal points of government activity, and no exclusive government district.

The dispersal of the members of court, and state administration, meant that the caliph had less control over his potentially powerful subjects than if they were confined to the palace complex, under his watchful eye. The caliphs possibly extended their supervision by employing a network of spies. For example, one anecdote describes how the wazir Ibn al-Furāt was enjoying a lavish party, when the famous singer Bidʿa arrived for a visit. The wazir quickly removed some valuable furnishings and took on a more serious demeanor, for he was concerned that the singer had been sent by the caliph to spy on him.[50] The caliph also employed a huge corps of eunuchs, some of whom were used as messengers, and probably spies as well. As we shall later see, the chamberlain and wazirs also employed informants. In general, it was not uncommon for people at court to know what was taking place in other parts of the city.

Because the ruling elite worked and lived in scattered parts of Baghdad, there was a great deal of human mobility and integration across the city. Since the distances between two officials sometimes made personal interaction inconvenient, people often communicated by letter or through verbal messages transmitted by proxies; this was particularly true for the caliph and the royal family, who rarely left the palace, and never deigned to visit anyone else's home. The messengers were frequently eunuchs, and occasionally female attendants, called *qahramānas*, probably because these individuals could enter any gendered space forbidden to other men. For the most part, though, people moved freely across the city, generally with a retinue in tow; the higher one's status, the larger the retinue. Mobility was not restricted to men, for court women also moved freely about Baghdad, and only certain specific categories of women were spatially confined.[51] Nor was mobility completely restricted after dark, which was an appropriate time for especially sensitive meetings that required the utmost secrecy. For example, when the bureaucrat Zanjī wanted to return a bribe he had accepted, fearing that his enemies would find out about it and tell his patron, he left his home in the middle of the night, taking

48. Miskawayh, *Tajārib*, 15.

49. Le Strange, *Baghdad*, map V (facing 107); at various crucial moments, we hear that the caliph sends messages to these officers, who were not located close enough to arrive quickly at the palace (Hilāl al-Ṣābī, *Wuzarāʾ*, 71).

50. Hilāl al-Ṣābī, *Wuzarāʾ*, 214–15.

51. There are numerous stories depicting female singers, palace servants, and attendants, and even female members of the royal family out in public, not to mention everyday activities of the female public. The only woman whom we hear about in our sources who was strictly confined to the palace was the royal mother; concubines, wives, and other female relatives of the caliph were likely confined as well, though we almost never hear about any such persons.

care that nobody would see him, traversed the east side of Baghdad and crossed the river toward the west side, where the man who had bribed him resided. Zanjī was momentarily delayed when he found the gate to the western suburbs locked and guarded, but he soon sneaked in when a messenger sent from the military chief to another official in the west side passed through. Zanjī then returned the bribe after some haggling, and went home.[52] This story demonstrates both the dispersion of court officials throughout Baghdad, and the relative ease of traversing the city, even at night.[53]

In a broader sense, the city of Baghdad was used by the court elite as a political stage. A variety of ceremonies took place in public: ostentatious processions honoring newly appointed officials or humiliating captured enemies; military parades that functioned as intimidating displays of force; and the torture, execution, and dismemberment of criminals. Each of these events demonstrated state authority over the city, and disseminated state ideology. The processions in particular wound throughout the city, and served the multiple functions of differentiating the court elite from the masses, and establishing relative status within the court elite.[54] The recurring processions in particular indicate that the best way for the court to assert social and political superiority was through a collective display of splendor: in short, social distinction required contrast. On these occasions the people of Baghdad served as the civilian backdrop for imperial grandeur.

Here we might raise the question of the separation of state and society. Scholars have asserted that by the middle of the third/ninth century, the Abbasid state was increasingly detached culturally and morally from the society over which it ruled. One goal of this study is to understand the complexities of this dichotomy, to look for the social, cultural, and ethical links between the Abbasid court and Baghdadi society. As indicated above, on a physical plane, state and society were enmeshed: indeed, the state used contact and juxtaposition with the rest of society precisely in order to affirm its own elite status.

The Court Community

The most important members of the court were those individuals and groups that had an impact on government policy, and shaped sociopolitical relations: the caliph, the royal

52. Hilāl al-Ṣābī, *Wuzarāʾ*, 217–21.

53. Among other such nocturnal stories, the jewelry merchant Ibn al-Jaṣṣāṣ visited the home of the wazir Ibn al-Furāt in the middle of the night in order to settle a personal quarrel (Hilāl al-Ṣābī, *Wuzarāʾ*, 125–28; al-Tanūkhī, *Nishwār*, 1:29–35).

54. Paula Sanders describes such processions for Fatimid Egypt in greater detail throughout *Ritual, Politics, and the City*, especially in ch. 2 ("The Ceremonial Idiom"). She states that Fatimid ceremonial differed from Abbasid ceremonial in that the latter took place almost entirely within the palace, and the few recorded public processions involved only wazirs (8). Though public processions might have been more important for the Fatimids, such events were also relatively common in Abbasid Baghdad of this era: every appointment of wazir or judge included a public procession, as did the departure of caliphs on military campaigns, which was particularly pronounced under the caliph al-Muʿtaḍid. There were also many elaborate processions for prisoners.

family, the palace staff, the military, the bureaucracy, and the judiciary. Each of these groups was professionally distinct, with virtually no overlap or mobility between groups. One clear indication of the strict separation that existed was the caliph al-Muqtadir's angry response to the suggestion that he appoint a *qāḍī* (judge) as wazir: "If I did that, I would be notorious among Muslim and heathen rulers. I would be thought of in one of two ways: either my state would be imagined to have no bureaucrat suitable for the wazirate, which would diminish [my] standing in their eyes; or I intentionally gave the wazirate over to the wearers of the *ṭayālīs* [the judges], which would be considered poor judgment."[55] This strict professional delineation was reinforced by birthright and nepotism, as by the late third/ninth century most bureaucrats, judges, and even many military commanders were trained (and sometimes appointed) by their fathers, so that court professions became virtual monopolies.[56] Lineage was therefore an extremely important social and political value. One commentator goes so far as to say that the state began to decline when unqualified men were appointed as judges: the people in question "had no knowledge and no [proper] paternity," which reflects the predominance of inherited training and status.[57] Those members of the elite who were not following a family profession—primarily manumitted soldiers—were usually imported from distant lands according to strict standards, and were not recruited locally. Professional distinctions were further enhanced by ethnic and religious differences, as the military was predominantly of foreign birth or parentage, the bureaucrats were largely Shiʿis or of Christian or Nabatean origin, whereas the judges had longer Islamic and orthodox lineages.[58]

We might add that since most people belonged to court either because of birth and family training (royalty, bureaucrats, and judges) or purchase (soldiers), they had not chosen to participate in court society of their own free will. This is worth keeping in mind when considering two issues: the desire and the ability of any given person to remove himself or herself from court society.

The court elite, while divided into distinct groups, was unified by a common code of etiquette, which differentiated the elite from commoners, but also served to differentiate between court groups and to systematize internal hierarchies. The space people occupied, their physical movement and interaction, their forms of speech and address,

55. Hilāl al-Ṣābī, *Wuzarāʾ*, 348.

56. There are numerous instances of sons inheriting positions from their fathers.
*For one in-depth example, see J. Bray's analysis of the Buhlūlid family in "Place and Self-Image."

57. al-Tanūkhī, *Nishwār*, 1:231. Yet another story in the *Nishwār* tells of how one official embarrassed a rival by publicizing the ignorance of his rival's father (al-Tanūkhī, *Nishwār*, 2:105–7).

58. Aside from the main groups discussed throughout this study—the bureaucrats, judges, and military—there were many other participants at court whose functions were less clearly defined, who benefited from less social cohesion, or who wielded little influence, individuals such as financiers, entertainers, boon companions, and intellectuals. Ideally the roles of these individuals and groups would be analyzed in conjunction with the better defined and generally more powerful social groups, but information on these court participants is limited and scattered and must await a later stage of research.

the clothes they wore and their manner of eating were all regulated and indicated relative status; these established patterns of behavior formed the basic framework of social and political interaction.[59] The most important category of regulated behavior involved physical interaction and spatial relations.[60] One powerful demonstration of relative status occurred when subordinates were given the honor of kissing the hands or feet or their social superiors. This practice exemplifies the manipulation involved in etiquette, for while permission to kiss somebody's body conferred prestige, the act itself was a clear demonstration of submission to a greater authority. An extension of this respect for the body of a superior was respect for the space surrounding them; thus, one was required to keep a distance from a social superior, and the invitation to approach closer and enter prohibited space was a sign of favor.[61] A more ubiquitous form of respect was standing up (or dismounting) upon greeting social equals, and remaining standing before social superiors. One interesting example of how the act of standing reflected social distinctions was that the general Abū al-Hayjāʾ was allowed to sit down when visiting the wazir ʿAlī b. ʿĪsā, but the general's son remained standing.[62] Respect for the physical presence of a social superior was even extended to his entire home, so that visiting someone's home was an expression of respect and even acquiescence, while the burning and looting of someone's residence signified disgrace.

Central to the paradigmatic valuation of physical presence and spatial relations was the person of the caliph.[63] His body, and even the ground in front of him, were kissed by only the highest officials of state; the space in front of him was left vacant during audiences, and only his immediate family, the wazir, and the military chief were allowed to sit in his presence. The caliph's private chambers were accessible to only select palace servants; as noted earlier, the interior of the palace complex was a series of increasingly inaccessible areas, and the entire complex was designed to exude an aura of authority. In other words, the social rank of any individual, starting with the caliph, radiated out-

59. The various forms of etiquette have been catalogued in the sources and in scholarship (Hilāl al-Ṣābī, *Rusūm*, especially ch. 4, "What They Wear"; Sanders, *Ritual*, ch. 2: "The Ceremonial Idiom"; and Sourdel, "Questions de cérémonial"). I will only briefly review the patterns that were most obviously relevant for sociopolitical competition at the Abbasid court.

60. As Lewis points out, the most common metaphors in Islamic and Western political language involve spatial relations (*Political Language*, 11). This was true not only in language, but in people's actions.

61. For example, when the wazir Ibn al-Furāt summoned a man whom he wished to honor, the man refused to approach the wazir, and then refused to sit in his presence, fearful of appearing pretentious (Hilāl al-Ṣābī, *Wuzarāʾ*, 228).

62. al-Tanūkhī, *Nishwār*, 2:149. There are numerous examples of court officials, and all members of society, for that matter, standing up in respect for social peers or those with higher status. One remarkable story, preserved by Ibn Khallikān, relates that Ibn al-Furāt used to stand up when a letter embossed by the caliph was brought to him (*Wafayāt*, 2:357).

*For the etiquette surrounding the practice of standing up on behalf of a social superior, see Hamori, "Rising to Greet You."

63. Sanders, *Ritual*, 32.

ward from one's body, through successive layers of space, to the gate and walls of one's residence.

Other important aspects of etiquette for the representation of relative status were speech (forms of address), and costume. All members of the court elite were expected to speak in a civil and polite manner, and this was especially true in the presence of social superiors. The most sensitive aspect of speech was the way in which people addressed one another. Elaborate distinctions in titles were used for addressing people of different ranks;[64] one would address a peer or someone higher rank by their *kunya* (teknonym), never by their personal name; and the highest-ranking men in the state—the caliph and the wazir—were generally addressed in third person. As for costume, each group commonly wore a distinct headdress and cloak, though there seems to have been a great deal of overlap in the clothes people wore.[65] In fact, costume does not figure prominently in politically oriented texts, and for sociopolitical purposes was a less malleable symbol than spatial relations or speech. The one respect in which costume was significant was that the caliph conferred cloaks of honor on all important appointees and others whom he wished to commend, so that they would literally wear the caliph's favor out in public. But this representation of status was only manipulated by the caliph and had few repercussions in sociopolitical competition.

Divergence from these standards of etiquette meant a disruption or challenge to relative status and was therefore presumptuous and insulting. The most noticeable divergences were naturally those that broke the most important aspects of etiquette. For example, when a brash young man from a distant branch of the royal family kissed the hand of the wazir, his subsequent suggestion that the wazir reciprocate was considered extremely rude.[66] Most divergences from etiquette had political overtones. When the disgraced minister Ḥāmid b. al-ʿAbbās arrived unexpectedly to the palace, the chamberlain Naṣr would not stand up for him. Naṣr apologized, knowing that Ḥāmid would be stunned by this rudeness, but explained that he could not risk standing for a man who had lost the caliph's favor.[67] The diminished status of bureaucrats was also marked by insults and curses during interrogations. Yet even these insults had to be tempered, for as the recently dismissed Ibn al-Furāt reminded his replacement Ḥāmid, inappropriate language inside the palace was an insult to the caliph.[68]

As the center of patronage and the bearer of highest status, the caliph periodically insisted on adherence to appropriate etiquette. Near the outset of al-Muʿtaḍid's caliphate, the newly appointed wazir ʿUbaydallāh b. Sulaymān stood up, within the wazir's

64. Forms of address are listed by Hilāl al-Ṣābī (*Wuzarāʾ*, 172–78).

65. Ahsan, *Social Life*, 29. An anecdote in the *Nishwār* (1:263) demonstrates that bureaucrats wore turbans, and judges wore *qalansuwas*; when someone wore the inappropriate clothing, others took notice and might find it comical.

66. al-Tanūkhī, *Nishwār*, 1:85; trans. Margoliouth, *Table-talk*, 52.

67. Miskawayh, *Tajārib*, 96.

68. Miskawayh, *Tajārib*, 62.

audience chamber, to publicly honor and thereby compensate a merchant who had done him favors; the caliph, irate, scolded his minister: "You degraded the wazirate by standing for a merchant? If he had been an important governor it would have been forbidden, or for a crown prince excessive!"[69] Similarly, when one of the caliph's eunuchs attended the judicial court but refused to maintain a proper distance, the offended judge sent him to al-Muʿtaḍid, who was outraged at this insolent servant.[70] Yet while the caliph insisted upon adherence to deference and etiquette, he was also bound by social norms that were not always to his advantage.[71]

Aside from a common code of behavior, the members of the court were unified by a shared intellectual culture. The sensitivity to forms of address was related to an intense appreciation of the spoken word. The most common form of leisure activity, both communal and private, was listening to the recitation of poetry. Frequently these poems were set to music by female singers, and court officials sometimes became so enamored of particular singers that they expended great wealth upon them.[72] Many people at court actively memorized and composed poetry themselves, which enhanced their prestige. Poetry could also be used for sociopolitical purposes: a timely and witty reply could curry favor, while biting criticism of a rival in verse (often written anonymously on paper) could be the basis of a successful plot.[73] In general, the ability to manipulate words, and employ rhetorical devices for a desired impact, was one of the most important skills at court;[74] we shall see how bureaucrats used rhetoric in plotting, counterplotting, and interrogation.

The ruling elite also appreciated the religious sciences. Bureaucrats and judges were often knowledgeable in Qur'an and hadith, and the study of these subjects provided contact with the religious elite who rarely appear in court sources. Such knowledge also had political uses, as religious texts were cited as defense during interrogations.[75] Finally, the elite enjoyed passing on stories from court tradition. These stories not only entertained, they also reinforced the corporate identity of the court, or of particular groups within

69. al-Tanūkhī, *Nishwār*, 1:79

*See Marmer, "Greed Is Good" for the specific relationships involved in this interaction.

70. al-Tanūkhī, *Nishwār*, 1:129.

71. For example, the caliph was not supposed to ask the wazir questions, as it would reflect ignorance; the wazir was responsible for supplying all necessary information that preempted questions. However, it was the caliph who was embarrassed by ignorance when the wazir failed (Hilāl al-Ṣābī, *Rusūm*, 31–32). As well, the caliph was not supposed to arrest a wazir after seeing him on a given day (Hilāl al-Ṣābī, *Wuzarāʾ*, 291).

72. al-Tanūkhī, *Nishwār*, 8:263–64.

73. For example, someone wrote a poem criticizing the courtier Ibn al-Ḥawārī, which so persuaded the caliph that this poem is cited as one reason for Ibn al-Ḥawārī's downfall (Miskawayh, *Tajārib*, 86–87).

74. "Some of the earliest Arabic classical writers ... speak of poetry and oratory as the two arts which the Arabs most admired and in which they most excelled. Both of them are of course arts of verbal persuasion; both were extensively used for political purposes" (Lewis, *Political Language*, 10).

75. For example, Hilāl al-Ṣābī, (*Wuzarāʾ*, 67, 115) records references to the Qur'an and hadith.

the court, and were usually didactic. Indeed, the most interesting aspect of analyzing an entertaining work such as the *Nishwār* is to recognize the morals that both the historical figures and the author al-Tanūkhī wish to convey.[76]

The comprehensive nature of court culture meant that "professional" and "social" activities often coincided, taking place in the same setting at the same time, indeed often becoming indistinguishable. Patrons not only expected their subordinates to perform governmental responsibilities, but also to serve as social companions. For example, one bureaucrat was in the habit of visiting the wazir ʿAlī b. ʿĪsā at home, accompanying him first to the mosque for prayer, later to an official reception at the royal palace, and finally back to ʿAlī's home for a meal.[77] The activities that most commonly combined social and political functions were eating and drinking. The provision of food was a sign of munificence and prestige; sharing a meal enabled a social superior to demonstrate patronage and develop intimacy with protégés.[78] The wazir Ibn al-Furāt frequently interrupted administrative sessions to eat or drink with his officials, and it was during this daily meal that confidants were expected to request favors.[79] This overlap between governmental and social activities had two main implications: first, patronage and power could be negotiated in almost any conceivable setting, which contributed to an atmosphere of constant tension; second, this overlap meant that it was difficult to distinguish between the professional and private spheres of court life.

The synthesis and commonality of shared court culture was reinforced at regular assemblies, usually at the palace complex. For cyclical events and rites of passage—circumcisions, weddings, appointments, and funerals—most of the court gathered, and we get a sense of the fundamental cohesiveness of court society.[80] Gatherings of the court could also function as public competitions for status and influence. On reception days

---

76. This raises two questions that will not be dealt with in this study: how people at court used stories to impart values; and how al-Tanūkhī organized these stories to give the work a moral focus. We should keep in mind that most of our material on the court has been framed several times: by the actual participants, by the transmitters, and by the authors/compilers of our texts. At each stage of transmission, material is selected and presented to convey a particular message.

*For the ways in which al-Tanūkhī and other court-oriented authors used anecdotes to shape and reaffirm corporate identity, see Wickham, "Administrators' Time," especially 432–33.

77. Hilāl al-Ṣābī, *Rusūm*, 14–15.

78. Lewis, *Political Language*, 18. Ḥāmid b. al-ʿAbbās took pride in the sumptuous meals he provided for visitors and spent an exorbitant amount of money feeding his own staff. Such extravagance was reportedly one of the reasons for his favor with the caliph al-Muʿtaḍid (Hilāl al-Ṣābī, *Wuzarāʾ*, 95), which seems oddly out of character for this caliph.

79. Hilāl al-Ṣābī, *Wuzarāʾ*, 261–62. Ibn al-Furāt so wanted his secretary Zanjī to eat with him, that he granted Zanjī's request to let a prisoner go free (Hilāl al-Ṣābī, *Wuzarāʾ*, 260). In a different setting, Ibn al-Jaṣṣāṣ the jewelry merchant became intimate with the Ṭulūnid ruler of Egypt by being the only person at court who could drink intoxicating beverages into the night, a trait that his Ṭulūnid patron highly admired (al-Tanūkhī, *Nishwār*, 2:314–15). The meal table was also a common setting for reconciliation (al-Tanūkhī, *Nishwār*, 2:283–85; 336–38).

80. A phrase often used in the sources is: "Leaders of state, commanders, bureaucrats, nobility, and

(Mondays and Thursdays), all bureaucrats, judges, and commanders congregated outside the palace complex; higher ranking officials and those in favor were called for a royal audience, while others were left outside.[81] Though government business was apparently conducted on these days, an equally important purpose for such gatherings was the massive demonstration of fealty to the caliph, acknowledged by important officials waiting outside the caliph's residence and public conferral by the caliph of favored status to those he summoned.

Yet the events with the greatest political tension were public interrogations, usually of fallen bureaucrats. These were the only occasions in which all the different social groupings at court competed openly for influence. We shall see, in these frequent and tense scenes of interrogation, how the different people at court attempted to assert their respective sociopolitical influence, first and foremost, the caliph himself.

Aside from interaction in public events, people from different social groups within the court elite also interacted in more casual settings and developed friendships. There are many examples of judges and bureaucrats who visited each other at work and at home, on holidays or for a daily meal or poetry recital. The sources even state that these men were friends, not just colleagues. Similar relationships existed between merchants/financiers and bureaucrats, and merchants/financiers and judges. These relations were particularly useful for bureaucrats, who, due to the vicissitudes of their profession, often needed to hide their money (and then themselves) in the homes of judges and merchants.[82] The caliph and the royal family did not develop these types of lasting friendships, as the royal family was severely restricted in mobility; more importantly, friendships might undermine the hierarchical relationship of royalty and subject, and might blunt the royal prerogative of manipulation. In general, any interaction with royalty, especially the caliph, necessarily involved status differentiation, and therefore precluded friendships.

The military is noticeably absent from this network of cross-professional friendships. The only commanders who cultivated relations with bureaucrats were members of the Ḥamdānid dynasty—we hear that Abū al-Hayjāʾ and his son were friendly with ʿAlī b. ʿĪsā,[83] and that al-Ḥusayn b. Ḥamdān got drunk with the wazir al-ʿAbbās b. al-Ḥasan;[84] no

---

judges," meaning all members of court society, save the royal family, such as when all these people attended the funeral of a general (al-Tanūkhī, *Nishwār*, 1:138).

81. al-Tanūkhī, *Nishwār*, 1:284. We hear frequently of official reception days, though such accounts do not provide details about the standard routines or procedures of such events.

82. For example, the wazir Ibn al-Furāt deposited money with both merchants and judges for safe keeping (Miskawayh, *Tajārib*, 66–67); years earlier, an indebted and desperate ʿUbaydallāh b. Sulaymān borrowed money from the merchant Ibn Abī ʿAwf, apparently also taking refuge in the latter's home. *For more on this relationship, see Marmer, "Greed Is Good," 7–11.

83. al-Tanūkhī, *Nishwār*, 2:148–51.

84. ʿArīb, *Ṣilat*, 26. On this occasion, al-ʿAbbās offended Ibn Ḥamdān, who later killed the bureaucrat for this slight—a particularly harsh example of the potential complications of social interaction.

other generals socialized with bureaucrats or judges.[85] This absence of casual social relations was probably due to the fact that the military elite was almost entirely imported, likely spoke poor Arabic, and were not granted literate or religious education, and thus could not participate in the more intellectually refined aspects of court culture. Nor did they have ties to other families, social connections that were inherited from past generations. The result is a sense that the military was largely isolated, socially and culturally, from the rest of the court.

We might add here that social interaction across professional groups had fewer political implications than social interaction within professional groups. This is probably because members of different professional groups had fewer reasons to compete. Furthermore, most cross-professional relations involved judges, who seemed to function as political buffer zones, and competed for influence far less than the rest of the court elite.

Beyond relationships that crossed professional lines, the court elite inevitably had some contact with the populace of Baghdad. Since court life involved a great deal of movement across the city, encounters with commoners were inevitable. We hear stories of the wazir Ibn al-Furāt riding through the city and receiving favors—a cold drink, or clean clothes—from ordinary citizens, whom he repaid generously for their kindness.[86] Similarly, ʿAlī b. ʿĪsā reportedly had a dream, encouraging him to give a bankrupt but pious businessman some money.[87] These stories, whether fictional or not, depict a social setting in which the elite had incidental contact with ordinary residents of Baghdad, and suggest that these commoners could gain access to high ranking officials when necessary. Yet the main purpose of these stories is to show the generosity of the court elite; and thus, like elaborate processions, these chance encounters with the nameless masses were simply a means of providing the elite with a counterpart upon whom they could expend their largesse and demonstrate their superior status.

In sum, the return of the imperial capital to a thriving metropolis created the challenge of distinguishing the court elite from the urban masses and maintaining the consolidation of government. On a spatial level the caliphs only partially succeeded in creating this division. They established a royal complex that became the focal point of court life; yet much of the court elite worked, socialized, and resided in various parts of Baghdad, and thereby maintained a certain distance—and hence independence—from the caliph. Despite this geographic dispersion, however, the court encompassed a unified, strictly defined group of people. The court elite remained distinct from their neighbors through heredity/nepotism, etiquette, intellectual culture, and displays of splendor; so, while the

85. We should distinguish between friendships and alliances. As we shall see, military officials frequently formed alliances, particularly with bureaucrats; yet we almost never hear of such officials attending poetry or music recitals, communal meals, visiting other members of the court for no apparent reason, or characterizing their relations in any way as friendly or intimate. All the relationships we witness involving military personnel are overtly political.

86. Hilāl al-Ṣābī *Wuzarāʾ*, 84–85, 239; also in al-Tanūkhī, *Nishwār*, 1:166–67; 7:235–36.

87. al-Tanūkhī, *Nishwār*, 2:243–45.

court was physically enmeshed within the expansive city of Baghdad, both socially and culturally the court strongly asserted its distinctiveness.

279–324 AH/892–936 CE: A Brief Chronology

The period from 279–324 AH (892–936 CE) was a time of tremendous contrasts, of glorious heights and unprecedented depths. The caliphate returned to Baghdad in 279/892, and the Abbasid Empire once more achieved the centralized power, wealth, and splendor of the earliest Abbasid caliphs. Over the next three decades the financial situation of the empire gradually declined; and by the mid-310s/920s the state was confronted by military incursions and financial insolvency. In 320/932, the longest-reigning Abbasid caliph was systematically humiliated and publicly murdered. Finally, in 324/936, facing military and economic chaos, another caliph granted administrative authority to the *amīr al-umarāʾ*, signaling the end of Abbasid control over the state.

The period begins with the caliphate of al-Muʿtaḍid, a firm and capable ruler who participated in military campaigns and inspired awe in his staff and subjects. His ten-year reign was characterized by governmental stability, expansion of Abbasid authority, and financial surplus. Two wazirs—ʿUbaydallāh b. Sulaymān (d. 288/901) and his son al-Qāsim (d. 291/904)—supervised administration, while Badr al-Muʿtaḍidī served as chief military officer for the entire reign. Al-Muʿtaḍid and his armies, on campaign for much of the decade, reasserted Abbasid control over Syria and the Byzantine border, all of Iraq, and western Iran; Abbasid suzerainty was once again recognized by the Ṭulūnids in Egypt, who renewed the payment of tribute to Baghdad. This control over lucrative provinces, combined with stable administration and agricultural revitalization, brought great wealth to Baghdad, and the caliph's private treasury reportedly contained ten million dinars at his death.[88]

Al-Muʿtaḍid was succeeded in 289/902 by his eldest son al-Muktafī, who had received extensive military and administrative training. We have very little information for the brief reign of this caliph, but the prosperity of the state seems to have continued. The Abbasid Empire regained authority over Egypt from the defunct Ṭulūnids and defeated the Qarmatian rebels from Oman that had been disrupting the trade routes of Arabia, Syria, and southern Iraq. Money continued to flow to the capital, and this caliph saved an additional six million dinars. The only significant change seems to have involved the style of governance. The wazir al-Qāsim b. ʿUbaydallāh (later succeeded by al-ʿAbbās b. al-Ḥasan) asserted more independence than in the previous reign and arranged for the dramatic execution of the general Badr in 289/902. For the remainder of al-Muktafī's caliphate, there was no predominant military commander. In 295/908, the chronically

88. For surveys of the reign of al-Muʿtaḍid, see H. Kennedy, "al-Muʿtaḍid," *EI2*; and Kennedy, *Prophet and the Age of the Caliphates*, 181–86; the idealized image of this caliph is explored further below.

ill al-Muktafī died after only six years on the throne, leaving no mature or experienced relative as an obvious successor.

Following a great deal of deliberation and scheming, al-Muktafī's thirteen-year-old brother Jaʿfar was appointed caliph, with the regnal title of al-Muqtadir. The accession of this inexperienced and impressionable youth ushered in a period of heightened competition for influence among various people at court. Less than a year after his appointment, al-Muqtadir faced an attempted coup that enjoyed broad support among court officials, who favored a more capable and mature candidate for the throne. Yet al-Muqtadir was restored as caliph due to the intervention of an elite corps of military clients, and went on to rule for twenty-five years, longer than any other Abbasid caliph.

For roughly the first ten years of al-Muqtadir's reign, the Abbasid state maintained the centralized power and prestige established by the previous two caliphs. Since the young ruler could not assert authority himself, several different members of the court supervised government affairs. The most prominent and influential individuals were the caliph's mother al-Sayyida, the general Muʾnis, the chamberlain Naṣr, and the wazirs Ibn al-Furāt and ʿAlī b. ʿĪsā, all of whom had long and noteworthy careers over the next two decades. Collectively, they presided over an impressive string of military victories: Fārs was recaptured in 298/910–911; the Fatimid invasions of Egypt in 301/913–914 and 305/917–918 were repelled; and the rebellious governors Ibn Ḥamdān (Mosul) and Ibn Abī al-Sāj (Armenia) were captured and jailed in Baghdad in 303/916 and 307/919–920, respectively. All these victories were celebrated by public processions in the capital. The height of this period of glory was the visit of Byzantine envoys in 305/917, which involved sumptuous decorations, impressive military formations, and the general glorification of Baghdad, the Abbasid caliph, and the Muslim empire.

Beneath the surface of this continued success, however, the financial situation of the state was declining. It seems that agricultural revenues tapered off; this loss of revenue, combined with the notorious extravagance of the impressionable new ruler and his entourage, created a severe budgetary imbalance. The problem was exacerbated by the constant turnover in the bureaucracy. Between 295/908 and 306/918, six wazirs were serially appointed and dismissed, and fiscal policy wavered between huge expenditures and high taxation (under Ibn al-Furāt), budget cuts and reduced taxes (under ʿAlī b. ʿĪsā), and simple incompetence (al-Khāqānī and Ḥāmid b. al-ʿAbbās). Knowing that their tenure would be relatively short, these wazirs and their subordinates embezzled huge amounts of money, which contributed to the financial strain. Military payments became erratic, leading to periodic riots. By 306/918 the state was nearly bankrupt, and the caliph resorted to appointing a wealthy provincial official (Ḥāmid b. al-ʿAbbās), expert at squeezing out tax money, to be his newest wazir.

In the years 307–311/919–923 the various tensions at court increased. The newly appointed wazir enhanced his personal wealth by hoarding grain and driving up prices, which provoked widespread rioting in 307/919. The court also became engulfed in intrigue. In late 309/922 the controversial religious figure al-Ḥallāj was interrogated and executed, despite enjoying the protection of important figures of state; and in 310/922–923 the assistant to the caliph's mother Umm Mūsā was arrested for plotting against the caliph. More importantly, the wazir Ḥāmid broke the rules of acceptable punishment, and tortured rival bureaucrats excessively. When Ibn al-Furāt and his son al-Muḥassin replaced Ḥāmid, they in turn instituted a reign of terror, murdering several important bureaucrats and even plotting against leading military commanders.

The year 312/924–925 marked the end of one court drama, and the beginning of more serious military developments. The violence of Ibn al-Furāt and al-Muḥassin forged unity among military leaders, who forced the caliph to execute the wazir and his son. From then through 320/932, eight different men served as wazir, and this instability meant that state finances could not be rehabilitated. That same year, an old threat reemerged from the Arabian Peninsula: the Qarmatians. These Shiʿi insurgents attacked the hajj, plundered the major urban centers of Basra, Kufa, and even Mecca, and generally terrified the populace of Baghdad. By 315/927 the Qarmatians were just barely thwarted from overrunning the capital itself. These Qarmatian incursions from the south were matched by Byzantines advances in the northwest, and Daylami incursions in the east.

During these years the caliph's relations with the military also deteriorated. In 315/927 the caliph apparently intended to assassinate the leading general Muʾnis but was prevented from this by the army's mobilization in support of its commander. Also, due to the financial insolvency of the state, soldiers were again not being paid regularly. These tensions erupted in 317/929 in a second coup attempt, as a coalition of military factions replaced al-Muqtadir with his younger brother al-Qāhir. As in 296/908, this coup proved to be temporary due to military divisiveness, and al-Muqtadir was returned to the throne; but this time the royal palace was pillaged, and the caliph's image was seriously tarnished.

The tension between al-Muqtadir and Muʾnis continued in the years immediately following this second failed coup. The caliph promoted bureaucrats and generals hostile to Muʾnis, and the latter countered by mobilizing troops, which usually forced the caliph to compromise. In 319/931 the two reached an impasse, and Muʾnis abandoned the capital. After a crucial victory against forces loyal to the caliph at Mosul, Muʾnis collected provincial tax revenues, attracted large numbers of troops, and marched on Baghdad. The caliph and his former leading general made attempts at reconciliation, but al-Muqtadir was continually dissuaded by Muʾnis's rivals. In 320/932 the two forces met in a climactic battle, which the caliph attended in order to inspire his troops. Yet Muʾnis's men carried the day, and in a remarkable scene the caliph was beheaded and dismembered in a field outside Baghdad.

This public disgrace, combined with financial ruin and military disunity, meant that caliphal authority had nearly come to an end. The new caliph al-Qāhir retained a measure of control by playing military factions against one another and even managed to have Muʾnis murdered; but before long the military turned on this duplicitous ruler, removed al-Qāhir from the throne, and gouged out his eyes. His successor al-Rāḍī, with virtually no money and facing military incursions from various directions, made little attempt at independent rule. In 324/936 he asked the general Ibn Rāʾiq, who had accumulated wealth in the provincial capital of Wāsiṭ, to come to Baghdad and undertake the administration of the state with the title *amīr al-umarāʾ*. This marked the official end of caliphal rule over the Abbasid Empire.[89]

Power Relations of the Abbasid Court

In the following chapters I examine the social dynamics characteristic of the most important social groups at the Abbasid court, and how these dynamics influenced the way members of these groups competed for power. The starting point for this analysis is the recognition that the fundamental principle underlying court relations was autocracy. The caliph had tremendous control over state affairs and personnel: he could appoint and dismiss subordinates, and change policies, virtually at will. The caliph was the linchpin of court politics; more than anyone else, he enforced the norms of social relations and could occasionally change them. Yet the caliph was also dependent upon the cooperation of capable subordinates. The challenge then for the caliph, and the driving force behind all court relations, was to delegate enough authority so that the state could function yet prevent his delegates—particularly the military and bureaucracy—from challenging his absolute authority.

In the first chapter I explore the foundations of caliphal power, and by extension the caliph's vulnerabilities. In subsequent chapters I will describe caliphal strategy for undermining the potential power of subordinates, particularly a strategy of divide and rule, which encouraged hostility between social groups and division within them. This strategy in turn shaped the internal dynamics of each group, and the ways in which members of these groups competed for power.

89. *Hugh Kennedy has subsequently written a lengthier narrative summary of the reign of al-Muqtadir, which largely highlights the same main events and trends (van Berkel et al, *Crisis and Continuity*, 16–17).

Chapter 1. The Caliph

Creating a Caliph

What makes a ruler powerful? The authority of any given ruler is a complex phenomenon, composed of many elements. On the one hand rulers must harness some force that projects them to the pinnacle of society and enables them, at least to a degree, to enforce their will. For most effective rulers this force is military support. On the other hand, rulers generally cultivate an image of majesty, an expression of authority that transforms ordinary mortals into extraordinary figures and thereby legitimizes rulership. In the words of Clifford Geertz, "majesty is made, not born."[1] Majesty, or the expression of authority, is constructed; and while this construction often involves standardized rituals, different rulers manage to exude different kinds of majesty. The particular expression of authority for any given ruler both reflects and influences the sociopolitical relations of the court they dominate.

In the following chapter I will follow the process by which a rather ordinary young man was transformed into the authoritative ruler of the Abbasid Empire. This particular young man, the prince Jaᶜfar b. al-Muᶜtaḍid, who ruled with the regnal title al-Muqtadir, had not been trained in the art of rulership as was customary with previous Abbasid heirs-apparent; nor did he naturally possess such skills. He was nevertheless catapulted to the caliphate, primarily because he inherited the most powerful force in the state: a network of patron-client relations. Once enthroned as the caliph al-Muqtadir (295–320/908–932), he cultivated an aura of authority, of "majesty," that would consolidate his control over the court and Abbasid society at large. Yet this expression of authority differed substantially from that of his father, al-Muᶜtaḍid, a divergence which subsequently influenced all court relations. In the second half of this chapter, "Destroying the Caliph(ate)," I show how al-Muqtadir contributed to a permanent change in the nature and expression of caliphal authority. This decisive change was the most important aspect of a general shift in the entire Abbasid sociopolitical system.

Al-Muᶜtaḍid: The Model Caliph

In order to see the shift in the expression of caliphal power with al-Muqtadir, I first explore the example set by his father, al-Muᶜtaḍid. The caliph al-Muᶜtaḍid (279–289/892–902) is generally considered the most successful Abbasid ruler between the period of anarchy at Samarra (247–257/861–871) through the Būyid takeover of Baghdad (334/946). He solidified Abbasid control over Iraq and western Iran, filled the state treasury, and

1. Geertz, "Centers, Kings, and Charisma," 124.

revived Baghdad as the imperial capital.[2] Due to these impressive successes, al-Muʿtaḍid is often portrayed in the sources as a model ruler.[3] In what follows I describe the aspects of caliphal authority that this "model ruler" projected, so admired by contemporaries. This pattern will then serve as a starting point for analyzing the process of change in the nature and expression of caliphal authority in the last half-century of independent Abbasid rule.

The cornerstone of al-Muʿtaḍid's power was his close relationship with the military.[4] He had been extensively trained for combat by his father al-Muwaffaq, and while still a prince was one of the leading generals in the Abbasid counteroffensive against the Zanj rebellion (255–270/869–883). During this long campaign, al-Muʿtaḍid reportedly demonstrated prowess and tactical acumen. He outmaneuvered the enemy on several occasions and undermined the morale of Zanj rebels by encouraging them to defect for money and gifts.[5] He was also known as a great marksman.[6] Most importantly, he displayed courage and leadership by leading his troops into battle. He was at the vanguard of every attack, continued fighting even when wounded, and was so eager to attack the enemy that he sometimes set out on an offensive before some of his troops were ready.[7] Al-Muʿtaḍid's firm leadership in this campaign established strong ties between him and the military elite.[8]

Upon accession to the caliphate, al-Muʿtaḍid continued to demonstrate military leadership, thereby retaining strong ties with the army. He spent more time on campaigns than any previous Abbasid ruler,[9] leading his army across Iraq and Syria, as well as to the Byzantine border. Al-Muʿtaḍid reportedly conducted systematic military reviews, evaluating the skill and subsequently determining assignments and salaries for every cavalryman.[10] He also seems to have acquired a great number of military slaves, for most of the military elite for the next generation were his freedmen.[11] In general, al-Muʿtaḍid represented the culmination of Abbasid military policy, whereby close ties between the caliph and his military clients would be the fundamental pillar of the Abbasid state.

Al-Muʿtaḍid's military efforts certainly impressed contemporaries, and his relentless defense of the state was quickly mythologized. In one anecdote, the caliph interrupted an

2. *For an in-depth look at al-Muʿtaḍid's financial policies, see al-Hasan, "Financial Reforms of the Caliph al-Muʿtaḍid."

3. *For analysis of al-Muʿtaḍid as an idealized ruler, see Malti-Douglas: "Classical Arabic Detective"; and Malti-Douglas, "Texts and Tortures"; as well as Bray, "Caliph and His Public Relations."

4. See Kennedy, "al-Muʿtaḍid," *EI2*; and Kennedy, *Prophet and the Age of the Caliphates*, 183.

5. al-Ṭabarī, *History*, 37:41, 43.

6. al-Ṭabarī, *History*, 37:21.

7. al-Ṭabarī, *History*, 37:18, 23, 42, 75.

8. *For an in-depth look at the depiction of al-Muʿtaḍid's military reputation, see Kennedy, "Caliphs and Their Chroniclers."

9. Kennedy, *Prophet and the Age of the Caliphates*, 183.

10. Hilāl al-Ṣābī, *Wuzarāʾ*, 21.

11. The examples of Muʾnis, Naṣr, and Nāzūk are discussed in greater length in ch. 4 below.

evening of drinking upon being informed that a Daylami force had infiltrated the Iranian city of Qazwīn. Al-Muʿtaḍid immediately summoned the wazir ʿUbaydallāh b. Sulaymān (who feared arrest) and gave detailed orders regarding the situation in Qazwīn. Yet the caliph remained distracted for much of the evening. When a boon companion asked why the caliph had interrupted his revelry and not simply waited until the following day to take action, al-Muʿtaḍid replied:

> I am beside myself with fear for the state, that [the Daylamis] may secretly penetrate Qazwīn—for they would gather there and conquer it, and it is the boundary between us and them.... That would lead to the destruction of the state. I thought to myself that if I delayed even an hour, all would be lost, [the Daylamis] would take possession of Qazwīn; and if they took it, they would rise up from beneath my throne, and would seize the imperial palace.[12]

This anecdote clearly demonstrates the caliph's dedication to, and personal supervision of, state security. According to another story, when al-Muʿtaḍid was told of a new rebellion in distant Ṭarsūs, he immediately left for the military encampment outside Baghdad without changing clothes and swore that he would not change his dress until he had apprehended the chief rebel.[13] These accounts reflect al-Muʿtaḍid's lasting image as the warrior-king par excellence.

Yet what is most striking about al-Muʿtaḍid is the extent to which he exuded authority. Naturally, his powerful presence was felt at court. His stern threats, such as a promise to kill security agents if they did not apprehend the Daylami infiltrator in Qazwīn,[14] certainly humbled state functionaries. We hear that one judicial official was reluctant to confront the caliph about state delinquencies in paying rent for land held by religious foundations (*waqf* endowments), even though at that time it was still taboo to harm members of the judiciary.[15] Even al-Muʿtaḍid's trusted wazir, ʿUbaydallāh b. Sulaymān, was terrified of the caliph and constantly feared removal.[16]

But al-Muʿtaḍid also succeeded in projecting his authority beyond the confines of the palace, out to the capital city, indeed the entire realm. One means of achieving this was to intimidate subjects by exposing them to his imposing presence in the palace. In one anecdote we hear that al-Muʿtaḍid abruptly interrupted a drinking session and went to an adjacent chamber to conduct an audience with a cotton merchant. The anecdote continues:

12. al-Tanūkhī, *Nishwār*, 1:319–21; also translated by Margoliouth, *Table-talk*, 168–70. We might note that al-Muʿtaḍid is made to predict exactly what happens fifty years later, and incredible foresight is indeed one of his consistently idealized traits. In this instance, the imperial palace is mentioned as a symbol of Abbasid rule.

13. al-Tanūkhī, *Nishwār*, 2:248.

14. al-Tanūkhī, *Nishwār*, 1:320.

15. al-Tanūkhī, *Nishwār*, 8:20–21.

16. al-Tanūkhī, *Nishwār*, 8:14.

> [The Caliph] put on a robe, took a spear in his hand, and sat as if terribly angry, so much so that we [his courtiers] feared him, despite our intimacy with him. An old man was brought in, and [the caliph] bellowed in a strong voice: "Are you the cotton merchant who said yesterday what you said?" Thereupon the merchant fainted, so [the caliph] had him removed to the side. When the man had recovered he was brought back, and [al-Muʿtaḍid] said: "Woe unto you! Did you say that the Muslims have nobody looking after their affairs? Then who am I, and what am I doing?"

The cotton merchant explained that someone had distributed clipped (undervalued) coins in the *sūq*, and that his criticism was directed at the *muḥtasib*, the market inspector; moreover, he repented of making the remark. The caliph promptly called for the *muḥtasib* and rebuked him severely, ordering him to ensure proper scales for verifying commercial transactions. The caliph then sent the old merchant home and returned to his courtiers. As in an earlier anecdote, here again one of his companions asked the caliph why he had stopped carousing and not simply delegated this investigation to a subordinate. Al-Muʿtaḍid replied:

> This sort of comment could have spread in the mouths of the populace ... and it would not be long before this generated resentment against the state and religion, and a revolt would break out against the authorities. There is no more effective way of stopping such a thing than to cut it out by the roots from the very start. This man, after his experience here, having fainted, will go out and magnify the rebuke he received, and will exaggerate the imposing and awe-inspiring presence he experienced, going beyond reality. The people will come to hear of the vigilance that we displayed, that the words of no man are unknown to me, that I will not neglect to interrogate the perpetrators [of such comments]. This will save me from taking many actions, since the people will be cautious and will control themselves. Thus, I have put a quick end to something, by words and actions, that left unchecked would have required harsh use of the sword.

Our narrator concludes his report by saying that the courtiers and all present praised the caliph effusively.[17]

This anecdote, like countless others, demonstrates al-Muʿtaḍid's diligence: he does not delay important affairs of state, he addresses them personally, and possesses uncanny foresight. Of greater interest for our purposes is how al-Muʿtaḍid projects authority to the general populace. He intentionally intimidates the cotton merchant, creating an "imposing and awe-inspiring presence," so that the merchant will spread the word that al-Muʿtaḍid has firm control of the state, that he is not the kind of ruler to underestimate or disparage. Special attention should be paid to the means by which al-Muʿtaḍid cre-

17. al-Tanūkhī, *Nishwār*, 1:326–28; also translated by Margoliouth, *Table-talk*, 172–74.

ates this "imposing presence:" the loud voice, the feigned rage, and the spear suggest awesome strength, and recall the caliph's military prowess; we will later see that the caliph al-Muqtadir, with a very different personality and an altogether different means of expressing authority, employs entirely different symbols. Finally, we should not dismiss this story as simply a dramatic performance that overwhelmed an innocent and naïve civilian. The narrator clearly states that the caliph's boon companions also felt intimidated, which suggests that al-Muʿtaḍid had a formidable character that was not solely the creation of his caliphal props.

Al-Muʿtaḍid also projected his awe-inspiring authority through public appearances. At the very beginning of his reign, on the holiday of Eid al-Adha, the caliph rode across Baghdad accompanied by a military escort, then led prayers and delivered the khutba or Friday sermon.[18] This procession, in which the new caliph led the military and performed the traditional rites of the ruler, was intended to convey to the audience, both state officials and the general populace, that al-Muʿtaḍid had taken firm control of the state. Similarly impressive processions were led by al-Muʿtaḍid throughout his reign.[19] As stated above, he went on many military campaigns; and upon setting out and returning from each one, he routinely camped outside the Shamsiyya Gate in northern Baghdad, crossing much of the city in military procession.[20] We have some idea of the impact of these processions on the populace, from an account related by the caliph himself:

> I saw myself in a dream leaving Baghdad with my army for the district of al-Nahrawān. Many onlookers were watching me. I passed by a man standing on a hill. He was praying and paid me no attention. I wondered about him and his lack of interest in my troops when all these people were watching them.[21]

The important point presupposed here is that these processions, and more specifically the caliph and his troops, were the focus of popular attention, which is why al-Muʿtaḍid was surprised that someone would show no interest. His awareness that somebody was not watching and the subsequent investigation as to the reason for this disinterest suggest that the caliph deliberately set out to make a strong impression on his subjects.

Aside from the processions, al-Muʿtaḍid's military reputation developed from the simple fact that he led his army into battle frequently, and always with success. Moreover, the caliph missed no opportunity to publicize his accomplishments, as each victory was celebrated by a dispatch that was read from the pulpits of the mosques of Baghdad,

18. al-Ṭabarī, *History*, 38:4.

19. Sanders makes this argument in the Fatimid context, noting that newly installed rulers traversed Cairo/Fustat at the head of the military, and performed religious rites reserved primarily for rulers (*Ritual*, 36–37, 61–62).

20. See, e.g., al-Ṭabarī *History*, 38:29, 88; al-Tanūkhī, *Nishwār*, 2:248.

21. al-Ṭabarī, *History*, 38:24.

occasionally according to the caliph's own narration.[22] Thus al-Muʿtaḍid continually reiterated his military might, and his successful rule, to an attentive populace.

Al-Muʿtaḍid also made physical demonstrations of his authority throughout the empire. He apparently loved to hunt, a symbolic means of asserting territorial control.[23] But the caliph's most obvious and concrete method of exhibiting authority was to travel across the state with the military. He ventured in virtually all directions, to al-Jazīra and al-Jibāl in northern Iraq, and as far away as Syria and Anatolia; he also visited Mosul at least three times. On many of these missions, he made several intermediate stops,[24] probably to make contact with local notables. Throughout the Abbasid Empire, the caliph's imposing presence, supported by his successful army, was tangible proof of his pervasive authority.

In summary, al-Muʿtaḍid was considered an outstanding ruler. His basis of power lay in close relations with the military; yet he also had a powerful personality that commanded profound respect. He used this combination of a forceful character and military might to project his authority throughout the state: a highly visible caliph in total control of the imperial palace, the capital city, and the entire realm.

Creating a New Caliph

I turn now to how al-Muʿtaḍid's son al-Muqtadir came to the throne, and the forms of authority he developed as caliph. I first analyze his life as a prince. We will see that this future caliph was not inherently born or even bred to assert authority: the authority he would wield as a caliph would have to be cultivated, constructed. I subsequently discuss the construction of this authority, founded upon two main elements: a network of military clients, inherited from his father; and an image of majesty. We will see how al-Muqtadir wielded these forms of authority and how they compared to the behavior of his father al-Muʿtaḍid. I then explore the repercussions of the differences between these two rulers.

Childhood: The Raw Material

Throughout Abbasid history, caliphs had usually undergone a period of preparation while they were still princes. Most royal children received symbolic honors, such as public celebration of their circumcisions and weddings, or oaths of allegiance, which asserted their superior status. Heirs apparent were often dispatched to govern provinces and/or to command armies, thus gaining practical experience for ruling an empire. Such missions also gave them a setting for acting as authority figures away from the presence

22. al-Ṭabarī, *History*, 38:16, 27, 76.

23. al-Tanūkhī, *Nishwār*, 3:260; Ibn al-Jawzī, *al-Muntaẓam*, 5:129.

24. For example, in al-Ṭabarī, *History*, 38:91, one of the caliph's lengthier journeys.

of their fathers, and for acquiring the trappings of power on a small scale, thereby emphasizing their status as rulers-in-the-making. During these missions, and even at home in Baghdad, princes acquired large retinues including experienced mentors and personal servants; this provided them with a loyal staff upon which to base their rule. By these various means, princes acquired the tools and personnel for administering the empire and developed an image of authority that would eventually legitimize their accession to the caliphate.[25]

Al-Muʿtaḍid had provided just such preparation for his eldest son al-Muktafī, who became caliph (289–295/902–908) upon his father's death. At the age of seventeen, al-Muktafī was appointed by his father as governor of Rayy and the surrounding regions, a task that he performed to al-Muʿtaḍid's satisfaction.[26] Five years later, at the age of twenty-two, al-Muktafī was put in charge of armies with the task of subduing regions along the Byzantine border;[27] he later led the military offensive against the rebellious eunuch Waṣīf.[28] Al-Muktafī thus acquired practical experience in administration and warfare. He also developed an image of authority. In one poem, he was referred to as "the *amīr* Abū Muḥammad who illumines with his splendor the darkest darkness,"[29] praise that was worthy of the caliph himself. With an established position of authority and a high public profile as heir apparent, al-Muktafī was able to assume the position of caliph upon his father's death with apparently no opposition or upheaval. Like several previous Abbasids, he had begun to assume the role and image of caliph before actually acquiring the office.

Al-Muktafī died of illness after a brief reign (289–295/902–908), and was succeeded by his younger brother, Jaʿfar al-Muqtadir (295–320/908–932).[30] The new caliph was only thirteen years old upon his accession and had little opportunity to prepare for assuming the caliphate. His father al-Muʿtaḍid, the person most likely to train him, had died when al-Muqtadir was only seven; his older brother al-Muktafī died only a few years later, without having made serious plans for a successor, as can be seen in the rather hasty search for an heir.[31] Thus even had al-Muktafī wanted to train his younger brother, which is unlikely since he would have probably preferred to promote his own sons, he simply died too soon and al-Muqtadir was too young. As a result, al-Muqtadir never appears in the sources as receiving any official duties or symbolic honors while still a prince; he

25. The best study of the training of heirs apparent is Chejne, *Succession to the Rule*. His analysis does not include the period under investigation here. The issue of princely training will be discussed in detail in the next chapter, which will concentrate on al-Muqtadir's children.

26. al-Ṭabarī, *History*, 38:14 (also see Rosenthal's footnote 83).

27. al-Ṭabarī, *History*, 38:76

28. al-Ṭabarī, *History*, 38:89.

29. al-Ṭabarī, *History*, 38:37.

30. The chaotic process by which this young prince was chosen as ruler of the empire and the relationships and strategies at work in this process are explored below.

31. Al-Muktafī was sick for several months, which was enough time for complicated intrigue around the choice of a successor. All the confusion over who would be al-Muktafī's heir shows that he had not prepared a candidate prior to falling ill.

received no training in rulership, established no ties of personal patronage, and occupied no setting for developing an image of authority. Al-Muqtadir thus lacked the skills, relationships, and image he would need as caliph.

One of the rare references to al-Muqtadir's childhood illustrates the point that the prince was not by his innate nature prepared to assume the role of caliph. The following story is narrated by the eunuch Ṣāfī al-Ḥuramī, one of al-Muʿtaḍid's intimate servants and later the protector of al-Muqtadir; the lengthy anecdote wonderfully illustrates the expectations of a royal father, and the importance of individual character:

> I was walking one day with al-Muʿtaḍid, who wanted to go to the quarters of the harem. When he reached the door of Shaghab, al-Muqtadir's mother, he stood, eavesdropped and then peeked from behind the curtain. Al-Muqtadir was there, roughly five years old, sitting surrounded by companions of roughly his age. There was a vine of grapes in a silver dish in front of him, at a time when grapes were very expensive. The boy ate one grape, then fed each of the group one grape at a time, in turns; when it was his turn he ate one grape just like the others, until the vine was finished.
>
> Al-Muʿtaḍid burst with anger and left without entering [the harem rooms]. I saw that he was distressed, and said "O Master, why did you leave? What overcame you?" He replied, "Ṣāfī, by God, if not for hellfire and dishonor, I would kill this boy today: killing him would be good for the [Muslim] community." So I said, "Master, God forbid! What did he do? God save you, Master, from the accursed devil." "Woe unto you!" he responded, "I know what I'm saying, I'm a man who has ruled the state, and set the world right after severe deterioration. Someday I will die, and I know that after my death the people will only choose one of my sons; they will enthrone my eldest"—meaning al-Muktafī—"but I don't think his days will be long, due to his illness"—meaning the Scrofula that infected his body—. "He will die soon; and the people will not want to take [the caliphate] from my children, but they will not find anyone older than Jaʿfar, and they will seat him while he is a boy. He is by nature generous: we have seen that he feeds children the same food that he eats, and made himself equal to them, with regard to something very expensive, even though children his age are usually stingy. Therefore women will dominate him, due to his close contact with them; he will distribute the money I have saved just as he distributed the grapes. He will waste the benefits of the world, will wreck it, and will lose the border regions; authority will be dispersed and rebels will appear, and there will come about the conditions for the removal of the state from the Abbasid family." I said, "Master, but God will preserve you so that he will grow up in your lifetime and reach maturity during your reign, and be educated in your knowledge and shaped by your character, and what you imagine will not come to pass." "Heed what I say," he responded, "for it will come to pass." That whole day he remained disturbed. Fate took its course: al-Muʿtaḍid died; al-Muktafī

> was appointed, but his time did not last and he died; and al-Muqtadir was chosen. The situation is exactly as al-Muʿtaḍid had described.[32]

On the most basic level, this story gives us our few details about al-Muqtadir's childhood. He apparently played in his mother's quarters and likely grew up under her care; this fact, plus the assertion of his "close contact" with women, suggest that al-Muqtadir spent a lot of time with his mother and her staff. As we might expect for a prince, al-Muqtadir enjoyed luxury, as the eating of grapes out of season on a silver dish attests. We also learn that he played with other children of lower status and was not confined to royal siblings. Finally, we might also note that al-Muʿtaḍid considered the welfare of the state a higher priority than that of his son, as he expresses a desire to kill al-Muqtadir for the good of the state.

This anecdote is especially interesting in that it assesses the perception of authority demonstrated by the young prince, relative to the kind of authority considered necessary for an effective caliph. On the one hand Prince Jaʿfar seems to dominate his social surroundings, as he controls the action taking place—the distribution of grapes—to his childhood companions. In this respect al-Muqtadir behaves like a royal child dictating to friends of lower status. He was also very generous, willing to share the grapes evenly. But the young Jaʿfar was ignorant of the grapes' value, which made his graciousness appear, especially to his father, as reckless extravagance. Al-Muʿtaḍid was clearly concerned that his son's generosity would lead to waste. But beyond this waste, al-Muʿtaḍid was angry that the prince had "made himself equal to them," by sharing with no regard for distinction of status. The boy had effectively renounced his elevated rank by failing to maintain distinctions between himself and others. He would make a bad ruler, for at least as a child, he did not grasp the importance of his superior status, and the need to constantly reassert it. Al-Muʿtaḍid is implicitly suggesting that status differentiation is the foundation of authority, which in turn upholds the state; and the young prince was clearly oblivious to this fundamental sociopolitical principle.

Ṣāfī sought to calm al-Muʿtaḍid's fears; and his suggestion, that the prince might be educated during his father's lifetime, reflects another basic sociopolitical assumption: that the conscious possession and assertion of superior status—the wielding of authority—can be taught and developed, and are not necessarily innate outgrowths of royal pedigree. This notion, that authority could be shaped, was the idea behind the apprenticeships of heirs apparent. Previous Abbasids had been trained to value, embody, and project superiority, and al-Muqtadir would likewise develop, over time, his own sense of grandeur. In other words, majesty may not be born, but it can be made. Unfortunately,

32. al-Tanūkhī, *Nishwār*, 1:287–88, also translated by Margoliouth, *Table-talk*, 152–54; a very similar version is in Ibn al-Jawzī, *al-Muntaẓam*, 6:70–72.

*A part of this text has subsequently been translated by van Berkel ("Vizier and the Harem Stewardess," 315; and van Berkel, "Young Caliph," 3–4).

al-Muqtadir's father and older brother died before he could be trained; he would have to develop such "majesty" as he would achieve while already in the position of caliph.

The story is clearly anachronistic, and in its hindsight establishes two themes that will be important for analysis of al-Muqtadir's caliphate. First, the anecdote creates a sharp dichotomy between al-Muʿtaḍid and al-Muqtadir and suggests a fundamental difference in character. Second, a direct link is established between the caliphs' respective characters, and the impact they have on the state; al-Muʿtaḍid "set the world right," while al-Muqtadir "will wreck it." There is a dual message here: responsibility for the decline of the state is squarely attributed to al-Muqtadir, which means that any analysis of this decline must begin with this caliph; and his failure was not strictly a matter of policy, but of character.[33]

The Foundations of Power: Patron-relations

When analyzing the emergence of al-Muqtadir as caliph, contemporary sources and modern scholars consistently emphasize the decisive role of various bureaucrats. This thesis usually has a corollary, according to which during the early years of al-Muqtadir's reign the bureaucracy was the dominant power at court.[34] I believe that these assertions are inaccurate, that they obscure the real force that stood behind al-Muqtadir's succession, namely a network of military clients. Below, I follow the events of 295 and 296 (August to December, 908), when al-Muqtadir was enthroned as caliph. My underlying argument is that bureaucrats were not in fact decisive in this historic development and were in a sense defeated; rather, it was a group of military clients, whom al-Muqtadir inherited from his father, who succeeded in installing their new patron. They, and not the bureaucrats, would remain the basis of al-Muqtadir's power throughout his reign.

Accession to the Throne

The process by which Jaʿfar al-Muqtadir was chosen to succeed al-Muktafī as caliph was very complicated. The different sources provide varying details, and a perfect chronology seems impossible to establish.[35] The immediate impression derived from the sources is that al-Muktafī's senior bureaucrats were in complete control of the selection of the new

33. *Letizia Osti similarly argues that "al-Muqtadir became the paradigm of the disastrous caliph" (in van Berkel et al, *Crisis and Continuity*, 51); she also points out the somewhat divergent presentation of the historian al-Ṣūlī, who—as tutor and later courtier to al-Muqtadir's son and successor—was more sympathetic to the now deceased caliph.

34. Kennedy, *Prophet and the Age of the Caliphates*, 187–88.

35. Bowen (*ʿAlī b. ʿĪsā*, 84–88), has presented a plausible narrative, and thus the complex events will not be related here in their entirety.

*Osti ("ʿAbbāsid Intrigues," 7–9), has compared the historical narratives of two specific historians, al-Ṣūlī and Miskawayh, for this specific event, arguing that Miskawayh attributes greater agency and

caliph. When al-Muktafī became seriously ill, "[the wazir] al-ʿAbbās b. al-Ḥasan began to consider whom he should appoint caliph."[36] He consulted with leading administrators: a certain Muḥammad b. Dāwud suggested ʿAbdallāh b. al-Muʿtazz, a mature member of the Abbasid royal family who was apparently favored by other state officials as well. ʿAlī b. ʿĪsā, a senior bureaucrat, abstained from expressing an opinion; but his colleague ʿAlī b. Muḥammad b. al-Furāt, in a blatant articulation of self-interest, discouraged the wazir from favoring Ibn al-Muʿtazz:

> "For God's sake do not appoint to this post someone who knows the home of one and the wealth of another, the garden of this person and the slave woman of that person, one person's property and another's horse; someone who has interacted with people, who is familiar and experienced in affairs, and who has calculated people's fortunes." The wazir asked me to repeat this a few times, then said: "So whom do you recommend?" I replied, "Jaʿfar b. al-Muʿtaḍid." "What do you mean!" he answered, "Jaʿfar is a boy." So I said, "Except he is the son of al-Muʿtaḍid. Why appoint a man who will command and forbid, understanding our finances, and take command of the administration by himself, considering himself independent? Why not give control to someone who will turn the administration over to you?"

Arguing for a weak caliph, Ibn al-Furāt nominated the young prince Jaʿfar, son of al-Muʿtaḍid.[37]

At some point the wazir al-ʿAbbās contemplated other candidates, and reportedly conducted negotiations with two additional senior Abbasids (Muḥammad b. al-Muʿtamid and Muḥammad b. al-Muʿtazz).[38] Yet by the time of al-Muktafī's death, al-ʿAbbās had decided upon al-Muqtadir; one source claims that al-ʿAbbās had decided to exploit the young caliph, while another says that al-ʿAbbās decided upon al-Muqtadir against his better judgement. Whatever his motives, "the wazir al-ʿAbbās appointed Jaʿfar to the caliphate."[39] Scholars have accepted and emphasized that the bureaucrats were responsible for the succession; as Hugh Kennedy summarizes: "the choosing of the new caliph reveals clearly where power now lay ... only the bureaucrats were involved in the decision making."[40]

---

responsibility to leading bureaucrats, than does al-Ṣūlī, who presents the caliph al-Muktafī as more influential in deciding the succession.

36. Miskawayh, *Tajārib*, 1; al-Hamadhānī, *Takmila*, 4.

37. Miskawayh, *Tajārib*, 2 (translated by Amedroz and Margoliouth, *Eclipse*, 2).

38. Al-ʿAbbās reportedly intended to appoint Muḥammad b. al-Muʿtamid and arranged for the judge Abū ʿUmar to witness the negotiations (ʿArīb, *Ṣilat*, 20), though for unknown reasons this appointment never came to fruition. Al-ʿAbbās is also said to have sworn allegiance to Ibn al-Muʿtazz even before the caliph al-Muktafī's death (ʿArīb, *Ṣilat*, 25).

39. Miskawayh, *Tajārib*, 3.

40. Kennedy, *Prophet and the Age of the Caliphates*, 187–88.

Yet there are several indications that the bureaucrats were not dominant in determining the succession. First of all, al-Muktafī himself had apparently arranged to have his younger brother Jaᶜfar succeed to the throne. Toward the beginning of his illness, al-Muktafī was told by Ṣāfī al-Ḥuramī that rumors were spreading of Ibn al-Muᶜtazz or Muḥammad b. al-Muᶜtamid taking power; Ṣāfī suggested imprisoning these two princes, presumably to prevent them from securing the caliphate. Al-Muktafī refused to imprison them, but the report startled him, so that "he feared that sovereignty would be removed from the children of his father."[41] Al-Muktafī apparently realized that he must ensure the continued rule of his immediate family by securing the succession for Jaᶜfar, so when his illness became severe, "he asked about his brother Jaᶜfar, and it was confirmed that [Jaᶜfar] was of legal age; so he summoned judges and had them witness that he appointed [Jaᶜfar] his successor."[42] This text makes it very clear that al-Muktafī chose al-Muqtadir as heir. The wazir al-ᶜAbbās is presented in this chronology as still favoring Muḥammad b. al-Muᶜtamid, and plays no part in al-Muktafī's selection of Jaᶜfar. Moreover, even Miskawayh's account, whereby the wazir al-ᶜAbbās took upon himself the task of choosing the heir, concludes that "al-ᶜAbbās b. al-Ḥasan inclined to Ibn al-Furāt's view [of promoting Jaᶜfar al-Muqtadir], which concurred with what al-Muktafī had [already] authorized, namely the appointment of his brother Jaᶜfar to the caliphate."[43] While Miskawayh does not discuss how or why al-Muktafī had decided upon Jaᶜfar, the historian does suggest that al-Muktafī's decision was independent of that of al-ᶜAbbās and Ibn al-Furāt, and even preceded the bureaucrats' consultations. Miskawayh's main focus is the bureaucrats at court, and here he is interested in showing the extent of Ibn al-Furāt's ambition and the influence of the bureaucrats generally; thus, he minimizes the fact that al-ᶜAbbās and Ibn al-Furāt had merely decided upon the candidate whom al-Muktafī, the dying caliph, had already chosen.

Furthermore, there was another powerful group at court who had a particular interest in al-Muqtadir and in fact ensured his succession: al-Muᶜtaḍid's military clients.[44] These men had been imported from distant lands and were trained by al-Muᶜtaḍid (and the latter's father al-Muwaffaq); they owed their powerful positions entirely to their personal relationship with the now deceased al-Muᶜtaḍid. They could only hope to retain their elite status if al-Muᶜtaḍid's children, and hence their masters by inheritance, occupied the caliphate. They had retained power during al-Muktafī's caliphate, and were no doubt intent on maintaining al-Muᶜtaḍid's line by arranging for Jaᶜfar b. al-Muᶜtaḍid's succession.

The first hint of this established interest-group at court is seen in the story presented earlier, when al-Muᶜtaḍid was furious that Prince Jaᶜfar was sharing grapes. He had told

41. ᶜArīb, *Ṣilat*, 21.

42. ᶜArīb, *Ṣilat*, 21; also in Ibn al-Jawzī, *al-Muntaẓam*, 6:67.

43. Miskawayh, *Tajārib*, 3.

44. These men are not identified by name until the year 296/908, when they defend al-Muqtadir from a coup attempt (see below).

Ṣāfī: "I know that after my death the people will only choose one of my sons;" and "the people will not want to remove [the caliphate] from my children."[45] He does not indicate, however, exactly who these "people" are, who specifically want his descendants to rule. But as the succession question developed, the identity of these "people" became clear. We have seen that this same Ṣāfī, al-Muʿtaḍid's most trusted *mawlā*, warned al-Muktafī of rumors concerning other claimants to the throne (Ibn al-Muʿtazz and Muḥammad b. al-Muʿtamid), and urged al-Muktafī to imprison them. Ṣāfī instigated al-Muktafī so as to ensure the succession of al-Muqtadir; and this provocation succeeded, as al-Muktafī began to worry about the preservation of his father's line and arranged for al-Muqtadir's accession.[46]

The clearest expression in the sources concerning the attitude of al-Muʿtaḍid's *mawlās* involves the wazir al-ʿAbbās's reported attempt to make Muḥammad b. al-Muʿtamid the candidate for the caliphate.[47] The wazir had supposedly decided that al-Muqtadir was too young to rule and wanted to appoint Muḥammad b. al-Muʿtamid. He hesitated, however, and waited for approaching troops from Khurasan, whose presence he wanted as support "against the military clients (*ghilmān*) of al-Muʿtaḍid."[48] Al-ʿAbbās realized that al-Muʿtaḍid's *mawlās* wanted al-Muqtadir as caliph, and would physically oppose any change in the succession arrangement; his plan could only succeed if he had military support capable of withstanding al-Muʿtaḍid's clients. As things turned out, Muḥammad b. al-Muʿtamid died before the Khurasanis arrived, and the young Jaʿfar al-Muqtadir was installed as originally planned. In sum: Al-Muʿtaḍid's *mawlās* wanted al-Muqtadir as caliph, and their imposing presence sufficiently intimidated the wazir al-ʿAbbās that his plan to replace al-Muqtadir was delayed and ultimately collapsed.

Finally, Ṣāfī even protected al-Muqtadir on the very day of enthronement: he retrieved Jaʿfar from the palace in which children of the caliphs lived,[49] and escorted him by boat to the royal palace. Along the way they passed the residence of the wazir al-ʿAbbās, whereupon al-ʿAbbās's servants urged Ṣāfī to bring al-Muqtadir into the wazir's home. Ṣāfī, suspicious of a plot to prevent al-Muqtadir's accession, avoided al-ʿAbbās's residence and went straight to the royal palace, where al-Muqtadir was subsequently invested as caliph.[50] Regardless of al-ʿAbbās's actual intentions, we see that Ṣāfī was de

45. al-Tanūkhī, *Nishwār*, 1:287.

46. ʿArīb, *Ṣilat*, 21. The term "*mawlā*" refers to the military slaves and freedmen frequently referred to in the sources, which I will occasionally translate as military "clients" (for further explanation, see Pipes, *Slave Soldiers*, ch. 1: "What Is a Military Slave?").

47. This part of the succession question is hard to place chronologically: ʿArīb has it before al-Muktafī's death, and Miskawayh has it after. Neither version is inherently preferable, and either way al-Muqtadir had already been chosen as successor, thus the precise timing does not affect the argument that follows.

48. Miskawayh, *Tajārib*, 4. "*Ghilmān*" refers to al-Muʿtaḍid's military clients, i.e., his *mawlās*.

49. The Ṭāhirid Palace in northern Baghdad, discussed in ch. 2 below.

50. ʿArīb (*Ṣilat*, 22): "Al-ʿAbbās b. al-Ḥasan called for Ṣāfī to bring al-Muqtadir into his home, where he resided on the Tigris, so that he could take him [al Muqtadir] down to the royal palace. But Ṣāfī

termined to install al-Muqtadir as caliph, and took all precautions to ensure that this should be achieved.[51]

The Ceremony of Investiture

Al-Muqtadir was given the oath of allegiance in the royal palace less than twenty-four hours after his brother's death, and officially became the caliph. Surprisingly, the sources provide few details about the ceremony which turned a prince into the Commander of the Faithful—we might therefore assume that our scant information represents the most important aspects of this momentous ritual. ʿArīb presents the fullest account:

> The oath of allegiance for al-Muqtadir was conducted in the Ḥasanī Palace. When he entered and saw the throne erected, he ordered a prayer rug, which was laid for him; he prayed four rak'ahs, and continued calling out loud for guidance [from God]. Then he sat on the throne, and people swore allegiance to him. Ṣāfī al-Ḥuramī and Fātik al-Muʿtaḍidī conducted the oath; the wazir al-ʿAbbās b. al-Ḥasan and his son were present until the oath was completed. Then [the deceased caliph] al-Muktafī was washed and buried.[52]

A few symbolic actions, probably standard for this ceremony, are emphasized in this report. First, and perhaps most important, is the invocation of God.[53] Al-Muqtadir prays to God and calls for guidance, thus infusing the ceremony with a divine presence and suggesting divine sanction of his appointment. The prayer also makes the new caliph appear

avoided al-ʿAbbās's home, fearing he would be tricked; and that was attributed to Ṣāfī's prudence and intelligence." Miskawayh: "The retainers of al-ʿAbbās called out to [Ṣāfī's] boatman to come inside. It occurred to Ṣāfī al-Ḥuramī that al-ʿAbbās only desired Jaʿfar to enter his palace because he had changed his mind with regard to the prince; fearing that the vizier might transfer his choice to someone else, Ṣāfī told the boatman not to go in, and drawing his sword said to the boatman: 'If you go inside, I will cut off your head.' So the boatman proceeded without stopping to the ruler's palace" (*Tajārib*, 3–4; translation from *Eclipse*, 3). Al-Hamadhānī's version (*Takmila*, 4) is very similar to Miskawayh's, only he adds that al-ʿAbbās's servants called for Ṣāfī so that they could change al-Muqtadir's clothes (again, it is impossible to know if this was al-ʿAbbās's innocent intention, or just the excuse used by his men in an attempt to fool Ṣāfī).

51. *Kennedy also hints at the decisive role of al-Muʿtaḍid's military clients in determining the accession of al-Muqtadir: "His accession had ultimately depended upon his brother's nomination and the determination of al-Muktafī and the *ghilmān* of the palace to keep the highest office in the hands of the children of al-Muʿtaḍid" (van Berkel et al, *Crisis and Continuity*, 21).

52. ʿArīb, *Ṣilat*, 22. This ceremony took place on Sunday, 13th of Dhu'l Qadah 295 (14 August, 908).

53. According to Emil Tyan, a major theoretical question concerning the oath of allegiance was whether it invested authority, or confirmed authority invested by God ("*Bayʿa*," *EI2*). I would think it was in the caliphs' best interests to support the latter theory, whereby God appointed new caliphs, and the community of Muslims recognized new appointments. This would suggest that an obligation to the caliph was virtually an obligation to God, and would make criticism, let alone forcible removal, of a divinely appointed ruler akin to sacrilege.

pious and worthy. Also, the caliph sits while everyone else presumably stands: indeed, the whole ritual is referred to as "sitting for the *bayʿa*."[54] As mentioned earlier, the act of remaining seated while others stand is a recurring symbol of honor and prestige in the sources; and it is worth noting here that the first physical expression of the distinction between ruler and subjects is that he sits while they stand. More generally, it is striking that the focus is entirely on al-Muqtadir, and not at all on his subjects. The few details describe his actions; we hear nothing of the subjects' physical location relative to the caliph, the content of their oath, or even the identity of those who participated beyond the vague term "the people."[55] The ritual is essentially about receiving allegiance, not granting it; the ceremony involves the creation of "The Caliph," not of a caliph-subject relationship. While the oath was supposed to establish a contract between ruler and ruled, this depiction of the *bayʿa* strongly suggests the crowning of an autocrat.

More important for our purposes, we see that Ṣāfī and Fātik, freedmen whose loyalty al-Muqtadir had acquired from his father, supervise the investiture—they are the most important figures to attend the ceremony. Though the wazir al-ʿAbbās is present, he has no obvious function. The central role granted to Ṣāfī and Fātik reinforces the argument that al-Muʿtaḍid's *mawlās* were the strongest force supporting the caliphate of al-Muqtadir.

The Failed Coup of 296/908

Only four months after the accession, al-Muqtadir's position as caliph was threatened by an attempted coup. While the sources differ widely in the details they provide, a fairly coherent picture nevertheless emerges.[56] Many of Baghdad's leading figures—"commanders, bureaucrats, and judges,"[57] most of whom had originally preferred Ibn al-Muʿtazz as al-Muktafī's successor—now decided to remove al-Muqtadir from the throne due to his youth, and to replace him with the more experienced Ibn al-Muʿtazz. Apparently the conspiracy was led by the secretary Muḥammad b. Dāwud and the warrior al-

54. Ibn al-Jawzī, *al-Muntaẓam*, 6:67; we have also seen that al-Muʿtaḍid told Ṣāfī that people would "seat" his oldest son, referring to the ritual of installation.

55. "*al-nās*" probably referring to the court elite. Descriptions of previous investitures include the various groups at court (the military, palace servants, the Hāshimīte extended royal family, etc.) who swore allegiance and even provide the names of participants. The point here is that for ʿArīb, and possibly for much of court society, this particular ceremony was about the ruler, not ruler-subject relations. This might reflect the assumption that allegiances were simply inherited, and/or an awareness that the oath itself was not, in practice, binding on either party.

56. One indication of the vast differences in historical narratives of this event: Ibn Khallikān, writing nearly four hundred years later, gives two alternative dates for the coup, and three possibilities for the regnal title of the pretender to the caliphate (*Wafayāt*, 2:41).

57. ʿArīb, *Ṣilat*, 24–25.

Ḥusayn b. Ḥamdān,[58] both of whom had a particular incentive in that they bore grudges against the wazir al-ʿAbbās b. al-Ḥasan.[59] The one point upon which all the sources agree is that the movement to replace al-Muqtadir with Ibn al-Muʿtazz enjoyed widespread support throughout the Baghdadi elite.[60]

The coup began when al-Ḥusayn b. Ḥamdān murdered the wazir al-ʿAbbās on the way to the rose gardens, but failed to kill al-Muqtadir, who had been playing at the polo grounds but escaped to the royal palace.[61] Ibn Ḥamdān informed his co-conspirators that al-ʿAbbās was dead, whereupon an elaborate gathering was convened at the official waziral palace for the swearing of allegiance to Ibn al-Muʿtazz.[62] Once again the sources emphasize that most of the important people of Baghdad were present, the only absentees being the secretary Ibn al-Furāt, and all of al-Muqtadir's personal clients.[63] The leading members of state swore allegiance to Ibn al-Muʿtazz in the presence of judges, and each member of the military was called upon by name to give the oath. Ibn al-Muʿtazz made a series of official appointments and then sent word to al-Muqtadir to vacate the royal palace, and go with his mother to the palace for princes; al-Muqtadir agreed, intending to leave the next day. ʿArīb summarizes the situation to this point: "People had no doubt that the affair was settled, since the people of state had all agreed upon it."[64]

But then the coup began to falter. The men attached to al-Muqtadir at his palace, mostly *mawlās* of his father al-Muʿtaḍid, faced with the removal of their new patron, decided to defend their own interests by resisting a change of caliph. They reportedly said to one another:

58. Miskawayh, *Tajārib*, 5; al-Hamadhānī, *Takmila*, 5. We saw earlier that Muḥammad b. Dāwud had suggested Ibn al-Muʿtazz to the wazir al-ʿAbbās as a candidate to the caliphate.

59. Ibn Dāwud had not received what he wanted (which is not specified) from the wazir al-ʿAbbās, so he sought Ibn Ḥamdān's assistance in removing al-Muqtadir (al-Hamadhānī, *Takmila*, 5). Ibn Ḥamdān, for his part, had been offended by al-ʿAbbās and determined to kill him (ʿArīb, *Ṣilat*, 26).

60. "Many of the commanders, secretaries, and judges agreed upon the removal of al-Muqtadir" (ʿArīb, *Ṣilat*, 25). Similar versions appear in al-Ṭabarī (*History*, 38:189); Ibn al-Jawzī (*al-Muntaẓam*, 6:69), and Ibn al-Athīr (*al-Kāmil*, 8:4).

61. Only a few sources assert that Ibn Ḥamdān tried to kill al-Muqtadir; see Miskawayh (*Tajārib*, 5) and Ibn al-Athīr (*al-Kāmil*, 8:5).

62. I noted in the introduction that the waziral palace was an important center of authority. Yet we will see that acquiring the caliphate meant occupying the royal palace complex, the *Dār al-Khilāfa*, which was the true center of authority.

63. Miskawayh: "There were present the commanders of the army, the heads of the bureaucrats ... the judges and notables, with the exception of Abū al-Ḥasan Ibn al-Furāt, and the persons attached to al-Muqtadir" (*Tajārib*, 5; translation: *Eclipse*, 5); al-Hamadhānī: "Leaders of state from among the bureaucrats, commanders and judges were present, and gave the oath of allegiance" (*Takmila*, 5). These "clients," who did not participate in the coup, were the *mawlās*—the military slaves and freedmen—who had been attached to al-Muʿtaḍid, and transferred allegiance to their original master's sons, first al-Muktafī and then al-Muqtadir, as was standard practice at the Abbasid court. See Pipes, *Slave Soldiers*, ch. 1: "What Is a Military Slave?"

64. ʿArīb, *Ṣilat*, 27.

> Friends, are we going to surrender control so easily? Why not fight off those who threaten us? Perhaps God will make them vulnerable to us.[65]

Thus, when al-Ḥusayn b. Ḥamdān came to the palace the next morning to remove al-Muqtadir, he was denied entry; and when he attacked the palace, al-Muqtadir's men held firm and successfully protected the caliph within the palace. Ibn Ḥamdān then unexpectedly abandoned the coup and returned with his troops to Mosul, amidst speculation that he had made a deal with al-Muqtadir. The caliph's loyalists, with new momentum, counterattacked under the command of Muʾnis al-Khādim.[66] They sailed in boats to the waziral palace, where Ibn al-Muʿtazz and his supporters were located, and began shooting arrows; the conspirators promptly scattered in fear.[67] The coup fell apart. Supporters of Ibn al-Muʿtazz now returned to al-Muqtadir with apologies or went into hiding; several people, most notably Ibn al-Muʿtazz, the pretender to the throne, and a few minor military figures were executed; other supporters of the coup attempt, secretaries, judges, even a merchant, were fined and pardoned.[68] Ibn al-Furāt was appointed as the new wazir, and the oath of allegiance to al-Muqtadir was renewed. Al-Muqtadir was once again recognized as caliph.

The failure of the coup, despite its broad support, has baffled historians. Muslim chroniclers explain al-Muqtadir's retention of the caliphate as divine will,[69] and "good luck" has even been invoked.[70] Yet important lessons can be drawn from these events. This coup was the first attempt by a broad spectrum of state officials to remove an Abbasid caliph and thus provides us with an opportunity to see popular perceptions and expectations of "a caliph," and the issues involved in changing the occupant of this office. Most obviously, the supporters of Ibn al-Muʿtazz wanted a capable and experienced man as ruler and sought to depose the young and impressionable al-Muqtadir for the good of society, though a few conspirators were motivated by personal grudges. The obvious assumption underlying this movement was that a caliph could and should be removed, if necessary, for the public good. More striking is the nearly universal disregard for the oath of allegiance that had been sworn four months earlier. We hear of only one man, the

---

65. Miskawayh, *Tajārib*, 6 (cf. translation: *Eclipse*, 6).

66. This is the first important appearance of Muʾnis as al-Muqtadir's leading general; he had previously been mentioned as one of the men who helped defend the palace hours earlier.

67. al-Ṭabarī (*History*, 38:190) and ʿArīb (*Ṣilat*, 28) report that Muʾnis indeed attacked (with arrows), prompting Ibn al-Muʿtazz's supporters to scatter. Miskawayh, however, specifically states that these supporters scattered upon seeing Muʾnis's boats approaching, before the attack had even begun (*Tajārib*, 6).

68. Miskawayh, *Tajārib*, 7.

*For the specific experience of Ibn al-Jaṣṣāṣ, a wealthy jewelry merchant who tried unsuccessfully to hide Ibn al-Muʿtazz when the coup failed, see Marmer "Asset Management."

69. ʿArīb, *Ṣilat*, 28. Miskawayh writes: "Then was accomplished which God had foreknown and foreordained, that al-Muqtadir should be established in the caliphate. The efforts and schemes of created beings to remove him were unavailing" (*Tajārib*, 8–9; translation: *Eclipse*, 9).

70. Kennedy, *Prophet and the Age of the Caliphates*, 193.

judge Ibn Abī al-Shawārib, who hesitated to give the oath to Ibn al-Muʿtazz, asking "what has al-Muqtadir done [wrong]?"[71] A host of other judges, as well as the famously pious secretary ʿAlī b. ʿĪsā, all swore allegiance to Ibn al-Muʿtazz, with no sign of any regret over breaking their previous oath to al-Muqtadir.

There is also absolutely no acknowledgment of the awesome audacity of replacing the Commander of the Faithful. In fact, I would suggest that al-Muqtadir was not really perceived as "The Caliph." True, he had received the oath of allegiance; but this was apparently withdrawn by the Baghdadi elite without any serious expressions of remorse or guilt. The oath had conferred only the title of "caliph" upon al-Muqtadir, but not the stature and authority which real caliphs possessed. In short, the court elite took the view that the creation of a caliph involved more than an oath of allegiance, and al-Muqtadir simply did not embody or project majesty.

As for explaining the failure of the coup, we should focus on the role of al-Muqtadir's protectors, the former *mawlās* of al-Muʿtaḍid. These men, especially Ṣāfī al-Ḥuramī, had ensured in the events leading up to al-Muqtadir's original investiture that their new patron should receive the caliphate. Now they confronted an attempt to replace al-Muqtadir with Ibn al-Muʿtazz, which, if successful, would leave them with no link to the head of state. Thus, it is no surprise that they took up arms to defend al-Muqtadir's reign, essentially to maintain their own position of power. First they protected the palace from external threat, then took the offensive and routed an ill-prepared opposition.

The supporters of Ibn al-Muʿtazz, by contrast, formed a political alliance; and while numerous, they were not cohesive. There is one report that before al-Muktafī's death, the wazir al-ʿAbbās had made a pledge to support the candidacy of Ibn al-Muʿtazz but abandoned this obligation when al-Muqtadir proved more personally beneficial. Similarly, al-Ḥusayn b. Ḥamdān, one of the instigators of the coup, abandoned his allies by leaving Baghdad, thereby weakening morale and depriving Ibn al-Muʿtazz's supporters of armed men and leadership. When confronted with a counterattack, the conspirators scattered, ignoring any commitment to one another and especially to Ibn al-Muʿtazz. Simply stated, the alliance supporting Ibn al-Muʿtazz fell apart as soon as it was exposed to external pressure.[72]

At the root of the difference between the supporters of al-Muqtadir and those of Ibn al-Muʿtazz was basically the difference between patron-client relationships, versus a political alliance. Al-Muqtadir's men were personally bound to the caliph and were dependent upon him; their senses of loyalty and self-interest coincided in support of their patron, and they were therefore prepared to fight on his behalf. Moreover, they had nothing to lose by doing so. As a self-contained group, they also shared common interests and years of experience and fought as a unit. The political alliance that opposed

71. ʿArīb, *Ṣilat*, 27.

72. We will see in chs. 4 and 5 that the caliphs encouraged division among subordinates, precisely so that such alliances could not be formed against caliphal power.

them was based upon momentary and disparate interests; the soldiers and bureaucrats backing Ibn al-Muʿtazz had no historical bonds either to him or to one another, nor were they defending interests specifically bound to one branch of the royal family. Certain individuals abandoned their commitments when their personal goals had been achieved or had changed, while those who remained committed had no unifying basis for military cooperation. In short, patronage defeated alliance as the most effective political force in Baghdad.

We can conclude from the events preceding al-Muqtadir's accession through the failed coup, that it was the loyalty and self-interest of al-Muqtadir's *mawlās* that installed him and ensured his status as caliph. Other political mechanisms had not worked in al-Muqtadir's favor: his birthright to the throne as the oldest remaining son of al-Muʿtaḍid, a kind of primogeniture, had not been recognized by the court elite; he was certainly not the most qualified or best prepared candidate for the caliphate; and his position as caliph was not respected even after he had officially acquired the office, as the oath of allegiance, one of the most celebrated honors a caliph received, was easily disregarded. Nor did bureaucrats have any hand in keeping al-Muqtadir on the throne. Rather, it was al-Muqtadir's personal retainers who brought about his accession to the throne and defeated all political opposition in securing his caliphate.

In somewhat broader terms, the coup represented an attempt to change the power relations of the state. As mentioned earlier, the fundamental pillar of Abbasid rule for at least a century had been a close personal bond between the caliph and the military, albeit with varying levels of effectiveness. Al-Muqtadir's accession was in keeping with this principle, for he was raised to the throne due to the particular interests of military clients. The coup was an attempt to revoke the primacy of these patron-client relations, to take the prerogative of selecting the caliph away from a small group of military personnel with strong personal interests. The conspirators asserted that qualification should determine succession; that the welfare of the state, based on consensus, should replace the parochial interests of one specific group as the fundamental principle of Abbasid rule. The failure of the coup meant a return to the status quo; and those groups that were not connected to the caliph through a bond of clientage, especially the bureaucrats, remained relatively weak. Patron-client relations remained dominant at court, and al-Muqtadir's status as the premier patron of the state was the primary basis for his power.

Developing an Image as "The Caliph"

Following the failed coup of 296/908, al-Muqtadir was once again officially recognized as caliph. Yet the oath of allegiance had proven to be an ephemeral commitment and might easily be abrogated once again. The widespread support for the coup had indicated that the court elite did not respect al-Muqtadir as head of state; if al-Muqtadir were to establish the permanence of his rule, and have any effective control over the empire, he would need to reinforce his position of authority by developing a more convincing persona as

"The Caliph," one exhibiting "majesty." I describe below the various ways in which al-Muqtadir developed and expressed his majesty. Underlying this analysis are two basic arguments. First, majesty is not simply a reflection or symbol of power: it creates power. A ruler enhances his coercive abilities by convincing his subjects that he is the rightful leader of society; persuading society to accept authority is the function of majesty. Second, the means of projecting majesty are neither static nor irrelevant; different rulers can create majesty by different means. We will see that al-Muqtadir had a radically different, and perhaps less effective means of projecting majesty than his father, and that this gave court politics a different texture.

The Generous Patron

As we have seen, al-Muqtadir's accession and survival as caliph depended upon his status as the most important patron in the state. He consolidated his position at court, both before and after the coup, by broadening his role as a benevolent patron. In accordance with Abbasid custom, the military was granted bonuses upon the investiture of a new caliph, a practice doubtless intended to encourage loyalty by showing the troops that their new patron was generous. In this particular instance, the bonus of three months' pay for the cavalry and six months' for the infantry was distributed twice, following each oath of allegiance.[73] As for the palace staff, al-Muqtadir conferred robes of honor upon servants whose status justified such a gift, as well as upon servants whose positions did not warrant robes. He also revived court traditions, suspended by his father al-Muʿtaḍid, of lavish food and drink, as well as the practice of distributing vast amounts of meat to the elite of society on certain holidays. Furthermore, he granted a monetary bonus to the Hāshimīs, the extended royal family, and increased their monthly stipends.[74]

While at this early stage al-Muqtadir's enthusiasm for giving presents brings to mind his father's worst fears, the young caliph learned with time to be a more skillful patron. One typical example was his handling of a Ṣaffārid soldier named al-Qattāl. In 298/910–911 this al-Qattāl was involved in a revolt in Fārs, was captured and imprisoned; yet in 302/914–915 al-Muqtadir had him released and robed, granted him a house and stipend, and ordered that he attend the royal palace on official audience days along with other courtiers. This practice, which al-Muqtadir followed to different degrees on a number of occasions, turned a once-troublesome rebel into a subservient courtier. In exchange for patronage—through royal pardon and financial assistance—al-Muqtadir received a public display of submission.[75]

---

73. ʿArīb, *Ṣilat*, 23, 29; Miskawayh, *Tajārib*, 4, 8. It should be noted that the accession bonus did not prevent military commanders from joining the coup attempt; we are not told if they received a bonus from the pretender Ibn al-Muʿtazz.

74. Miskawayh, *Tajārib*, 13.

75. al-Ṭabarī, *History*, 38:195; ʿArīb, *Ṣilat*, 49.

Religious Leader

Al-Muqtadir also aspired to the role of pious Muslim and promoter of Islam. Certain standardized rituals, like the prayer before the oath of allegiance, and the affirmation of the caliph's authority in the khutba during Friday prayers, encouraged the association of the caliph with religion. This association was generally enhanced by the use of the Friday mosque as a site of caliphal authority. Al-Muqtadir emphasized this association in various ways. One of his earliest orders was to destroy a lucrative marketplace, which generated large tax revenues, to clear more space for public prayer.[76] He also imposed strict regulations on non-Muslims upon receiving complaints of growing Christian influence in the bureaucracy.[77] In 303/915–916, al-Muqtadir endowed royal revenues as religious foundations (*waqfs*) for the holy cities of Mecca and Medina, a symbolic measure witnessed by the judges and leading residents of Baghdad.[78] Following the example of his mother, al-Muqtadir also provided the funding for a hospital.[79] Finally, he gave large donations to charity on the occasion of important military victories, such as Muʾnis's defeat of the Fatimids in Egypt in 302/914–915, and much later on the dramatic withdrawal of Qarmatian forces from Iraq in 315/927.[80]

To some extent, the construction of al-Muqtadir's image—via court etiquette, patronage, and religious symbolism—followed commonly used patterns within the Abbasid dynasty. However, as I argue below, the nature of al-Muqtadir's participation in these levers of image-making, or rather, his absence and nonparticipation, made him very different than previous caliphs, especially compared to his father al-Muʿtaḍid.

Defender of the Empire

The strongest image projected by al-Muqtadir was as defender of Islam. In the previous half-century, the Abbasids had lost control over much of their empire; and the two preceding caliphs, al-Muʿtaḍid and al-Muktafī, had developed reputations as successful caliphs by spending much of their energies in recapturing Abbasid territories. Such military successes continued for the first decade of al-Muqtadir's reign and provided him excellent opportunities to bolster his prestige as Commander of the Faithful. There were various ways in which military victories were linked to the caliph and construed as signs

76. ʿArīb, *Ṣilat*, 24; Ibn al-Jawzī, *al-Muntaẓam*, 6:69.

77. ʿArīb, *Ṣilat*, 30; Ibn al-Jawzī, *al-Muntaẓam*, 6:82. Fischel, in *Jews in the Economic and Political Life of Medieval Islam*, refers to the passage in Ibn Taghrībirdī, *al-Nūjūm*, which expands on this topic more than earlier sources: "Al-Muqtadir ordered that Jews and Christians not be allowed to serve [the state] except as doctors and bankers." He also enforced a dress code for these religious minorities (Ibn Taghrībirdī, *al-Nujūm*, 3:165, under year 296/908–909).

78. Ibn al-Jawzī, *al-Muntaẓam*, 6:130.

79. Ibn al-Jawzī, *al-Muntaẓam*, 6:146; (also referred to by editor of Ibn Khallikān, *Wafayāt*, 2:45n2).

80. ʿArīb, *Ṣilat*, 53; Miskawayh, *Tajarib*, 180.

of his inspired command and pervasive authority. One simple method was glory by association: victorious commanders would return to Baghdad and be honored by the caliph, as when al-Muqtadir presented Muʾnis with a robe, necklace, and the title *"al-Muẓaffar"* ("The Victorious") following the latter's second triumph in Egypt in 308–309/920–921.[81] This ritual reasserted the caliph's status as patron of a successful client, and by extension claimed that his servant's victory was actually the caliph's victory. Another common method was to announce conquests from the minbars of mosques; and while the sources do not provide explicit details, we might speculate that these announcements were made in conjunction with proclamations of the caliph's authority, as in the khutba.[82]

Victory Parades

The most prominent means of publicity, recorded numerous times in the sources, was the parading of prisoners through the streets of Baghdad. In 298/910–911, at the beginning of al-Muqtadir's reign, a Muslim victory over Byzantine forces was celebrated when captive "heathen" were paraded on camels through the city streets, carrying banners bearing gold and silver crosses.[83] Later that year, the rebel Subkarā and his protégé al-Qattāl were brought to Baghdad, and the reconquest of Fārs was thus celebrated:

> Al-Qattāl, Subkarā's assistant, was brought to Baghdad on an elephant, wearing a long *burnūs*,[84] preceded by thirteen prisoners on camels wearing cloaks and burnooses of embroidered silk; and Waṣīf [the victorious commander] was robed and given a jeweled necklace. Then Subkarā entered [the city], his entrance being attended by the wazir Ibn al-Furāt and the rest of the commanders.... He was carried on an elephant, and paraded in a long burnoose lined with fur, and a man playing cymbals, followed by al-Layth b. ʿAlī[85] on another elephant. Then Ibn al-Furāt was robed and carried. It was a memorable day.[86]

One of the more unusual and elaborate processions followed the suppression in 303/916 of the suddenly rebellious Ḥamdānid family:

---

81. Miskawayh, *Tajārib*, 76. There are numerous such examples in the sources.

82. There are many examples of military victories being announced from "the *minbar*," probably meaning during the khuṭba of the Friday prayers. For example, in 309/921–922 "the written messages concerning the rout of the Fāṭimids were read from the minbars: (al-Hamadhānī, *Takmila*, 22); in 310/922–923, "there were successive victories for the Muslims on land and at sea [over the Byzantines], and the dispatches were read from the minbars to that effect (al-Hamadhānī, *Takmila*, 29).

83. ʿArīb, *Ṣilat*, 34.

84. According to Dozy the classical term *burnūs* referred to a cap, which sometimes had an extension that hung over the shoulders (*Vêtements*, 73–74). It later came to mean a coat with an attached hood.

85. Also a Ṣaffārid, who had been captured and paraded the previous year.

86. ʿArīb, *Ṣilat*, 34–35.

> Al-Ḥusayn [b. Ḥamdān] was led on a camel, crucified on a *niqnīq*....[87] A man rotated this *niqnīq* so that al-Ḥusayn revolved right and left. He wore a wide silk cloak that concealed the man rotating the *niqnīq*, who therefore could not be seen. [Al-Ḥusayn's] son ... was carried on a camel, wearing a silk cloak (*qabā*)[88] and a burnoose; he had refused to put the burnoose on his head, but al-Ḥusayn had told him: "Put it on, my son, for your father has forced many of the people you see here to wear a burnoose," referring to al-Qattāl and other Ṣaffārids.... Abū al-ʿAbbās Muḥammad b. al-Muqtadir [the crown prince] rode, in front of him Naṣr the Chamberlain with the royal staff, behind him Muʾnis and [the wazir] ʿAlī b. ʿĪsā ... following a huge group of the military wearing black.... They reached the palace, and [al-Ḥusayn] stood before al-Muqtadir.[89]

We possess the most information for the procession commemorating the defeat of Ibn Abī al-Sāj in 307/919–920. Miskawayh relates that "Ibn Abī al-Sāj was brought into the city in triumph from the Shamsiyya gate, mounted on a camel with a burnoose on his head, the army marching in front of him, until they reached the palace. There he was made to stand before al-Muqtadir."[90] ʿArīb adds that Ibn Abī al-Sāj wore the silk cloak that ʿAmr b. al-Layth the Ṣaffārid had previously worn, as well as bells, and rode on a two-humped camel. The spectacle was apparently very humiliating, since "people were saddened by what was done to him, for he had not done anything bad to the men he had captured."[91] Al-Hamadhānī also reports that Ibn Abī al-Sāj was publicly proclaimed "a rebel against the ruler."[92] Finally, al-Tanūkhī preserves an account that sheds more light on what was probably common practice in such processions. In this account, Abū Bakr the Qur'an reciter reported that he went outside Baghdad to meet Muʾnis on the day before the latter brought Ibn Abī al-Sāj into the city. He told Abū Bakr to ride in front of the prisoner and read from the Qur'an. So, the next day, when Ibn Abī al-Sāj was paraded in a burnoose, Abū Bakr recited, "Such is the chastisement of your Lord when He chastises communities in the midst of their wrong; grievous, indeed, and severe is His chastisement," and other Qur'anic verses of a similar nature.[93]

---

87. As Margoliouth explains, this is "apparently the name for some erection of wood" on which people were crucified (*Eclipse*, 42n1).

88. This is a tight cloak. See Dozy, *Vêtements*, 352–362; Ahsan, *Social Life*, 41–42.

89. ʿArīb, *Ṣilat*, 57–58; also in Miskawayh, *Tajārib*, 37–38, and al-Hamadhānī, *Takmila*, 16, with only minor variations.

90. Miskawayh, *Tajārib*, 49–50; translation from *Eclipse*, 53. Miskawayh clearly states that this took place in 307/919–920, though he records this under the year of 304/916–917, as part of a long string of events involving Ibn Abī al-Sāj. Other sources confirm that this procession took place in 307/919–920, e.g., ʿArīb, *Ṣilat*, 77.

91. ʿArīb, *Ṣilat*, 77.

92. al-Hamadhānī, *Takmila*, 18.

93. Translation of the Qur'anic passage from Yusuf Ali, *The Holy Quran: Text Translation and Commentary*, 11:102. The anecdote appears in al-Tanūkhī, *Nishwār*, 4:114–16, and in Ibn al-Jawzī's *al-Muntaẓam*, 5:81.

These prisoner processions are the main examples we possess of political propaganda, as preserved in the sources. The basic purpose of the processions was obviously to publicize military victory and humiliate the vanquished. The events attracted a lot of attention, as the parades were elaborate, including elephants, large contingents of the army, and leading state officials. The prisoners were degraded by a variety of means: Byzantine prisoners were forced to display their religious symbol, the cross, in defeat, while al-Ḥusayn b. Ḥamdān was subjected to the bizarre humiliation of being rotated on a crucifix of some sort. The shame of defeat was most clearly expressed in costume, as several men are described as wearing silk garments, while virtually everyone is paraded in a burnoose, which was viewed as a powerful symbol of humiliation.[94]

The more subtle purpose of the processions was to emphasize the triumph of the caliph. Everyone understood that the prisoners had rebelled against the central government, essentially denying al-Muqtadir's authority; thus, their defeat was implicitly al-Muqtadir's victory, a reaffirmation of the caliph's authority. This message was also conveyed more explicitly: al-Hamadhānī informs us that Ibn Abī al-Sāj was denounced as a rebel against the caliph, and now he had been vanquished. Moreover, the processions usually headed toward and concluded at the *Dār al-Khilāfa*, where the prisoners were forced to stand before the caliph in homage. Thus, a display of submission to the caliph was the conclusion, and climax, of the entire ritual. Finally, the connection between the caliph and God is also invoked. The Qur'anic verses read during Ibn Abī al-Sāj's parade referred to God's punishment of those who disobey him; rebelling against al-Muqtadir was equated with disobeying God, and the degrading procession and subsequent imprisonment are tantamount to divine punishment.

The processions demonstrated, in a more general way, that the caliph was the focal point of society. The extravagant parades began at the outskirts of Baghdad and progressed toward the symbolic center, the royal palace. Alongside the prisoners and army, leading figures of state—the crown prince, the wazir, senior generals, and the chamberlain—rode along with the court elite in a mass movement toward the caliph, all of society paying homage to its ruler. Al-Muqtadir was the patron par excellence: he forced vanquished rebels to wear humiliating hoods, while he endowed favored subjects with

94. Note that Ibn Ḥamdān's son refused to wear the burnoose until ordered to do so by his father. Rosenthal, in his translation of al-Ṭabarī, explains the significance the burnoose: "The costume, mentioned frequently in connection with captured rebels, mainly heretics who were displayed in triumph, appears to have the significance of branding them as effeminate and, in particular, as dressed in a manner not proper for Muslims," (*History*, 8:13n75). The same costume was used extensively in al-Muqtadir's reign for men who were not considered heretics. From these texts I see no connection with effeminacy. Dozy does not indicate that the burnoose, in its classical usage, was humiliating; he demonstrates that, in later centuries, the hooded cloak called *burnūs* was worn extensively in the Middle East, with no negative connotations. Some of his examples suggest that the color of the burnoose indicated social class (*Vêtements*, 73–74). This leaves us with the question whether in our texts it is the burnoose itself that is humiliating, or some combination of specific fabric, decoration, and/or color.

fabulous robes and necklaces. Everyone was symbolically decorated according to their behavior vis-a-vis the caliph; everyone received an identity based upon their relationship with the caliph.[95]

However, we should note the contrast in both style and substance from the shaping of caliphal authority of the previous generations. Unlike his father, the young al-Muqtadir did not participate in these military campaigns or public processions: he was the passive object in his palace.

The Byzantine Delegation

The most impressive event staged in this early part of al-Muqtadir's reign was the reception in 305/917 of a visiting Byzantine delegation. The Byzantine envoys were hosted in a guest palace and were provided with all sorts of luxuries. Upon requesting an audience with the caliph, they were told that they must first meet with the wazir Ibn al-Furāt. The envoys were conducted through the streets of Baghdad, lined with troops, to the wazir's palace; he received them, seated, in a magnificently decorated chamber.[96] Ibn al-Furāt eventually agreed to let the envoys see the caliph, and undertook extensive preparations for the royal audience. The impressive event was recorded by a number of sources:

> Ibn al-Furāt told al-Muqtadir that the envoys would be brought to him and instructed him how to respond [to their requests]. He then commanded all officials, generals, and the rest of the army to ride in the direction of the imperial compound, and to line the streets on horseback from the (guest) palace of Saʿīd to the royal palace. They rode and took up this formation, in their best clothes and full combat gear. The wazir further ordered that the courtyards and passages of the palace be filled with armed men, and the whole complex furnished magnificently. He made sure that every detail was carried out and then summoned the envoys to present themselves. They rode to the palace, and witnessed along the way the impressive military display, with its large numbers of well-dressed, fully equipped soldiers. They reached the palace and were taken into a corridor which led to a courtyard, then turned into another corridor which led to a courtyard wider than the first. The chamberlains led them

95. Prisoner processions were certainly not new under al-Muqtadir and took place under various caliphs. For example, under al-Muʿtaḍid, vanquished rebels were paraded through the city to the royal palace in 281/894 (al-Ṭabarī, *History*, 38:13); and in 283/896 this caliph camped outside the city with his troops and publicly displayed a Khārijite rebel (al-Ṭabarī, *History*, 38:29). Here we should note that al-Muʿtaḍid did something that al-Muqtadir would never do, namely to appear outside the palace for the display of a prisoner. Other features make these processions particularly noteworthy under al-Muqtadir: they are described as highly elaborate, they occur frequently in the early part of his reign, and they involve the participation of the political elite.

96. This is one example of how the official waziral palace, north of the royal complex, was an alternative focus of status and authority.

> through corridors and courtyards until they were weary from walking, and out of breath. These corridors and courtyards were filled with pages and eunuchs.
>
> Finally, they approached the chamber in which al-Muqtadir was located. The officers of state stood according to their different ranks, while al-Muqtadir was seated on his throne. Abū al-Ḥasan Ibn al-Furāt stood near him, and Muʾnis al-Khādim and the other eunuchs stood to his right and left. Upon entering the chamber, the envoys kissed the ground and stood where Naṣr the Chamberlain instructed. They then delivered their master's letter, proposing a prisoner exchange. The wazir replied for [the caliph] that he accepted the proposal out of compassion for the Muslims, and the desire to get them released, and wished to obey God in freeing them. He added that the caliph would send Muʾnis to attend [the exchange]. When the envoys left the royal presence, they were presented with silk coats embroidered with gold.[97]

This one event combines in it the variety of symbolism that constituted the complex image of "The Caliph." First of all, al-Muqtadir is presented as the champion of Islam. The obvious goal of this elaborate procession was to assert the superiority of the Muslim ruler over the Byzantine envoys, and by extension their Christian lord, indeed, the superiority of Islam over Christendom. Certainly, this spectacle of the grandeur of Islam was intended to humble the visiting Christians; yet the more important audience was al-Muqtadir's own subjects, who no doubt appreciated the assertion of Muslim superiority, as orchestrated and personified by their glorious ruler.

The caliph's concern for Muslim interests was also made more explicit, as the wazir said that al-Muqtadir consented to a prisoner exchange "out of compassion for the Muslims," acting "out of zeal to obey God." Thus, the pious and conscientious caliph had asserted the greatness of Islam. The success of this message for the local audience is reflected in the variety of sources that report the event and considered it important. For Muslims, this event was a triumph for Islam; and this triumph would be glorified for centuries by historians.

The structure of the event was designed to accentuate the inaccessibility of the caliph, and hence his superiority. The envoys were not allowed to see al-Muqtadir until they had first met with the wazir Ibn al-Furāt; only after several days of waiting, and through the mediation of the wazir, were they granted a royal audience. Once inside the palace, the envoys were conducted through endless corridors and courtyards before reaching the audience chamber, again stressing the effort which one must expend simply to enter the caliph's presence. Once in al-Muqtadir's presence, "they were forced to stand [at a distance] from the caliph ... the wazir stood in front of him, the translators also stood and addressed the wazir, and the wazir addressed the caliph."[98] Thus the

97. Miskawayh, *Tajārib*, 53–55 (similar translation in *Eclipse*, 58–59). Parallel, abbreviated versions appear in: ʿArīb (*Ṣilat*, 64–65); Hilāl al-Ṣābī, (*Rusūm*, 16–18); Ibn al-Jawzī (*al-Muntaẓam*, 6:143–44); Ibn al-Athīr (*al-Kāmil*, 8:107); al-Khaṭīb (*Tārīkh*, 1:100–105); and Ibn Zubayr (*al-Dhakhāʾir*, 161–64).

98. ʿArīb, *Ṣilat*, 64.

envoys not only stood in the caliph's presence along with everyone else, and were not allowed to approach him; they did not even speak with al-Muqtadir directly but always through the mediation of the wazir.

Like the prisoner processions, the reception of the Byzantine envoys also made the caliph the focus of Baghdadi society. Soldiers lining the streets formed a human arrow that pointed toward the palace and the caliph. Indeed, "all the officials, civil and military" were ordered "to ride in the direction of the imperial palace." The result was a human wave that reiterated the status of the caliph's residence as the center of authority; and the participation of the representatives of the court elite in this human wave expressed their submission, and the submission of the entire society, to the caliph.

Finally, we should note that the construction of al-Muqtadir as "The Caliph" was successful despite the fact that he himself did not plan the symbolic show. Miskawayh is very clear that Ibn al-Furāt orchestrated this event: he met first with the envoys and emphasized the difficulty of obtaining a royal audience; he made the preparations for the elaborate procession and decoration of the palace; he even instructed al-Muqtadir how to respond to the envoys' proposals. During the audience, the wazir spoke on behalf of the caliph, and stood between him and the visitors. Thus, Ibn al-Furāt was in complete control. From this realization we can propose two hypotheses. First, the construction of the caliph's image was not strictly or even primarily al-Muqtadir's doing, but was undertaken by his wazirs, indeed by the whole of court society, and utilized traditional court culture; this was not about giving a unique individual a personal image, but rather inserting an otherwise nondescript young man into a traditional, prefabricated image. Second, Ibn al-Furāt's responsibility for the preparations had the effect of making the caliph appear inaccessible, somehow above the petty concerns of preparations and negotiations, too important for other human beings to have direct contact with him. This impressive combination of images—as a pious man, the champion of Islam, the focal point of society, the bearer of superior status—proved to the Byzantine envoys and to all of Baghdadi society that al-Muqtadir had truly become "The Caliph."

We should nevertheless note that the image cultivated for al-Muqtadir differed drastically from that of his father. Both men used court ritual to heighten their senses of majesty. Al-Muʿtaḍid, in confronting the cotton merchant, had projected awesome strength with a spear, a commanding voice, and constant governmental supervision. Al-Muqtadir, by contrast, was distant and silent during the Byzantine visit. The vast differences between the two caliphs would become more apparent in the second half of al-Muqtadir's reign.

Conclusion: Creating a Caliph

As noted earlier, the construction of al-Muqtadir's authority involved many elements. Yet two elements were fundamental to his aura of majesty: the sanctity of the office of the caliph, and his personal inaccessibility. These two principles were intertwined and mutually supportive. Al-Muqtadir's inaccessibility was implicitly justified by his supposed sacredness, and at the same time served to enhance the myth of his sanctity.

This inaccessibility had several layers. First of all, the caliph was ensconced in the palace. While elaborate processions took place outside and usually included the most powerful men in the empire, al-Muqtadir always remained within the palace. Moreover, this was true not only during processions, but at virtually all times: al-Muqtadir rarely left the palace, eschewed public appearances. He never led the military on campaign, and thus never participated in a military procession. As far as we know he never left Baghdad. Nor do we have evidence that he ever led public prayers, or presided over the court of complaints (the *maẓālim*), which would have made him visible to the populace.[99] He also apparently did not attend important funerals, even those of his own immediate family, since the distinguished people in attendance are generally named, and the caliph is not among them.[100] On those rare occasions when al-Muqtadir did leave the royal palace, he remained within the palace complex, at the polo field or the military parade grounds, and thus was not seen by the populace.[101]

Indeed, the caliph's public appearances were so rare that Ibn al-Jawzī specifically records when al-Muqtadir was seen outside the royal compound. We are told that al-Muqtadir first appeared before the masses in 301/913–914, in a procession, over five years after his accession;[102] this is in sharp contrast to his father al-Muᶜtaḍid's first public procession within six months of becoming caliph. We hear of no more appearances for another five years, until in 306/918–919 there were rumors that al-Muqtadir was sick. He rode from the palace to the Shamsiyya Gate, and then took a boat downstream back to the palace, "so that [the people] would see him and calm down."[103] We get the impression that al-Muqtadir was so unaccustomed to being in public, and the populace so unused to seeing him, that he occasionally had to participate in a staged event simply to reassure his subjects that he was still alive. For the populace, the caliph was nearly always

99. I am not aware of any systematic study of public appearances and ritual participation of different caliphs; this is one step in that direction. Many Abbasid caliphs did participate in military processions and lead Friday prayers; al-Muqtadir, unlike his father, apparently did neither.

100. In 305/917–918 his daughter died, "and the family of the Ruler was present, as were people of all ranks." In the same year, his cousin al-Qāsim b. Gharīb died, "and none of the commanders or distinguished people were absent from the funeral." Rounding out the year, al-Muqtadir's uncle Gharīb died, "and present at his funeral were the wazir, his entire retinue, and the commanders and judges" (ᶜArīb, *Ṣilat*, 68–69). I believe that if al-Muqtadir had attended any of these funerals, ᶜArīb would have mentioned him specifically. The one possible exception is his daughter's funeral, if al-Muqtadir is included in "the ruler (*sulṭān*)'s family." By contrast we have a detailed description of the famed Hārūn al-Rashīd's participation in his mother's funeral, when he walked from his palace to the cemetery barefoot (al-Ṭabarī, *History*, 30:107).

101. Miskawayh, *Tajārib*, 5; ᶜ*Arīb*, *Ṣilat*, 51.

102. Ibn al-Jawzī, *al-Muntaẓam*, 6:121.

103. Ibn al-Jawzī, *al-Muntaẓam*, 6:147.

"absent;" and I will argue that this "absence" was an intermediate stage on the path to caliphal irrelevance.

Al-Muqtadir's reclusiveness in the palace reinforced the conception that the palace itself embodied authority, even sanctity. Both in popular conception and in speech, the image of the palace represented the image of the caliph, and the two were interchangeable. In the prisoner processions and the Byzantine visit, all of society headed toward the palace; the intention and effect were clearly to assert the superiority of the caliph. Yet the caliph was invisible to most of society; he could only be addressed publicly via the symbol of his palace, thus people honored the caliph by honoring his palace, and in the process the dwelling acquired the authority of its occupant. This symbiosis was articulated frequently, as when al-Muqtadir's personal guard considered themselves "the protectors of the caliph and the palace," or when Muʾnis referred to submission to the caliph's authority as a "return to the caliph's gate."[104] In subsequent chapters we will see that occupation of the palace was the most concrete means of seizing authority.

The second layer of inaccessibility was the difficulty of reaching the caliph's presence once inside the palace. The Byzantine envoys were shepherded around endless palace corridors until they were finally conveyed to the audience chamber. This was a common theme of court life: we hear of many instances throughout al-Muqtadir's reign when people gained entry to the palace but failed to see the caliph. As we shall see, this problem was particularly severe for bureaucrats, since they, unlike many other court dignitaries, always required permission for an audience, and sometimes could not gain admission at critical moments. Below we will see that the chamberlain and eunuchs enjoyed great influence precisely because they could navigate this space more freely, and largely controlled access to the caliph.

The final layer of inaccessibility was the space immediately surrounding the caliph. We saw above that the Byzantine envoys were not allowed to approach the caliph beyond a certain distance, and that a precise pecking order determined who could approach his physical body. Deference to the caliph was sometimes expressed by kissing the ground in front of him, though the most common recognition of the caliph's authoritative space was the practice of standing while the caliph sat. All these regulations originated in the understanding that the caliph's body was sacrosanct. The ultimate definitive act of defying and negating caliphal authority was to invade his space and defile his body.

These layers of inaccessibility—the palace, the audience chamber, the space surrounding the caliph's body—were reiterated on a daily basis and were the central message of ceremonial occasions. They fostered among both the populace and the court elite a sense that al-Muqtadir was the primary authority of the state. Of course, previous caliphs had manipulated such themes of sanctity and inaccessibility; effective rul-

104. ʿArīb, *Ṣilat*, 168. Again, I note that the image of the palace as a representation of caliphal authority was not new under al-Muqtadir and is surely a common image in world rulership. My aim is to show how this representation was expressed and manipulated, and differed from caliph to caliph.

ers must strike a balance between inaccessibility, which heightens their special status, and active control of the organs of government that enable them to impose their will. My goal here is to assess the kind of balance forged by al-Muqtadir and to understand the relative weight of common court rituals in the construction of his authority. In my view, al-Muqtadir developed an unusual degree of passivity and withdrawal and did not balance these attributes with displays of awe-inspiring assertiveness in the manner of previous caliphs. There were an unusual number of court ceremonies in the early years of al-Muqtadir's reign, and they all revolved around and emphasized the caliph's inaccessibility and sanctity. In addition, the issue of access would recur throughout court life, especially at critical moments. In short, inaccessibility was al-Muqtadir's primary means of demonstrating authority.[105]

We can see this best through a comparison with al-Muʿtaḍid, for the two caliphs demonstrated authority in nearly opposite ways. Al-Muʿtaḍid made numerous public appearances, participating in military processions, leading prayers, and delivering the khutba; al-Muqtadir, by contrast, made few public appearances, none of them similar in character to those of his father, preferring to remain in the royal palace. Al-Muʿtaḍid led processions, al-Muqtadir was the destination of processions; al-Muʿtaḍid traveled with his army to dominate provinces and capture rebels, whereas al-Muqtadir had rebels brought to him in the palace. Al-Muʿtaḍid terrified the cotton merchant into submission, while al-Muqtadir impressed the Byzantine envoys by not talking with them. In general, al-Muʿtaḍid demonstrated authority by tireless activity, whereas al-Muqtadir founded his authority on inactivity; more abstractly, al-Muʿtaḍid manipulated symbolism to further his power, but with al-Muqtadir, the caliph became a symbol in and of itself.

We should not take this to mean that al-Muqtadir had no authority, for he did. From what we read in the sources, the various people at court honored the caliph's wishes, and implemented his decisions; this caliph may have been pliable, but everyone recognized that it was his favor that had to be courted, and his mind that they had to convince. Ironically, in the first half of his reign al-Muqtadir asserted his authority most often by changing wazirs. True, other forces were involved in these personnel changes, as we shall later see; yet the fact remains that it was the caliph's ill will that toppled any given wazir, his poor judgment that determined the successor, his lack of commitment to bureaucrats in general that kept the wazirate in flux. During each of these personnel changes, the issue of accessibility to the caliph was paramount. The main point here is that different caliphs constructed and wielded different kinds of authority. The particular configuration and expression of authority for any given caliph—in this instance al-Muqtadir—influenced the way people at court behaved. Al-Muqtadir's case is particularly important, for he was

105. *Maaike van Berkel has also argued that al-Muqtadir was remarkably inaccessible ("Politics of Access," esp. 31–32). She argues that the parallel ideal of accessibility, which earlier caliphs had also pursued, in demonstrating their supervision of society, was transferred in this era to the caliph's representatives: the wazir.

instrumental in bringing about a permanent change in the nature of caliphal authority, which was one aspect, perhaps the most important aspect, of a changing sociopolitical system.

The Destruction of the Caliph[ate]

Above I have tried to demonstrate two distinct elements of al-Muqtadir's authority as caliph: the possession of military force, based upon personal bonds with military clients; and the ritualized construction of an aura of majesty, calling upon divine sanction, the defense of Islam, and the sacredness and inaccessibility of the ruler. In what follows, I show that as the financial and military crises confronting the Abbasid state worsened, al-Muqtadir's authority over the state was increasingly challenged. At key moments the caliph is forced to assert one aspect of his authority, and the two basic elements, patronage and majesty, come into conflict. The resulting political drama revolves around the question of whether the caliph is ultimately responsible for obligations to clients, or if his inherent right to rule, cultivated in an image of majesty, supersedes these obligations. Muʾnis, the caliph's most important client, is forced to decide at what point he is justified and benefits by severing the bond to al-Muqtadir. Gradually the caliph's status as patron and his image of majesty deteriorate and both are ultimately shattered. The twin pillars of patronage and majesty upon which al-Muʿtaḍid had invigorated caliphal power disintegrated; and the Abbasid caliphs would never regain the same level of effective authority.

The Decline of the State

The Abbasid state started to decline noticeably around the year 306/918, and by 311/923 began a severe plunge. At first al-Muqtadir was absolved of responsibility for this decline, and his image remained unblemished. For the most part he had delegated important governmental functions to the wazirs, so they were the obvious scapegoats; moreover, he did not have strong personal attachments to bureaucrats, so they were easy for him to replace. The earliest of these problems were financial in nature. In 306/918, the wazir Ibn al-Furāt had no available funds to pay rioting cavalry, due to the expenditures incurred in the failed attack against Ibn Abī al-Sāj to reclaim Azerbaijan and restore the payment of tax revenues which this rebel had withheld. When Ibn al-Furāt asked al-Muqtadir for funding from his private treasury, the caliph indignantly refused, saying that military payments were entirely the wazir's responsibility.[106] Ibn al-Furāt was also blamed for

106. Miskawayh, *Tajārib*, 56; Ibn al-Jawzī, *al-Muntaẓam*, 6:147. Also partly related by al-Hamadhānī (*Takmila*, 19). Al-Muqtadir refused to help Ibn al-Furāt with the payments, even though it was the caliph who insisted upon the costly war in Azerbaijan, while the wazir had opposed this decision.

Muʾnis's subsequent defeat, as somehow being in league with the rebel.[107] Ibn al-Furāt's supposed responsibility for the fiscal and military crisis was among the reasons he was dismissed from office. Then during the years 307–309/919–921 there was a food shortage that resulted in price riots. The populace vented its fury primarily at the new wazir Ḥāmid b. al-ʿAbbās, stoned him in public, and attacked his home. The caliph calmed the populace, and implicitly blamed the wazir by issuing a public announcement that Ḥāmid had been removed from important posts.[108] On several other occasions, we hear that military factions, and even Abbasid family members, physically abused wazirs over financial grievances.[109] On all these occasions, the caliph assumed no responsibility, and was never the object of criticism.

The caliph and the Baghdadi populace also focused blame upon the wazir when the state began to suffer from foreign incursions. Early in 312/924, the Qarmatians attacked the hajj caravan on its way back from Mecca to Iraq; many Baghdadis were killed or taken prisoner, including generals and members of the royal family, and a large amount of the caliph's possessions and money was seized. The chamberlain Naṣr, in a conference with the caliph, blamed the wazir Ibn al-Furāt for interfering with military deployment; a Baghdadi mob then stoned Ibn al-Furāt's boat and publicly called him "the older Qarmatian."[110] The wazir pleaded with al-Muqtadir that he could not have prevented the Qarmatian attack: a similar attack occurred in al-Muktafī's reign, but that caliph had not blamed his wazir.[111] Yet al-Muqtadir was apparently convinced of Ibn al-Furāt's guilt, for the wazir was soon thereafter dismissed. As he was being transported to the palace for imprisonment, the populace again stoned him and proclaimed that "the older Qarmatian had been arrested."[112] Society had found its scapegoat. But there was only so long the caliph's image could remain intact as the state sank deeper into financial chaos and was subject to military threat.

---

107. Miskawayh, *Tajārib*, 47.

108. Miskawayh, *Tajārib*, 75.

109. Armed units (the *rajjāla*, explained further in ch. 4) attacked ʿAlī b. ʿĪsā's home in 303/915–916, seeking raises (ʿArīb, *Ṣilat*, 58.); they also rioted against al-Khāqānī (the younger) in 312/924, but since he had no money, he would not ride to attend the palace for months, probably out of fear (al-Hamadhānī, *Takmila*, 47). A group of Abbasids verbally abused Ibn al-Furāt in 304/917 (ʿArīb, *Ṣilat*, 62) and actually attacked ʿAlī b. ʿĪsā in 306/918–919 (ʿArīb, *Ṣilat*, 75, Ibn al-Jawzī, *al-Muntaẓam*, 6:146), on both occasions because their stipends were late. I discuss these events in the next chapter on the royal family.

110. Miskawayh, *Tajārib*, 122. "The older Qarmatian" apparently refers to the fact that the Qarmatian leader at this time was a very young man. Naṣr specifically accused Ibn al-Furāt of scheming to get Muʾnis out of Baghdad, which is why the wazir had convinced the caliph to dispatch Muʾnis to Raqqa. This accusation is true. But Naṣr's further claim, that Muʾnis's absence made the hajj caravan more vulnerable, seems improbable, if not ridiculous. The hajj had been protected by troops who were defeated by the Qarmatians. Muʾnis probably would have remained in Baghdad had he not been sent to Raqqa and thus could not have defended the pilgrims against the Qarmatians anyway; and even Muʾnis's capacity to vanquish the Qarmatians is questionable, given that nobody could defeat them for a decade.

111. Miskawayh, *Tajārib*, 124.

112. Miskawayh, *Tajārib*, 126.

Tense Patron-Client Relations: The Compromise of 315/927

The first indication that al-Muqtadir's stature was faltering, came with increasingly tense relations with the leading general Muʾnis. In 315/927, a rumor was spread that al-Muqtadir was planning to kill Muʾnis, supposedly ordering eunuchs to trap Muʾnis in the royal palace, when the general came to bid the caliph farewell before departing for border raids; the supposed plan was for palace eunuchs to strangle him, but it would be announced publicly that Muʾnis had fallen in a cellar and died. Because of these rumors, Muʾnis stayed away from the palace, and much of the military congregated at his home, until even the royal palace was emptied of troops. In an attempt to prevent a rebellion, al-Muqtadir wrote Muʾnis an autograph letter, swearing that the rumors were false. Muʾnis was apparently convinced, as he dismissed all soldiers from his home, and wrote back to al-Muqtadir that he was not at fault for the mobilization, since he had not summoned the soldiers. The crisis ended when Muʾnis came to al-Muqtadir in the palace, kissed the ground in front of the caliph, as well as his hand and foot; al-Muqtadir in turn swore his good intentions and devotion to Muʾnis.[113]

The brief crisis sheds light on the relationship between al-Muqtadir and Muʾnis, and their relative power in Baghdad. First, we see that the caliph was fairly weak compared to his powerful general. If al-Muqtadir had indeed intended to kill Muʾnis, he needed to devise a plot on his own territory, in the royal palace, and could not simply have Muʾnis seized and executed; and if the plot were successful, he would have to announce that an accident had occurred, for he could not risk the consequences—probably a general mutiny—if it were known that Muʾnis had been murdered. As the crisis developed, Muʾnis was surrounded by loyal troops, while even those soldiers assigned to the palace abandoned their posts in support of the general. These men might have been frustrated that their salaries were late.[114] In any case, al-Muqtadir clearly did not command the loyalty of a substantial military force, and Muʾnis did; in a confrontation between the two, al-Muqtadir was obviously more vulnerable.

Yet the crisis was defused because of the strong personal relations between the two men. Al-Muqtadir tried to pacify Muʾnis by writing to the general, in his own hand, and swearing that reports of his animosity were untrue. Both by writing and by swearing, al-Muqtadir compromised his dignity as caliph; and it was precisely this symbolic expression of humility vis-à-vis his general that successfully placated Muʾnis. The general then dispersed his troops and responded defensively that he was not to blame for the concentration of force, that he was not guilty of challenging the caliph. The two men were finally reconciled in a very personal interaction. Muʾnis demonstrated deference to al-

113. Miskawayh, *Tajārib*, 160–61; al-Hamadhānī, *Takmila*, 51; Ibn al-Jawzī, *al-Muntaẓam*, 6:205–6. Only the latter reports that Muʾnis kissed the caliph's hand and foot. ʿArīb does not include a report of this crisis at all but instead transmits a report that al-Sayyida was plotting to kill Muʾnis by trying to infiltrate his supporters with an assassin (*Ṣilat*, 133).

114. Miskawayh, *Tajārib*, 160.

Muqtadir by kissing the ground at the caliph's feet; al-Muqtadir's gesture, however, was extraordinary: he swore that he had good intentions toward Muʾnis, thereby assuming the grave responsibility of taking an oath in defending his own loyalty. The relationship here was not one of supreme ruler and humble servant, but rather of mutual obligation, as developed between patron and client. In short, al-Muqtadir compromised the majesty of his office in order to reinforce his personal bond with Muʾnis, thereby neutralizing a volatile situation.[115]

The Coup of 317/929

Up until the year 317/929, al-Muqtadir's relations with Muʾnis and his image of majesty had been under strain but remained intact. Yet in this year al-Muqtadir was threatened by a second coup attempt, which, though it failed, did irreversible damage to the caliph's authority. As with previous events, the sources present very different accounts, and a completely reliable chronology is difficult to achieve.[116] The various stages of the coup reflect different political values regarding the image of the caliph and his relations with subjects, and the issues involved in removing a mature caliph and installing a substitute. Given the complexity of these events, and the variety of political values under scrutiny, I analyze each stage of the coup separately.

Prelude to the Coup

The trouble began when three of the state's leading military figures—the Chief of Police Nāzūk, the general Abū al-Hayjāʾ b. Ḥamdān, and Muʾnis—were estranged from al-Muqtadir.[117] There are indications in the sources that al-Muqtadir was beginning to favor his own first cousin, Hārūn b. Gharīb, at the expense of these other military figures; perhaps, in view of his weakness in the crisis of 315/927, al-Muqtadir had devised a policy of

---

115. We should note the importance of spatial metaphors for expressing political intentions. Muʾnis was expected to come to the palace to bid farewell to al-Muqtadir before departing on a campaign, as a sign of allegiance to the caliph. His refusal to attend the palace signaled disobedience, and the beginning of a crisis. The crisis was then defused when Muʾnis reaffirmed his allegiance by coming to the palace. As well, loyalty to the caliph was emphasized by kissing the ground, that is, honoring the space inhabited by the caliph.

116. ʿArīb (*Ṣilat*, 139–44) and Ibn al-Jawzī (*al-Muntaẓam*, 6:221–22) give one version, while Miskawayh (*Tajārib*, 189–200) and al-Hamadhānī (*Takmila*, 59–62) present another; Ibn al-Athīr (*al-Kāmil*, 8:200–207) combines the two versions to an extent but adheres more closely to that of Miskawayh and al-Hamadhānī.

117. According to ʿArīb (*Ṣilat*, 139), Nāzūk claimed that he had been treated poorly by al-Muqtadir; another reason for his estrangement was a fight between his men and those of the general Hārūn b. Gharīb, who was al-Muqtadir's first cousin. After this battle, Nāzūk remained conspicuously absent from the royal palace (Miskawayh, *Tajārib*, 188). Ibn Ḥamdān was angry about being removed from a provincial post (reported in all the sources).

empowering his relatives to reduce dependence upon Muʾnis and other clients. Muʾnis, on his way south to confront the Qarmatians, was informed that the caliph was going to replace him as chief *amīr*, whereupon he returned to Baghdad, went straight home, avoiding the royal palace.[118] At some point he took his army out to the Shamsiyya Gate, where he was met by additional armed supporters, including Nāzūk, Abū al-Hayjāʾ and their men; the large force then moved to the *muṣallā* (oratory) outside the city walls.[119] Muʾnis wrote to al-Muqtadir, stating that "the army complained bitterly of the amount of money and land wasted upon the eunuchs and women of the court, and of their participation in the administration [of the state]; he demanded their dismissal, removal from the palace, and seizure of their possessions."[120] Al-Muqtadir was frightened by the accumulation of forces at the *muṣallā*, and responded to Muʾnis with a long letter of appeasement and self-defense:

> In the name of God.... May God give me benefit from you, and not deprive me of you, nor show me any hostility from you.... As for you, Abū al-Ḥasan [Muʾnis] the Conqueror, may I never lose you! You are my teacher and my elder, whom I will continue to favor, honor, befriend, and support, whether this trouble comes between us or not, and whether the bonds between us be broken or preserved. I hope that you will not doubt this when you think about it and question your soul, and that you will banish all evil thoughts.... Now what our friends propose regarding the eunuchs and women—to remove them from the palace and banish them, cancel their stipends, deprive them of their fortunes, and make them turn over their money and estates to the rightful owners—that is a proposal, which, if they considered and examined it, they would realize is unjust. Still,

118. ʿArīb, *Ṣilat*, 139; al-Hamadhānī, *Takmila*, 57; Ibn al-Jawzī, *al-Muntaẓam*, 6:221. All the sources state that Muʾnis avoided going to the royal palace (most indicate that Muʾnis was in Raqqa, while only ʿArīb says that he was going to fight the Qarmatians). ʿArīb is alone in saying that Nāzūk and Abū al-Hayjāʾ told Muʾnis of al-Muqtadir's plan to replace him, while the other sources report that he heard this from his supporters.

119. This mobilization of troops is not completely clear. The sources agree that when Muʾnis returned home and avoided the palace, al-Muqtadir's son Abū al-ʿAbbās and the wazir Ibn Muqla went to greet the general. ʿArīb adds that al-Muqtadir sent them to express his longing for Muʾnis, no doubt an attempt to calm the distrustful general. But this goodwill was undermined when, according to ʿArīb, Muʾnis's house was attacked by a group of infantry that he thought was sent from the royal palace and instigated him to mobilize his troops. The other sources do not have this episode, and do not explain Muʾnis's mobilization. The sources then agree that Muʾnis left his home and camped outside the Shamsiyya Gate (the northernmost gate, near Muʾnis's palace), probably as a way of threatening or signaling revolt. The sources also agree that Muʾnis was joined by Nāzūk and Abū al-Hayjāʾ. However, Miskawayh (*Tajārib*, 189) and al-Hamadhānī (*Takmila*, 58) are alone in saying that these combined forces moved to the *muṣallā*, the site used for prayers during the festival following Ramadan. The *muṣallā*, according to Le Strange (*Baghdad*, 204–5), was situated west of the Shamsiyya Gate.

120. Miskawayh, *Tajārib*, 189 (this is my translation, a similar but redacted/modernized version of *Eclipse*, 213; there are parallel versions in al-Hamadhānī (*Takmila*, 58–59) and Ibn al-Athīr (*al-Kāmil*, 8:200).

> I am so anxious to concur with them, and determined to please them, that I agree to the extent feasible with regard to [the women and eunuchs]; so I am giving orders for the seizure of some of their fiefs, for the abolition of their privileges, for the subjection to assessment of the land which they hold at a fixed rate, and for the removal from the palace of all whom it is permissible to expel, while those who remain shall not be permitted to interfere with my administration.... I will also personally investigate the affairs of the elite and the commoners, and act with justice and benevolence. I shall rely on no wazir or intermediary whatsoever; I shall supervise the collection of funds, proper extraction and expenditure, and guard against reduction. I will exert myself, and resist enemies both far and near. I have hitherto neglected this duty only because I relied on you and delegated my functions to you, and was confident that you were my partners.... Had I known that this would be regarded as a fault on my part, and as a crime for which I would be held guilty, I would have confronted these difficulties, without delay or hesitation. As for you, most of your fortune comes from me; I would not stop favoring you, which I regarded in the past and still consider as small compared with your merits. Indeed, I prefer to increase your favor. God knows my good intentions regarding all of you and is witness that I long to fulfill your utmost aspirations.... As for Abū al-Hayjāʾ, Nāzūk, and the rebels generally I have nothing but forgiveness, mercy, and reprieve. I may claim from you that oath of allegiance which you have affirmed time and again; whoever has sworn allegiance to me has sworn it to God, so that whosoever violates that oath violates an oath to God. I also may claim gratitude for favors and benefits that I have conferred upon you, obligations and kindnesses which I hope you will acknowledge and consider binding, and for which you will display gratitude and not the reverse.... As you know, I am reliant upon you, and ready to favor you.... But if you are resolved on defiance, antagonism, stirring up strife, and renewing disorder, then I give you a free hand, sheathe my sword, and declare before God that I will not stretch my arm against any one of you; I will rely upon God to help, aid, and protect me. [I will not abandon the right which God has granted to me; and I will follow the example of ʿUthmān b. ʿAffān, God bless him, when he did not leave his home and did not give up his right when he was abandoned by his followers and helpers].[121] This then is my plea before God, and his grace is the reason for my hopes of success in this world and the next.[122]

The correspondence between Muʾnis and al-Muqtadir continued, and the caliph granted the generals' request that Hārūn b. Gharīb, the caliph's ascendant first cousin, be expelled from Baghdad. Here the sources seriously diverge: Miskawayh reports that al-Muqtadir assigned Muʾnis to a provincial governorship, Muʾnis began to head for the province, but

121. Amedroz and Margoliouth indicate that there is confusion in this part of Miskawayh's text. The bracketed words are my addition from the parallel text in al-Hamadhānī.

122. Miskawayh, *Tajārib*, 189–92 (translation by Amedroz and Margoliouth, 213–17).

then suddenly stopped, and returned once again to Baghdad. According to ʿArīb, however, when the men at the *muṣallā* received al-Muqtadir's letter, they decided to reenter Baghdad and speak with the caliph in person. Al-Muqtadir prepared for the encounter by dismissing his armed guards, sitting on the throne reading the Qur'an, surrounded by his sons, and ordered the doors to the palace opened and nobody prevented from entering. Muʾnis, however, again decided to avoid going to the palace, so he returned to his home. Everyone thought that the crisis had been averted.[123]

The letter quoted above is fascinating for how it reveals al-Muqtadir's own perceptions of his role as caliph, as well as his understanding of his relationship with important military clients.[124] On one level, al-Muqtadir wanted to placate disaffected generals by addressing their criticisms of court administration. He accepted the accusations of maladministration and agreed to reforms; he refused to expel the eunuchs and women of the court, but did commit himself to seizing some properties, limiting privileges, and tightening fiscal assessments, implicitly acknowledging that financial abuses did indeed exist. He also agreed to restrict the influence of court personnel in administration, again recognizing undue interference in affairs of state. Al-Muqtadir further promised to take more control of financial affairs himself, stating, "I will rely on no wazir or intermediary whatsoever; I shall supervise the collection of funds." Finally, he confesses to having "neglected" certain duties, probably referring to the military defense of the state, and suggests that this neglect was seen as "a crime for which he [was] held guilty." Remarkably, al-Muqtadir even accepts the possibility that he was personally to blame for maladministration and the severe security crisis. In general, al-Muqtadir acknowledged that his administration was defective and promised to make improvements. Wazirs were no longer the focus of blame; al-Muqtadir was finally accepting responsibility for the dysfunction within the state.

This document tells us even more about al-Muqtadir's perception of his relationship with leading generals, especially Muʾnis. While al-Muqtadir addressed the generals' practical criticisms regarding administrative failures, and promised changes, his letter focused more on the caliph's relationship with Muʾnis and the latter's supporters. Al-Muqtadir believed, perhaps for good reason, that the real problem was not curing court corruption, but ensuring the loyalty of military commanders.[125]

Al-Muqtadir claimed the loyalty of his commanders on several grounds. The primary basis for loyalty was the patron-client relationship that had been strengthened over the course of many years. Al-Muqtadir reaffirmed his strong bond to Muʾnis, acknowledging

123. ʿArīb, *Ṣilat*, 140–41.

124. This aspect of the letter is also discussed by Mottahedeh, *Loyalty and Leadership*, 40–41.

125. The generals seem to have multiple and conflicting goals in threatening the caliph. They first want eunuchs and women removed; then they are temporarily satisfied with the expulsion of Hārūn, the caliph's cousin; and finally, they want the caliph himself removed. In ch. 4, I argue that this inconsistency results from conflicting personal agendas. The commanders active in this event were not unified in purpose; indeed, they were actually competing with one another as well as with the caliph.

that he was indebted to Muʾnis for acting as his mentor, promising to continue favoring his mentor regardless of political circumstances. Al-Muqtadir recognized the vulnerability of these relations, as he admits the possibility that "the bonds between us [might] be broken." Because of this vulnerability, al-Muqtadir asserts that he deserves loyalty out of gratitude, stating that "most of your fortune comes from me," and "I also may claim gratitude for favors and benefits that I have conferred upon you." Finally, he continues to have his clients' best interests in mind, as "God knows my good intentions regarding all of you and is witness that I long to fulfill your utmost aspirations." These notions of mutual support and gratitude constituted the personal bond between al-Muqtadir and Muʾnis and are invoked to encourage loyalty.

Al-Muqtadir also invokes the legal obligation of loyalty to the caliph. He states, "I may claim from you that oath of allegiance which you have affirmed time and again," arguing that beyond a traditional patron-client bond, these men have also sworn obedience to him. Furthermore, this obligation is not only to the caliph, but to God: "whoever has sworn allegiance to me has sworn it to God, so that whosoever violates that oath violates an oath to God." In a sense, al-Muqtadir is pulling multiple levers: if the bond of patronage would not prove compelling enough to ensure loyalty, then the legal obligation might. In the process, al-Muqtadir shifts the emphasis from a personal relationship between himself and Muʾnis, to an impersonal obligation linking subject to caliph and subject to God.

Al-Muqtadir concludes with a final form of legitimacy and claim for loyalty: his God-given right. He tells the commanders that if they abandon their patron and their oath, "I will not give up the right that God has granted to me." Rather, he would follow the example of the caliph ʿUthmān and suffer martyrdom at the hands of rebels in defense of his right to be caliph. He concludes: "This is my plea before God ... the reason for my hopes of success in this world," arguing that the ultimate foundation for his legitimacy is divine will. Al-Muqtadir had presented a multilayered case for why he deserves loyalty: he has been a generous patron and will continue to be so in the future; he has received an oath of allegiance, valued as an obligation to God; and he simply has the God-given right to be caliph. Yet he ends with this divine sanction. Al-Muqtadir is basically asserting that if his relations with military clients break down, he has the sanctity of his office to fall back upon.

Al-Muqtadir's emphasis on divine sanction is also reflected in his preparation for a confrontation with the military figures. He dismisses his armed guards, sits on his throne with a Qur'an in his lap, and allows anyone to enter his presence. He has called upon the various elements of his majesty, in typically passive fashion, and challenges his clients to defy this majesty. It is as if al-Muqtadir thought that the image of authority could overcome the breakdown in patron-client relations.[126]

126. One basic point that emerges from the beginning of the coup is, once again, the political overtones of location and movement. Muʾnis expressed his estrangement from al-Muqtadir by not visiting

The Coup

The caliph's appeal to bonds of patronage, legal obligation, and divine sanction proved ineffective. Within days of the initial mobilization, Muʾnis, Nāzūk, Abū al-Hayjāʾ, and a large part of the military once again gathered either at the Shamsiyya Gate or the *muṣallā*.[127] Here the sources seriously diverge: Miskawayh and al-Hamadhānī suggest that Muʾnis was in charge of this renewed mobilization, while ʿArīb states that Nāzūk was in control, and forced Muʾnis to join the nascent rebellion.[128] In any case, the commanders brought their troops into Baghdad and headed for the palace, whereupon the entire palace staff fled; the conspirators then invaded the palace, without dismounting, while the caliph hid with his sons in an interior chamber. The sources agree that al-Muqtadir was eventually removed from the palace, along with his mother, aunt, sons, and concubines, and was sent to Muʾnis's palace. ʿArīb, however, provides more detail: Nāzūk was searching for al-Muqtadir in the royal compound, and Muʾnis, perhaps alarmed at what might happen, located the caliph and sent him and his family to Muʾnis's own home for protection. During the next few days, the royal palace was ransacked by the invading troops. In the meantime, al-Muqtadir's brother Muḥammad b. al-Muʿtaḍid was brought from the palace of Ibn Ṭāhir, was given the oath of allegiance, and was proclaimed caliph with the title al-Qāhir. Various appointments were made to important posts. Then, only after al-Qāhir was already appointed, several of the generals who led the coup gathered at Muʾnis's palace and forced al-Muqtadir to abdicate.[129]

This coup gives us another glimpse of the political symbolism involved in deposing a caliph. First of all, we once again see the high value placed on authoritative space: the royal palace is consistently perceived as the primary symbol of caliphal authority, and al-Muqtadir is effectively removed from the caliphate when he is removed from the palace. Moreover, the termination of his unique status was signaled by the desecration

---

the palace when he returned to Baghdad. He then increased the tension by going out to the *muṣallā*, a symbolic act of rebellion, where he was met by much of the military. Finally, Muʾnis's return to Baghdad suggested that the crisis was over, and his return home was intended to calm the populace and the caliph. Yet Muʾnis had again avoided going to the palace, unlike two years before when his reconciliation with al-Muqtadir was enacted by a personal visit to the caliph; Muʾnis's absence from the palace suggested that the political crisis had not been resolved.

127. Miskawayh says the Shamsiyya Gate; ʿArīb says the *muṣallā*; and al-Hamadhānī skips this detail. The dating of this event in the sources is confused: Ibn al-Athīr records the date as the tenth of Muharram, Miskawayh has it as the eleventh, and ʿArīb says the thirteenth. The differences concerning these first few details suggest the impossibility of establishing a precise narrative, and it is difficult to know if any one account, or any particular detail, is completely accurate. There is also little precision regarding which military units participated in the coup.

128. Miskawayh, *Tajārib*, 192–93; al-Hamadhānī, *Takmila*, 59 (this version is particularly vague); ʿArīb, *Ṣilat*, 141. There will be more evidence supporting ʿArīb's view, though it is difficult to understand how Nāzūk could force Muʾnis to participate.

129. ʿArīb, *Ṣilat*, 142; Miskawayh, *Tajārib*, 194.

of the palace, as the invading troops entered while mounted—a vulgar expression of disrespect—and pillaged the compound. Al-Qāhir's accession to the caliphate is likewise achieved by his occupying the palace. Indeed, the historical descriptions concentrate far more on how al-Qāhir was brought to the palace than on the ceremony of investiture,[130] for the possession of authoritative space defined "The Caliph" more than receiving the oath of allegiance. Unlike the coup of 296/908, however, the conspirators now considered the implication of breaking their oath to al-Muqtadir, and thus forced him to abdicate, in effect canceling their oaths. Yet this abdication was not a prerequisite for the installation of a new caliph, since all the sources report that al-Muqtadir's resignation was at least a day after al-Qāhir's accession. Also, the document verifying this resignation was kept secret, and was not needed for publicity purposes to justify the appointment of a new caliph.[131]

The Countercoup

Similar to twenty years earlier, this coup also failed within a matter of days. Nāzūk, now acting as both chamberlain and chief of police, managed to alienate different sectors of the military. He removed two military factions that had been assigned to the palace,[132] and then was late in paying the accession bonus to the regular troops. The disgruntled soldiers took revenge only two days after the installation of al-Qāhir, during the first official reception day. They attacked Nāzūk in a palace courtyard and killed him, then stormed the rest of the palace, yelling "al-Muqtadir the Victorious."[133] The palace staff once again fled, and al-Qāhir managed to escape to the palace of Ibn Ṭāhir; Abū al-Hayjāʾ however, was killed while defending the new caliph. In the meantime, some soldiers went to Muʾnis's home—he had been conspicuously absent from the festivities at the royal palace—and requested that al-Muqtadir return to the royal palace. At first al-Muqtadir declined, fearing a plot; but Muʾnis insisted, and al-Muqtadir "resumed possession of the

130. See esp. Miskawayh, *Tajārib*, 193.

131. The judge Abū ʿUmar gave the document to his son and told him not to show it to anyone. When his son responded that everyone already knew about the resignation, Abū ʿUmar replied that the future cannot be foreseen, so the prudent action was to keep the document concealed. Later, when al-Muqtadir returned to the throne, Abū ʿUmar brought him the document and informed the caliph that nobody had seen it, which greatly pleased the caliph, who rewarded Abū ʿUmar by appointing him as chief Qāḍī (Miskawayh, *Tajārib*, 194). This story gives us a few pieces of information: the official abdication was documented on paper, probably like the oath of allegiance; it did not precede the appointment of a new caliph, and was not publicized, thus making it seem of questionable importance; but despite its possible trivial value, al-Muqtadir was glad that nobody had seen it.

132. The *maṣāffi* infantry who were camped outside the palace, and the *ḥujarī* guards stationed inside the palace. Nāzūk replaced them with men who served under him as chief of police.

133. Miskawayh, *Tajārib*, 196. ʿArīb has a slightly different version: "We only want al-Muqtadir as our caliph" (*Ṣilat*, 143).

palace."[134] The severed heads of Nāzūk and Abū al-Hayjāʾ were publicly paraded, amid the cry: "this is the recompense for someone who rebels against his master and is ungrateful for his benefits."[135] Al-Muqtadir, once again ensconced in the palace, received a new oath of allegiance, and promised to pay the military accession bonuses that Nāzūk had failed to distribute.

Thus, the coup was overturned by disillusioned troops who, seeking greater pay, inexplicably preferred the return of the old caliph. There were rumors that Muʾnis was actually behind the reinstatement of al-Muqtadir. We have already heard hints that Muʾnis was forced by Nāzūk to participate in the storming of the palace, and that Muʾnis sent al-Muqtadir to his own home in order to protect the deposed caliph. In addition, Muʾnis did not attend the official reception day, when the countercoup took place, suggesting that he knew what was planned and chose not to defend the new caliph.

These pieces of evidence are supported by ʿArīb, who reports: "it was said that Muʾnis al-Muẓaffar, seeing that Nāzūk was dominating affairs, sent for the leaders of the infantry and conspired with them regarding what they did, for he did not want al-Muqtadir's deposal to be finalized. This is why he hid [al-Muqtadir] and did not sleep out of his company from the time he brought [al-Muqtadir] into his home."[136] Ibn al-Athīr expands upon this interpretation, suggesting that Muʾnis opposed the coup from the very beginning:

> It was said that Muʾnis al-Muẓaffar was not influential in the removal of al-Muqtadir, but agreed with the group [of rebelling commanders] contrary to his own thinking, for he knew that if he opposed them he could not help al-Muqtadir. So he agreed with them to gain their trust. He then plotted with the *maṣāffī* and *ḥujarī* soldiers and contrived with their commanders to do what they did, so that al-Muqtadir was returned to the caliphate.... Al-Muqtadir trusted him, such that when [al-Muqtadir] was carried back from Muʾnis's palace to the royal palace, and he saw the large number of people fighting, he returned to Muʾnis's house due to his trust in him, and reliance upon him. For if Muʾnis did not love al-Muqtadir, he would have attended al-Qāhir along with the rest of the group, but he was not with them, as we have related; and he would have killed al-Muqtadir when the latter was sought at [Muʾnis's] home in order to be returned to the caliphate.[137]

These reports suggest that Muʾnis never wanted al-Muqtadir deposed and schemed skillfully for the failure of the coup. Of course, the antagonism felt by much of the military

134. Miskawayh, *Tajārib*, 199. This is yet another example in which the royal palace functions, linguistically, as the symbol of caliphal authority.

135. Miskawayh, *Tajārib*, 199; translation from *Eclipse*, 224.

136. ʿArīb, *Ṣilat*, 143.

137. Ibn al-Athīr, *al-Kāmil*, 8:206–7. In addition to this evidence, a reference to this coup in al-Tanūkhī's *al-Faraj* (2:52) mentions only Abū al-Hayjā' and Nāzūk as leading the coup.

for the new regime made a countercoup possible. Yet given the variety of evidence, and the speculation of these two sources, it does not seem excessive to suggest that Muʾnis was the guiding force behind the reversal of fortunes. Once again Muʾnis had protected al-Muqtadir's status as caliph.[138]

Looking at the coup as a whole, we can contrast al-Muqtadir's claims for his own legitimacy as caliph with the values and behavior of his military commanders. In his letter to Muʾnis and subsequent actions, al-Muqtadir had called for loyalty based upon several forms of obligation and legitimacy, culminating in his divinely sanctioned right to rule. Yet al-Muqtadir's military supporters in effect rejected al-Muqtadir's claims to legitimacy. They removed him from the throne, and from the palace, and disgraced his supposedly sacred space. They also nullified the oath of allegiance. While the desecration of the palace and the forced resignation suggest that the soldiers acknowledged and valued these symbols of authority, the military simultaneously proved that such symbols of authority could be breached or disregarded. In general, the majesty of the ruler, buttressed by divine sanction, was completely rejected. The one firm pillar that kept al-Muqtadir's caliphate intact was the bond of patronage with Muʾnis, who defended al-Muqtadir from deposal for the second time.[139] In sum, the symbolism of the caliphate was impressive to an extent, and al-Muqtadir had mistakenly chosen to emphasize this symbolism; but the real foundation for al-Muqtadir's rule was still the patron-client relationship that made him the benefactor of a powerful—and clever—military commander.

Shattering the Image of "The Caliph"

Though the coup had failed, the temporary deposal of al-Muqtadir damaged his image and prestige, and we subsequently see overt expressions of disrespect. The *maṣāffī* infantry who had returned al-Muqtadir to the palace and the caliphate considered themselves the caretakers of the caliph, no longer his subjects. They would not allow al-Muqtadir or the wazir Ibn Muqla to move about without constant accompaniment, and the caliph could not refuse any of their requests.[140] Their haughty attitude vis-à-vis the caliph is widely reported. Ibn al-Athīr preserves some of their more arrogant remarks, which he

138. Waines suggests that Muʾnis played a waiting game and remained inconspicuous while the coup was still young. Once Nāzūk's scheme had clearly failed, Muʾnis reinstalled al-Muqtadir ("Caliph and Amir," 79). This theory is controverted, however, by the statements of ʿArīb and Ibn al-Athīr, and there is much logic behind the assertion that Muʾnis was intent on keeping al-Muqtadir on the throne. Muʾnis undoubtedly had a long-standing attachment to al-Muqtadir that would not be simple, psychologically, to abrogate; and Muʾnis surely understood that his interests were better suited by this caliph than by a replacement with whom he had no established link. In general, I think we should be careful not to underestimate the sense of loyalty that certain military clients actually felt.

139. I might add here that this bond of patronage did not necessarily make Muʾnis "loyal" to al-Muqtadir per se. Rather, this long-tenured patron-client bond fixed Muʾnis's interests in a particular patron. Muʾnis defended al-Muqtadir in defense of his own interests.

140. ʿArīb, *Ṣilat*, 148.

labels "things that caliphs do not tolerate," such as: "he who raises a donkey up to the roof can lower him," and "if al-Muqtadir does not give what we demand, we will attack him, as he deserves."[141] These soldiers now brazenly insulted the caliph, asserted the right to replace him if they so desired, and even threatened him with bodily harm. Al-Muqtadir obviously resented this attitude, and instigated another military faction against the *maṣāffīs*, who were beaten, disbanded, and banished.[142] But the caliph's image had been irreparably damaged. The comments by the *maṣāffī* troops indicate that al-Muqtadir was no longer considered the inherently rightful caliph, but merely a temporary occupant of that post.

We also see the decline in al-Muqtadir's status among the broader Baghdadi populace. In 319/931, a band of criminals and commoners attacked the royal palace, burned down a gate, and breached the walls.[143] This sort of violence directed at the palace—the public symbol of the caliph—had been very rare in the past;[144] but once the military had invaded and pillaged the palace in 317/929, the royal edifice lost a great deal of its mystique for the general public, who now dared to attack it as well. Then in 320/932, al-Muqtadir was verbally abused by residents of border regions, and by the Baghdadi populace, because of the deteriorating security situation. ʿArīb reports this event in great detail:

> The people from the Byzantine border region and al-Jibāl (northwest Iran) gathered at the ruler's palace, calling the people of Baghdad to fight. They reported that the Daylamīs and Byzantines were oppressing them, though the *kharāj* tax was still collected from them and everyone else for the protection of the general populace and defense against their enemies. But they were perishing, as were their border towns, and their enemies lorded over them. People were moved by this and similar reports. The populace was stirred up and went to the Friday mosque in the City of al-Manṣūr,[145] broke the railings of the caliph's enclosure and the minbar, and thwarted the khutba. They also pounced upon Ḥamza the khatib and stoned him until he bled, damaging the skin of his face; they dragged him by the legs, yelling: "You adulterer! You pray on behalf of a man who neglects the affairs of Muslims! He is too preoccupied with singing and illicit sex to look to the affairs of the holy cities and the frontier towns! He distributes the money of God to the enemies of God and does not fear divine punishment or anticipate the hereafter!"[146]

141. Ibn al-Athīr, *al-Kāmil*, 8:216.

142. The elimination of the *maṣāffīs* is described in great length in the sources.

143. ʿArīb, *Ṣilat*, 157.

144. One example is the riots during food shortages in the years 307–309/919–921.

145. This is the original Friday mosque the caliph al-Manṣūr built in the Round City (whence "City of al-Manṣūr") when he founded Baghdad some 150 years earlier. The mosque maintained its status as one of the central mosques of Baghdad, despite the disrepair of the rest of the Round City. See Le Strange, *Baghdad*, 33–36.

146. ʿArīb, *Ṣilat*, 173–74.

The people of the empire were now holding al-Muqtadir personally responsible for military and security setbacks, for they paid taxes to ensure defense of their lands and the caliph was not fulfilling his side of the social contract. The populace expressed its dissatisfaction by attacking the Friday mosque—a site of caliphal authority—and abusing the official who asserted the caliph's authority in the khutba. The accusations against al-Muqtadir show how far his image of majesty had plummeted: he was said to value illicit sex over the holy cities, and to have no consideration for God's final judgment. This was clearly not the pious figure who, in countless ceremonies and public proclamations, had asserted a close relationship with God, at least not in the minds of al-Muqtadir's subjects.

Yet, while al-Muqtadir's majestic image was falling apart, he still occupied the caliphate and controlled the state. The primary foundation of his power had always been his standing as the master of important military clients, and only a complete rupture in the patron-client relationship could remove him from the caliphate for good. Muʾnis had kept him in power, and it would be Muʾnis who removed him.

Severing the Patron-Client Bond

The tension between Muʾnis and al-Muqtadir continued to grow in the years following the failed coup of 317/929, as the two feuded over the appointment of state officials. First al-Muqtadir removed the minister Ibn Muqla, fearing his inclination toward Muʾnis; but Muʾnis strenuously opposed al-Muqtadir's candidate, al-Ḥusayn b. al-Qāsim, so they compromised on a third man.[147] Then in 319/931 Muʾnis asked the caliph to banish Yāqūt and his son, military officers who were acquiring a great deal of influence. Al-Muqtadir initially refused; but when Muʾnis once again gathered troops at the Shamsiyya Gate, and attracted deserters from the royal palace, the caliph capitulated and expelled Yāqūt and his son to provincial posts.[148] The relationship was aggravated once again when the caliph managed to appoint al-Ḥusayn b. al-Qāsim to the wazirate. This new wazir and Muʾnis continually plotted against one another; at one point, Muʾnis and al-Muqtadir almost struck a deal whereby al-Ḥusayn would be dismissed, but al-Muqtadir objected to certain conditions. All this intricate political scheming suggests that al-Muqtadir was searching for a way to curb Muʾnis's influence at court. Two specific points are worth noting: Muʾnis periodically mobilized troops in order to threaten the caliph, who invariably backed down; and though Muʾnis clearly held the upper hand, he never even hinted at a desire to replace the caliph.

The final showdown between al-Muqtadir and Muʾnis resulted from the return of the recently expelled generals Yāqūt and Hārūn b. Gharīb to Baghdad.[149] When Muʾnis heard

147. Miskawayh, *Tajārib*, 203–5.

148. Miskawayh, *Tajārib*, 209–11.

149. The sources disagree as to whether the wazir or the chamberlain recalled them. In either case, we might assume, as Muʾnis did, that the caliph was behind this recall.

that his bitter rivals were returning to the capital, he demonstrated his disapproval by again mobilizing at the Shamsiyya Gate. This time, however, al-Muqtadir did not back down or compromise. First, he gathered his own military forces at the palace, attracting large numbers by promising bonuses and forgiving soldiers who were out of favor. He then participated in a public procession designed to win popular support:

> When the prayers at the Friday mosque were completed, al-Muqtadir rode between the afternoon and evening prayers in a cape and black turban, with a parasol shading his head. His seven oldest sons rode with him, as did all the emirs and generals. He went from the Bāb al-Khāṣṣa to the majlis alongside the parade grounds, where a silk tent was erected for him. He entered it, then left, and appeared before the populace, calling for people to support him.[150]

This is the only procession in which the caliph participated since 306/918–919, thirteen years earlier, that is recorded in the sources I have seen, and the timing was crucial. Al-Muqtadir had apparently resolved to confront Muʾnis and thus made a powerful demonstration of authority by appearing in public, actively wooing popular support.

As the crisis developed, Muʾnis was reluctant to break from al-Muqtadir and tried several times to reconcile with his patron. Immediately following the caliph's public appearance, Muʾnis sent a letter stating that he was not being disobedient but was fleeing from enemies. The caliph, however, refused to receive Muʾnis's messenger, who was imprisoned and beaten; Muʾnis was thus further estranged, and led his troops north toward Samarra.[151] Once there, he again adopted a conciliatory tone, stating: "I am not rebelling against my master, nor am I running from him. Rather, this group of people has pursued me and dominates my master."[152] Muʾnis decided to remain at a distance and told his troops that they could "return to the caliph's gate" if they wanted, which they rejected. But the caliph remained hostile, sending provincial governors an order to capture Muʾnis, leading to a crucial battle between Muʾnis and the Ḥamdānids, where Muʾnis overcame a tremendous numerical disadvantage and won an impressive victory. Soldiers stationed in Baghdad began to desert and join Muʾnis in the north; after nine months of waiting, the strengthened general headed back to Baghdad. Within only miles of the capital, he again offered a compromise, writing:

150. ʿArīb, *Ṣilat*, 167. The Friday mosque that al-Muqtadir attended, one of several in Baghdad, was within the palace complex (*Dār al-Khilāfa*); as previously noted, this caliph almost never ventured outside the palace compound. The procession described by ʿArīb thus took place within the palace complex, but because it followed the Friday prayers (when the general public was allowed to attend the mosque within the complex) it became a public event.

151. This campaign will be discussed in more detail in ch. 4, which focuses on internal military relations.

152. ʿArīb, *Ṣilat*, 168.

> I am not rebelling against the Commander of the Faithful nor breaking allegiance. I withdrew due to the pursuit of my enemies, who surround [the caliph]. I have come to his gate with his men, not in rebellion or seeking bloodshed. I have heard that my master will attack me, but no good will come of that for either party, only fragmentation, loss of men, destruction, and death. So, my master, order that the soldiers receive their stipends, and pay them. They will then approach and reconcile with him.[153]

Al-Muqtadir was inclined to accept this solution. But several of his supporters did not want Muʾnis back in Baghdad and thus forced the caliph to reject the offer. The final opportunity for compromise had passed.

The messages that Muʾnis sent al-Muqtadir reflect the general's perception of his relationship with the caliph. The fact that Muʾnis tried on several occasions to reconcile with him and avoid a confrontation, suggests that he was reasonably satisfied with the political status quo, and did not want any drastic changes. He sought to receive pay for his troops, and the expulsion of his enemies from Baghdad; but at no point does Muʾnis mention that al-Muqtadir should be replaced. In fact, Muʾnis was very defensive regarding his questionable intentions vis-à-vis the caliph; he reiterated several times that, although he had distanced himself from Baghdad and mobilized troops, his intention was not to rebel against his patron. This continued insistence by Muʾnis shows that he truly valued his own loyalty to the caliph and did not want this loyalty questioned.

We also see the nature of the relationship, which obligated Muʾnis, in his own mind, to be loyal: al-Muqtadir was first and foremost his master, to whom he owed the debt of a favored client. True, Muʾnis does recognize al-Muqtadir's larger identity as "The Caliph," addressing him once as "The Commander of the Faithful." Yet Muʾnis almost always refers to al-Muqtadir as "my master," for it was al-Muqtadir's role as a personal patron that commanded Muʾnis's respect and gratitude; this was the basis for their relationship. Muʾnis had no intention of replacing "The Caliph," indeed he was not interacting with that official per se. Rather, Muʾnis saw this crisis as a rupture in his personal relationship with his master and thus tried to reconcile with al-Muqtadir within the context of their patron-client bond.

The Final Battle

In contrast to Muʾnis's search for a patron-client dialogue, al-Muqtadir assumed the role of a symbol, of "The Caliph," that is, he emphasized royal majesty over patronage. In the final confrontation with Muʾnis, al-Muqtadir's main function was to act as a symbol around whom his troops would rally, and before whom rebellious soldiers would take flight. At first, al-Muqtadir considered abandoning Baghdad to consolidate his forces elsewhere; but his leading general, Ibn Yāqūt, argued that the caliph should go out to the

153. ʿArīb, *Ṣilat*, 175. Muʾnis addresses the caliph in the third person.

encampment of his troops and motivate them to fight, as Muʾnis's supporters would not dare oppose the caliph in the field of battle. Al-Muqtadir was apparently not convinced that his presence would prove decisive. He replied to Ibn Yāqūt: "You are a messenger of the devil!" The caliph nevertheless agreed to leave the palace and join his troops at the Shamsiyya Gate.[154]

Al-Muqtadir made his way to the Shamsiyya Gate in a procession that was rich in symbolism. A number of Baghdadis who saw the caliph leave his palace and cross through the city provide this detailed report:

> He was wearing a silver silk Tustari khaftan, a plain black turban, with the Prophet's cloak hung over his shoulders, in front and in back. He also bore *Dhū al-Fiqār*, the Prophet's sword (God bless and keep him), as well as his sword belt of red leather. In his right hand were the signet ring, and the [Prophet's] staff.... Beside him was his son Abū Aḥmad ʿAbd al-Wāḥid, wearing a multicolored silk Byzantine caftan, and a white turban. Behind him was the wazir al-Faḍl b. Jaʿfar b. al-Furāt, and in front of him were white flags and black banners ... and white and yellow flags carried by the *Anṣār*, who had spears topped with copies of the Qur'an. Al-Muqtadir went in this fashion until he reached the canal in Shamsiyya.[155]

Since al-Muqtadir was now trying to protect his caliphate from a "rebel," this procession and its symbolism served to assert the various aspects of al-Muqtadir's legitimacy as caliph. First of all, the display of the Prophet's cloak, sword, belt, and staff demonstrates that al-Muqtadir has inherited the Prophet's possessions and hence bears the Prophet's authority. Al-Muqtadir also asserts his status as an Abbasid (and thus his family relation to the Prophet) via the black banners which are carried in the procession, and the black turban. Finally, the procession, and by extension al-Muqtadir's reign, is endowed with divine sanction. The ostentatious display of Qur'ans, and the recitation of Qur'anic passages, implied that the caliph was accompanied by divine words, and was empowered by the directives of the divine text. In general, the procession was filled with an atmosphere

154. Miskawayh, *Tajārib*, 235; al-Muqtadir reportedly had a similar conversation with the chamberlain, Ibn Rāʾiq. When the caliph was preparing to leave the palace, Ibn Rāʾiq told him, "Hurry master, so that the people will see you," to which al-Muqtadir responded pessimistically, "Where am I rushing to, you face of evil fortune" (ʿArīb, *Ṣilat*, 176).

155. ʿArīb, *Ṣilat*, 177. Briefer accounts in other sources also emphasize that the caliph wore heirlooms from the Prophet, and was accompanied by royal banners, by the *Anṣār* carrying Qur'anic texts, and even by Qur'an readers reciting verses aloud (Miskawayh, *Tajārib*, 235; al-Hamadhānī, *Takmila*, 69; Ibn al-Jawzī, *al-Muntaẓam*, 6:243; Ibn al-Athīr, *al-Kāmil*, 8:242). The use of the Qur'an on spears evokes the memory of the caliph Mu'āwiya's troops at the historic battle of Ṣiffīn, and might symbolize a plea for arbitration. Amedroz/Margoliouth mention in a footnote that the "*Anṣār*" might refer to aristocratic families from Medina. I have no alternative explanation; the term rarely appears in the context of Baghdadi society in this era.

of sanctified Islamic authority; and the man who bore the Prophet's objects of authority and surrounded himself with the words of the Qur'an, was surely the legitimate caliph.

Al-Muqtadir's symbolic value was also emphasized during the battle itself. At the outset of the conflict, al-Muqtadir did not actually reach the battlefield, but remained with his retinue on a hill at a safe distance. As the battle progressed, al-Muqtadir's generals sent him emphatic requests to approach the front, arguing that "if Muʾnis's followers see you, they will desert."[156] The message was reiterated by another officer, who kissed the ground beneath the caliph's horse and said to him, "if the [enemy] see you, they will be routed."[157] Apparently al-Muqtadir's generals were convinced that the rebels would not continue to fight if they were confronted by the caliph and fully recognized that they were rebelling against caliphal authority: they would be intimidated by the image of the caliph, and could not disobey him in his presence.

Al-Muqtadir was not convinced of the impact of the caliphal image and repeatedly refused to approach the battlefield. At one point he wanted to abandon the scene altogether, but a general beseeched him, "Commander of the Faithful, there is hand-to-hand combat; if you leave, the men around you will be routed!"[158] Al-Muqtadir remained, so as not to damage morale; he was again urged to come to the front lines by his own troops: "We want to see our master, so that we can fling ourselves upon those dogs."[159] Al-Muqtadir eventually agreed to approach the battlefield, but he arrived too late: his troops were already in disarray, and the caliph found himself without military protection. Reportedly accompanied only by commoners, he urged his supporters to fight on his behalf, pleading with them in the name of God and the Prophet.[160] But his desperate calls were to no avail, and the enemy fell upon the caliph.

To summarize: in the prelude to this battle, and during the actual fighting, al-Muqtadir's primary role was as a symbol, to embody "The Caliph," and thereby inspire loyalists to defend his reign. His commanders told him time and again that loyalist troops would be inspired by seeing the caliph, and the rebellious forces would not dare to fight in the presence of society's figure of authority. Al-Muqtadir's role as a figurehead was emphasized by the procession to the battlefield, which was much more a performance, a parade of legitimacy, than the mobilization of a commander-in-chief.

If we accept that al-Muqtadir's personification of "The Caliph" could have been decisive, we might blame his fear and subsequent delay in approaching the battlefield for the defeat of his troops.[161] But this is questionable, given the evidence in the sources regard-

156. Miskawayh, *Tajārib*, 235; al-Hamadhānī, *Takmila*, 70. Literally: "they will ask you for safe conduct."

157. Miskawayh, *Tajārib*, 236 (similar translation: *Eclipse*, 266).

158. ʿArīb, *Ṣilat*, 178.

159. Miskawayh, *Tajārib*, 236; abbreviated version in al-Hamadhānī, *Takmila*, 70.

160. ʿArīb, *Ṣilat*, 179. The text also says, "he rubbed a Qur'an in his own face," which is difficult to visualize, though the intention of invoking divine support is clear.

161. Here we might note how very different al-Muqtadir was from his militaristic father. The fact

ing the relative sizes of the opposing forces.[162] In any case, reliance upon al-Muqtadir for any kind of military leadership or inspiration was misplaced; he had never served this function before: in fact, we have no indication that he ever saw a battlefield before in his life, let alone leading soldiers to victory. The main point is that al-Muqtadir was put into a position for which he had no experience, where there was no precedent for him to succeed. His function as a military symbol was simply inappropriate.

In different terms, Muʾnis's approach to Baghdad represented a rupture in the patron-client bond that was, from al-Muqtadir's childhood, the foundation of his rule. Muʾnis had made very clear that this is how he viewed the current crisis, and that he wanted reconciliation with his master. Yet al-Muqtadir, under the influence of jealous advisors, chose not to repair this relationship, and did not address this crisis as involving a personal bond between himself and his client. Instead, al-Muqtadir asserted the authority of his office, "The Caliph," displaying the various aspects of his majestic persona. The image of "The Caliph," and the authority this image projected, was supposed to be a more powerful basis for the caliphate than al-Muqtadir's role as the supreme master of the state. This strategy failed. In the end, al-Muqtadir was caliph because of a personal bond of patronage; when this personal relationship was superseded by an assertion of royal majesty, his authority as caliph fell apart.

Death of "The Caliph"

Now that al-Muqtadir was stranded on the battlefield, he could only rely upon the sanctity of his office for protection. This sanctity proved to be ineffectual. The first of Muʾnis's commanders to reach al-Muqtadir was ʿAlī b. Yalbaq. Upon seeing the caliph, he dismounted, addressed al-Muqtadir respectfully as "My master, the Commander of the Faithful," kissed the ground in front of al-Muqtadir and then kissed the caliph's knee.[163] Thus even at the moment of the revolt's impending victory, this high-ranking officer adhered to standard etiquette in honoring the caliph. Yet, immediately following this demonstration of respect, the sanctity of the caliph was impugned. A group of Berber soldiers surrounded the caliph and unsheathed their swords—a blatant sign of disrespect, a

that al-Muqtadir's advisers encouraged him to come to the battlefield, despite his lack of experience and inclination, suggests that they had an expectation of "The Caliph" as military leader. This expectation no doubt derived from the model established by al-Muʿtaḍid.

162. There are several reports that al-Muqtadir's generals fought very hard, regardless of al-Muqtadir's absence. We have also seen several times that the caliph's troops were not especially loyal, and were mostly interested in being paid; there is thus little reason to believe that they would be particularly inspired by the caliph's presence. In any event, none of this changes the fact that al-Muqtadir was definitely put into a position of leading his troops as a symbol.

163. Miskawayh (*Tajārib*, 236) is the only source that relates Ibn Yalbaq's actual words. Other details are recorded in al-Hamadhānī (*Takmila*, 70), and Ibn al-Athīr (*al-Kāmil*, 8:242).

desecration of sacred space.[164] Shocked by this threat to his person, al-Muqtadir reacted incredulously, shouting: "Curse you, I am The Caliph!"[165] Here al-Muqtadir articulates a notion of self-identity that almost goes without saying: his person and his office were one and the same, he was "The Caliph," and any threat to him was an affront to the dominant figure in society.[166] It was as if the assertion itself of this identity should protect him. But the Berbers were not impressed by this assertion and responded: "We know who you are, you riffraff, you are the caliph of the devil!"[167] They did not dispute that al-Muqtadir was "The Caliph," they simply rejected any assumption that the caliph was necessarily sacrosanct, or worthy of immunity. In threatening al-Muqtadir, they were challenging the office of the caliph itself.

After violating the caliph's space and addressing him crudely, the soldiers proceeded to desecrate the supposedly unassailable body. First they slashed his right shoulder, so that he lost his grip on the Prophet's sword; they then systematically stripped the caliph—figuratively and literally—of those symbols of authority that were worn on his person: "One of [the Berber horsemen] took the sword from his hand, and another took off the mantle and the caftan, while a third demanded the signet ring, which [al-Muqtadir] turned over to him."[168] The attackers proceeded to dismember the caliph's body: "one of them struck and wounded him in the forehead with a sword, so that al-Muqtadir took out his shirt sleeve to wipe the blood from his face; then another hit al-Muqtadir on the left hand, severing his thumb, which tumbled through his hand and fell to the ground."[169] The Berbers completed the slaughter by knocking al-Muqtadir to the ground, and cutting off his head.[170]

Al-Muqtadir's reign was finally over, ended by rebellious troops who were totally indifferent to the supposed sanctity of his social position.[171] The contrast between the actions of Ibn Yalbaq and those of the Berbers is striking: for whereas the former afforded

164. Ibn al-Athīr reports that they unsheathed their swords (*al-Kāmil*, 8:242); ʿArīb adds that they were mounted, which was also disrespectful.

165. Miskawayh, *Tajārib*, 237; al-Hamadhānī, *Takmila*, 70; Ibn al-Athīr, *al-Kāmil*, 8:242.

166. Here I am trying to explore a very fine point: I want to understand how people in this society came to identify with their social function, status, occupation. To what extent could they conceive of occupying a different status in society, of not being fixed in their particular profession? I imagine many rulers, like al-Muqtadir, believe that they are the ruler, that they have no other possible status or function in society, and that they cannot distinguish between their personal identity and their public role.

167. Ibn al-Athīr, *al-Kāmil*, 8:242.

168. ʿArīb, *Ṣilat*, 179.

169. ʿArīb, *Ṣilat*, 179.

170. ʿArīb, *Ṣilat*, 179; Miskawayh, *Tajārib*, 237; al-Hamadhānī, *Takmila*, 70; Ibn al-Athīr, *al-Kāmil*, 242.

171. Ibn Yalbaq's actions during the killing are uncertain; he is not said to have participated, but Ibn al-Athir reports that he had signaled to the Berbers, who then killed al-Muqtadir. Muʾnis apparently had not ordered that al-Muqtadir be killed, as we will see below. It is noteworthy that the desecration of the caliph was performed by outsiders, not members of the court elite.

the caliph great symbolic authority, the Berbers proved that the sanctity and authority of the caliph could be summarily dismantled.

The desecration of the caliph continued even after al-Muqtadir's death. His head was raised on a sword, and then on a stake;[172] the Berbers continued to curse him while parading his head around the battlefield.[173] The ultimate degradation then befell his body: all of his clothes were stripped, including his undergarments, so that he was left naked, his genitals exposed. His corpse remained in this state until a laborer passed by, covered the body with hay, dug a grave on the spot, and buried the corpse without leaving a marker. Al-Muqtadir was totally disgraced in death: his corpse was abandoned, naked; torso and head separated. There was no funeral; the only witness of his ignominious burial was a simple laborer, and the location of his grave remained unknown. Al-Muqtadir's head was taken to Muʾnis, who grieved upon hearing of his master's death.[174]

The series of events in which al-Muqtadir was killed, and his body disposed of, was a systematic reversal of his construction as "The Caliph." The layers of symbolism attached to his person were abruptly stripped, and he was symbolically transmuted back into an ordinary man. First his sacred space was violated, addressed rudely, and his prophetic and dynastic heirlooms seized; then his body was abused, and his blood shed like that of a common man; and his head was severed and paraded like that of a criminal. In the end, al-Muqtadir was abandoned in a state of the most banal humanity, naked, his penis revealed for all to see. "The Caliph" had reverted to an ordinary man.[175]

Conclusion: Regicide or Revolution?

Was the killing of al-Muqtadir simply a violent change of rulers, the victory of one military faction (Muʾnis) over another (Hārūn, Yāqūt, and others)?[176] Was it comparable in nature to previous regicides in Abbasid history? Or did this murder represent, indeed accelerate, a change in the sociopolitical system?

---

172. Miskawayh, *Tajārib*, 237; al-Hamadhānī, *Takmila*, 70; Ibn al-Athīr, *al Kāmil*, 8:242.

173. Ibn al-Athīr, *al-Kāmil*, 8:242.

174. Miskawayh, *Tajārib*, 237; al-Hamadhānī, *Takmila*, 70; Ibn al-Athīr, *al-Kāmil*, 8:242–43. ʿArīb (*Ṣilat*, 180) gives a completely different version: al-Muqtadir's naked body was brought to Muʾnis, united with the head, and given to the judge Ibn Abī al-Shawārib to deal with. ʿArīb also gives three different possibilities for the site of al-Muqtadir's grave, saying that at one of them people prayed for the caliph and built a mosque on the site. This account is very dubious, since the other sources all say that al-Muqtadir was buried by a laborer where he was killed. Moreover, ʿArīb cannot say for sure where the body was buried.

175. *Osti hints that this violent death perhaps engendered a measure of historical empathy for al-Muqtadir: "The final redeeming quality of the caliph was his martyrdom, with which his purity was completed" (in van Berkel et al, *Crisis and Continuity*, 58).

176. I take the phrase in the title from Walzer, *Regicide and Revolution*, which explores how the trial and execution of Louis XVI destroyed not only the king, but kingship. I explore this question here with reference to the caliphate.

One could argue that the events of 320/932 constituted a violent version of earlier attempted coups and were in keeping with traditional patterns of Abbasid politics. The murder was performed by low-ranking soldiers (Berbers), who posed no threat to the political order. Conveniently, Ibn Yalbaq observed proper etiquette toward the caliph even on the battlefield, while Muʾnis, far from the scene, voiced dismay that his patron had been murdered. In short, the commanding officers could be absolved of guilt for the misguided assassination. They then enthroned a new caliph—al-Muqtadir's brother al-Qāhir—swore allegiance to him, and the traditional order was restored.

On the other hand, this regicide was significantly different from previous murders of caliphs, in that this murder was accompanied by a public process of "humanization." Earlier caliphs, such as al-Amīn and al-Mutawakkil, were killed in the privacy of their palaces; if aspects of their sanctified status were defiled, this was not made public. Al-Muqtadir, by contrast, was systematically stripped of his special identity—his space was invaded, his clothes and caliphal props removed, his body hacked to pieces—all of which took place where it could be witnessed publicly, in a field just outside Baghdad. The particular disgrace experienced by al-Muqtadir is reflected in the fate of his corpse: unlike other caliphs, al-Muqtadir did not receive a proper burial. Indeed, his body was left naked in public, an embarrassment that was unprecedented in Abbasid history. The majesty of this particular caliph had been publicly and systematically destroyed.

But to what extent was the desecration of al-Muqtadir important for the office of the caliph in general? Traditional wisdom has held that the Abbasid caliphate suffered a dramatic and irreversible decline in 324/936 when the caliph al-Rāḍī submitted financial and military control of the empire to Ibn Rāʾiq, giving him the title of *amīr al-umarāʾ*. David Waines has shown that a process of economic and social decline preceded this event, that the appointment of an *amīr al-umarāʾ* was primarily a convenient marker for historians.[177] I wish to contribute to this conception of the process of decline by demonstrating that the caliphate of al-Muqtadir, epitomized by the manner of his death, accelerated the fundamental sociopolitical changes that eventually culminated with the appointment of the *amīr al-umarāʾ*.

First of all, al-Muqtadir's death was the definitive end to profound respect for the majesty of caliphs. The public desecration of all the symbols of authority amounted to the ultimate demystification of the figure of "The Caliph." We are told that al-Qāhir, al-Muqtadir's successor, was entirely restricted in terms of the actions he could take and the places he could go and dominated by the chamberlain and the senior general. True, al-Qāhir was able to play one military faction against another, wielding a small measure of influence; yet he was not inherently respected because he was the caliph. Less than two years after his accession, al-Qāhir was blinded by leading military figures, who openly disfigured the caliph and did not hide behind anonymous "Berbers"; some years

177. Waines, "Internal Crisis," 282–87.

later al-Qāhir was reduced to begging in the streets of Baghdad, a symbol of the depths to which the caliphate had fallen.[178]

The earliest sources already view the death of al-Muqtadir as an important watershed in the history of the Abbasid state. Al-Hamadhānī, echoing an argument also made by Miskawayh, states: "What Muʾnis did—that is, striking al-Muqtadir in the face with a sword—was the reason enemies became insolent with the caliph."[179] Ibn al-Athīr adds that "what Muʾnis did was the reason border peoples were brazen toward the caliphs, and [the reason] for their desire for something that had not occurred to them previously; the esteem [of the caliph] was damaged, and the authority of the caliphate was weakened."[180] It was the public affront to the sanctity of the caliph—the violent "slap in the face," as it were—that irrevocably damaged the authority of the caliph, and subsequently the state as a whole. In short, "The Caliph" had been desanctified, humanized; and Muslim historians considered this such a monumental change that they presented this event as one cause, or at least a prominent marker, for the decline of the Abbasid caliphate.

The accusations of historians directed at Muʾnis, despite universal agreement that he was not on the battlefield, hints at another important sociopolitical development: the complete rupture of patron-client relations. More than anything else, the killing of al-Muqtadir was the ultimate renunciation of a *mawlā*'s bond to his patron. Muʾnis's involvement in the killing is complex. Certainly, he remained detached from the murder scene and expressed genuine grief—after all, this was the violent termination of a long relationship with his patron, a man to whom he likely had an emotional attachment. The change in caliph also threatened his position as chief commander given the unpredictability of a new ruler. In a sense, Muʾnis represented the prototypical client: he continually referred to al-Muqtadir as his master, and for years avoided replacing the caliph despite enormous interpersonal tensions.

Yet Muʾnis was clearly held responsible by contemporaries for al-Muqtadir's death; even if he was not actually present, and proclaimed the killing a tragic mistake, he had nevertheless confronted his master and sent troops against him in battle. For contemporaries, Muʾnis was the definitive client who had severed the bond with his master. The process occurring here is what we might call "self-manumission,"[181] the realization by military clients that they have little incentive or moral imperative to remain loyal to a master, in this case the ultimate master, the caliph. Muʾnis himself never fully achieved this realization. He was the last of a generation when clients developed emotional bonds with patrons, bonds that were strong enough to maintain a sociopolitical structure of

178. Miskawayh, *Tajārib*, 292. The loss of majesty was nearly complete by the reign of al-Rāḍī (322–329/934–940); for while Waines argues that al-Rāḍī could wield power by playing on the rivalries of different commanders, he acknowledges that this caliph did not have the power to change personnel of his own will, a power that al-Muqtadir generally did possess ("Caliph and Amir," 134).

179. al-Hamadhānī, *Takmila*, 70; Miskawayh, *Tajārib*, 237.

180. Ibn al-Athīr, *al-Kāmil*, 8:243.

181. This is based upon an idea developed by Pipes in *Slave Soldiers*, 20–21.

power that so obviously contradicted the reality of who actually possessed military might. Muʾnis's younger contemporaries experienced a different sociopolitical environment, in which the caliph received a degree of symbolic respect, and in political terms was a somewhat useful ally, but certainly did not command the loyalties of military clients. As Waines has shown, the caliph remained a political actor; but after al-Muqtadir, the caliph was no longer the center of authority.

Chapter 2. The Royal Family

Identifying the Royal Family: The *Hāshimiyya*

Throughout early Abbasid history, the extended royal family was generally referred to as "*Banū Hāshim*," or "the *Hāshimiyya*."[1] The exact origin of the term *Hāshimiyya* is disputed;[2] however, already under the earliest Abbasid caliphs, and certainly during the period investigated here, the *Hāshimiyya* were the distinguished descendants of the family of the Prophet, encompassing both Abbasids and ʿAlids. As relatives of both the Prophet and the Abbasid caliph, the *Hāshimiyya* enjoyed elite status at the Abbasid court. The earliest Abbasid caliphs had employed their relatives as governors in an attempt to consolidate control of the empire within Abbasid hands; this practice was gradually phased out, however, as the caliphs became fearful of internal opposition, and preferred to delegate authority to personal clients.[3] Yet the *Hāshimiyya* retained a prominent, if largely ceremonial, role at court. They attended important state events, such as investitures,[4] abdications,[5] the granting of safe conduct,[6] and public processions,[7] often serving as official witnesses. On occasion they even took collective political action in support of a particular caliph or caliphal candidate.[8]

---

1. See B. Lewis, "Hāshimiyya," in *EI2*. I take these two terms to be equivalent and interchangeable. The second term, "*Hāshimiyya*," is far more common in the sources for the period under consideration here.

2. There is general agreement that the term originated in the Abbasid propaganda campaign against the Umayyads. M. Sharon and F. Omar, in their research on the Abbasid *daʿwa*, claim that the term refers to the followers of Abū Hāshim (hence "*Hāshimiyya*"), who transferred their loyalties to Muḥammad b. ʿAlī the Abbasid. Patricia Crone, however, argues that "*Hāshimiyya*" derived from *Hāshim*, the Prophet's ancestor, and thus suggests a movement in favor of the Prophet's extended family. This second interpretation is definitely how *Hāshimiyya* was understood in later Abbasid times—that is, referring to the family of the Prophet. B. Lewis states: "In Abbasid times the name *Hāshimiyya* was applied to the family of the Prophet in general but more specifically to the Abbasids themselves, and the sectarian connotation of the term was lost in an oblivion from which it was rescued only by modern scholarship" ("Hāshimiyya,"in *EI2*).

3. See Lassner, *Shaping*, 87–90.

4. For example, attending the ceremony of investiture, of al-Muʿtazz (al-Ṭabarī, *History*, 35:113), or afterward were witnesses that his corpse bore no incriminating scars (al-Ṭabarī, *History*, 35:165).

5. For example, the abdication of princes al-Muʿtazz and al-Muʾayyad from succession (al-Ṭabarī, *History*, 34:212).

6. For example, when Hārūn al-Rashīd granted safe conduct to an ʿAlid rebel (al-Ṭabarī, *History*, 30:117).

7. For example, when Hārūn al-Rashīd, the *Hāshimiyya*, military commanders, bureaucrats, and notables went to the outskirts of Baghdad to greet the minister al-Faḍl b. Yaḥyā (al-Ṭabarī, *History*, 30:148).

8. In 201/816–817, they, along with military commanders, encouraged Ibrāhīm b. al-Mahdī to declare

As royalty, the *Hāshimiyya* commanded respect both at court and among the populace. The caliphs had an obvious interest in promoting Hāshimī exceptionalism, and thus, at least in the early Abbasid era, the execution of kinsmen was considered taboo.[9] Hārūn al-Rashīd expressed this sentiment when confronting a royal adversary: "By God, if it were not for sparing the blood of the Hāshimītes, I would cut off your head."[10] A more elegant expression of Hāshimi status was uttered by a poet praising Hārūn al-Rashīd: "You see around him the rich masters of the house of Hāshim, just as the shining stars surround the full moon."[11] The *Hāshimiyya* were widely respected among the masses as well. During the civil war and siege of Baghdad in 251/865, the *Hāshimiyya* convened outside the home of the governor of the city, Muḥammad b. ʿAbdallāh b. Ṭāhir, because their stipends had not been paid. They yelled at the governor that he had better deliver their stipends, or "we will open the city gates and let in the Turks, and none of the people of Baghdad would oppose us." Their threat was effective, and the governor was forced to negotiate, for the populace truly would not oppose the *Hāshimiyya*, even in surrendering the city.[12]

We derive a more detailed view of the *Hāshimiyya* in the reign of al-Muʿtaḍid from the budget of 279–280/892–893. Two entries concern the extended royal family:

> The salaries of the Hāshimī shaykhs, men of high rank, and khaṭībs, specifically those of the Friday mosques of [Baghdad]: 600 dinars per month, 20 dinars [per day].
>
> The stipends of the entire *Banū Hāshim*, including Abbasids and Talibids, as al-Nāṣir [al-Muwaffaq], God bless him, had allotted to them: to every one of their children, male and female, one dinar a month for every person. He ordered that [the money] be taken from the revenue of his property known as *Nahr al-Muwaffaqī*. Al-Muʿtaḍid, God bless him, cut their stipends to 1/4 dinar per month. They numbered, in Baghdad, 4,000 people: 1000 dinars per month, 33 1/3 dinars per day.[13]

Here we have some basic information about the royal family. First, this passage confirms that the *Hāshimiyya* included both Abbasids and ʿAlids (referred to as Talibids); we also see an internal social hierarchy: the elite (shaykhs), which included the *khaṭībs* of Baghdad, were listed as distinct from the larger royal community, numbering roughly four

himself as caliph, in opposition to al-Maʾmūn; many years later they tried to gather support for the caliph al-Muhtadī against the Turkish military (al-Ṭabarī, *History*, 32:50–53; 37:107).

9. See Lassner, *Shaping*, 46.

10. al-Ṭabarī, *History*, 30:234. Abbasid caliphs occasionally killed fellow Abbasids, and especially ʿAlids. But the killing of royalty, as suggested by this quotation, remained taboo and was often disguised. For example, the deposed caliph al-Muʿtazz was starved and suffocated; and the *Hāshimiyya* were called to witness that his body had not been scarred (al-Ṭabarī, *History*, 35:165).

11. al-Ṭabarī, *History*, 30:307.

12. al-Ṭabarī, *History*, 35:87–88.

13. al-Ṣābī, *Wuzarāʾ*, 25. Mez discusses the stipends of the *Hāshimiyya* (*Renaissance*, 149–52).

thousand people.[14] This is also the most concrete evidence we have of royal stipends, that elite Hāshimīs received generous salaries, while the bulk of the royal family received only a small amount of money. In fact, these stipends were reduced 75 percent by al-Muʿtaḍid, probably just one instance of his budget-cutting. The stipends were later increased by al-Muqtadir;[15] but as we shall see, they were not always paid.

The *Hāshimiyya* seem to have played a minimal political role in this period. They are never mentioned in the sources for the reigns of al-Muʿtaḍid and al-Muktafī; we do know, however, that the Abbasid Ibn al-Muʿtazz was a prominent courtier: he was a close friend of two wazirs, and was supposedly well-informed about state affairs, enough so that he was considered a competent candidate for the caliphate during the attempted coup of 296/908.[16] Perhaps al-Muqtadir recognized the threat that Hāshimīs like Ibn al-Muʿtazz posed to his rule, so he further reduced Hāshimī presence at court, which would explain why we rarely hear reference to the extended royal family during the dramatic political events or even the daily affairs of al-Muqtadir's reign.[17] I would assume that the *Hāshimiyya* participated in court events, in keeping with traditional ceremonial, but their presence was no longer important and thus was not noted. For example, we have the brief comment that al-Muqtadir forgave those of his relatives who had participated in the coup of 296/908; yet in all the detailed accounts of this coup, and the lists of men who participated, not once are any members of the *Hāshimiyya* mentioned, either as individuals or as a group.[18] In other words, they almost certainly took part, but were not worth mentioning by name. In short, the political impact of the *Hāshimiyya* for this period is so minimal that it is not even worthy of historical record.

On the other hand, there are indications that the *Hāshimiyya* still commanded broad social respect. One of al-Muqtadir's first acts as caliph was to distribute money to them and increase their stipends, in keeping with traditional practice.[19] In a completely dif-

14. We will see empirical evidence of this division, as well as the fact that khatibs were selected from within the *Hāshimiyya*.

15. ʿArīb, *Ṣilat*, 23; Miskawayh (*Tajārib*, 13) says this was Ibn al-Furāt's decision (he told al-Muqtadir to give the order). This is not surprising, since at the beginning of his reign al-Muqtadir, as a very young man, was probably not making any independent decisions.

16. For more on Ibn al-Muʿtazz, known primarily for his poetry, see B. Lewin, "Ibn al-Muʿtazz" in *EI2*. We might recall that Ibn al-Furāt had opposed Ibn al-Muʿtazz's candidacy precisely because the latter was well-informed and would leave no authority to the bureaucrats. The men who participated in the attempted coup of 296/908 thought he was highly qualified for the caliphate.

*For recent research on Ibn al-Muʿtazz, see Bray, "Ibn al-Muʿtazz and Politics."

17. The only occasion upon which al-Muqtadir is reportedly accompanied by other Abbasids was during the final confrontation with Muʾnis in 320/932, when al-Muqtadir's retinue on the battlefield included four of his cousins (ʿArīb, *Ṣilat*, 178). Thus, on the one hand we can confirm the obvious, that these Abbasid relatives existed and had some connection with the caliph and the state; on the other hand, there is absolutely no information to be found about such men.

18. Miskawayh, *Tajārib*, 13.

19. Miskawayh, *Tajārib*, 13; ʿArīb, *Ṣilat*, 23.

ferent context, a judge who sought to embarrass a colleague gathered official legal witnesses, *Hāshimiyya*, merchants, and bureaucrats to have them meet his colleague's uneducated father; here the *Hāshimiyya* were included among the social elite of Baghdad.[20] Finally, we possess a letter from a Hāshimī in Baghdad to his financial agent, referring to himself as "your lord, Abū ʿAlī b. al-Ḥasan b. ʿAbd al-ʿAzīz, cousin of the Prophet;" here the inclusion of Abū ʿAlī's impressive pedigree was no doubt intended to command the respect of delinquent villagers, and urge them to pay rent.[21] These bits of evidence are certainly insufficient for reconstructing the status of the *Hāshimiyya* in this period; yet they do indicate that, in all likelihood, the *Hāshimiyya* retained a large measure of respect due to their lineage, even though their participation in political events was virtually insignificant.

Official Appointments

Though the *Hāshimiyya* of the late third/ninth and early fourth/tenth centuries were no longer governors, and are rarely mentioned during important political events, they nevertheless held several official appointments at court. In the following pages I identify and describe these offices and try to assess the extent to which officeholders could wield influence at court. As we shall see, their functions were manipulated in such a way that officeholders shouldered responsibilities without acquiring power; their public activity actually served to distinguish and elevate the caliph above his royal kinsmen.

The Naqīb

Throughout the Abbasid period, the *Hāshimiyya* had a representative of sorts, called the *naqīb*.[22] The political theorist al-Māwardī (d. 450/1058), in his *Ahkām al-sulṭāniyya*, discusses the general principles of this position.[23] The purpose of a *naqīb* is to protect the bearers of superior lineage, first and foremost, from people of inferior descent. A *naqīb* can be appointed by the caliph, or one of his delegates, such as a wazir, based upon the following guidelines:

> When the person making the appointment wants to appoint a *naqīb* for the Talibids (ʿAlids), or a *naqīb* for the Abbasids, he should choose the best of their

20. al-Tanūkhī, *Nishwār*, 2:105. The term used by al-Tanūkhī is "*al-baṭnayn*," which the editor ʿA. Shāljī explains refers to the ʿAlids and the Abbasids.

21. al-Tanūkhī, *Nishwār*, 7:189.

22. Massignon, "Cadis et Naqībs", presents a list of the men who held this office from 132/750 to 656/1258. Unfortunately, he does not cite any sources, nor does he discuss the functions of this officer. Biographies of some of these men appear in al-Khaṭīb's *Tārīkh Baghdād*, but only on one occasion is the man in question mentioned as being a *naqīb*.

23. For information regarding this political theorist, see C. Brockelmann, "al-Māwardī" in *EI2*.

> family, with the best qualities and the most superior mind. He is appointed over them in order to combine leadership and administration. They will follow his leadership, and their affairs will be organized under his administration.

Al-Māwardī then presents a long list of the *naqīb*'s duties: he should keep a register of all living family members, noting births and deaths; ensure that all members behave as appropriate for their status, and that widows marry only their social equals; adjudicate criminal cases involving Hāshimīs, and civil cases between them, with the authority to admonish but not punish those found guilty; represent family members in ordinary litigation; administer *waqf*s (religious foundations) in the family's honor; and finally, administer the property of minors, and care for the insane or otherwise incapacitated.[24]

The first appearance of a *naqīb* during this period in contemporary sources is in a death notice, and provides interesting details about the office, the way it was acquired, and the power of the *Hāshimiyya* in general:

> At the end of this year [301/914], Aḥmad b. ʿAbd al-Ṣamad b. Ṭūmār al-Hāshimī died. He had been the *naqīb* of the Banū Hāshim, the Abbasids and the Talibids. Then the brother of Umm Mūsā[25] was appointed to the post; but the *Hāshimiyya* made a big stir about this and requested that the position previously held by Ibn Ṭūmār be returned to his son Muḥammad b. Aḥmad. Their request was granted. Aḥmad b. ʿAbd al-Samad [Ibn Ṭūmār] was 82 years old on the day he died.[26]

We learn a good deal about the *naqīb* from this death notice. First of all, at this point in time the *naqīb* represented the entire Hāshimī extended family, both Abbasids and ʿAlids.[27] From this text we might infer that it was standard practice for a son to inherit

24. al-Māwardī, *Aḥkām*, 96. Unfortunately, al-Māwardī's description is ahistorical, so we cannot derive from him an understanding of how this office actually functioned. The list of the *naqīb*'s responsibilities is described in Bowen, *ʿAlī b. ʿĪsā*, 74–75, who has borrowed it from von Kremer, *The Orient under the Caliphs*. Mez emphasizes the *naqīb*'s judicial function in the later fourth/tenth century (*Renaissance*, 148).

25. This is Abū Bakr Aḥmad b. al-ʿAbbās al-Hāshimī, often referred to as the brother of Umm Mūsā (since she was the more influential personage). He also led the hajj, was in charge of prayers in the holy cities (Mecca and Medina) and Basra, and was also in charge of the prayers at the Ruṣāfa mosque in Baghdad (al-Khaṭīb, *Tārīkh*, 4:328).

26. ʿArīb, *Ṣilat*, 47. Al-Hamadhānī (*Takmila*, 16) also records this information, but with several differences: he says that Ibn Ṭūmār is the Abbasid *naqīb* (not the *naqīb* of the Banū Hāshim); that he was ninety-two years old at death, not eighty-two; and that his death was in the year 302/914–915 instead of 301/914. In this case, as in several others, I prefer ʿArīb's version and consider al-Hamadhānī's report to be inaccurate. We will also see that Ibn Ṭūmār could not possibly have been *naqīb* for the Abbasids to the exclusion of the ʿAlids.

27. Bowen also recognizes this (*ʿAlī b. ʿĪsā*, 74). According to Massignon ("Cadis et Naqībs"), a separate ʿAlid *naqīb* was appointed in 305/917–918, due to the influence of the wazir Ibn al-Furāt, but does not cite the evidence. I have been able to confirm the existence of two officeholders for the year 325/937, but not earlier (Ibn al-Jawzī, *al-Muntaẓam*, 6:292). Mez also points out that, in the fourth/tenth century,

the office of *naqīb* from his father, since the *Hāshimiyya* object when Ibn Ṭūmār's son does not receive the post, and request that it be "returned" to him, implying that it was rightfully his in the first place.[28] More importantly, the brief dispute over the new appointment suggests that the office of *naqīb* was somewhat desirable. In fact, as we shall later see, Umm Mūsā was deeply involved in court intrigue; she and her brother were later arrested for scheming to acquire the caliphate on behalf of someone in their immediate family. In this light, Aḥmad b. al-ʿAbbās's attempt to become *naqīb* was perhaps one element in a larger family plan to accumulate power, and suggests that the office of *naqīb* was more influential than we might otherwise know. Finally, the fact that general consensus among the *Hāshimiyya* succeeded in imposing their favored candidate suggests that the *Hāshimiyya* could not be disregarded, even if opposed by an important faction like Umm Mūsā's family.[29]

We possess minimal historical evidence regarding the function of the *naqīb*. In one brief reference, the older Ibn Ṭūmār led prayers at the funeral of ʿUbaydallāh b. ʿAbdallāh b. Ṭāhir, a distinguished Baghdadi from the Ṭāhirid family;[30] and he is also cited as an authority on the intellectual soirees convened by the wazir ʿAlī b. ʿĪsā.[31] These two bits of information reflect the *naqīb*'s involvement in the social life of the Baghdadi elite, as we might expect. The fact that he led prayers—a task usually reserved for an official imam or khatib—might reflect that the *naqīb* also possessed some form of religious authority.

Aside from these passing references, we possess one detailed account of the *naqīb*'s activities at the Abbasid court. The story runs as follows: an unknown aristocratic young man, claiming to be of ʿAlid descent, approached the caliph's uncle, Gharīb, saying that he had secret information to convey to the caliph. After much hesitation and deliberation in the palace, the stranger was allowed to speak with al-Muqtadir in private and was provided with a temporary residence and servants. The caliph then summoned Ibn Ṭūmār, "*naqīb* of the Talibids,"[32] as well as other shaykhs from the ʿAlid family, all of

---

the post was divided into two, one for each branch of the extended royal family (Abbasids and ʿAlids), but he cannot date this split (*Renaissance*, 148–49). Massignon adds that Ibn Ṭūmār was a descendant of the Abbasid Muḥammad b. Ibrāhīm and hence was a distant relative of the reigning branch of the Abbasid family.

28. In this respect the office of *naqīb* was similar to posts in the bureaucracy, judiciary, and even the military, where transmission of posts from father to son was very common. Massignon's information ("Cadis et Naqībs") makes clear that inheritance was common, though not completely consistent. It is also worth noting that the *naqīb* generally served until death, even at a very old age; this is also true for other court officials, such as *qāḍīs*.

29. It is impossible to know who actually made this appointment, but the wazir would be a safe guess. We shall see that, on several occasions, wazirs were eager to satisfy the *Hāshimiyya*.

30. ʿArīb, *Ṣilat*, 40 (in Shawwal of the year 300/913).

31. Yāqūt, *Muʿjam al-udabāʾ*, 5:279. Also in Bowen, *ʿAlī b. ʿĪsā*, 75.

32. This would seem to be Aḥmad b. Muḥammad, the younger Ibn Ṭūmār, since his father is said to have died the previous year (unless we accept al-Hamadhānī's version, in which the older Ibn Ṭūmār died this very same year). The specific identity—father or son—is not relevant for my analysis.

whom were informed of the stranger's story. They went to the stranger's guest quarters (incidentally, he insulted them by not standing up when they arrived); Ibn Ṭūmār questioned him about his lineage, finding it dubious. The *naqīb* then noticed that the stranger's sword was new; he confiscated the sword, showed it around the Baghdad markets until a swordsmith identified the stranger as the son of a provincial bureaucrat. The family was apparently not ʿAlid, for the young man began to shake spasmodically, and his father arrived and begged the wazir, now in charge of concluding this affair, for mercy. When the wazir promised not to punish the impostor, the Banū Hāshim made an uproar, demanding that the impostor be disgraced publicly and severely punished. They were appeased as the false claimant was paraded on a camel on both sides of Baghdad, and imprisoned.[33]

This account proves that the Hāshimī *naqīb*, though an Abbasid, also represented the ʿAlid side of the family, for here he is specifically called "*naqīb* of the Talibids," and is an authority on ʿAlid lineage.[34] In fact, Ibn Ṭūmār's sole function here is to verify the stranger's ʿAlid descent—something of a test, to ascertain the veracity of the supposed secret information. Ibn Ṭūmār also appears as a clever man, for he reveals the impostor by means of the latter's sword. Most importantly, we see the value attached to Hāshimī, and more specifically ʿAlid lineage: the *Hāshimiyya* insist that the impostor be punished, for falsely claiming ʿAlid descent is a grave social transgression. They also wanted him paraded, as a reminder to the populace of the honor of ʿAlid status, and the gravity of making false claims. Finally, we might note that Hāshimī insistence sways the wazir, who acquiesces to their demand and punishes the impostor.[35]

These are the only references to the *naqībs* of this period. In the two main references, Ibn Ṭūmār is summoned to the royal palace to investigate the supposed ʿAlid descent of strangers; he serves as an "expert on ʿAlid affairs" for the caliph. We should note that, in these limited accounts, the *naqīb* is primarily serving the caliph's needs, not representing the interests of the *Hāshimiyya*. In fact, the most startling fact is his general absence, for as we shall see, the *Hāshimiyya* appear several times in this period complaining of severe financial problems, but not once does the *naqīb* appear as a spokesman on their behalf. In short, the *naqīb* seems to possess negligible political influence.

33. ʿArīb, *Ṣilat*, 49–50 (year 302/914–915). A very brief account is also preserved in Ibn al-Jawzī, *al-Muntaẓam*, 6:127–28.

34. That the same *naqīb* also represented the Abbasid extended family is seen in the title attributed to the elder Ibn Ṭūmār, and the undisputed Abbasid lineage of Aḥmad b. al-ʿAbbās, who was briefly appointed to the post. In addition, al-Hamadhānī clearly labels Ibn Ṭūmār as *naqīb* of the Abbasids.

35. The *naqīb* performed a similar duty three years later, when a deserter from the army of Ibn Abī al-Sāj came to Baghdad, and claimed ʿAlid descent. Ibn Ṭūmār once again interrogated the deserter, presumably to verify his supposed ʿAlid lineage. In this instance as well, the man was found to be lying and was turned over to the chief of police for punishment (ʿArīb, *Ṣilat*, 67, in year 305/917–918). In both cases, the imposters seem to claim ʿAlid descent assuming that this higher social status would preempt suspicion of their dubious stories.

Leaders of Ritual, Political Propagandists

In addition to the post of *naqīb*, the *Hāshimiyya*—or more precisely, the extended Abbasid family—held other, ritual-oriented positions: those of khatib and imam of the Friday mosques, and official leader of the hajj.[36] I assume that these positions were also held by Hāshimīs in previous periods of Abbasid history.

In combing through the identities of these officeholders, we can make some generalizations. First of all, these posts were held exclusively by Abbasids, with no exceptions. Moreover, the officeholders were concentrated in one particular Abbasid family, especially the position of khatib/imam of the various Baghdadi mosques. From the information available, the pulpits in Baghdad were dominated in the years 300–333/912–945 by the descendants of a certain ʿAbdallāh b. ʿUbaydallāh b. al-ʿAbbās;[37] in the later 320s/930s, the pulpits were held exclusively by al-Ḥasan b. ʿAbd al-ʿAzīz and his two sons, Abū Bakr and ʿUthmān.[38] Interestingly, like the *naqīb*, the family that dominated these positions was only distantly related to the reigning caliph.[39]

The actual functions performed by the holders of these offices are not always clear. The role of the Abbasid leading the hajj is never described in the sources of this period, though this was, most likely, a strictly symbolic appointment and involved no military responsibilities; when the hajj required military protection, troops were sent under the command of military figures.[40] Some of the men who led the hajj apparently also led prayers on infrequent occasions, such as funerals or festivals, which were not conducted

36. All these office holders are referred to as "*Hāshimīs*," but on closer investigation they all belong to the Abbasid family. Mez, discussing a somewhat later period, notes that "the office of the leader of prayers in towns was mostly held by [the *Hāshimiyya*]," and "the very lucrative position of the leadership of the annual pilgrimage caravan was always held by a Hashimid" (*Renaissance*, 150). Regarding terminology, the different sources seem to use the terms *khaṭīb* and *imām* interchangeably, with certain men described by both terms; there is never a case of these two terms referring to different individuals for the same mosque at the same time.

37. In fact, the only men not of this family to control a pulpit were Muḥammad b. Jaʿfar b. al-ʿAbbās, the imam of al-Manṣūr's mosque, who was appointed in the mid-third/ninth century; his son Jaʿfar, who held office for less than a year; and Aḥmad b. al-ʿAbbās, brother of the powerful Umm Mūsā, who also held office for only a few years.

38. This information is gathered from a letter he wrote, preserved by al-Tanūkhī, (*Nishwār*, 7:186–189), in which he refers to himself and his sons as *imāms* of different mosques. One interesting note: his four sons were named Abū Bakr, ʿUmar, ʿUthmān, and ʿAlī, obviously in honor of the first four caliphs.

39. The common ancestor for al-Muʿtaḍid and his sons, and the khatibs they appointed was Muḥammad b. ʿAlī, father of the first two Abbasid caliphs. Other points worth mentioning: positions did not usually pass from father to son, but among cousins; a few men were khatibs/imams and leaders of the hajj at the same time; men usually held office until they died; most of the information about these men involves their status as hadith transmitters; and several of these men are mentioned as adhering to the Shāfiʿī school of law.

40. For example, in 312/924 Abu al-Hayjāʾ the Ḥamdānid commanded troops in escorting the hajj, and was completely responsible for security (Miskawayh, *Tajārib*, 120, 139).

in the Friday mosques and thus not necessarily the jurisdiction of the khatibs/imams.[41] As for the khatibs appointed to the Friday mosques, they presumably delivered the weekly sermon and led prayers on Fridays.[42] Their role had a particularly strong affiliation with the state, for not only was the khatib technically the replacement of the caliph, he also usually included in his sermon the name of the reigning caliph, which was at once a symbol of obedience and legitimization. It was possibly also the khatib who made important state announcements, such as the reports of military victories. In a sense he acted as the official state propagandist.

Because the khatib habitually legitimized the caliph and was one of the few state representatives (along with judges) in regular contact with the public, he often served as the object of popular frustrations. At various times in Abbasid history, the populace expressed discontent by preventing delivery of the khutba, and/or interrupted Friday prayers; we might surmise that the disruption of these proceedings involved a good deal of hostility or violence directed at the khatib. During the severe political decline of the early fourth/tenth century, such abuse of the khatib reached extremes. In 307/919–920, when inflation triggered riots, the populace expressed its frustration by attacking the mosques and breaking the minbars, which, because of their association with the khutba, were symbols of state authority. Also, Ibn al-Jawzī reports that "the commoners" prevented the imam from conducting the prayers on Fridays,"[43] and Ibn Kathīr clarifies that "the commoners assaulted ... the khatib."[44]

As the security situation in the empire unraveled, and people of all social classes experienced economic stress and witnessed political violence, the khatib consequently encountered greater hostility. We saw in chapter 1 that residents of border towns and the commoners of Baghdad joined in attacking al-Manṣūr's mosque in 320/932, break-

41. For example, when al-Faḍl b. ʿAbd al-Malik prayed at the funeral for a certain Muṣʿab b. Isḥāq (ʿArīb, *Ṣilat*, 69–70, year 306/918–919); or when Isḥāq b. ʿAbd al-Malik led leading state figures in holiday prayers at the *muṣallā* (Ibn al-Jawzī, *al-Muntaẓam*, 167).

42. See J. Pedersen, "Khaṭīb," *EI2*. Regarding the fact that khatibs performed the sermon and prayers instead of the caliphs, he states: "In the time of the Abbasids, as early as Hārūn al-Rashīd, the caliph left it to the qāḍīs to deliver the sermon at the service, while he himself was a listener." D. Sourdel adds: "The caliph was the *imām* par excellence and conducted the Friday prayers in the great mosque. At the end of the 3rd/9th century, however, he was exercising this function only in the great mosque of the caliph's residence, leaving to delegated officials the task of conducting the prayers and performing the *khuṭba* in the other great mosque of the capital" ("*Khalīfa*," *EI2*). Just to update these explanations: we know that al-Muʿtaḍid delivered the khutba at least once, though we do not know if he did so regularly. Al-Muqtadir apparently did not lead the service in the mosque of the caliph's residence, although his son al-Rāḍī would do so as caliph. Finally, the khatibs of this period were definitely not *qāḍīs*.

43. Ibn al-Jawzī, *al-Muntaẓam*, 6:156; similar versions in al-Hamadhānī, *Takmila*, 21; Miskawayh, *Tajārib*, 73–74; and Ibn al-Athīr, *al-Kāmil*, 8:116–17. During these riots, the populace also attacked other public institutions and was only stopped by the military in urban battles.

44. Ibn Kathīr, *al-Bidāya*, 131.

ing the caliph's enclosure, the minbar, and preventing the khutba. On this occasion ʿArīb describes the violence in detail:

> They also pounced upon Ḥamza the khatib and stoned him until he bled, damaging the skin of his face. They dragged him by the legs, yelling: You adulterer! You pray on behalf of a man [the caliph] who neglects the affairs of the Muslims, being too preoccupied with singing and illicit sex to look into the affairs of the holy cities and the frontier towns![45]

Here we clearly see that, in the eyes of the populace, the khatib is associated with the caliph; since he legitimizes the caliph in his sermon, he becomes the personal representative of the caliph. The populace thus vents its frustrations on the khatib and beats him. Finally, the honor of the Hāshimī khatib was undoubtedly impugned: not only was he beaten, he was also defamed, labeled an "adulterer." In short, the khatibs served as representatives of the state; and as society became more chaotic, these Hāshimīs were subject to increasing violence and humiliation.

To conclude, I offer certain hypotheses regarding the implications of these positions occupied by members of the Abbasid family. The presence of Abbasids in such symbolic positions as leading the hajj and supervising mosque rituals served to extend the prestige of the ruling house, and especially that of the caliph. On the one hand members of the Abbasid family held authority in religious settings on a daily basis, which projected Abbasid authority deeper into society; on the other hand the caliph himself was released from his technical duties and could remain in the royal palace, enhancing his image of secluded majesty.[46] This arrangement also emphasized the superiority of the caliph within the royal family, as he delegated authority to other Abbasids, who legitimized the superior status of the caliph, in the process humbling themselves, and in a sense renouncing their claims to the throne.

How should we interpret the fact that all Abbasid officeholders were only very distantly related to the caliph, men we never hear of in other sociopolitical contexts? Perhaps these positions were considered mildly degrading and not suitable for the higher-ranking Abbasid family members. After all, as the most accessible extension of the caliph's authority, these men were exposed, precisely in order to shield the caliph from any public accountability. Just as the wazir was the focal point of government responsibility, the khatib was the focal point of Abbasid moral responsibility; and just as the wazir encountered violence in difficult times (as we shall see in ch. 5), so did the khatib. In this respect, the Abbasid identity of the khatibs did not immunize them from popular resent-

45. ʿArīb, *Ṣilat*, 173–74. Ḥamza the Khatib is Ḥamza b. al-Qāsim b. ʿAbd al-ʿAzīz, who had been put in charge of prayers at the Manṣūr mosque in 311/923–924 (al-Khaṭīb, *Tārīkh*, 8:181–83). He would also obtain posts in other mosques; he died in 335/947.

46. As argued in the previous chapter, the manipulation of this form of majesty differed by caliph: al-Muʿtaḍid was more of a "public" ruler, asserting his authority through his actual presence, which is why we have evidence that he delivered the khutba, while his son al-Muqtadir did not.

ment; they were treated like any other state official, regardless of supposed elite social status and lineage.

Problems with Their Stipends

The circumstances under which the *Hāshimiyya* appear most frequently in the sources of this period are when their stipends have been delayed. We have already seen that during the siege of Baghdad in 251/865 the local Abbasids complained publicly, even using harsh language and threatening to surrender the city, because they were not receiving government payments.[47] Their plight no doubt resulted from the financial difficulties brought about by civil war. Similarly, the chronic fiscal chaos of al-Muqtadir's reign often led to the suspension of Hāshimī salaries; but in this unstable period the ensuing confrontations became violent. ʿArīb reports the first two such occasions in some detail. The first, in 304/917, occurred immediately after Ibn al-Furāt had been appointed wazir for the second time, and was riding to the Friday mosque:

> The *Hāshimiyya* yelled at him, "We have been abandoned!" and made an uproar about their stipends. Ibn al-Furāt ordered the people accompanying him not to speak with them, so [the *Hāshimiyya*] became abusive in their language. Al-Muqtadir found this reprehensible and ordered that the men of rank[48] be prevented from entering the royal palace. So the Hāshimī elders went to Ibn al-Furāt and apologized to him, saying "this was the doing of ignorants among us." He spoke with the caliph on their behalf, until the latter forgave them. He attached to Ibn al-Furāt a unit of the *ḥujarī* soldiers to ride in his retinue and accompany him wherever he went.[49]

The problem recurred only two years later, in 306/918, when Ḥāmid b. al-ʿAbbās was wazir and ʿAlī b. ʿĪsā was serving as his deputy:

> A group of *Hāshimiyya* pounced upon ʿAlī b. ʿĪsā when their salaries were overdue, as he was leaving the home of Ḥāmid b. al-ʿAbbās. They spoke abusively and defamed him, tore his cloak and dismounted him. Some military commanders came to his rescue, attacked [the *Hāshimiyya*] and gave them a severe beating. This reached al-Muqtadir, who took aggressive action against them: he banished them to Basra, shackled on a prison barge (after one of them had been whipped), and ordered that they be incarcerated in the jail.
>
> When they arrived, the governor (*amīr*) of Basra, Sabūk al-Ṭūlūnī, sat them chained on donkeys, and put them in a building alongside the prison. He spoke pleasantly to them, made them promises, and distributed money to them,

47. al-Ṭabarī, *History*, 35:87–88.
48. "*aṣḥāb al-marātib*" apparently a reference to high-ranking Hāshimīs.
49. ʿArīb, *Ṣilat*, 62.

> though he kept all of this secret. Then the message for their release arrived, whereupon Sabūk al- Ṭūlūnī treated them very well: he summoned them, had food prepared for them, gave them presents, and rented water transport for them. They had been in Basra for ten days. [The wazir] Ḥāmid, as well as Umm Mūsā, her brother [Aḥmad], and ʿAlī b. ʿĪsā had visited them.[50]

At two later dates the *Hāshimiyya* protested in the streets, again because their salaries had been delayed, but for these incidents we possess few details.[51]

These reports tell us quite a bit about the status of the *Hāshimiyya* at that time. First of all, the earliest incident confirms what we have already seen, that the *Hāshimiyya* had an internal hierarchy, comprising both "ignorants" and "elders."[52] Also, all these incidents indicate that many of the *Hāshimiyya* were financially dependent on government stipends, and did not have sufficient alternative funds; when the state went bankrupt and delayed Hāshimī stipends, these people were left poor and somewhat desperate.

We acquire even more insight regarding Hāshimī relations with the important men of state. Most strikingly, the *Hāshimiyya* apparently had little or no official recourse to the caliph or wazir, or any influential personage for that matter, and thus had to express their grievances in public, on the streets. Moreover, the *naqīb* is never mentioned as having contact with the heads of state, whether to voice the grievances of his extended family or to take responsibility for misbehavior. Either the *naqīb*'s negotiations with the government were unsuccessful, or, more likely, he was simply not summoned, for his function was to assist the caliph in questions of identity or lineage, not to represent the *Hāshimiyya* in their financial concerns. In any case, the *Hāshimiyya* clearly did not have a satisfactory means of lobbying important government officials.

With no official means of expressing discontent, some of the *Hāshimiyya* resorted to confronting and even attacking the wazir.[53] Here the wazir is again acting as the focal point of government responsibility and is thus the object of popular frustration. Indeed, the prestige of the wazir was so low in this era, and the plight of the *Hāshimiyya* so severe, that Hāshimīs not only abused ministers verbally, they even physically attacked ʿAlī b. ʿĪsā. Also, the *Hāshimiyya* are so distanced from the caliph that not only can they not approach him for help, they do not even blame him for their distress. The caliph once again

---

50. ʿArīb, *Ṣilat*, 75–76. A much briefer version appears in Ibn al-Jawzī, *al-Muntaẓam*, 6:147, albeit with two key additions: al-Muqtadir had ordered the Hāshimī stipends canceled; and ʿAlī b. ʿĪsā spoke to the caliph on their behalf, resulting in the return of the banished men to Baghdad. This incident is summarized (without analysis) by Mez, *Renaissance*, 152.

51. Ibn al-Jawzī, *al-Muntaẓam*, 6:195 (in the year 313/925); Ibn Taghrībirdī, *al-Nujūm*, 232.

52. This internal stratification within the *Hāshimiyya* would be more pronounced in the Būyid period; following another instance of civil strife, several members of the extended Abbasid family were arrested, including "the prominent men ... and the scoundrels and scum" (al-Tanūkhī, *Nishwār*, 1:86–88).

53. ʿAlī b. ʿĪsā, while not technically the wazir in 306/918–919, was in charge of the bureaucracy as "deputy" for the incompetent Ḥāmid b. al-ʿAbbās; as such, ʿAlī controlled the fate of Hāshimī stipends.

appears as a distant, unblemished figurehead, which leaves the wazir to face the realities of socioeconomic crisis.

While the caliph is not held responsible for the plight of the *Hāshimiyya*, he does not remain uninvolved: indeed, he responds to the abuse of a state official by disciplining members of the extended royal family, despite their privileged status. He is willing to employ physical punishment: at least one man was whipped, and others were shackled. The more important form of punishment, however, was distancing the *Hāshimiyya* from the royal palace. In 304/917 al-Muqtadir threatened to prevent distinguished Hāshimīs from entering the palace, which prompted them to apologize; in 306/918–919 they were removed even further, to Basra. Maintaining a presence at the Abbasid court was crucial for the *Hāshimiyya*: they derived their prestige, and to an extent their funding, by association with the court; banishment was thus a potentially severe blow to their social standing.[54]

Despite these indications of weakness, the *Hāshimiyya* seem to emerge from these incidents still commanding a great amount of societal respect. In direct contrast to the punitive attitude of the caliph, the wazirs appear anxious to appease the *Hāshimiyya*. In the first incident, Ibn al-Furāt interceded with the caliph on their behalf, thereby overturning the restriction from entering the palace; and in the second incident, ʿAlī b. ʿĪsā convinced al-Muqtadir to recall the *Hāshimiyya* from Basra. The wazir's consideration for the *Hāshimiyya*, despite suffering from Hāshimī hostility, suggests a certain ingrained, long-standing respect for the extended royal family, irrespective of their political powerlessness. We also see that the *Hāshimiyya* were honored by the *amīr* of Basra and were visited by the ministers ʿAlī b. ʿĪsā and Ḥāmid b. al-ʿAbbās, as well as by fellow Abbasids Umm Mūsā and her brother Aḥmad, within the span of ten days. Thus, while the *Hāshimiyya* faced desperate financial problems, and were publicly chastised and subordinated by the caliph, they retained an important degree of social recognition from leading state officials.

This combination of high status and minimal political and economic influence is best revealed by an anecdote dating from shortly after al-Muqtadir's death, within the first week of his successor al-Qāhir's reign:

> Al-Qāhir sent for al-Mutawakkil's sons, the sons of other caliphs, and the sons of sons (grandchildren). They were brought to him; he had them approach close to him and ordered that they sit while [the temporary wazir] al-Kalwādhī administered the oath of allegiance. Then Hārūn b. ʿAbd al-ʿ Azīz b. al-Muʿtamid[55] addressed [al-Qāhir], after shaking his hand, congratulating him, and blessing him. He said: "Commander of the Faithful, alienation (*jafwa*) has harmed your family, damaged them, and impacted their conditions. They do not ask for land

54. We should note that al-Muqtadir never agrees to renew the Hāshimī stipends, or at least never authorizes an announcement to that effect.

55. This is one of the Abbasids in al-Muqtadir's retinue during the final battle with Muʾnis (see chs. 1 and 4).

> grants or the restoration of property and previous conditions but will be satisfied with the distribution of their stipends." [Al-Qāhir] replied, "I command that they be distributed, and I will not be satisfied with that for all of you, since what I have heard about your affairs troubles me." They collectively thanked him for these words. Abū ʿAbdallāh Muḥammad b. al-Muntaṣir also spoke for them, and they all prayed on [al-Qāhir's] behalf.[56]

On the one hand this report shows that certain members of the royal family—the immediate offspring of previous caliphs—are still highly respected. Al-Qāhir wishes to receive their pledge of allegiance in person, due to their elevated social status, and further honors them by insisting that they come close and sit in his presence. He also grants their request without hesitation and commits himself to promoting their interests more broadly. Yet the anecdote actually emphasizes the plight of the extended royal family. Their financial troubles are now obvious. Hārūn b. ʿAbd al-ʿAzīz refers to the poor economic conditions of the extended royal family, and implies that they desperately need money, while al-Qāhir himself says that he is concerned about their state of affairs. We might speculate that ʿArīb relates this event precisely in order to highlight the problems of the royal family: that is, the incident is not historically noteworthy because the Hāshimīs took an oath of allegiance to the new caliph, but rather because grandchildren of Abbasid caliphs were publicizing their poverty.[57]

Indeed, the conflicting images of this anecdote are telling: high ranking Abbasids taint a ritualized and dignified ceremony with their mundane and humiliating financial problems. The impression we receive is that the *Hāshimiyya* had few opportunities to express or address their grievances in the palace, and could not wait for a more appropriate occasion; thus, they took advantage of this opportunity, when their presence was ensured by tradition for ritual purposes to ask the caliph for help.

On a final note, this report suggests that the *Hāshimiyya* suffered from deliberate sanctions by al-Muqtadir. Hārūn b. ʿAbd al-ʿAzīz mentions the return of Hāshimī properties, likely seized during al-Muqtadir's long reign; moreover, he states that the royal family has suffered from alienation and estrangement. We might hypothesize that the three preceding caliphs—al-Muʿtaḍid, al-Muktafī, al-Muqtadir—had deliberately removed the *Hāshimiyya* from favor. So Hārūn b. ʿAbd al-ʿAzīz was asking for more than renewed stipends, but more generally for a change in policy, a return to closer relations between the extended royal family and the caliph. Despite al-Qāhir's good intentions, however, we shall see that the long-term fate of the *Hāshimiyya* was rapidly declining.

56. ʿArīb, *Ṣilat*, 183

57. We might recall that the *Hāshimiyya* oath of allegiance for al-Muqtadir, twenty-five years earlier, was not recorded by any historians, though it almost certainly took place.

Conclusion: The Decline of Royalty

Though there are only occasional references to the *Hāshimiyya* for the period of al-Muqtadir's reign, we can still obtain a sense of the social position held by the extended royal family, and the ways in which they were impacted by the vicissitudes of that era. We should first note that there is virtually no information about Abbasids closely related to al-Muqtadir, whether as political strongmen, governors, or boon companions. The only men of royal blood that received appointments—khatibs/imams and leaders of the hajj—were distant relatives of the caliph, and possessed no political power. There is also no evidence of the *Hāshimiyya* as witnesses to important political events; even the *naqīb*, ostensibly an appointed court official, was absent when the royal family needed access to the caliph. In short, the *Hāshimiyya* seem to have lost virtually all political power and influence. Nevertheless, we should not ignore the several indications that the *Hāshimiyya* still possessed an honorable status in Baghdadi society; they held important symbolic posts and were respected by the highest officials of the state.

By all indications, the decline of the Abbasid state had a severely adverse impact on the *Hāshimiyya*. Many of them were dependent on the state for stipends, and as the fiscal crisis worsened, their livelihoods were threatened. When their stipends were delayed, the *Hāshimiyya* protested publicly and defamed important officials, on one occasion even attacking a senior bureaucrat; as punishment, they were themselves beaten by soldiers. In response to these events, the caliph rebuked his relatives and temporarily banished them from the center of power. As khatibs, the *Hāshimiyya* occasionally encountered the hostility of a frustrated populace, and on at least two occasions a khatib was physically attacked. In general, members of the *Hāshimiyya* became involved in the civil unrest and violence that became an increasing part of Abbasid politics and Baghdadi society.

In more abstract terms, the *Hāshimiyya* were dependent upon the Abbasid state, both for their stipends, and for the legitimacy of their privileged social status. At the same time, however, they had virtually no involvement in the operation of the state, while filling marginal positions that made them the most accessible representatives to a sometimes-hostile populace. In short, the *Hāshimiyya* comprised a very vulnerable sector of the state and suffered accordingly even as they commanded respect, which somewhat mitigated the damage resulting from the state's collapse.

Thus, the status of the *Hāshimiyya* under al-Muqtadir was declining, but only gradually. This was an intermediate stage; the dramatic decline of the *Hāshimiyya* occurred under Būyid rule. The relatively good position of the *Hāshimiyya* in the early part of the fourth/tenth century is demonstrated by successive stories in al-Tanūkhī's *Nishwār*. The first is narrated by the senior bureaucrat ʿAlī b. ʿĪsā:

During one of my wazirates,[58] Abū Bakr Muḥammad b. al-Ḥasan b. ʿAbd al-ʿAzīz al-Hāshimī[59] gave me a note with a difficult request, and kissed my hand ... I considered how to satisfy [this request] without bringing rebuke upon myself. As I was riding, an idea occurred to me, so I dismounted. But Muḥammad b. al-Ḥasan grabbed my hand and said: "May I be banished from the Abbasid family if the wazir stops riding, unless he first signs my request, or kisses my hand as I kissed his." I signed [the petition] for him while standing but was surprised by his poor manners and great impudence.[60]

The first thing we notice in this story is that Muḥammad b. al-Ḥasan had access to the wazir and could make a request at the highest official level. Indeed, ʿAlī b. ʿĪsā is eager to fulfill the difficult request, though he struggles to find a solution without compromising himself. Moreover, ʿAlī agrees to sign the document despite Muḥammad's rudeness: apparently his desire to satisfy the Hāshimī overcame his disgust with the latter's behavior. We are left with the impression that Muḥammad, with the elite status of a Hāshimī, could get away with impolite behavior toward the wazir, and still get his wishes fulfilled.

Al-Tanūkhī contrasts this situation by then presenting a story from several decades later, under Būyid rule, which he narrates himself:

> I saw the same Abū Bakr Muḥammad b. al-Ḥasan in the year 350 [961]—and the times had completely reversed his fate and that of his family—in the presence of [the wazir] Abū Muḥammad al-Muhallabī. The *ʿayyārūn*[61] had rioted in Baghdad, and incited great civil discord; it began as a row within the Banū Hāshim ... between an Abbasid and an ʿAlid, over wine, and the ʿAlid had been killed. His family was aroused, and civil disorder broke out as the commoners got involved. It became a big ordeal, so that Daylami (Būyid) soldiers had to be stationed in the city quarters. It was a dreadful affair. As the disorder continued, Abū Muḥammad [the wazir] arrested most of the Abbasids—including prominent men, the *ʿayyārūn*, and the scum—even seizing among them a number of righteous Hāshimī *qāḍīs* and official witnesses. One of them was Muḥammad b. al-Ḥasan b. ʿAbd al-ʿAzīz.
>
> The wazir [al-Muhallabī] sat one day to interrogate them, and force them to name the *ʿayyarūn*, *aḥdāth*,[62] and those bearing weapons among their group, in order to arrest them and release everyone else.... The qāḍī Abū al-Ḥasan Muḥammad b. Ṣāliḥ al-Hāshimī was present, and began to argue against this in respectful language, softening [the wazir] al-Muhallabī and befriending him. But [Muḥammad b. al-Ḥasan the Hāshimī] repudiated this approach, and spoke

58. ʿAlī served twice as wazir: in 301–304/913–917 and 314–316/927–928, so the anecdote takes place in one of these periods.

59. A senior Abbasid, who served as khatib/imam, reported to have built a mosque in the *Ḥarbiyya* quarter (Ibn al-Jawzī, *al-Muntaẓam*, 7:171).

60. al-Tanūkhī, *Nishwār*, 1:85; also translated by Margoliouth, *Table-talk*, 52.

61. According to F. Taeschner, *ʿayyārūn* means "rascal, tramp, vagabond ... from the 9th to 12th centuries it was the name of certain warriors" ("*ʿayyār*," *EI2*). The sense here would still seem to be pejorative.

62. "*aḥdāth*," lit. "youths," probably a euphemism for troublemakers.

> in rude, crude, harsh language.... I heard [the wazir] respond to him: "You sucker of this and that, don't give us your ignorance and craziness! As if I have not known you for a long time! I know your stupidity and that of your father, how you dishonor the wazirs' assemblies!... As if you think al-Muqtadir is still on the throne, and I am one of his wazirs. Don't you know that the man who sits on the throne now is Muʿizz al-Dawla the Daylamī, who sees the shedding of your [Hāshimī] blood as a way to get close to God, and your value as that of a dog!"

Al-Tanūkhī continues: Muḥammad b. al-Ḥasan was dragged out of the palace by his legs, banished to Oman, and eventually put under house arrest back in Baghdad; and his Hāshimī relatives were forced to provide all the information they had concealed. As a result, a group of young Hāshimīs were imprisoned in harsh conditions and many perished; the rest were freed only after the wazir al-Muhallabī died.[63]

By the mid-fourth/tenth century, then, the standing of the *Hāshimiyya* had dramatically changed. Al-Tanūkhī states that the fate of Muḥammad b. al-Ḥasan, and the *Hāshimiyya* in general, had been completely reversed since the days of Muḥammad's arrogance toward ʿAlī b. ʿĪsā. The setting for this later anecdote is a trivial dispute that engulfed the Abbasid and ʿAlid extended families, spreading to the Baghdadi riffraff in a flurry of urban violence. The main message, though, is the change in Hāshimī official status: when Muḥammad b. al-Ḥasan had been rude to ʿAlī b. ʿĪsā, the latter was perturbed, but still acquiescent; decades later, however, the Būyid wazir al-Muhallabī would not suffer Muḥammad's insolence: he has the man dragged away and banished, and his compatriots sent to rot in prison. The current Būyid ruler (Muʿizz al-Dawla) disdains the *Hāshimiyya*, delights in harming them and thinks of them as dogs. Daylami control of the state had brought a complete reversal in the status of the *Hāshimiyya*: where they were once honored for their lineage, they are now despised by the heads of state. They had begun to suffer during the reign of al-Muqtadir; their ultimate loss of state patronage and social status occurred with the removal of the Abbasid dynasty from power.

The Princes

I turn now to the caliph's closest male relatives: his sons and brothers, and to a small extent his uncles and cousins.[64] In the chapter on the caliph we saw that princes were generally trained and prepared for the caliphate. Here we will take a more detailed look

63. al-Tanūkhī, *Nishwār*, 1:86–88; also translated by Margoliouth, *Table-talk*, 53–54 (in which the profanity is purged). Mez refers to several incidents in which al-Muhallabī disciplined both Abbasid and ʿAlid family members, especially the former; he also discusses the strength of the ʿAlid community, relative to Abbasid weakness, in the later fourth/tenth and fifth/eleventh centuries (*Renaissance*, 152–54). For more on the Būyid minister al-Ḥasan b. Muḥammad (d. 352/963), see K. Zetterstéen, "al-Muhallabī," *EI2*.

64. Female relatives will appear in the next section, though sisters and daughters are almost never mentioned in the sources for this period.

at the upbringing and training of princes, the relations they developed among themselves, and the ways in which the caliph used the princes for his own purposes. A few key themes will emerge: first, there is inevitable tension among close male relatives, all of whom potentially compete for the same office; second, the training of princes, which would influence their eventual style of rulership, closely follows the patterns of rulership established by their fathers; and finally, the caliph used the princes to consolidate his own power, primarily by reinforcing the legitimacy of inheritance.

The Sons of the Caliph

The period under investigation includes three sets of related families: those of al-Muᶜtaḍid, al-Muktafī, and al-Muqtadir, each with his own children. Regarding the families of the first two caliphs we have very little information. We saw in chapter 1 that al-Muᶜtaḍid trained his eldest son, the future al-Muktafī, in administration and warfare, and provided him a setting for establishing majesty; his younger son Jaᶜfar (the future al-Muqtadir) was not trained, and other sons (including the future al-Qāhir) are never even heard of, probably due to their young age at their father's premature death. As we might expect, the difference in training directly influenced a prince's future behavior as caliph: al-Muktafī ruled in the same hands-on, aggressive style of his father al-Muᶜtaḍid, while al-Muqtadir was reclusive and willing to delegate authority. Regarding the reign of al-Muktafī, I have found no information whatsoever regarding royal children. Fortunately, the situation changes under al-Muqtadir, and we possess many references to his children. With this information we can reconstruct various aspects of the lives of princes and assess their participation at court.[65]

Al-Muqtadir's first children were born just over a year after he became caliph. ᶜArīb records the following events: "In Muharram of this year [297/909], a son was born to al-Muqtadir. He ordered that the [baby's] name be written on banners, shields, dinars, dirhems, and placards; however, the child did not survive."[66] A second son was born only three months later: "on Wednesday night, the fifth of Rabi al-Thani in the year 297 [909], Abū al-ᶜAbbās Muḥammad al-Rāḍī billāh was born to al-Muqtadir, at Dayr Ḥanīnāᵓ, before daybreak."[67] These brief reports provide insight into perceptions concerning royal parentage and childbirth. First of all, the phrase "a son was born to al-Muqtadir," used in both birth notices, implies that the children belong to the caliph, and the mother is simply the caliph's vessel for creating children; she is not mentioned and for historical purposes does not exist. The name of Abū al-ᶜAbbās's mother is recorded, however, when

65. There are several reasons why we have information about al-Muqtadir's sons. Due to his long reign, his sons reached maturity while he was still alive, and three of them later became caliphs themselves, so that information about their youths is preserved. Also, the historian ᶜArīb takes an unusual interest in all aspects of court society but begins his narrative only from the outset of al-Muqtadir's reign.

66. ᶜArīb, *Ṣilat*, 31.

67. ᶜArīb, *Ṣilat*, 33.

he later becomes caliph, as is true for his younger brothers who would reign after him. These women are not historically noteworthy as either the concubines of the caliph or as the mothers of princes, but do become so once their sons acquire the caliphate; by extension these mothers acquire the potentially powerful position of "mother of the caliph." We might note in passing that there is confusion about the date of Abū al-ʿAbbās's birth, with at least three different possibilities;[68] this is not uncommon in Islamic historiography, suggesting an indifference to birthdays and precise ages, even among royalty and future rulers.

Al-Muqtadir fathered at least ten sons, five of whom (if not more) were alive by 302/914–915.[69] From infancy a hierarchy was established for these princes, and particular importance was attached to the eldest son.[70] The only two births recorded by ʿArīb were those of the first-born, who died in infancy, and of Abū al-ʿAbbās, who survived as the eldest of al-Muqtadir's children; no other births are mentioned, suggesting that younger sons were less important, and of lower rank, at least once an eventual successor survived. The birth of the first-born was publicized with state symbols, presumably establishing him as the official heir apparent; we might presume that this was also done for the second birth, since the first-born son had already died. Indeed, as we shall see, during al-Muqtadir's reign Abū al-ʿAbbās was by far the most prominent prince and was predictably the first of al-Muqtadir's three sons to become caliph.[71] Thus an orderly succession, based upon primogeniture, had been planned from the birth of the caliph's oldest son.

---

68. ʿArīb, above, claims the fifth of Rabi al-Thani; Ibn al-Jawzī (*al-Muntaẓam*, 6:265) has the third of Rabi al-Thani; and al-Khaṭīb al-Baghdādī (2:142, *Tārīkh*) gives the month of Rajab. There is general agreement, however, that younger brother Ibrāhīm (al-Muttaqī) was born in Shaban 297/910 (Ibn al-Jawzī, *al-Muntaẓam*, 6:316; al-Khaṭīb, *Tārīkh*, 6:51).

69. We have a list of al-Muqtadir's sons from ʿArīb (*Ṣilat*, 180): (1) Abū al-ʿAbbās, Muḥammad al-Rāḍī, (2) al-ʿAbbās, Abū Aḥmad, (3) Hārūn, Abū ʿAbdallāh, (4) ʿAbd al-Wāḥid, Abū ʿAlī, (5) Ibrāhīm, Abū Isḥāq al-Muttaqī, (6) al-Faḍl, Abū al-Qāsim al-Muṭīʿ, (7) ʿAlī, Abū al-Ḥasan, (8) Isḥāq, Abū Yaʿqūb, (9) ʿAbd al-Malik, Abū Muḥammad, (10) ʿAbd al-Ṣamad.

It is unclear if this list is organized by age, with the oldest children first. Abū al-ʿAbbās was definitely the oldest surviving son (born in Muharram or Rabi al-Thani 297/909), and Ibrāhīm al-Muttaqī was born in Shaban of the same year. Thus, if this list is organized by age, the sons listed second, third, and fourth would have been born between Rabi al-Thani and Shaban, a period of only four months. My inclination is to believe that ʿArīb does indeed list the princes according to age, meaning that al-Muqtadir fathered many children within just over a year of becoming caliph, possibly to ensure a successor (and giving some credence to the accusation that he spent much of his time with women in the harem). Several sources report that al-Muqtadir circumcised five of his sons in 302/914–915 (Ibn al-Jawzī, *al-Muntaẓam*, 6:127; Ibn Kathīr, *al-Bidāya*, 122; al-Hamadhānī, *Takmila*, 15). Al-Muqtadir had at least one daughter, who died in 305/917–918 (ʿArīb, *Ṣilat*, 68); we have no systematic list or other references to daughters.

70. Chejne states that this is common in Abbasid history, but not the rule (*Succession to the Rule*, 54).

71. This is not mentioned in the sources, but a coin preserved in the British Museum has the inscription "Abū al-ʿAbbās, son of the Commander of the Faithful" on one side, and the name of the caliph, "al Muqtadir billāh." on the other. The coin is reproduced by Bowen, *ʿAlī b. ʿĪsā*, pl. II, opposite p. 99.

Residence

While the princes were children, they probably lived in *Dār al-Khilāfa*, the royal palace complex. In chapter 1 we saw that the young prince Jaʿfar al-Muqtadir was playing in his mother's quarters, and it is reasonable to assume that royal children lived with their respective mothers in the harem of the caliphal palace, or at least in apartments within short distance of their mothers. Additional pieces of evidence support this assumption: when prince Abū al-ʿAbbās, aged four, embarked on a procession in 301/913–914, he reportedly left from the Ḥasanī palace, likely where he and his brothers were raised.[72] A fire in the royal complex in 314/926–927 reportedly burned down the residences of the princes.[73]

At an early age, however, the princes acquired residences of their own. In 306/918–919, when the wazir Ḥāmid b. al-ʿAbbās moved back to his hometown of Wāsiṭ, the caliph gave the vacant waziral palace in the Mukharrim neighborhood to crown prince Abū al-ʿAbbās.[74] In 307/919–920, other princes also acquired palaces: one palace was purchased from the governor of Mosul, for thirty thousand dinars, on behalf of Ibrāhīm b. al-Muqtadir, while additional homes were selected for the caliph's remaining children.[75] However, it would seem that some of al-Muqtadir's younger children remained in the royal palace, for during the coup of 317/929 a few were removed from the palace along with their father, also accompanied by their grandmother al-Sayyida.[76]

Ownership and/or residence outside the royal complex enabled princes to assert independent political identities, and to begin to develop the administrative skills and aura of majesty that they would need as rulers; however, it also increased the possibility of their participation in a coup against their father. Thus, when al-al-Muqtadir was told in 319/931 that Muʾnis intended to transport Abū al-ʿAbbās to Syria and proclaim him as a countercaliph, al-Muqtadir transferred the prince from the Mukharrim palace to the royal complex, presumably to keep a closer watch over him.[77] After al-Muqtadir was killed, a later wazir (Ibn Muqla) eliminated these potential bases of independent

72. ʿArīb, *Ṣilat*, 43 (translated below).

73. Ibn al-Jawzī, *al-Muntaẓam*, 6:201.

74. al-Hamadhānī, *Takmila*, 21. Five years later Ibn al-Furāt was appointed wazir for the third time, and requested that the official waziral palace be returned to him; al-Muqtadir granted the request, and there is no indication as to where prince Abū al-ʿAbbās moved, but he was again living in this same palace in the year 319/931 (al-Hamadhānī, *Takmila*, 32; Ibn al-Athīr, *al-Kāmil*, 8:232–33). Other historians (such as Miskawayh) state that Ḥāmid vacated the waziral palace in 307/919 but make no mention of the transfer of this property to the crown prince.

75. The prince Ibrāhīm, who later reigned as the caliph al-Muttaqī (329–333/940–944), apparently received his palace from Muḥammad b. Isḥāq b. Kindāj, the governor of Mosul (see al-Khaṭīb, *Tārīkh*, 6:51–52; Ibn al-Jawzī, *al-Muntaẓam*, 6:153).

76. ʿArīb, *Ṣilat*, 141.

77. Ibn al-Athīr, *al-Kāmil*, 8:232–33.

power by destroying all the homes of al-Muqtadir's children.[78] I discuss the fate of these younger princes, who were no longer the children of the reigning caliph but potential rivals to their older brother, further below.

Education and Training

We can piece together a tentative picture of the princes' upbringing, education, and training. As mentioned earlier, adolescent princes were likely under the care of their mothers, the potential foundation for strong mother-son bonds. As we shall soon see, al-Muqtadir's early attachment to his mother Shaghab developed into complete devotion, and she consequently wielded substantial power at court. The prince Abū al-ʿAbbās, al-Muqtadir's oldest son, seems to have followed in his father's footsteps: when he became caliph, he was also influenced by his mother Ẓalūm; we might assume that this close relationship began when Abū al-ʿAbbās was a child in his mother's care.[79] In fact, Ẓalūm was later buried next to her dead son.[80]

The transition from child to prince-in-training was marked by a public rite of passage. In 302/914–915, at five years of age, Abū al-ʿAbbās and four of his brothers were circumcised, honored with a lavish celebration, and then given schooling. Their teacher was the famous grammarian Ibrāhīm al-Zajjāj, who had previously tutored the wazir al-Qāsim b. ʿUbaydallāh b. Sulaymān, and thereby acquired many contacts at court.[81] At some point, the princes were assigned to different officials for further training. Many years later, the general Muʾnis referred to Abū al-ʿAbbās as his protégé;[82] yet Muʾnis could not have been a full-time mentor, since he was usually commanding military units in the provinces, and Abū al-ʿAbbās is generally described as a literary man with no obvious military instincts or training. We have more information for the prince Hārūn:

> Al-Muqtadir had entrusted [Hārūn] to Naṣr the chamberlain for training and assigned him to [Naṣr's] chambers. When Naṣr died, Yāqūt [the general] became

---

78. ʿArīb, *Ṣilat*, 185.

79. Abū al-ʿAbbās, now the caliph al-Rāḍī, was convinced by his mother to release a prisoner. We will see below, that the attachment of a son to his mother became proverbial, such that court elites avoided appointing caliphs with living mothers, concerned that these royal mothers would have a dominant role at court.

80. Ibn al-Jawzī, *al-Muntaẓam*, 6:325.

81. For the circumcision, see al-Hamadhānī, *Takmila*, 15; Ibn al-Jawzī, *al-Muntaẓam*, 6:127; Ibn Kathīr, *al-Bidāya*, 122 (the latter mentioning al-Zajjāj). The biographies of al-Zajjāj (d. 310/922) do not mention the fact that he tutored al-Muqtadir's sons (see al-Khaṭīb, *Tārīkh*, 6:89–93; Ibn Khallikān, *Wafayāt*, 1:28–29).

82. Ibn al-Athīr, *al-Kāmil*, 8:244. We will see below that Abū al-ʿAbbās received a government appointment, and Muʾnis was dispatched to act on his behalf.

> responsible for his affairs as Naṣr had been previously; Naṣr had given him presents and had become intimate with him.[83]

One example of this intimacy was that Naṣr had bought a large tract of land, valued at thirty thousand dinars, and gave it to Hārūn. Naṣr then organized a party at this new estate in honor of both Hārūn and Abū al-ʿAbbās, attended by leading military figures, and upon which Naṣr spent a tremendous amount of money.[84] From this information we see that the two highest-ranking princes were in some way attached to two of the most important figures at court; both Muʾnis and Naṣr no doubt cultivated their status as mentors, which would ensure their continued prominence at court if their protégé became caliph. We might also note that bureaucrats did not play the role of counselor or tutor, as they had performed under earlier caliphs; this is one more indication of their relative weakness in court politics in this era.

Unfortunately, we do not know what sort of training Abū al-ʿAbbās or Hārūn actually received. A third prince, ʿAbd al-Wāḥid, was certainly trained for combat, since he is mentioned in the fateful battle of 320/932 between the forces of al-Muqtadir and Muʾnis, having fought boldly on his father's side. Following this defeat, ʿAbd al-Wāḥid briefly commanded troops in a short-lived rebellion against the next caliph, al-Qāhir.[85] However, he is the only prince to appear in battle; it therefore seems that the princes Abū al-ʿAbbās and Hārūn did not receive extensive military training from Muʾnis and Naṣr.[86]

Retinues

As the princes matured, they acquired personal retinues. For this aspect of princely life we have good information for the eldest son Abū al-ʿAbbās. In 301/914, when the powerful commander Muʾnis al-Khāzin died, "his men were joined to the detachment of Abū al-ʿAbbās b. al-Muqtadir."[87] Here we see that a troop of soldiers had previously been assigned to the four-year-old prince, and that this troop was expanded, probably on a continual basis, by transferring men from the ranks of deceased generals. A similar situation occurred in 311/923–924, when the high-ranking and wealthy general Yānis al-Muwaffaqī died. Naṣr the chamberlain advised al-Muqtadir to send prince Abū al-ʿAbbās to Yānis's palace to supervise prayers and burial and assume command of Yānis's

83. ʿArīb, *Ṣilat*, 154.

84. ʿArīb, *Ṣilat*, 154–55.

85. ʿArīb, *Ṣilat*, 177–79; al-Hamadhānī, *Takmila*, 74; Ibn al-Athīr, *al-Kāmil*, 8:248–50.

86. *Osti has recently added several details to the education of the princes in the time of al-Muqtadir, based in part on the writing of al-Ṣūlī: see her chapter "Culture, Education and the Court," in van Berkel et al, *Crisis and Continuity*, especially 205–12.

87. ʿArīb, *Ṣilat*, 45. This Muʾnis is not Muʾnis al-Muẓaffar, the senior commander who lived well beyond al-Muqtadir's caliphate, and appears throughout this research. Miskawayh reports that Muʾnis al-Khāzin commanded nine thousand horsemen (*Tajārib*, 20).

troops. On this particular occasion Ibn al-Furāt convinced the caliph not to implement this plan.[88] Nevertheless, Naṣr's suggestion demonstrates that troops were continually added to the prince's retinue.

Aside from military units, the princes were also accompanied by intellectual and social companions. One interesting anecdote reflects the politics of companionship, and the tension between princes. In 318/930, Prince Hārūn planned to travel to eastern provinces, and asked the courtier and poet al-Ṣūlī to be among his companions. This disturbed Abū al-ʿAbbās, who apparently had a close relationship with this courtier; so al-Ṣūlī, protecting his relations with the older prince, gave Hārūn an excuse that he could not go, whereupon the latter was angered and stopped favoring al-Ṣūlī.[89] This brief report informs us that Hārūn had a retinue of traveling companions that included nonmilitary figures; moreover, both Abū al-ʿAbbās and Hārūn developed a personal relationship with al-Ṣūlī, and were jealous of one another for the poet's attention. Finally, al-Ṣūlī made a calculated decision to appease Abū al-ʿAbbās and lose Hārūn's favor, for Abū al-ʿAbbās was the higher-ranking prince who might become caliph and was therefore the more important patron. Indeed, Abū al-ʿAbbās and al-Ṣūlī remained close for years to come, as Abū al-ʿAbbās asked the poet to help him choose a throne name (al-Rāḍī);[90] al-Ṣūlī subsequently became one of al-Rāḍī's favored boon companions.[91] Thus we see that from a very early age the princes, and especially the heir apparent, acquired military supporters and social companions who were intended to attend them for decades.

In order to maintain separate households, and pay social companions and military units, the princes obviously needed an income. In fact, the stipends allotted to the princes were among the more sensitive financial issues at court. These stipends are usually discussed at the same time as those of the caliph himself and the caliph's mother. Aspirants to the wazirate—especially Ibn al-Furāt—offered increases to the salaries of al-Muqtadir, al-Sayyida, and the princes; by contrast, ʿAlī b. ʿĪsā was dismissed in part for cutting these salaries.[92]

---

88. ʿArīb, *Ṣilat*, 115–116. This incident is also mentioned by Mottahedeh (*Loyalty and Leadership*, 87) and will appear again in ch. 4.

89. ʿArīb, *Ṣilat*, 155–56. In the end Hārūn did not leave Baghdad.

*Osti discusses the relationship between the princes and al-Ṣūlī, especially from the tutor/courtier's perspective, in "Remuneration of a Court Companion" (esp. 93–94).

90. Ibn al-Jawzī, *al-Muntaẓam*, 6:266.

91. *For an extensive analysis of al-Ṣūlī's participation at court, including his relationships with Abbasid princes, see Osti, *History and Memory*.

92. Miskawayh, *Tajārib*, 42–44, 85. Ibn al-Furāt promised to pay the caliph 1000 dinars daily, plus 333 1/3 dinars for al-Sayyida, and 166 2/3 dinars a day for the princes Abū al-ʿAbbās and Hārūn (*Tajārib*, 42).

There are several other indications that the princes controlled substantial amounts of money: for example, control of prince Abū al-ʿAbbās's financial affairs was lucrative enough that one wazir appointed his son to this task; this prince also gave one of his teachers, a certain al-Baghawī, a lot of money (Ibn al-Jawzī, *al-Muntaẓam*, 6:266). Prince ʿAbd al-Wāḥid owned properties (Ibn al-Athīr, *al-Kāmil*, 8:250); and Muʾnis argued that Abū al-ʿAbbās should be appointed caliph following al-Muqtadir's death, for "his

Sibling Rivalry

The account described above, in which Abū al-ʿAbbās and Hārūn compete for the attention of al-Ṣūlī, suggests that princes developed rivalries. Such rivalries were natural, given that princes were potentially competitors for the throne. Once one brother became caliph, his siblings' status changed from "sons of the caliph" to "brothers of the caliph." This change increased the potential threat posed by siblings, since a fully mature royal brother could be the focus of intrigues and coups. Caliphs of this era therefore distanced their brothers from court activity by confining them to the palace of the Ṭāhirids, in the northern outskirts of Baghdad.[93] When the caliph al-Muktafī died, his brother Jaʿfar (al-Muqtadir) had to be brought from the Ṭāhirid palace to the *Dār al-Khilāfa*, the royal complex. The same was true for al-Muqtadir's brother al-Qāhir, who was retrieved from the Ṭāhirid palace in both 317/929 and 320/932.[94] In fact, security at the Ṭāhirid palace was so tight that the general Abū al-Hayjāʾ was at first refused entry in 317/929, and had to obtain a special pass from Muʾnis in order to retrieve al-Qāhir.[95] In later times, deposed caliphs joined royal siblings in the Ṭāhirid palace.[96] This expulsion from court obviously did not fully prevent rebellious officials from replacing the caliph with a royal sibling; but it did ensure that these siblings could not easily initiate intrigue.

Despite these tensions, royal siblings seem to have developed strong emotional bonds. We have seen that Abū al-ʿAbbās—the eventual caliph al-Rāḍī—feuded with his brother Hārūn; yet when Hārūn died in 325/937, al-Rāḍī, now caliph, grieved heavily for his departed brother, and temporarily banished the doctor responsible for Hārūn's care.[97] Abū al-ʿAbbās had also quarreled with his brother Abū Isḥāq (subsequently the caliph al-Muttaqī), but later apologized for harming his younger sibling.[98] The best example of the tension between brothers, and the inclination toward forgiveness, followed the failed coup of 317/929. After al-Muqtadir had been restored to the throne, he summoned his brother al-Qāhir—who had temporarily replaced him on the throne—for a conversation. He brought al-Qāhir close to him, invited him to sit, kissed his forehead, and initiated the following reconciliation:

---

grandmother, the mother of al-Muqtadir, and his brothers ... would be glad to pay money" for his appointment (Miskawayh, *Tajārib*, 241–42).

93. The location of this palace is mentioned by Yāqūt, *Muʿjam al-buldān*, 2:256. Lassner (*Topography*, 251n4) and Le Strange (*Baghdad*, 120) note that this palace was primarily used as a prison in this era.

94. Miskawayh, *Tajārib*, 193; al-Hamadhānī, *Takmila*, 59; Ibn al-Athīr, *al-Kāmil*, 8:201. ʿArīb (*Ṣilat*, 182) adds that al-Qāhir escaped from the royal palace during the countercoup of 317/929 and returned to the Ṭāhirid palace.

95. Miskawayh, *Tajārib*, 193.

96. Al-Qāhir lived there after being deposed (al-Khaṭīb, *Tārīkh*, 1:339–40; Ibn al-Jawzī, *al-Muntaẓam*, 6:368). The prince al-Muttaqī also lived there before his appointment to the caliphate (Ibn al-Jawzī, *al-Muntaẓam*, 6:316).

97. Ibn al-Jawzī, *al-Muntaẓam*, 6:288.

98. al-Khaṭīb, *Tārīkh*, 2:144–45.

> al-Muqtadir: "My brother, I know that you have done nothing wrong, that you were coerced..."
>
> al-Qāhir: "Commander of the Faithful, by my soul, remember the bond of kinship between you and me."
>
> al-Muqtadir: "By the soundness of the Messenger of God, no evil will come to you from me, and nobody will harm you while I am alive."

Al-Muqtadir then entrusted his mother al-Sayyida with supervision of al-Qāhir, and she treated the repentant sibling very kindly; so even after al-Qāhir had betrayed his older brother by agreeing to replace him on the throne, al-Muqtadir forgave his brother and promised to protect him.[99]

Functions of the Princes

As discussed in the previous chapter on the caliph, royal princes were usually given assignments in which they could accumulate military and administrative experience, and develop an image of authority, facilitating the transition to ruling an empire.[100] Like previous princes, Abū al-ʿAbbās b. al-Muqtadir officially received an important governmental post when he was still a child: in 301/913–914, al-Muqtadir appointed his four-year-old son over the defense of the Maghrib and Egypt.[101] Abū al-ʿAbbās was obviously too young to perform any task, so he was represented by his mentor Muʾnis, who was in Egypt in 302–303/914–916 and 307–309/920–922 repelling Fatimid invasions. We can be certain that Abū al-ʿAbbās did not join Muʾnis in Egypt, for in 307/920 he accompanied Muʾnis only as far as the general's encampment on the way out of Baghdad;[102] and in 309/922 he greeted Muʾnis upon the latter's return from Egypt.[103] We could easily attribute Abū al-ʿAbbās's absence in these instances to his young age; yet in 318/930, al-Muqtadir again robed and appointed Abū al-ʿAbbās to Egypt, and again Muʾnis is said to have performed the prince's duties, even though the prince was now over twenty years old.[104] Likewise, Hārūn b. al-Muqtadir was robed in 318/930 and appointed to Fārs and Kirmān, yet al-Ṣūlī informs us that Hārūn never went out to these provinces either.[105] In short, it seems that

99. Ibn al-Athīr, *al-Kāmil*, 8:206; similar interaction between the brothers in al-Hamadhānī, *Takmila*, 61.

100. Examples of this can be found throughout Chejne's work, *Succession to the Rule*.

101. ʿArīb, *Ṣilat*, 43; al-Hamadhānī, *Takmila*, 13; Miskawayh, *Tajārib*, 32; Ibn al-Athīr, *al-Kāmil*, 8:176, Ibn Taghrībirdī, *al-Nujūm*, 182. The nature of this post is not precisely clear, for, as is often the case, the sources use differing terminology. However, the position seems to have ranked above the governor, for according to Lane-Poole, Abū al-ʿAbbās's representative Muʾnis "had been dictator of Egypt for some years and had deposed and set up governors as he pleased" (*History of Egypt*, 81).

102. ʿArīb, *Ṣilat*, 79, who states this took place at the end of the month of Ramadan.

103. al-Hamadhānī, *Takmila*, 22.

104. Ibn al-Athīr, *al-Kāmil*, 8:223.

105. ʿArīb, *Ṣilat*, 154–55.

neither of the senior princes who were appointed to provincial posts ever left Baghdad to perform their duties, regardless of their age.

In fact, with all the military crises of the period, particularly the later conflicts with the Byzantines and the Qarmatians, we never hear of any of the princes involved in military actions. This seems especially strange since we know that at least Abū al-ᶜAbbās had troops attached to him. The only prince we hear of on the battlefield is ᶜAbd al-Wāḥid, defending his father's caliphate, and even then, this prince was alone from among his brothers.

The princes did, however, perform political missions in Baghdad on behalf of their father the caliph. In 310/922–923, when ᶜAlī b. ᶜĪsā was sick, Hārūn b. al-Muqtadir came to visit the respected bureaucrat and brought a message from his father. On this occasion ᶜAlī b. ᶜĪsā in turn showed respect for the prince, as he took great effort to stand up when Hārūn arrived, presumably reluctant to sit in the presence of a high-ranking member of the royal family.[106] Prince Abū al-ᶜAbbās undertook a more important and delicate mission in 317/929. When Muʾnis had heard rumors that he would be replaced as chief commander, and returned to his palace in Baghdad, al-Muqtadir sent Abū al-ᶜAbbās and the wazir Ibn Muqla to convince Muʾnis of the caliph's good intentions and continued favor. Perhaps al-Muqtadir employed Abū al-ᶜAbbās in this instance because of the prince's relationship with Muʾnis: the general had technically been filling the prince's provincial posts for years, and Muʾnis would later refer to Abū al-ᶜAbbās as his protégé. In any case, these two examples show that al-Muqtadir used the princes as intermediaries with important state officials, especially when the caliph wanted to convey a personal message to someone's home but was restricted by etiquette from leaving the palace and delivering the message in person.[107]

The princes appear most frequently in the sources as participants in public processions. On those occasions when princes received appointments or conveyed messages, the accompanying procession is often described in detail, and sometimes even seems like the most important aspect of the entire event.[108] For example, when Abū al-ᶜAbbās was appointed over the Maghrib and Egypt at age four, the appointment was celebrated by an impressive parade:

> Abū al-ᶜAbbās Muḥammad b. al-Muqtadir rode from the Ḥasanī palace, while in front of him was the banner that al-Muqtadir had given him over the Maghrib. Accompanying [the prince] were all the commanders, the *ghilmān*, the *ḥujarī* infantry, and many eunuchs, all surrounding his mount. On his right was ᶜAlī b.

---

106. Ibn al-Jawzī, *al-Muntaẓam*, 6:166.

107. In fact, after Hārūn visited ᶜAlī b. ᶜĪsā, the caliph considered coming to pay a visit himself, which would have been an extraordinary break from protocol and this particular caliph's seeming aversion to leaving the royal palace. Indeed, ᶜAlī was shocked by this idea, so he had Muʾnis convince al-Muqtadir to cancel the visit (Ibn al-Jawzī, *al-Muntaẓam*, 6:166).

108. *N. El Cheikh has subsequently concurred with this observation ("To Be a Prince," 213).

> ʿĪsā [the wazir], Muʾnis was on his left, and Naṣr the chamberlain was in front of him. He traveled along the main road, and returned via the river, with the cavalcade accompanying him.[109]

This elaborate procession was intended to honor the prince, even though he was only four years old and would not fill the post to which he was assigned. What's more, the procession included the most powerful men in the state: the wazir, the chamberlain, and the chief military commander. Several years later, Hārūn b. al-Muqtadir's visit to the sick ʿAlī b. ʿĪsā involved a similar procession: "He rode to visit ʿAlī ... and with him were Muʾnis, Naṣr al-Qushūrī [the chamberlain], and the leading pages. The road was carpeted for him from the riverbank to [ʿAlī's] reception room."[110] The decoration of the road indicates that Hārūn's journey was a distinguished event; also, Muʾnis and Naṣr could have visited ʿAlī b. ʿĪsā any time they chose, but on this occasion they were accompanying Hārūn, that is, they were honoring the prince, not necessarily ʿAlī. Eight years later, when Hārūn was appointed to Fārs and Kirmān, he again rode "accompanied by the wazir and the military."[111]

Abū al-ʿAbbās also appears in processions not specifically devoted to him, in which his primary function is to add royal dignity to the proceedings. In 303/916, as part of the prisoner parade for the rebel al-Ḥusayn b. Ḥamdān, Abū al-ʿAbbās rode in the streets of Baghdad, accompanied by Naṣr, Muʾnis, ʿAlī b. ʿĪsā, and a throng of soldiers. Seven years later, in 310/922–923, Abū al-ʿAbbās rode to the *muṣallā* for the feast day of Eid al-Fitr; here again he was accompanied by the wazir Ḥāmid b. al-ʿAbbās, ʿAlī b. ʿĪsā, Muʾnis, and the military.[112]

In general, these processions were intended to honor the princes: they made the princes the center of an elaborate event and surrounded them with the most important men of state. In fact, the glorification of the princes was often more the focus of attention, and hence more important, than the event the processions were supposedly celebrating.

As al-Muqtadir's caliphate collapsed, the princes assumed a role as symbols of sanctity, echoing the role played by their father. In 317/929, when al-Muqtadir heard that rebellious troops were approaching the palace, he dismissed all armed guards, opened the gates of the palace, and sat on his throne, reading the Qur'an, surrounded by his sons.[113] Al-Muqtadir was consciously projecting an image of sanctity, the holiness of "The Caliph," which the insurgents presumably would not dare intrude upon; the princes who surrounded the caliph were a part of his image: they were caliphs-in-waiting, bearers of

109. ʿArīb, *Ṣilat*, 43. The story continues: a commoner interrupted the procession in order to perfume the prince's horse.

110. Ibn al-Jawzī, *al-Muntaẓam*, 6:166.

111. Ibn al-Athīr, *al-Kāmil*, 8:223.

112. Ibn al-Jawzī, *al-Muntaẓam*, 6:167.

113. ʿArīb, *Ṣilat*, 140.

superior status based upon royal descent and ritual sanctification, symbols of authority that the military would presumably not confront. In a sense, the princes swathed the caliph in an additional layer of sanctity. They were obviously not defending their father in a physical sense, for he had abrogated armed defense by removing his guards, and the princes were surely not intended to face the army in battle alone.

The princes served a similar symbolic function in 320/932, at the end of their father's reign. Several days before the fateful battle against Muʾnis's forces, al-Muqtadir made an impressive public display after Friday prayers, riding across the royal compound, preceded by his seven oldest sons, and accompanied by military officers and commanders.[114] Here again we know that the princes were not participating as commanders of the military, for only one of these sons participated in the battle that took place just days later.[115] The princes had no military function; rather, they were offshoots of the caliph, little spheres of symbolic authority that surrounded and enhanced the ultimate authority, the caliph. Thus, in the decisive moments of al-Muqtadir's caliphate, the princes functioned as symbols, not in an administrative or military capacity.

Conclusion: Grooming Future Caliphs

Most of the references in the sources demonstrate that an image of authority was deliberately fashioned for the royal princes, and especially for the heir apparent. The construction of this image began at birth: the oldest son, as heir apparent, was publicized on coins and banners, thus immediately being linked to the caliph and the state. The subsequent circumcision of the princes was an expensive and elaborate event, emphasizing that these were the most important children of the realm. From an early age, the princes, especially Abū al-ʿAbbās, received official state appointments, and developed large retinues, which again reinforced their elite status and theoretical power within the state; high-ranking officials, such as Muʾnis, were technically in subordinate position to the princes. Finally, the many public processions made the princes the focus of important state rituals; and by accompanying them—that is, riding to the side or in front of a prince—the wazirs, commanders, and chamberlain were always situated in relation to the prince, secondary figures to his central image, the elite of society subordinated to the royal family. By these various means the princes developed an image of authority second only to that of the caliph.

Why were the princes granted elite status, and publicly glorified? We might assume that al-Muqtadir felt an impulse shared by many rulers, and parents in general, to preserve his own power and the power of his family by transmitting it to his children. According to this logic, the princes were honored in order to make them viable candidates

114. ʿArīb, *Ṣilat*, 167. Members of the public were present to see this procession, as they had just attended prayers at the Friday mosque within the royal compound.

115. ʿArīb, *Ṣilat*, 177; al-Hamadhānī, *Takmila*, 69.

for the caliphate. By elevating the princes—and one heir in particular—the caliph also simplified the future succession, which under the Abbasids was sometimes chaotic for lack of systematic guidelines. I do think the glorification of the princes served a more subtle role in support of al-Muqtadir's rule: they were props for the present, not just forward planning or a safeguard for the future. The glorification of the princes reinforced two political principles that supported al-Muqtadir's claim to the caliphate: first, the notion that inheritance—immediate blood relation—was the appropriate means of determining a successor; and second, that this particular branch of the Abbasid family should rule. Both these arguments would bolster al-Muqtadir's claim to the caliphate, particularly vis-à-vis pretenders from other branches of the royal family (like Ibn al-Muʿtazz, of the ill-fated coup of 296/908), since al-Muqtadir was the oldest surviving male of the Muʿtaḍidī branch of the family. Al-Muqtadir thus used the princes to assert the political principle of succession, which in effect changed the caliphate from being the possession of the extended Abbasid family to being the birthright of a specific branch: the Muʿtaḍidī bloodline.

The princes also served the caliph on another level. We have seen that the princes were most prominent in public processions; just as the wazir was the caliph's administrative representative and the khatib/imam his representative for Islamic ritual, the princes served to disseminate caliphal majesty in public while he personally remained distanced in the palace. The princes were primarily referents to the caliph, projections of his sovereignty, for he was the sole source of their status; when they appeared in public, they made the majesty of the caliph more tangible to the populace, a concrete vision of royal grandeur. Yet the actual source of sanctity and greatness remained in the palace, his stature heightened by his inaccessibility and the exaggerated imagination of his subjects.

Ironically, the public appearance of the princes reinforced their subordination to the caliph. While the caliph constructed the princes' image of authority and status as heir apparent, they necessarily became potential threats as figureheads for a coup; their subordination to the reigning caliph had, therefore, to be periodically reasserted. By repeatedly being honored in public, the princes were ceremonially feted with elite status yet were shown to be inferior to the more distant and inaccessible caliph.

Perhaps the most important conclusion from our source material, however, is that al-Muqtadir's princes developed an image of authority but did not develop the commensurate administrative and military skills necessary to be effective rulers. In this respect they were close reproductions of their father, who became a powerful symbol as "The Caliph," but did not take an active role in governance—certainly in comparison to his father—and abstained from military affairs. As the oldest surviving prince and heir apparent, Abū al-ʿAbbās was honored a number of times in public processions and was even accompanied by military chiefs; yet as far as we know he never journeyed to the provinces or took personal command of any military units. He played the role of a nascent commanding officer, gradually acquiring a personal military detachment; but he never actualized this role and never led troops into battle despite plenty of opportunities. Indeed, when al-Muqtadir was most in need of military support, in 317/929 and 320/932, the primary role of the princes was as secondary props, standing by the caliph in purely symbolic displays of authority and sanctity. The princes and the heir apparent, like the caliph, had become hollow figures: they acquired all the trappings of power, such as appointments and retinues, but developed none of the military or administrative skills for implementing rule. For previous princes such as al-Muʿtaḍid and al-Muktafī, an image of authority was the by-product of military training and was a tool for implementing effective rule; for al-Muqtadir and his princes, the image of authority gradually became an end in itself.

Royal Women

Scholarly discussions of royal women have usually concentrated on wives and concubines. I broaden the discussion here by analyzing the role of the caliph's mother and her extended female retinue and consider two basic questions: how did their participation differ from that of men? and to what extent were there meaningful differences among women? This period is particularly advantageous for such an analysis, since the caliph al-Muqtadir's mother was a powerful figure at court. This broadened assessment of women will reveal that different women held different status at court, which resulted in differing opportunities and limitations, nuancing our understanding of how women could wield power.[116]

Wives, Concubines, and Mothers

During the first decades of Abbasid rule, the most prominent women at court were the wives of the caliphs.[117] Umm Salama and Umm Mūsā, wives of the caliphs al-Saffāḥ and al-Manṣūr, benefited from favorable stipulations in their marriage contracts, so that they could demand monogamy and respect from their powerful husbands.[118] A generation later, al-Khayzurān and Zubayda took advantage of the devotion of their respective male partners, the caliphs al-Mahdī and Hārūn al-Rashīd, respectively, to become promi-

---

116. *In the past two decades, since undertaking this research, several articles have addressed the role of women at al-Muqtadir's court. Van Berkel argues against the common conception that powerful women were especially harmful to the state, noting that they built networks, as did the male participants at the Abbasid court ("Yet, looking behind the disapproving comments of contemporaries makes it possible to catch a glimpse of the advisory, mediatory, and negotiating functions women could fulfill at al-Muqtadir's court," "Young Caliph," 14). See also the articles of El Cheikh, "Revisiting the Abbasid Harems," and "Qahramāna in the Abbasid Court," as well as her chapter "Harem" in van Berkel et al, *Crisis and Continuity*. Her findings concur with mine.

117. Comprehensive surveys include Abbott, *Two Queens*; Walther, *Woman in Islam*; and Ahmed, *Women and Gender*.

118. Ahmed, *Women and Gender*, 77–78.

nent figures in court life. While these women were respected by their husbands, and made important contributions to court culture, they seem to have had little influence on the affairs of state; the one woman who apparently did intervene in political affairs, al-Khayzurān, is shown as asserting her influence most strongly in the caliphate of her son al-Hādī. According to al-Ṭabarī, "al-Khayzurān used to exercise her authority over him in all his affairs, without consulting him at all."[119] During al-Hādī's brief reign, leading men of state came to al-Khayzurān's residence in the palace to ask for favors, which so annoyed her son the caliph that he scolded her: "It is not dignified for women to involve themselves in affairs of state."[120] The tension between mother and son became so severe that al-Khayzurān is accused of having poisoned al-Hādī, thereby bringing about the accession of her favored son, Hārūn al-Rashīd.[121]

In some respects, al-Khayzurān represents a turning point in the nature of female participation at the Abbasid court, for she embodies the two major trends that would henceforth characterize this participation. First, concubines of slave origin increasingly predominated over wives of Arab ethnicity as the favored consorts of the caliphs. This change has been noticed by many scholars; but we should not overlook the fact that caliphs continued to marry free-born women from among the social elite.[122] For example, the caliph al-Maʾmūn staged a sumptuous wedding celebration for his marriage to Būrān, the daughter of the important minister al-Ḥasan b. Sahl; and al-Muʿtaḍid married the Ṭulūnid princess Qaṭr al-Nadā, a union that was reported and described by many historians due its important political significance.[123] Al-Muqtadir himself had at least one free-born wife. I suspect that these well-known examples reflect a broader reality: Abbasid

119. al-Ṭabarī, *History*, 30:42.

120. al-Ṭabarī, *History*, 30:42.

121. al-Ṭabarī, *History*, 30:42–45.

122. Ahmed (*Women and Gender*, 83–84) explains the decline in importance of free-born wives, but generalizes this as the loss of female power, which is not quite accurate. Abbott argues that "Acquiring a wife was a much more serious undertaking than stocking up on concubines who could be discarded, given away, or even killed without any questions raised. A wife had her legal rights to property settlement. She had 'family connections.' These considerations were to lead, in the none too distant future as history goes, to fewer and fewer royal marriages. With few exceptions the royal concubine reigned almost supreme in the caliphal palace" (*Two Queens*, 67). I agree with Abbott's logic about the potential complications of royal marriage; yet the historical record shows that some caliphs still married, precisely for family connections. Abbott's statement should not be taken to mean that concubines altogether replaced wives, or that the two were mutually exclusive. Clearly marriage provided additional benefits beyond sexual gratification or procreation, which was the primary purpose of concubines. Similarly, I would amend her assertion that the decline of wives allowed the concubines to "reign supreme." I contend that the most powerful women at the court were the mothers of caliphs, not concubines (even though these mothers largely originated as concubines). Women derived their power from a mother-son relationship, not a caliph-spouse/concubine relationship. On an additional note, Mez claims that caliphs of the fourth/tenth century rarely married free women (*Renaissance*, 364); this was not true for al-Muqtadir or his father al-Muʿtaḍid.

123. See, for example, al-Ṭabarī, *History*, 38:3, 19–20.

caliphs continued to take free-born wives, most likely to solidify political alliances. These wives, however, never seem to be involved in state affairs, and are certainly not described as commanding the same respect that early Abbasid wives did. More importantly, the sources never inform us if these wives bore children, meaning that none of the theoretical offspring were raised as heirs-apparent, and none became caliphs. As far as we know, from the accession of al-Maʾmūn (year 198/813) through the Būyid takeover (334/946), all Abbasid princes and caliphs were the children of concubines.[124] Given the fact that royal wives did exist, we might conclude that there was a conscious policy to procreate, and preserve the Abbasid dynasty, with slave-concubines and not with free-born wives.

While concubines became more prominent than free-born wives, they were not the most important women at court. Rather, the second trend that typifies the third/ninth century Abbasid court is the increasing power of the caliph's mother. As noted above, al-Khayzurān reached the height of her power during the reign of her son al-Hādī. The most influential of these "queen mothers" seem to have emerged in periods of political instability. For example, during the period of chaos at Samarra (247–257/861–871), the wealthiest individuals at the court were the mothers of the caliphs al-Mustaʿīn and al-Muʿtazz; they used their money to wield political influence.[125] What's more, despite the cyclical violence that afflicted the military, bureaucrats, and even the caliphs of that period, these wealthy women emerged unscathed, with much of their fortunes intact. It seems that these women benefited from certain unspoken rules at court: as royal mothers they were not in contact with the rest of the court elite, which created the illusion that they were beyond the boundaries of political intrigue; and as females they were protected by the taboo against harming women. In short, while everyone else at court engaged in continual conflict, these mothers were able to acquire fortunes and wield power but were never subject to retribution. In such periods of chaos, the royal mother was arguably the most powerful member of the court, or at minimum, the least susceptible to political scheming.[126]

Muslim historians noticed that mothers of caliphs were often important individuals. When describing a change of caliph, most historians record the full name of the new caliph and then immediately mention the name and legal status of his mother. For example, Ibn al-Jawzī writes: "The caliphate of al-Muqtadir billāh: his name was Jaʿfar b.

124. This has been noticed by many scholars, such as Mez (*Renaissance*, 364), and Shāljī, the editor of al-Tanūkhī's *Nishwār* (5:12). However, I have not yet seen anyone suggest that this was a deliberate policy. In other words, scholars seem to assume that princes were born of concubines, because these were the only women with whom the caliphs cohabited; wives were supposedly undesirable. But as I have noted, a few caliphs did indeed wed, and yet none of the wives bore children, as far as we can tell. Thus, concubines were, intentionally, the preferred mothers for princes.

125. For example, Qabīḥa, the mother of the caliph al-Muʿtazz, intervened to prevent the arrest of a bureaucrat (al-Ṭabarī, *History*, 35:161–62).

126. *El Cheikh has subsequently noted the same phenomenon: "The most powerful person in the Abbasid harem tended to be the mother of the caliph" ("Caliphal Family," 334).

al-Muʿtaḍid billāh, his *kunya* was Abū al-Faḍl, and his mother was an *umm walad* named Shaghab."[127] Such information was not limited to specific cases of prominent mothers, but was habitually recorded by historians for all caliphs.[128] These records always include the mother's name (often with variants), and her legal status (almost always *umm walad*); some historians also mention her ethnic origin—usually Greek, but sometimes Turkic—and Ibn al-Jawzī also notes whether or not she lived during her son's reign. We might add that these same historians never systematically name the wives and/or concubines of a given caliph; women such as Shaghab are only identified in relation their son, not their husband/master. That is, royal women were not noteworthy, and by extension not influential, as wives or concubines to ruling caliphs, but only as mothers.[129]

In fact, the "mothers of the caliphs" became something of a distinct historiographic theme. Ibn al-Zubayr, in his *Kitāb al-Dhakhāʾir*, includes a section entitled "What mothers of the caliphs bequeathed and possessed," in which he discusses the wealth of several royal mothers; but he includes no comparable section on wives or concubines. Instead, the few royal women who were not "mothers" that Ibn al-Zubayr does mention are included in the chapter on mothers, which suggests that as a group they were far less important and should therefore be subsumed by the "mother" category.[130]

This trend of powerful mothers reached its climax in the reign of al-Muqtadir. During the reign of this young caliph, his mother Shaghab, generally referred to as al-Sayyida, was one of the most powerful and lasting members of the court. Her influence, and that of her female staff, is particularly striking in contrast to the nearly complete absence of information regarding wives and concubines. A lengthy anecdote in al-Tanūkhī's *al-Faraj baʿd al shidda* makes this discrepancy in power very clear: a secretary of the prince Ibrāhīm b. al-Muqtadir had fallen in love with a singer who belonged to the caliph. The smitten secretary could not work, so the prince's mother (Umm al-Muttaqī) decided to intervene: she asked al-Sayyida to approach the caliph about selling the singing woman to the secretary. Al-Sayyida scorned this request and later mocked the secretary.[131] This anecdote demonstrates that Umm al-Muttaqī, an *umm walad* of the caliph, had less influence over al-Muqtadir than his mother, and generally appears as al-Sayyida's social inferior. Thus, while this period is known for its powerful women, it was more precisely the royal mother, and not the caliph's consorts, who achieved prominence.

---

127. Ibn al-Jawzī, *al-Muntaẓam*, 6:67; similar in al-Ṭabarī, *History*, 38:187; ʿArīb, *Ṣilat*, 22; al-Masʿūdī, *Murūj*, 248; al-Khaṭīb, *Tārīkh*, 7:213.

128. This is definitely true for al-Masʿūdī, ʿArīb, al-Hamadhānī, and Ibn al-Jawzī.

129. On this point, Walther generalizes that "power hungry mothers took over the business of state for their young or weak and incompetent sons on more than one occasion in the world of Islam" (*Woman in Islam*, 82). Von Kremer's attitude is similar.

130. Ibn al-Zubayr, *al-Dhakhāʾir*, 235ff.

131. al-Tanūkhī, *al-Faraj*, 4:309–311. The story also shows the close relationship between the prince and his mother.

Al-Sayyida, Umm al-Muqtadir: Political Influence

As was common with royal princes, al-Muqtadir was very attached to his mother, and spent a lot of time with her in childhood and throughout his reign. We saw in the previous chapter that as a young prince, Jaʿfar (later al-Muqtadir) was found playing in his mother's quarters, and likely grew up in her care. In fact, mother and son probably continued to live in the same residence and changed residences together when necessary. During the coup of 296/908, al-Muqtadir was told to vacate the royal palace and move with his mother to the palace of Ibn Ṭāhir; so apparently she was living in the palace complex and was expected to move with her son.[132] The same was true twenty years later: in the coup of 317/929, al-Sayyida was removed from the palace along with al-Muqtadir, this time accompanied by his consorts and children.[133] This close proximity enabled frequent contact between mother and son throughout his caliphate. According to reports from the year 312/924, an intruder was found sitting on the roof of a palace "that belonged to al-Sayyida, where al-Muqtadir frequently sat with her."[134] Not only did al-Muqtadir visit his mother, she also used to visit him on what was apparently a regularly scheduled basis, for on one occasion when she appeared to ask for a special favor, his first words were: "Milady (*Sittī*), this is not the [regular] time for your visit."[135] The respect and sentiment that al-Muqtadir felt for his mother is further demonstrated by his reception for her on such visits: "it was his practice when he saw her to stand up for her, hug her and kiss her on the head, and seat her beside himself in the place of honor."[136]

Given al-Muqtadir's youth and inexperience upon becoming caliph, and likely attachment to his mother, it is not surprising that she was involved in state affairs during the early part of his reign; indeed, contemporary historians emphasize the dominance of women and servants in this period. Al-Masʿūdī states that al-Muqtadir "received the caliphate when he was young, inexperienced and spoiled, and was not interested in affairs of state and had no control at all; the women, servants and others dominated affairs."[137] Miskawayh adds that "al-Muqtadir was devoted to his pleasures and avoided men, shunned male companions and singers, and was intimate with women, so that the harem and servants dominated the state."[138] These insinuations of female influence are corroborated by a report from 299/911–912, following the removal of Ibn al-Furāt from the wazirate. When a certain Ibn Thawāba wished to torture Ibn al-Furāt to extract fines, he had to ask permission from the powers-that-be: "*al-Sāda* (their highnesses)—by which he referred to al-Muqtadir, his mother al-Sayyida, Khāṭif [his aunt], and Dastanbūya, *umm*

132. Miskawayh, *Tajārib*, 6.
133. ʿArīb, *Ṣilat*, 141; Miskawayh, *Tajārib*, 193.
134. Miskawayh, *Tajārib*, 118.
135. Ibn al-Jawzī, *al-Muntaẓam*, 6:74. *Sittī* is a common term of respect in addressing women.
136. Ibn al-Jawzī, *al-Muntaẓam*, 6:74.
137. Al-Masʿūdī, *Tanbīh*, 377.
138. Miskawayh, *Tajārib*, 13 (slightly different translation by Amedroz, *Eclipse*, 15).

walad of al-Muʿtaḍid—for at the time they were in control of affairs due to al-Muqtadir's young age."[139] They consented to the torture of the fallen wazir; when the torture became excessive, these women were again petitioned to have the punishment stopped. Thus al-Muqtadir's mother, along with other royal women, was very much involved in court politics, giving orders to very important state officials.[140]

Since al-Muqtadir remained attentive to his mother over the course of his reign, she retained a great deal of influence over state affairs. On many occasions we hear that people with requests or complaints contacted both the caliph and his mother, to the extent that the phrase "al-Muqtadir and al-Sayyida" becomes almost formulaic. For example, when a stranger claiming ʿAlid descent approached the general Gharīb demanding an audience with the caliph, Gharīb "went to al-Muqtadir and to al-Sayyida, and informed them of this affair."[141] Al-Muqtadir and al-Sayyida were most commonly approached in the course of political intrigues: enemies of the influential Umm Mūsā told "al-Muqtadir and al-Sayyida" that Umm Mūsā was plotting for a change in the caliphate;[142] a letter criticizing the wazir al-Khāqānī was brought to al-Muqtadir and al-Sayyida;[143] and a high-ranking servant (Mufliḥ the eunuch) pressured al-Muqtadir and al-Sayyida into allowing the torture of the ex-minister Ḥāmid b. al-ʿAbbās.[144] Al-Sayyida is never mentioned as having made final decisions; yet the fact that historians repeatedly refer to her alongside the caliph in the context of crucial political moments suggests that, at the very least, she served as supreme counselor to her son, if she did not in fact make such decisions alone. Moreover, in all the cases mentioned above, the rumors or accusations brought to al-Muqtadir and al-Sayyida resulted in the fall of important court officials: that is, al-Sayyida was not simply collecting gossip, she was asked to make substantial changes in court personnel.

Indeed, on several occasions we see that al-Sayyida played a crucial and often decisive role in court politics. In one relatively trivial incident, the general Hārūn b. Gharīb (al-Sayyida's nephew) had arrested his own secretary for embezzlement. The secretary's brother complained to al-Sayyida's sister, who in turn informed al-Sayyida; she had the secretary brought to the palace and released. Here we see that al-Sayyida was the logical person to complain to about injustices, and she dared to cross a leading general, her own relative, by releasing his employee.[145] On more important occasions, al-Sayyida managed

139. Miskawayh, *Tajārib*, 90 (similar translation in *Eclipse*, 99); al-Khaṭīb, *Tārīkh*, 5:51–52. Dastanbūya and Khāṭif will appear again below.

140. Walther writes, "When [al-Sayyida's] son came to power in 908 [C.E.] at the age of 13, he was still so much a child and dependent on her that the government was de facto in her hands." She continues, "This did not change very much either when the khalif became older" (*Woman in Islam*, 82).

141. ʿArīb, *Ṣilat*, 49 (in year 302/914–915).

142. Miskawayh, *Tajārib*, 84; ʿArīb, *Ṣilat*, 108; Ibn al-Jawzī, *al-Muntaẓam*, 6:166.

143. Miskawayh, *Tajārib*, 142.

144. ʿArīb, *Ṣilat*, 112, in the year 311/923.

145. Miskawayh, *Tajārib*, 163–64.

to arrange senior appointments for her personal favorites. We are told that Ḥāmid b. al-ʿAbbās contacted Naṣr the chamberlain and al-Sayyida, even promising them money, in a successful attempt to attain the wazirate.[146] A few years later, in 312–313/924–925, when al-Khāqānī was sick and unable to continue as wazir, the general Muʾnis suggested ʿAlī b. ʿĪsā as his replacement, while al-Sayyida and her sister recommended al-Khaṣībī, who was subsequently appointed.[147]

Al-Sayyida's most impressive power, given the instability of the period, was the ability to protect very important men who had fallen out of favor. Early in al-Muqtadir's reign, the fabulously wealthy jewelry merchant Ibn al-Jaṣṣāṣ was imprisoned, and millions of dinars were confiscated from him. According to his own report, he languished in incarceration and began to give up hope of being freed, when one day a servant appeared and declared that Ibn al-Jaṣṣāṣ was to be released. He continues the report: "I was led through the caliph's apartments, heading toward the residence of al-Sayyida, for it was she who had released me, having interceded on my behalf." After being released, he wrote to al-Sayyida complaining about his poor conditions, and asked that several containers, which held one hundred thousand hidden dinars, be returned to him from the royal palace. She promised to talk to al-Muqtadir about this. After a few days Ibn al-Jaṣṣāṣ reminded her of this request; she informed the fortunate jewelry merchant that al-Muqtadir had ordered the containers returned to him. Ibn al-Jaṣṣāṣ thereby recovered a small part of his fortune.[148]

In the latter half of al-Muqtadir's reign, as state finances deteriorated and internal scheming reached a peak, al-Sayyida began to intervene in the most serious of crises. In 311/923–924, the vengeful wazir Ibn al-Furāt had convinced al-Muqtadir to banish the general Muʾnis to Raqqa and then encouraged the caliph to arrest Naṣr the chamberlain in order to seize the latter's wealth. As Miskawayh reports:

> Al-Muqtadir agreed to turn [Naṣr] over to [Ibn al-Furāt]. This information reached Naṣr. He turned to al-Sayyida and requested help; so she spoke with her son, saying: "Ibn al-Furāt has already distanced Muʾnis from you, and he is your sword and the person you most trust. Now he wants to sabotage your chamberlain, to control and repay you for what you did to [Ibn al-Furāt] previously—by withdrawing your favor and disgracing his harem. I would like to know whom you would ask for help against him if he has evil intentions toward you, such as deposing you or controlling you, given the evil he has displayed and the exaggerated behavior of his son, beyond all bounds." Naṣr had gone home, distributed his money in deposits, and gone into hiding. Al-Sayyida wrote to him to

146. Miskawayh, *Tajārib*, 57. Al-Hamadhānī, (*Takmila*, 19–20) says that Ḥāmid contacted al-Sayyida's agent in Wāsiṭ.

147. Miskawayh, *Tajārib*, 143. The appointment eventually took place toward the end of 313/925.

148. al-Tanūkhī, *Nishwār*, 7:233–234; *al-Faraj*, 2:112–13.

*I expand upon the career of Ibn al-Jaṣṣāṣ in a forthcoming article, "Asset Management," which includes analysis of the jewelry merchant's relationships at the Abbasid court.

> return to the royal palace. [Naṣr] trusted [her], returned, and humbled himself before Ibn al-Furāt and his son.[149]

Apparently al-Sayyida changed the caliph's mind regarding Naṣr, for the chamberlain was not arrested, and thus at least one of the fixtures at court remained in office. Al-Hamadhānī concludes that "Naṣr's position remained weak, and al-Sayyida protected him."[150]

Al-Sayyida's intervention was not always successful. Earlier in 311/923–924, al-Muqtadir had been uncertain whether or not to turn over the ex-minister Ḥāmid b. al-ʿAbbās to Ibn al-Furāt and his son al-Muḥassin, by whom Ḥāmid would certainly be tortured. Ḥāmid asked to be imprisoned in the palace, so as to avoid abuse; al-Sayyida supported his request, telling the caliph that there was no harm in sequestering Ḥāmid in the palace. Mufliḥ the eunuch argued that Ḥāmid should be turned over to the Banū al-Furāt. In this instance al-Muqtadir agreed with Mufliḥ and not with al-Sayyida, and sent Ḥāmid to the Banū Furāt, who tortured and eventually poisoned him.[151] But five years later, when al-Muqtadir had come to believe that ʿAlī b. ʿĪsā was a Qarmatian spy and ordered that he be whipped, al-Sayyida convinced her son that the accusations against ʿAlī were groundless, and the caliph canceled the intended punishment.[152]

In all the cases described above, influential members of the court elite—Ibn al-Jaṣṣāṣ, Ḥāmid, ʿAlī, and especially Naṣr—were no longer capable of defending themselves, and received help from al-Sayyida. She acquired her influence due to access and strong ties to al-Muqtadir: in every instance she personally spoke with him and usually convinced him of her own opinion. Moreover, al-Sayyida's intervention usually countered the policies of the current wazir, and in every instance she argued against a decision that the caliph had already made. In other words, she took bold political stands. In general, al-Sayyida seems like one of the solitary stable forces at court; she retained her influence while a parade of important figures came in and out of favor, and used her power to protect government officials, thereby limiting the damage of the constant scheming at court.[153]

149. Miskawayh, *Tajārib*, 117.

*This anecdote is also partially translated by van Berkel, "The Young Caliph," (12), to demonstrate the influence of the caliph's mother.

150. al-Hamadhānī, *Takmila*, 43.

151. Miskawayh, *Tajārib*, 97; al-Hamadhānī, *Takmila*, 34.

152. Miskawayh, *Tajārib*, 187; al-Hamadhānī, *Takmila*, 57.

153. ʿArīb alone reports that, in the year 315/927, Muʾnis believed that al-Sayyida was plotting to kill him and therefore requested permission to leave Baghdad (*Ṣilat*, 133); other sources report rumors that the caliph himself was trying to kill Muʾnis. I cannot understand why al-Sayyida would want to kill Muʾnis: this type of scheming against a pillar of the state seems out of character for al-Sayyida. We have already seen that she disliked the previous removal of Muʾnis from Baghdad. At any rate, this report reinforces the unanimous view that al-Sayyida was a very powerful figure, who could conceivably plot against the most senior general in the state, and force him to flee.

Wealth

Like previous royal mothers, al-Sayyida was immensely wealthy. Ibn al-Jawzī begins her death notice by saying that "she had a tremendous amount of money, too large to count. The yearly revenue from her properties was one million dinars."[154] What's more, al-Sayyida managed to accumulate this wealth in a period when the state continually experienced financial crises, and revenue was declining. Indeed, as the state fell into bankruptcy, she became an alternative source of funds: in 315/927, when the Qarmatians were approaching Baghdad and al-Muqtadir urgently needed to assemble the military, the wazir ʿAlī b. ʿĪsā told the caliph:

> No money is left in the private treasury, so for God's sake, Commander of the Faithful, go talk to al-Sayyida so that she will contribute the money she has saved for hard times—for that time has arrived.

Al-Muqtadir spoke with his mother, and she gave him at least five hundred thousand dinars.[155] Despite this huge outlay of cash, al-Sayyida still possessed extensive funds, for during the coup of 317/929, soldiers seized six hundred thousand dinars that she had hidden in a mausoleum.[156] In short, through the end of al-Muqtadir's reign, al-Sayyida was probably the richest person at court, and even the caliph had to ask her for financial support to keep the state intact.[157]

Naturally, al-Sayyida seems to have acquired her wealth due to her relationship with the caliph. Ibn al-Zubayr reports that, "as for Shaghab, the mother of al-Muqtadir, her son granted her abundant properties in parcels"—this was the origin of the estates that produced huge yearly revenues.[158] She, like other members of the royal family and state employees, also received a regular salary. We get some idea of the amount of her stipend from Ibn al-Furāt's promise to pay the caliph 1000 dinars daily, while al-Sayyida would receive 333 1/3 dinars,[159] fully one-third as much money as the caliph, over and above her real estate income. Ibn al-Furāt's promise also shows that al-Sayyida's stipend was considered an important issue: it was discussed at the same time as the caliph's stipend.

154. Ibn al-Jawzī, *al-Muntaẓam*, 6:253; Ibn al-Zubayr (*al-Dhakhāʾir*, 238), states seven hundred thousand dinars.

155. Miskawayh, *Tajārib*, 181 (slightly different translation in *Eclipse*, 204); al-Hamadhānī, *Takmila*, 55; Ibn al-Jawzī, *al-Muntaẓam*, 309; Ibn al-Zubayr says that this occurred in 318/930, not 315/927, and that she gave six hundred thousand dinars; ʿArīb reports that al-Sayyida contributed as much as three million dinars for the battle against the Qarmatians (*Ṣilat*, 183–84).

156. Miskawayh, *Tajārib*, 193; al-Hamadhānī, *Takmila*, 59; Ibn al-Jawzī, *al-Muntaẓam*, 6:222.

157. The only other person that reportedly possessed riches on the same scale was the merchant Ibn al-Jaṣṣāṣ; but his wealth was confiscated in 302/914—relatively early in al-Muqtadir's reign—leaving al-Sayyida as the wealthiest individual in Baghdad for some fifteen years, as far as we can tell.

158. Ibn al-Zubayr, *al-Dhakhāʾir*, 238.

159. Miskawayh, *Tajārib*, 42. The stipends for al-Sayyida, the princes, and other female relatives for the year 306/918–919 also appear in Hilāl al-Ṣābī, *Rusūm*, 24.

Finally, al-Sayyida received presents from high-ranking officials.[160] Here again, the precise value of such gifts is not really relevant; rather, the fact that any gesture made to the caliph was also made to al-Sayyida, that they were treated as a pair, reflects the common perception that al-Sayyida was also a supreme authority, even if of somewhat lesser status. In such instances, her position of authority brought about increasing wealth.

Al-Sayyida used her wealth for a variety of purposes. We have already seen that, during a military crisis, she contributed a huge amount of money for the benefit of the state. In addition, Ibn al-Jawzī reports that "she used to donate as charity most of [her money], and was devoted to affairs involving the *ḥajj*."[161] In 306/918–919 al-Sayyida financed a new hospital, whose monthly budget was six hundred dinars; we can evaluate her generosity by the fact that al-Muqtadir and Ibn al-Furāt also endowed new hospitals, each of which had a smaller monthly budget of two hundred dinars.[162] When the Qarmatians failed to capture the town of al-Hīt, al-Muqtadir and al-Sayyida reportedly gave one hundred thousand dirhems to charity.[163] Aside from supporting charitable endeavors, al-Sayyida spent a lot of money on court luxuries. Unfortunately, we do not seem to have information on such court splendor, other than the report that after al-Muqtadir's death, al-Sayyida possessed many trunks full of clothes, jewelry, and perfume worth one hundred thirty thousand dinars.[164]

Family

As was common in this era, al-Sayyida used her position at court to promote her own family. The sources never explicitly state that al-Sayyida helped her relatives; yet some of them became very important figures, which they could only have achieved as a result of her influence: after all, they were of foreign, slave origin and had no other court connections. We have already seen that al-Sayyida's sister Khāṭif was among "their highnesses" who controlled the state during al-Muqtadir's youth.[165] She apparently remained influential for many years, since in 313/925 she, along with al-Sayyida, contrived the

160. For example, a senior bureaucrat named al-Mādhrā'ī brought gifts for al-Muqtadir, al-Sayyida and ʿAlī b. ʿĪsā during Ramadan of the year 306/919 (ʿArīb, *Ṣilat*, 75); Ibn Bisṭām came from Egypt to Baghdad in 307/919–920, and brought gifts for both the caliph and al-Sayyida (ʿArīb, *Ṣilat*, 78); and the wazir al-Khaṣībī reported giving presents on Nawrūz of year 315/927 to al-Muqtadir, the princes, al-Sayyida and her sister Khāṭif, and other court officials (Miskawayh, *Tajārib*, 156).

161. Ibn al-Jawzī, *al-Muntaẓam*, 6:253.

162. Ibn al-Jawzī, *al-Muntaẓam*, 6:146, 174. Also referred to by editor of Ibn Khallikān, *Wafayāt*, 2:45 footnote 2. Mez (*Renaissance*, 377) also notes these new hospitals, but states that al-Muqtadir's new hospital had a monthly budget of two thousand dinars (and not two hundred). Mez uses Ibn al-Jawzī as one of his sources, yet in the edition I am using the budget is clearly stated as being only two hundred dinars.

163. Miskawayh, *Tajārib*, 180; Ibn al-Jawzī says that al-Muqtadir, al-Sayyida and ʿAlī b. ʿĪsā each gave fifty thousand dirhems (*Ṣilat*, 210).

164. Miskawayh, *Tajārib*, 243–44.

165. Miskawayh, *Tajārib*, 90.

appointment of al-Khaṣībī to the wazirate.[166] Khāṭif was also given a present at *Nawrūz* along with the caliph, al-Sayyida, the princes, and high-ranking servants.[167] Her honored status almost certainly derived from association with al-Sayyida: for example, we have seen that Khāṭif complained to al-Sayyida about the unjust treatment of a certain secretary, which resulted in the man's release. This kind of access to al-Sayyida, and hence a connection to influence, is what made Khāṭif an important person.[168]

The members of al-Sayyida's family who rose highest in the state were her brother Gharīb, and his son (al-Sayyida's nephew) Hārūn. These two men were among the highest-ranking generals of the period. Gharīb first appears in the failed coup of 296/908, when he is listed as one of the commanders who remained loyal to al-Muqtadir.[169] Since Gharīb is never mentioned before this event, we might speculate that he received an important post immediately following al-Muqtadir's accession, probably due to the influence of al-Sayyida. Two years later, when Badr al-Ḥuramī died, Gharīb was appointed to his posts, becoming the second-ranking general, after Muʾnis.[170] When Gharīb died in 305/917, his funeral was attended by the leading officials of the state.[171] Gharīb's posts were turned over to his son Hārūn, who played a prominent role at court through the end of al-Muqtadir's reign; indeed, al-Muqtadir intended to appoint Hārūn as the chief general, which triggered the coup of 317/929. In general, al-Sayyida's male relatives became a powerful force in the Abbasid state, and her family seems to have formed something of a small dynasty. With her leverage as mother of the caliph, al-Sayyida was able to transform her family from its humble origins into one of the most powerful families of the state.[172]

The Staff

Al-Sayyida's influential position at court, and consequent financial prosperity, meant that she required an extensive staff. One position that was especially prestigious and lucrative was al-Sayyida's personal secretary. For example, Abū al-Ḥasan Muḥammad b. ʿAbd al-Ḥamīd is described as "the secretary of al-Sayyida, one of the men who had been offered the wazirate and turned it down. He was wealthy and stingy, among the lead-

166. Miskawayh, *Tajārib*, 143.

167. Miskawayh, *Tajārib*, 156.

168. Indeed, the sources rarely refer to Khāṭif by name, but call her "al-Sayyida's sister"—a clear indication that she was essentially the sibling of the truly important individual. We also hear that al-Sayyida's uncle, Aḥmad b. Badr, was among the noteworthy hostages taken by the Qarmatians in 312/924–925 (Miskawayh, *Tajārib*, 120, 139); but I can find nothing more about him.

169. Miskawayh, *Tajārib*, 6; al-Hamadhānī, *Takmila*, 5.

170. al-Hamadhānī, *Takmila*, 9.

171. ʿArīb, *Ṣilat*, 69. One of Gharīb's sons, named al-Qāsim, died earlier in the same year, and his funeral was also well attended.

172. *El Cheikh has also summarized the powerful role of al-Sayyida during the caliphate of al-Muqtadir (in van Berkel et al., *Crisis and Continuity*, 168–74; and in El Cheikh, "Caliphal Family," 334–36).

ing bureaucrats upon whom affairs and ministries (*dīwāns*) were dependent. Al-Sayyida seized one hundred thousand dinars cash from his estate."[173] Thus it would seem that al-Sayyida's secretary was a senior bureaucrat, ranking high enough, in theory, to become wazir. Abū al-Ḥasan likely realized that working for al-Sayyida was more lucrative than acting as wazir, so he turned down the latter job. Al-Sayyida's next secretary, Aḥmad b. ʿUbaydallāh al-Khaṣībī, initially used this position as a springboard for attaining the wazirate. According to ʿArīb, al-Khaṣībī took firm control of al-Sayyida's affairs, and consequently his influence grew. Eventually he was recommended for the wazirate by al-Sayyida and her sister Khāṭif and received the appointment "due to his position in the service of al-Sayyida."[174] But al-Khaṣībī found that the wazirate was more strenuous and less lucrative; as a result, he "wished that he had not been appointed to the wazirate when he left the service of al-Sayyida ... which was more profitable for him than [working] for the caliph."[175] In short, al-Sayyida's affairs were so prosperous, and the state's affairs so dismal, that being al-Sayyida's secretary was more attractive than being wazir.[176]

Al-Sayyida also employed a network of female assistants in the palace, who were called "*qahramānas*." The term itself is difficult to define; in general, these women seem to have been personal assistants to al-Sayyida, but held a variety of responsibilities, and enjoyed a large degree of independence. At least one of the *qahramānas* was free born—indeed, she was a member of the Abbasid royal family—while others were possibly of slave origin; but pedigree seems to have been of little importance in becoming a *qahramāna*, and they were certainly not al-Sayyida's slaves. As we shall see, the term does imply an official post. On the other hand, several active female court officials are referred to as *qahramānas* at the same point in time, and their responsibilities were so fluid that it is difficult to pinpoint whether this was a particular post, a general status, or something in between.

Fāṭima

The first we hear of these women is in 298/910–11, in the following death notice:

173. ʿArīb, *Ṣilat*, 79–80.

174. ʿ*Arīb, Ṣilat*, 127; Miskawayh, *Tajārib*, 143. ʿArīb says that Naṣr and Thumal helped him acquire the wazirate, and since Naṣr and Thumal were allied with al-Sayyida, it is possible they all colluded on this appointment.

175. ʿArīb, *Ṣilat*, 128.

176. Al-Sayyida's next, and possibly final secretary was ʿAbd al-Raḥmān b. Muḥammad b. Sahl, who proved to be more competent than al-Khaṣībī, retrieving some funds for al-Sayyida that al-Khaṣībī had neglected (ʿArīb, *Ṣilat*, 128; Miskawayh, *Tajārib*, 143). We know that al-Sayyida employed a network of agents to oversee her vast land holdings. Her agent in Wāsiṭ was reportedly befriended by Ḥāmid b. al-ʿAbbās during his push to become wazir. Additional references to men appointed as al-Sayyida's agent and/or personal secretary: the wazir al-ʿAbbās b. al-Ḥasan gave his son this post (ʿArīb, *Ṣilat*, 23, year 295/908), and Ibn al-Furāt granted it to his close ally, Ibn Muqla (al-Hamadhānī, *Takmila*, 18, year 304/917).

> In this year, Fāṭima the *qahramāna* drowned in her boat, under the bridge, on a windy day. She had married her two daughters to [commanders] Bunayy b. Nafīs and Qayṣar, who attended her funeral, as did various commanders and judges. Al-Sayyida appointed Umm Mūsā the Hāshimī as *qahramāna* in her place; [Umm Mūsā] acted as intermediary between al-Sayyida, al-Muqtadir, and [the wazir] Ibn al-Furāt.[177]

Ibn al-Jawzī adds that al-Muqtadir had been angry at Fāṭima the *qahramāna* this same year and seized her money, "and she had a lot of money, hundreds of thousands of dinars."[178] These are the only references to Fāṭima that I have been able to find, yet they provide important information. First of all, Fāṭima seems to have been in al-Sayyida's service, and the title "*qahramāna*" resembled an official post, for when Fāṭima died al-Sayyida was responsible for appointing another woman in her place. Perhaps she performed the same function that her replacement Umm Mūsā undertook: acting as a messenger linking al-Sayyida and the caliph with the wazir. We also know that Fāṭima was quite wealthy, possessing hundreds of thousands of dinars; she also held a high rank in society, since she married her daughters to prominent generals, and her funeral was attended by important men of state. The fact that she reportedly arranged marriages of alliance for her daughters provides some insight into her personal life: obviously she had children; she was probably a free woman or would not have had the right to decide her daughters' fate; and she was possibly widowed, given that she seemingly conducted the marriage agreement herself. Fāṭima was also known by the caliph, and was involved in court affairs, at least to the extent that she managed to anger the caliph. Finally, we know that she was not confined to the palace, for she died while traveling along the river. In general, the image we derive is of an independent-minded, wealthy, and honored woman, a trusted subordinate of the caliph's mother.

Umm Mūsā

The woman who took Fāṭima's place, Umm Mūsā, became one of the most important figures at the Abbasid court. According to Ibn al-Zubayr, "[Umm Mūsā] was close with the mother of al-Muqtadir before he was appointed to the [caliphate]. Her fortunes prospered, so that she dominated the realm and the wazirate, and had the power to command and forbid. She received vast grants of land and owned precious properties that brought her large revenues. She also controlled important appointments."[179] Perhaps Umm Mūsā initially established a presence at court, and developed a relationship with al-Sayyida,

177. Miskawayh, *Tajārib*, 20 (similar translation in *Eclipse*, 22); also in al-Hamadhānī, *Takmila*, 9 (but citing the year 297/909–910), and Ibn al-Athīr, *al-Kāmil*, 8:62.

178. Ibn al-Jawzī, *al-Muntaẓam*, 6:112 (year 299/911–912).

179. Ibn al-Zubayr, *al-Dhakhā'ir*, 239–40; Ibn al-Athīr says that "Umm Mūsā the Hāshimī was made a *qahramāna* in al-Muqtadir's palace and brought letters from al-Muqtadir and his mother to the wazir.

because of her status as an Abbasid: she was a descendant of the first Abbasid caliph Ibrāhīm al-Saffāḥ.[180] In any case, it is worth noting that a respected member of the extended royal family chose to work as messenger for the caliph's mother, reflecting the desirability and social cache of this position.

Umm Mūsā performed a variety of tasks for al-Sayyida and the caliph. Miskawayh reports that she acted as a link between the caliph, al-Sayyida, and the wazir; Ibn al-Athīr clarifies that she transmitted letters between these people.[181] Umm Mūsā continued in this function for several years, as in 306/918–919 we are told that she delivered a note from the caliph to the wazir Ḥāmid b. al-ʿAbbās.[182] She also served as representative for both al-Sayyida and al-Muqtadir at the interrogation of Ibn al-Furāt in 299/911–912, and it was Umm Mūsā who was sent to "their highnesses"—al-Muqtadir, al-Sayyida, and the others—for permission to torture the former minister.[183]

Umm Mūsā was also assigned wider responsibilities by the mother of the caliph. According to al-Shābushtī, "when ʿUbaydallāh b. ʿAbdallāh b. Ṭāhir died ... Shaghab, al-Muqtadir's mother, sent Umm Mūsā the *qahramāna* to his children and harem. She consoled them on [Shaghab's] behalf, covered him in an impressive shroud, donated a thousand dinars and a thousand dirhems for his burial, and took control of all his affairs."[184] Here we again see Umm Mūsā representing al-Sayyida, in a location where the latter would certainly not venture: outside of the palace, in a private home. This assignment, however, was more complex, in that Umm Mūsā contributed money and also assumed the responsibility for ʿUbaydallāh's family.[185] Again we get the impression that al-Sayyida's subordinates were granted substantial authority.

Umm Mūsā's most impressive assignment in al-Sayyida's service also took place outside the confines of the royal palace: in a public procession. ʿArīb describes the event:

> [In 307/919–920] Umm Mūsā the *qahramāna* rode with presents that Umm al-Muqtadir had ordered her to prepare, as a gift for the daughters of Gharīb the [caliph's] uncle, on occasion of their dual marriage to the sons of Badr al-Ḥammāmī. Umm Mūsā (paraded) in a huge procession, including cavalry and infantry. In front of her were twelve horsemen, six with saddles and bridles decorated in gold, the other six in silver; each horseman had a servant at his

---

We mention her because she later had power in the state, which requires mention of her, otherwise she would be ignored" (*al-Kāmil*, 62).

180. Ibn al-Zubayr, *al-Dhakhāʾir*, 239–40.

181. Miskawayh, *Tajārib*, 20; Ibn al-Athīr, *al-Kāmil*, 8:62.

182. al-Hamadhānī, *Takmila*, 20.

183. al-Khaṭīb, *Tārīkh*, 5:51–52.

184. al-Shābushtī, *Kitāb al-Diyārāt*, 79 (this took place in the year 300/912–913).

185. This ʿUbaydallāh and his family were the descendants of the powerful Ṭāhirid family, prominent in Baghdad for much of the previous century. Hence, Umm Mūsā was actually tasked with supervising the affairs of this once-noble family.

> side, wore a gold belt, and swords with gold hilts.... [They carried] one hundred thousand dinars ... all of it a gift on behalf of the brides to their husbands.[186]

The gift that Umm Mūsā prepared involved a tremendous amount of money. We cannot know if this money belonged to al-Sayyida or Umm Mūsā, almost certainly the former, yet the account demonstrates that Umm Mūsā was trusted with huge funds. Her presence at the center of such an elaborate procession suggests that Umm Mūsā was recognized as an honorable figure of state. In fact, Umm Mūsā's function here is somewhat reminiscent of the royal princes: she represents al-Sayyida, both in the palace and in important public events, while the mother of the caliph remained in seclusion, just as the princes conducted certain missions for the caliph that highlighted the latter's inaccessibility.

At the same time that Umm Mūsā was performing duties on behalf of al-Sayyida, she gradually became involved in the political scheming at court. Within a year of replacing Fāṭima, Umm Mūsā was delivering messages to the caliph on behalf of people seeking appointments and plotting against current officials.[187] Such access to the caliph, and the willingness to provide favors, made Umm Mūsā an important figure in the palace. She also had personal protégés: in 299/911–912, she tried to convince the caliph to replace the wazir al-Khāqānī with a client of hers, named Ibn Abī al-Baghl. She nearly succeeded, for al-Muqtadir sent Umm Mūsā's brother to bring Ibn Abī al-Baghl from the provinces for appointment as wazir. Al-Khāqānī managed to foil the plan but as a result, "Umm Mūsā the *qahramāna* stopped favoring the wazir Abū ᶜAlī al-Khāqānī and he feared that she might ruin him," so he appointed her protégé Ibn Abī al-Baghl and a relative to provincial posts.[188] These men continued to enjoy her patronage and protection, for the new wazir Ibn al-Furāt dismissed all the officials of the previous minister, except for Ibn Abī al-Baghl and his relative, "due to the interest which Umm Mūsā had in them."[189] In fact, these two men remained in office until Umm Mūsā fell from power, at which time they were immediately dismissed.

Umm Mūsā even had enough influence to arrange for the dismissal of the wazir ᶜAlī b. ᶜĪsā, in the year 304/917. Apparently the two had a personal confrontation: in one account, ᶜAlī scolded Umm Mūsā's brother for spending seven thousand dinars each month; indeed, "Umm Mūsā had been friendly to ᶜAlī b. ᶜĪsā until he criticized [her brother]." This friendliness now turned to hostility.[190] The tone of this passage implies that Umm Mūsā favored the wazir, and not the other way around: that is, she had the higher status. Miskawayh provides a different version of their conflict:

---

186. ᶜArīb, *Ṣilat*, 78.
187. Miskawayh, *Tajārib*, 24–25.
188. Miskawayh, *Tajārib*, 22; Ibn al-Athīr, *al-Kāmil*, 8:64.
189. Miskawayh, *Tajārib*, 42.
190. ᶜArīb, *Ṣilat*, 58. Ibn al-Jawzī adds that there was great antipathy between Umm Mūsā and ᶜAlī (*al-Muntaẓam*, 6:138).

> [ʿAlī] received a visit from Umm Mūsā the *qahramāna*, who wished to arrange with him the sum to be distributed to the harem and court attendants, for Eid al-Adha. ʿAlī b. ʿĪsā was not receiving visitors, and his chamberlain did not announce her, but dismissed her politely instead. This made her very angry; and when ʿAlī b. ʿĪsā heard of her arrival and departure, he ordered someone to find her and apologize, hoping that she might return. But she refused and went to al-Muqtadir and al-Sayyida, inciting them against him with accusations. As a result, al-Muqtadir dismissed him from office and arrested him.[191]

Here we see that Umm Mūsā was directly responsible for ʿAlī's dismissal, which she achieved thanks to her close relations with the caliph and his mother. Indeed, ʿAlī was well aware of Umm Mūsā's influence, for he desperately tried to appease her by promptly sending an apology.

While Umm Mūsā's power grew, her brother Aḥmad b. al-ʿAbbās also acquired official responsibilities. In 299/911–912 he was sent to bring Ibn Abī al-Baghl, the new candidate for the wazirate, from the provinces; and in 301/913–914 he was appointed as *naqīb* of the *Hāshimiyya*, though this appointment was immediately canceled. In subsequent years he received permanent posts: by 307/919–920 he was the imam of the Ruṣāfa mosque and led the hajj, both of which he performed until his sister, and he along with her, fell from favor. He also managed to acquire, and spend, seven thousand dinars a month, at a time when his Hāshimī relatives were complaining of poverty.[192] We can assume that Aḥmad's good fortune was due to his sister's connections—he is almost always referred to as "Umm Mūsā's brother," which clearly implies that his status was a function of hers. None of his appointments suggests that Aḥmad b. al-ʿAbbās had the kind of power commanded by Gharīb, al-Sayyida's brother; yet in a fashion similar to al-Sayyida, only on a smaller scale, Umm Mūsā parlayed her influence into honorable positions for her brother.

We have seen several indications that Umm Mūsā and her brother had access to large amounts of money. In fact, the sources make very clear that Umm Mūsā and her family were wealthy. Ibn al-Zubayr records that Umm Mūsā and her brother held properties with annual revenues of one hundred thousand dinars.[193] Indeed, when the family fell from power in 310/922–923, the net worth of their properties and possessions is said to have been one million dinars, and another report claims two million.[194] A special bureau

191. Miskawayh, *Tajārib*, 40 (similar translation in *Eclipse*, 45); also in Ibn al-Athir, *al-Kāmil*, 98. We should note here another of Umm Mūsā's functions: she was involved in deciding the budget for the holiday. A similar story appears in Hilāl al-Ṣābī, when Umm Mūsā disturbed a policy meeting about the invasion of Egypt, in order to discuss court finances (*Wuzarāʾ*, 380–81).

192. ʿArīb, *Ṣilat*, 78–80. Before these official appointments, he was responsible in 305/917 for prayers at the funeral for Gharīb, al-Sayyida's brother (ʿArīb, *Ṣilat*, 69).

193. Ibn al-Zubayr, *al-Dhakhāʾir*, 240.

194. One million: Miskawayh, *Tajārib*, 84; Ibn al-Zubayr, *al-Dhakhāʾir*, 240; al-Hamadhānī, *Takmila*, 31. Miskawayh (*Tajārib*, 240) includes a list of finances at the end of al-Muqtadir's reign and includes two million dinars seized from Umm Mūsā and her family.

was even established to oversee the funds seized from Umm Mūsā's family.[195] It is most likely that Umm Mūsā acquired this wealth while in al-Sayyida's service. Ibn al-Zubayr hints that she received properties after al-Muqtadir became caliph, meaning once she had become a *qahramāna*; and it is difficult to believe that an Abbasid would have served as an employee, even for the caliph's mother, if she had been wealthy beforehand. We might therefore conclude that, like her predecessor Fāṭima, Umm Mūsā and her family became rich as a result of her position in al-Sayyida's service.

By 310/922–923 Umm Mūsā was so prominent at court, that she reportedly attempted to influence the succession to the caliphate. We hear that Umm Mūsā had married her niece to a great-grandson of the caliph al-Mutawakkil, who was very wealthy and was being trained for the caliphate by ʿAlī b. ʿĪsā.[196] Umm Mūsā spent vast sums of money on the wedding—yet another indication of her wealth—hosting officials from across the empire for more than ten days.[197] Umm Mūsā's enemies told al-Muqtadir and al-Sayyida that the *qahramāna* was plotting to make her new son-in-law the caliph.[198] According to a different version, al-Muqtadir fell sick in 310/922–23, and Umm Mūsā wrote to a relative, probably this same son-in-law, informing him that he would soon become caliph.[199] In any case, al-Muqtadir and al-Sayyida considered the threat posed by Umm Mūsā to be realistic, and therefore arrested her, along with her brother Aḥmad and a sister. The wealth of the family was seized; they remained in prison until 314/926–927, when Umm Mūsā's brother and sister died, and she alone was released.[200] We hear nothing more about Umm Mūsā after this point, other than that she was confined to her home, and received a small portion of her possessions in return.[201]

Umm Mūsā's dramatic fall shows just how powerful she had become in court politics. It is difficult to know if she really plotted to overthrow or replace al-Muqtadir; the sources seem to indicate that these were just the accusations of her enemies. Yet the important point is that al-Muqtadir and al-Sayyida believed such a plot was possible, that is, they recognized that Umm Mūsā was well situated to promote a candidate for the caliphate. Indeed, Umm Mūsā had a particularly powerful status: not only was she a high-ranking official employed by the caliph and his mother, she was also a Hāshimī, and thus had links to the rest of the royal family, and relatives who were, theoretically, eligible for

195. Miskawayh, *Tajārib*, 84.

196. This is the only reference I have seen to this prince and his caliphal aspirations. It is very hard to believe that ʿAlī b. ʿĪsā was promoting a candidate for the caliphate when prince Abū al-ʿAbbās was clearly the heir apparent.

197. Miskawayh, *Tajārib*, 83–84; Ibn al-Athīr, *al-Kāmil*, 8:137. The date of the wedding is never stated.

198. Miskawayh, *Tajārib*, 83–84; also in Ibn al-Jawzī, *al-Muntaẓam*, 6:166.

199. ʿArīb, *Ṣilat*, 108–9; Ibn al-Jawzī, *al-Muntaẓam*, 6:166.

200. ʿArīb, *Ṣilat*, 129; al-Hamadhānī, *Takmila*, 49.

201. al-Hamadhānī, *Takmila*, 49. ʿArīb (*Ṣilat*, 129) says that she received property that had been confiscated—likely only a small part of her assets, for in 316/928 the bureau that managed property taken from Umm Mūsā still existed (ʿArīb, *Ṣilat*, 136). Muʾnis later made a request on her behalf, probably for money (al-Hamadhānī, *Takmila*, 63).

rulership. She combined two of the highest statuses in society: court official, and royalty. The Abbasid caliphs had carefully excluded members of the royal family from positions of power, and Umm Mūsā's example shows why: the combination of power and legitimacy was a potent threat to the reigning caliph, even if embodied by a woman.

If Umm Mūsā's threat to the caliph is remarkable, so was the end result: she was imprisoned, interrogated, and likely tortured into relinquishing her wealth. She served an extended prison sentence; both of her siblings died while incarcerated, and her inquisitor was known for cruelty. More importantly, this is the first example I am aware of in which an Abbasid woman was arrested. In summary, Umm Mūsā had made an unusual rise to power in Abbasid court, and subsequently suffered an unusual, if not unique, demise.[202]

Thumal

Another of al-Sayyida's *qahramānas* was called Thumal. Wiebke Walther argues that Thumal was a slave, since her name comes from the root "to intoxicate;"[203] I have found no other evidence that she was of slave origin, though we shall soon see that she previously served as *qahramāna* for an Abbasid general, which suggests that *qahramānas* were not employed exclusively by al-Sayyida or by women. We first hear of Thumal in 306/918–919, when al-Sayyida gave her an extraordinary assignment:

> In this year, al-Sayyida, Umm al-Muqtadir, ordered that her *qahramāna*, known as Thumal, sit in the Ruṣāfa [mosque] to hear complaints, and examine the documents of the people on every Friday. The public disliked this, were repulsed by it and denounced it greatly. On the first day that she sat (held session), she commanded no authority; but the second time she sat, the judge Abū al-Ḥasan was present, thereby legitimizing her authority and promoting her. She issued directives; those with complaints benefited, and the people became accustomed to her adjudication and jurisdiction, which they had previously shunned.[204]

This brief report encapsulates the remarkable extent to which specific women exercised authority in the Abbasid court in this era, as Thumal was tasked with supervising the court of complaints, which had once been the prerogative of the Abbasid caliph himself; and her authority was legitimized by one of the senior judges in Baghdad.

Thumal also seems to have been partially responsible for al-Sayyida's bureaucratic affairs. Thumal had her own secretary: the same al-Khaṣībī who was later promoted to being al-Sayyida's secretary, and eventually wazir.[205] When al-Khaṣībī became wazir and

202. *El Cheikh also summarizes the career of Umm Mūsā ("Qahramāna," 46–52).
203. Walther, *Woman in Islam*, 82.
204. ʿArīb, *Ṣilat*, 71.
205. ʿArīb, *Ṣilat*, 79–80.

al-Sayyida needed a new secretary, she asked Thumal to find a replacement, and it was this *qahramāna* who appointed Abū Yūsuf ʿAbd al-Raḥmān b. Muḥammad.[206]

Perhaps Thumal's most surprising role was that of female interrogator. When Umm Mūsā was arrested, she was turned over to Thumal for the standard battery of questioning and punishment that was designed to extract the fortunes of dismissed officials. On this occasion Miskawayh describes Thumal as "a woman who had a reputation for cruelty, having been the *qahramāna* of Aḥmad b. ʿAbd al-ʿAzīz b. Dulaf, who used to turn over to her the female servants and eunuchs that had incurred his displeasure. She became notorious for her harshness and the severity of her punishments."[207] Befitting this reputation, Thumal managed to extract from Umm Mūsā and her family one million dinars.

In addition to these various responsibilities, Thumal, like Umm Mūsā, became involved in politics, though on a more modest scale. Apparently she allied with Naṣr the chamberlain to promote common candidates for the wazirate: in 312/924, they were influential in convincing al-Muqtadir to appoint al-Khāqānī,[208] and then in 313/925, she and Naṣr again teamed up in support of her former secretary, al-Khaṣībī.[209] There is evidence that Thumal was respected in court circles—which we might expect, given her various responsibilities—for the new wazir al-Khaṣībī is said to have been honored by the people, due both to his position in the service of al-Sayyida, and the favor granted him by Thumal.[210] Finally, we hear a remarkable appraisal from ʿArīb, summarizing Thumal's standing: "she had influence over al-Muqtadir."[211] Thus Thumal, like Fāṭima and Umm Mūsā, performed a variety of functions, acquired political influence, and held a generally respected status at court, including with the caliph himself, largely as a consequence of serving as one of al-Sayyida's *qahramānas*.

Zaydān

The only other *qahramāna* mentioned in the sources is Zaydān. Apparently, she served at court for much of al-Muqtadir's reign (she appears from 299/911 through 317/929), though she is the only *qahramāna* not explicitly connected to al-Sayyida, and we cannot know the identity of her patron at court. Nor is it clear if she was of free or slave origin.

---

206. ʿArīb, *Ṣilat*, 118; Miskawayh, *Tajārib*, 143. In fact, as mentioned earlier, this ʿAbd al-Raḥmān recovered funds for al-Sayyida that al-Khaṣībī had neglected; this apparently embarrassed Thumal, since al-Khaṣībī had originally been her secretary and rose to prominence with her assistance.

207. Miskawayh, *Tajārib*, 84 (translation from *Eclipse*, 93). Aḥmad b. ʿAbd al-ʿAzīz b. Abī Dulaf was a prominent general from at least the mid-260s, who served as governor of Isfahan from 266 through 276 (al-Ṭabarī, *History*, 37:2, 159). I have found no information whether Thumal was in his service in Baghdad, or elsewhere.

208. Miskawayh, *Tajārib*, 127.

209. ʿArīb, *Ṣilat*, 126.

210. ʿArīb, *Ṣilat*, 127.

211. ʿArīb, *Ṣilat*, 126—specifically related to her impact on the appointment of senior bureaucrats.

Whatever her precise status, it would seem that Zaydān held a respected social position, like the other *qahramānas*, for when the wazir al-Khaṣībī distributed presents on *Nawrūz* to al-Muqtadir, al-Sayyida and the princes, Zaydān is one of the few additional state officials mentioned as receiving a gift.[212]

Like the other *qahramānas*, Zaydān had more than one function at court. Among her responsibilities was supervision of the jewelry treasury. The importance of this post can be seen in the following crisis: ʿAlī b. ʿĪsā, recently appointed wazir, asked the caliph what had become of a particularly valuable string of beads. Al-Muqtadir ordered that it be brought from the treasury; when it was not found, ʿAlī pulled it out of his sleeve and revealed that it had been found in an Egyptian marketplace. The implication was that someone had stolen and sold the beads. Al-Sayyida was gravely disturbed by this incident; as a result, "Zaydān the *qahramāna* fell under suspicion, for nobody had access to the jewelry treasury except for her."[213] This particular string of beads was worth thirty thousand dinars.[214] With such valuables under her supervision, Zaydān was certainly recognized as having an important position at court, and if she were indeed guilty of stealing this or other pieces of jewelry, she was probably very rich. We might add, however, that Zaydān was not arrested, for she was still working in the palace in the years following this incident.

We hear of Zaydān more frequently in the context of what was probably her primary responsibility: jailer of the royal palace. The highest state officials, upon dismissal, were usually put in her custody. Bureaucrats such as Ibn al-Furāt (in 299/911, 306/918, and 312/924)[215] and ʿAlī b. ʿĪsā (304/917, 311/923, and 316/928)[216] were repeatedly incarcerated by Zaydān, as were rebellious generals, such as al-Ḥusayn b. Ḥamdān (303/915–916)[217] and Ibn Abī al-Sāj (307/919–920).[218] These important detainees were put in Zaydān's charge partly for their own benefit, as she kept them confined within the royal palace—where they were generally granted protection and better living conditions than in alternative Baghdadi jails. This is made clear by the standard report of such incarceration: for example, "[Ibn Abī al-Sāj] was held in the palace in the custody of Zaydān the *qahramāna*, who treated him well."[219]

Due to the many years which Ibn al-Furāt spent in Zaydān's custody, the two developed an alliance of sorts, and Zaydān habitually served as Ibn al-Furāt's informant. In

212. Miskawayh, *Tajārib*, 156. This took place in the year 315/927.

213. ʿArīb, *Ṣilat*, 130; Ibn al-Jawzī *al-Muntaẓam*, 6:70. This occurred during the year 315/927.

214. ʿArīb states thirty thousand; Ibn al-Jawzī reports three hundred thousand dinars, but this latter number is almost certainly a mistake.

215. Miskawayh, *Tajārib*, 22, 58, 87.

216. Miskawayh, *Tajārib*, 40, 89,185; al-Hamadhānī, *Takmila*, 32, 56.

217. Miskawayh, *Tajārib*, 38; Ibn al-Athīr, *al-Kāmil*, 93.

218. Miskawayh, *Tajārib*, 50; al-Hamadhānī, *Takmila*, 18.

219. Miskawayh, *Tajārib*, 50 (similar translation in *Eclipse*, 53). Similarly, after Ibn al-Furāt had undergone torture, he was transferred to Zaydān, who took good care of him (Miskawayh, *Tajārib*, 22).

306/918–919, Zaydān discovered that the caliph desired Ibn al-Furāt's money but was reluctant to torture the ex-minister. She gave Ibn al-Furāt this information, so he devised a way of giving the caliph part of his fortune, thereby preempting interrogation and torture.[220] At roughly the same time, Zaydān found out that the judge Abū ʿUmar had betrayed Ibn al-Furāt by relinquishing money that the minister had entrusted to him for safe-keeping. She again informed Ibn al-Furāt, and he later demanded compensation from Abū ʿUmar's private funds.[221] Finally, she helped the imprisoned Ibn al-Furāt scheme against the official Ibn al-Ḥawārī, by delivering messages to the caliph and providing funding for the intricate scheme.[222] In general, we get the impression that Zaydān had unusual access to information involving the caliph's affairs. Thus, while she was not politically active on the scale of Umm Mūsā or even Thumal, Zaydān seems to have taken advantage of her position at court in support of personal goals.[223]

To summarize what we know about the *qahramānas*: they were most prominent in the service of al-Sayyida and al-Muqtadir but were not limited exclusively to these patrons. The most striking feature of the *qahramānas* is the variety of functions they performed. Umm Mūsā was the special messenger of al-Sayyida and al-Muqtadir to wazirs, but she was also involved in the court budget and took control of Ṭāhirid family affairs. Thumal was involved in al-Sayyida's bureaucracy, but specialized as a female interrogator, and surprisingly took charge of adjudicating in the court of complaints. Zaydān was both the jewelry treasurer and the custodian of the state's most important prisoners. Due to these important responsibilities and subsequent court influence, they all had access to vast sums of money; at least a few of them became quite wealthy. Most importantly, the *qahramānas* used their high rank to indulge in political scheming, to the extent that Umm Mūsā and Thumal intervened in the appointment and dismissal of wazirs, and Umm Mūsā was even recognized as posing a threat to the caliph himself.

The most crucial point, though, is that these women were influential in what is often described as a male realm, or social and political circles of the court elite that were presumed to be off limits to women. As we have seen, such assumptions are inaccurate. First of all, the *qahramānas* were obviously not limited to one part of the palace: Umm Mūsā's main purpose was to shuttle back and forth between al-Sayyida, the caliph, and other ranking officials. They also ventured outside the royal palace complex in official capacity: Umm Mūsā led a procession and visited the Ṭāhirid home while conducting their family affairs, while Thumal officiated weekly at the court of complaints. In short, these

220. Miskawayh, *Tajārib*, 66.

*Zaydān's role as mediator has been analyzed in greater detail by van Berkel, "Vizier and the Harem Stewardess," 317–18, also highlighting the existing relationship between her and Ibn al-Furāt.

221. Miskawayh, *Tajārib*, 67–68.

222. Miskawayh, *Tajārib*, 87–88.

223. *El-Cheikh also analyzes Zaydān's role at court, emphasizing the relationships she established while acting as jailer. She suggests that Zaydān possibly reported directly to the caliph al-Muqtadir ("Qahramāna," 43–46).

women do not seem to have suffered from spatial restrictions. Moreover, they had very close contact with a variety of men, under all sorts of circumstances. All the *qahramānas* had access to the caliph and spoke with him directly. They also interacted on a daily basis with important officials, clearly developing relationships and alliances. Umm Mūsā delivered messages to several wazirs, was present at the interrogation of Ibn al-Furāt, and was a regular visitor to the office of ᶜAlī b. ᶜĪsā. Thumal worked closely with al-Sayyida's secretaries, and schemed with Naṣr the chamberlain. Zaydān's main profession was caring for male prisoners. Some of these women also employed male secretaries, and most likely entire staffs.

Possibly the most impressive example of female presence in supposedly "male" domain was Thumal's adjudication in the court of complaints, where she must have been in constant contact with men of all statuses. Her jurisdiction over this court was unusual, which is why the populace at first criticized and avoided her; but it was her authority they rejected, not necessarily her physical presence, and once a judge legitimized her authority, the populace quickly accepted her jurisdiction. Thus, just as freedom of movement was largely unrestricted, the *qahramānas* suffered few limitations on their interactions with men.

In fact, the interaction between these women and a variety of men seems so commonplace in the sources that the supposed dichotomy between "male space" and "female space" within the Abbasid court needs to be revised. It would seem that certain types or classes of women were restricted, but others were not. Indeed, one reason why the *qahramānas* became so important was that al-Sayyida, by virtue of being the mother of the caliph, could not move about the palace or interact freely with men; she needed intermediaries, who necessarily had to be women. In other words, it was precisely the restrictions on al-Sayyida which made other women prominent. The whole issue of female space and female restriction is in large part actually about social status: certain women, like certain men (the caliph, for example) experienced limitations, while other women enjoyed greater freedom.[224]

Conclusion: Women and Power

As mentioned earlier regarding powerful Abbasid women from previous eras, influential women at court had specific advantages over men, in that they were considered somewhat sacrosanct or "off limits"; that they could acquire money, and scheme, with little threat of retaliation. The woman with the best position at court was the caliph's mother, who enjoyed unique status as the individual with the closest of relations with the caliph. The mother and her associates achieved notable power in the reign of al-Muqtadir, for

224. *El-Cheikh has come to a similar conclusion: "It was through their mobility to move outside the confines of the harem that they managed to forge alliances and develop links that furthered their interests" ("Qahramāna," 54).

his young age at accession meant considerable influence for close relations, while the chronic financial crises later in his reign enabled certain women to become both among the wealthiest and safest people at court. Women used their resulting leverage to become integrated into court politics by scheming for and against wazirs, assuming judicial posts, and even purportedly plotting against the caliph himself.

Paradoxically this integration into court politics, particularly at a time of extreme turmoil, meant that women gradually lost their sacrosanct status. One manifestation of this change was that women were blamed for the decline of the state. Before the coup of 317/929, disgruntled generals charged that women and eunuchs of the palace were ruining state finances.[225] In 320/932, when Muʾnis suggested that al-Rāḍī should be appointed to the throne, a colleague responded: "After all the trouble we have had to get rid of [a caliph] with a mother, aunt, and eunuchs, are we going to return to the same situation!" Al- Rāḍi's candidacy was therefore dropped.[226] Muslim historians and modern scholars have picked up on this theme and attributed the decline under al-Muqtadir to excessive female influence.[227]

Furthermore, women became subject to the violence that plagued court life. Already in 299/911–912 Ibn al-Furāt's harem was mistreated; and in 306/918–919, al-Muḥassin's wife was tortured until she paid her husband's fine.[228] Similarly, when Umm Mūsā was imprisoned for treason, she was subjected to harsh treatment until a fine was extracted. Most incredible of all was the fate of al-Sayyida. After her son was murdered, she was incarcerated by the new caliph al-Qāhir, who wanted money from her. When she claimed to be penniless, "he beat her with his own hand, hung her [upside down] by one foot, and continued to beat her excessively on the sensitive (*ghāmiḍa*) parts of her body."[229] Men who witnessed al-Sayyida's condition "thought about the changes that time had brought." Now even women were subject to the vicissitudes and violence of the court.

225. Miskawayh, *Tajārib*, 189.
226. Miskawayh, *Tajārib*, 242 (similar translation in *Eclipse*, 272).
227. ʿArīb, *Ṣilat*, 24; Miskawayh, *Tajārib*, 13; Bowen, *ʿAlī b. ʿĪsā*, 102.
228. Miskawayh, *Tajārib*, 20.
229. Miskawayh, *Tajārib*, 243 (slightly different translation in *Eclipse*, 274).

Chapter 3. Palace Officials

The focus of this chapter is on palace functionaries, those individuals whose primary roles at court involved a permanent position within the caliphal palace. The huge palace complex obviously required a large and varied staff; according to a list of expenditures compiled during al-Muᶜtaḍid's reign, the palace employed people of all professions, from craftsmen (smiths, tailors, iron workers, shoemakers, and armorers) to menial laborers (water carriers and stable workers).[1] Boon companions (historians, astrologers, entertainers, etc.) were also on the caliph's payroll and frequented the palace. For some numerically large staffs, the sources provide statistics, albeit of questionable precision: during al-Muktafī's reign there were supposedly ten thousand eunuchs, and under al-Muqtadir this number increased to eleven thousand, comprising seven thousand blacks and four thousand whites (Slavs).[2] During the visit of the Byzantine ambassadors, there were reportedly seven hundred chamberlains in the palace.[3] The largest single group was the palace guard, divided into units, including the *rijāla al-maṣāffiyya* ("*maṣāffī*s"), and the *ghilmān al-ḥujariyya* ("*ḥujarī*s"), who together numbered well into the tens of thousands for the whole of this period.[4]

The two most important members of the palace staff were the chief chamberlain (*ḥājib*) and the senior eunuch (*khādim*).[5] Each of these men controlled large staffs: the chamberlain was responsible for several hundred subordinates and seems to have been in charge of the *massāfī* units. Likewise, the leading eunuch presumably supervised the other thousands of palace eunuchs, and commanded detachments of the *ḥujarī* soldiers. Two of the issues I explore in this chapter are precisely what kind of control each of

1. Hilāl al-Ṣābī, *Wuzarā'*, 21–23.

2. Hilāl al-Ṣābī, *Rusūm*, 14. Al-Khaṭīb (*Tārīkh*, 1:99–100) reports the existence of eleven thousand eunuchs in one report; but in another anecdote from a different source, al-Khaṭīb reports a total of seven thousand eunuchs: four thousand white, three thousand black (*Tārīkh*, 1:101). For a convincing argument that *khādim* means eunuch, see Ayalon, "On the Eunuchs in Islam," 74–86.

3. Al-Khaṭīb, *Tārīkh*, 1:101

4. D. Sourdel, "Ghulām" in *EI2*, mentions the existence of these two units. The *ghilmān al-dār*, which Lassner states are identical to the *ḥujarī*s (*Topography*, 267n7), are said to number twenty thousand during the reign of al-Muktafī, while the *maṣāffiyya* numbered roughly five thousand (Hilāl al-Ṣābī, *Rusūm*, 8, 14). The terms *ḥujariyya* and *maṣāffiyya* are not easy to define precisely. Scholars have suggested that the *ḥujariyya* (from *ḥujar*, "rooms") were the guards of the royal palace, and/or were housed in the innermost areas of the complex, and that the *maṣāffiyya* were stationed at the outer part of the palace complex. I discuss their functions at greater length below. For a review of this confusing material, see Lassner, *Topography*, 267–68.

5. I have not yet seen any reference to the "chief eunuch" as an official appointment or title. By the senior eunuch, I mean the individual, (often titled "*al-Ḥuramī*," but not always) who was the most prominent at any given time.

these two men exercised over both their subordinates and the military units entrusted to them, and what sort of effective power they derived from this control. However, there seems to have been a fundamental difference between chamberlains and eunuchs: in this period, the former were often trained soldiers with experience in warfare and military patronage, while the latter probably rose through the ranks of palace service.[6] This difference seems to match the distinction established by Daniel Pipes between "military slaves" (which suits the chamberlains) and "government slaves" (the eunuchs), which he discusses at length:

> Despite the high standing and power which government slaves share with military slaves, the two groups are fundamentally different. Whereas government slaves are chosen from among the ruler's servants, military slaves are soldiers. Government slaves cannot build up a power base of their own and almost never threaten their master; military slaves, however, can develop such a base from within their own corps and use it to stand up to the ruler. The difference here is explained by origins, not functions, for government slaves can take on military duties and military slaves often receive administrative appointments. Yet, even when they have military command, government slaves remain merely the agents of their master; military slaves in administrative or political positions, however, retain their military base and can build up independent political power from it. Their military connections, group solidarity, and close ties to the ruler propel them into a wide variety of positions—as personal counselors, top administrators, provincial governors, special agents, confidential agents, and so on. In case after case they enter the ruler's entourage, go on dominate the court, then the central government, and sometimes even take over the realm itself. These many opportunities are uniquely open to military slaves.[7]

Pipes acknowledges that, as in the case described above for this period, the two different types of slaves can enjoy both administrative and military command. He posits, however, that the military slave, because of his independent base of power, possesses a distinct advantage over the government slave with more means to dominate a caliph. This analysis by Pipes generalizes about a large swathe of time; my goal here is to investigate the nuances of this dichotomy, and ultimately its accuracy. What were the relations between eunuch and chamberlain? To what extent did each of them manipulate and benefit from administrative authority, and military command? In general, what links did each have with military power, and what other kinds of relationships did they cultivate?

6. Sourdel states that chamberlains since the time of al-Muʿtaṣim were often Turkish pages ("Ghulām," *EI2*). There is plentiful evidence regarding the military origins of different chamberlains during the Abbasid period, but I have not yet seen evidence regarding the training of eunuchs for this period.

7. Pipes, *Slave Soldiers*, 12.

The Reigns of al-Muʿtaḍid and al-Muktafī

There is very little information about specific palace officials under al-Muʿtaḍid and al-Muktafī, and it is therefore difficult to grasp the dynamics involved in palace relations. Our main piece of information involves the appointments made by al-Muʿtaḍid after receiving the oath of allegiance:

> Al-Muʿtaḍid then appointed his page Badr as chief of police, ʿUbaydallāh b. Sulaymān b. Wahb as wazir, and Muḥammad b. al-Shāh b. Mikāl as chief of the guard. He also appointed Ṣāliḥ, who was known as (Ṣāliḥ) al-Amīn, as chief chamberlain (*ḥājib*) for both the inner circle of notables (*khāṣṣah*) and the commoners (*ʿāmmah*). Ṣāliḥ took the place of Khafīf al-Samarqandī.[8]

Typical of this era regarding caliphal appointments, there is no mention of a chief eunuch, so we might conclude that either no such official position existed, and/or the position of the chief eunuch was not as important as those mentioned above. As for the new officials, Ibn Mikāl and Ṣāliḥ al-Amīn—the two most important officials within the palace—are rarely heard again. Ṣāliḥ, the chamberlain, was put in charge of Baghdad on two occasions when the caliph left on campaigns, which shows that this position involved important responsibilities.[9] Yet neither Ibn Mikāl nor Ṣāliḥ appears as a confidant of the caliph, or as important political actors in any respect.

Badr and Khafīf, however, are presented in the sources as retaining prominence throughout al-Muʿtaḍid's reign. According to one anecdote, al-Muʿtaḍid had originally planned to appoint Badr as the chamberlain, but as al-Ṭabarī's account makes clear, this intention changed.[10] Franz Rosenthal concludes that, though the chamberlain usually held higher rank than the police chief, "the new caliph felt that he needed a man with military experience whom he trusted completely in the office of chief of security."[11] Thus Badr, al-Muʿtaḍid's most important *mawlā*, was not posted in the palace but in metropolitan security, and became al-Muʿtaḍid's most powerful general.

Khafīf seems to have been a soldier of slave origin (*ghulām*), for he was sent along with other commanders on campaign during the caliphate of al-Muʿtamid. When al-Muʿtaḍid acceded to the throne, Khafīf (temporarily) lost his position as chamberlain, yet remained close to the caliph. He reports that he and al-Muʿtaḍid rode together alone on a hunt, when the latter boldly slew a lion;[12] on a few occasions al-Muʿtaḍid entrusted

8. al-Ṭabarī, *History*, 38:1.
9. al-Ṭabarī, *History*, 38:7,73.
10. Ibn al-Jawzī, (*al-Muntaẓam* 5:123) also has Ṣāliḥ as the chamberlain.
11. al-Ṭabarī, *History*, 38:1n1.
12. They had been separated from the rest of the hunting party (al-Tanūkhī, *Nishwār*, 3:260; also in Ibn al-Jawzī, *al-Muntaẓam*, 5:129). This story is one of many legends shaping the image of al-Muʿtaḍid as an ideal ruler: in this case, a brave yet humble warrior.

Khafīf with sensitive duties.[13] At some point Khafīf was reinstated as chamberlain, for in 287/900 we hear that "Khafīf the *ḥājib* of al-Muʿtaḍid" witnessed the discussion between Badr and al-Muʿtaḍid regarding a new wazir. We might note that Khafīf had no say in this matter, while Badr convinced the caliph to appoint al-Qāsim b. ʿUbaydallāh. Nevertheless, al-Muʿtaḍid demonstrated particular intimacy with Khafīf, for as his two *mawlās* were leaving his presence, he called back Khafīf, and said to him: "Did you see what just took place ... Badr will be killed by none other than al-Qāsim." Al-Muʿtaḍid shared his uncannily accurate prediction with Khafīf.[14]

The only other palace official we hear of in any detail is Ṣāfī al-Ḥuramī, who appears in anecdotes alongside al-Muʿtaḍid in the women's chambers, as well as alongside al-Muʿtaḍid (and later al-Muktafī) during the caliph's fatal illness.[15] In the story translated in a previous chapter, involving the prince al-Muqtadir giving away grapes, we saw that Ṣāfī was a trusted confidant of the caliph al-Muʿtaḍid, for the latter told Ṣāfī of his impulse to kill the prince. Indeed, Ṣāfī was sufficiently respected by the caliph that he could present an alternative point of view and tried to calm his master.[16] We might also note that Ṣāfī's prominence resulted precisely from his status as a eunuch, and his subsequent privilege of accompanying the caliph into the harem. We also hear that Ṣāfī to some degree controlled access to the caliph, for a judicial official who needed to speak with al-Muʿtaḍid about caliphal delinquence in paying for use of *waqf* property had to first receive permission for an audience from Ṣāfī.[17]

To briefly summarize the condition of palace officials under al-Muʿtaḍid, based upon admittedly limited information: the chamberlain was not necessarily the caliph's most intimate confident, but—at least in the case of Khafīf—possessed some military experience; the change of chamberlains (Ṣāfī to Khafīf) is not mentioned in any source; and, in general, neither the chamberlain nor any other palace official we know of played an important political role under a dominant caliph.

This situation changes somewhat under al-Muktafī, as both Khafīf (who remained chamberlain) and Ṣāfī are attributed active political roles. Khafīf assumed the role of protector of the bureaucratic Furāt family (the Banū al-Furāt), who at the time were struggling for control of financial affairs against the Jarrāḥ family.[18] According to Hilāl al-Ṣābī, "Khafīf al-Samarqandī saw to the affairs of the two Banū al-Furāt (Abū al-ʿAbbās and Abū

13. For example, Khafīf was told to investigate the blasphemy of a servant belonging to the caliph's Christian doctor (al-Ṭabarī, *History*, 38:43).

14. Ibn al-Jawzī, *al-Muntaẓam*, 5:134–35.

15. For example, the anecdote described below, involving the prince Jaʿfar b. al-Muʿtaḍid (al-Tanūkhī, *Nishwār*, 1:287–91; see also the presence of Ṣāfī during the caliphs' illnesses (al-Ṭabarī, *Return*, 103; ʿArīb, *Ṣilāt*, 19–21). Bowen considers Ṣāfī the "Chief Eunuch" (*ʿAlī b. ʿĪsā*, 88).

16. As noted earlier, even if this story is highly embellished, the close relationship between Ṣāfī and the caliph is likely based in widely known fact.

17. al-Tanūkhī, *Nishwār*, 8:20–22.

18. Noted by Bowen, *ʿAlī b. ʿĪsā*, 66–67.

al-Ḥasan), assisted them and strengthened them, so that few people jealous of Abū al-Ḥasan would open their mouths against him."[19] Khafīf had several opportunities to help the Banū al-Furāt. In one instance, he said to al-Muktafī: "The previous caliph could not manage without the Banū al-Furāt ... how could you possibly manage without them?"[20] Later, when the elder Ibn al-Furāt (Abū al-ʿAbbās) died, and al-Muktafī decided with the wazir al-Qāsim to appoint Abū al-Ḥasan to his brother's post, Khafīf overheard the conversation and sent word to Abū al-Ḥasan informing him of the impending appointment. Khafīf apparently did not want to be known as the bureaucrat's informant, for he told Abū al-Ḥasan to keep this news quiet until informed officially.[21] Khafīf then protected Ibn al-Furāt while accompanying al-Muktafī on a hunting expedition; he warned the caliph that the new wazir al-ʿAbbās b. al-Ḥasan was plotting to seize Ibn al-Furāt's property, and convinced the caliph to revoke an order to that effect.[22] Here again Khafīf sent a eunuch to inform Ibn al-Furāt of what had transpired. In general, we see that Khafīf supported Ibn al-Furāt; his close proximity to the caliph made him privy to information that the bureaucrat was not.

Khafīf almost certainly died during al-Muktafī's reign, for by the year 295/908 we are told that Sawsan had become this caliph's chamberlain.[23] Sawsan, like his predecessor, was actively involved in court politics: multiple sources note that "Sawsan al-Ḥājib was involved in control [of the state] alongside [the wazir] al-ʿAbbās b. al-Ḥasan."[24] This however is the only information we possess about him for this reign.

Ṣāfī al-Ḥuramī is also credited with political involvement. Someone accused al-ʿAbbās b. al-Ḥasan of plotting for the wazirate, with the help of Ṣāfī and a woman in the harem, before the wazir al-Qāsim had died.[25] We cannot know if this accusation was true, but if reflects a general perception of Ṣāfī's role and certainly his access to power. Ṣāfī was especially important once al-Muktafī became ill: as we have seen, he informed the caliph of rumors that two Abbasid princes were mobilizing support, thereby prompting the caliph to ensure the succession of his younger brother, Jaʿfar al-Muqtadir.[26] Ṣāfī also removed the signet ring from the dying caliph, and turned it over to the wazir.[27] In gen-

19. Hilāl al-Ṣābī, *Wuzarāʾ*, 154.
20. Hilāl al-Ṣābī, *Wuzarāʾ*, 162; also quoted by Sourdel (*Vizirat*, 336).
21. Hilāl al-Ṣābī, *Wuzarāʾ*, 249; Sourdel, *Vizirat*, 362.
22. Hilāl al-Ṣābī, *Wuzarāʾ*, 251.
23. ʿArīb, *Ṣilat*, 23. We never hear of Khafīf again, which is why I assume he died. It is nevertheless interesting to note that until this point, the transitions between chamberlains are not mentioned in the sources. Ibn al-Jawzī, who usually lists each caliph's chamberlains, does not mention al-Muktafī's appointee in *al-Muntaẓam*.
24. Hilāl al-Ṣābī, *Wuzarāʾ*, 31. Also in Miskawayh, *Tajārib*, 12, and noted by Bowen, *ʿAlī b. ʿĪsā*, 96. I am not certain that Sawsan's influence began during al-Muktafī's reign, or in the few months of al-Muqtadir's reign when al-ʿAbbās was still wazir.
25. al-Tanūkhī, *Nishwār*, 8:156; mentioned by Sourdel, *Vizirat*, 360.
26. ʿArīb, *Ṣilat*, 20–21.
27. ʿArīb, *Ṣilat*, 19; Sourdel, *Vizirat*, 365.

eral, Ṣāfī acquired influence due to his proximity to the caliph, and this power increased as the caliph became sick and immobile. When al-Muktafī finally died, it was Ṣāfī who brought Prince Jaʿfar to the palace, protected him along the way, and took part in conducting the oath of allegiance.

Thus, in summary, both chamberlains and the senior eunuch began to exercise political influence in the reign of al-Muktafī. We might note that both Khafīf and Ṣāfī were reportedly involved in bureaucratic scheming, and both men seemingly benefited from close access to the caliph. But the extent of their recorded involvement is limited, and we do not get much of a picture of the mechanisms of power in the palace. Political involvement by palace officials would increase under al-Muqtadir, which allows for deeper analysis of the power structure in the palace.

Al-Muqtadir: The Early Years

The accession of the thirteen-year-old caliph in 295/908 meant that the court had a very weak center of authority, which induced broader and brazen competition for influence, including among the palace staff. For this early period, it is difficult to distinguish clearly between palace functionaries, and military personnel posted in the palace. For example, in the defense of the palace during the coup of 296/908, we hear that Ṣāfī al-Ḥuramī, Muʾnis al-Khāzin, Muʾnis al-Khādim, Gharīb the royal uncle, and Sawsan the chamberlain all played leading roles; here we see the overlap between palace and military service, for Ṣāfī and Sawsan, with palace appointments, fought during the countercoup. Sawsan was particularly important, for he had originally supported Ibn al-Muʿtazz, but was disappointed with this pretender and returned to al-Muqtadir, and was credited with a crucial role in reversing the coup.[28] In addition, the two men named Muʾnis—both of whom clearly commanded military units—are mentioned as defending the palace, and it is difficult to know if their positions meant that they actually occupied an office of some sort within the palace.

Sawsan and Ṣāfī seem to have had particularly strong positions in the palace. One anecdote reveals that both men disliked Muḥammad b. Dāwud, a bureaucratic partisan of Ibn al-Muʿtazz who was in hiding after the failed coup, and whom the new wazir Ibn al-Furāt was trying to protect. Sawsan and Ṣāfī informed al-Muqtadir of a man who knew Ibn Dāwud's location; this informant was brought to the palace and threatened with execution if he did not reveal Ibn Dāwud's hiding place. The frightened informant arranged a rendezvous with Ibn Dāwud, then reported the time and location to Sawsan and Ṣāfī; these latter ordered the city police to arrest Ibn Dāwud and had him executed.[29] Thus Sawsan and Ṣāfī had managed to manipulate the caliph and an intimidated informant in

---

28. al-Tanūkhī, *al-Faraj*, 3:199–200.

29. Miskawayh, *Tajārib*, 9–10 (Bowen, *ʿAlī b. ʿĪsā*, 94; Sourdel, *Vizirat*, 74n4); Hilāl al-Ṣābī (*Wuzarāʾ*, 30) also preserves a different version, in which Ibn Dāwud approached the palace out of distrust for Ibn

overcoming Ibn al-Furāt's plans. The wazir obviously recognized the potential power of these men, for he then bribed Sawsan not to stir up trouble against ʿAlī b. ʿĪsā, another bureaucrat whom the wazir was protecting.[30]

The tension between Sawsan and Ibn al-Furāt quickly came to a head. As usual, the accounts of the final showdown vary: ʿArīb states that Sawsan became overbearing and haughty, and the caliph distrusted him;[31] according to Miskawayh and Hilāl al-Ṣābī, Sawsan was actually disaffected by his limited participation in government under Ibn al-Furāt, and plotted with some *ḥujarī* soldiers to assassinate the wazir in the royal palace.[32] In either scenario, Sawsan's potential power was threatening to both Ibn al-Furāt and al-Muqtadir, and the wazir convinced the young caliph that Sawsan should be killed. The sources describe the arrest of Sawsan in some detail:

> Al-Muqtadir rode out to the square[33] with Takīn al-Khāṣṣa, Nāzūk, Gharīb [the royal uncle], Rāʾiq, and Yāqūt.[34] Ibn al-Furāt had promised Takīn to appoint him over Egypt in return for assistance against Sawsan. Sawsan suspected a plot against him ... so he entered the square but did not dismount. He played polo with the caliph for a while; he then approached Ṣāfī al-Ḥuramī, who seemed to be sick.[35] Muʾnis al-Khāzin followed him; and when [Sawsan] dismounted [to assist] Ṣāfī in the corner of the square, Takīn al-Khāṣṣa pounced on him.[36]

Takīn then continues with a first-person account:

> When [Sawsan] approached Ṣāfī, I followed as if accompanying him. When he dismounted, I stretched out my arm toward his belt as if to lean on him; then I pulled at it, took out a knife I was carrying and cut off [his belt], leaving his sword in my hand. The soldiers (*ghilmān*) removed what he was carrying, and we pushed him into the gateway of the square, whereupon he wept. The eunuchs took up arms and were charged with protecting his house. All the soldiers in his service gathered, alongside his subordinates; a eunuch went out

al-Furāt. He came to the chamberlain, probably to seek protection or a caliphal audience. Sawsan, however, simply informed the caliph, and Ibn Dāwud was arrested and executed.

30. Hilāl al-Ṣābī, *Wuzarāʾ*, 29.

31. ʿArīb, *Ṣilat*, 29; initiative by the caliph seems unlikely, given his young age and near-universal consensus that al-Muqtadir did not act independently in the first years of his reign.

32. Miskawayh, *Tajārib*, 12; Hilāl al-Ṣābī, *Wuzarāʾ*, 31,155–56. It is odd that the chamberlain would plot with the *ḥujarīs*, given that he was supposedly in charge of the *maṣāffī* units. In general, the functions and allegiances of military units in this period are very confused, and possibly beyond clarification.

33. This is the polo grounds, or drill area for military review, both within the palace complex; the young caliph would not have left the confines of the palace grounds.

34. All these men would become influential commanders in the early years of al-Muqtadir's reign.

35. In a slightly different narrative, ʿArīb specifies that Ṣāfī feigned illness.

36. Hilāl al-Ṣābī, *Wuzarāʾ*, 155–56. Similar in ʿArīb (*Ṣilat*, 29–30) but he does not list all the commanders involved in the arrest.

> to them and announced: "Our Master [al-Muqtadir] says to you, 'You are my soldiers (*ghilmān*) and my favored troops (*khāṣṣatī*); he [Sawsan] is but my slave and possession. I heard information about him that required my taking action against him, but I will treat you well.'" They responded: "Our Master is the authority!" They dispersed, and nothing was heard from them again.[37]

This was the orchestrated and deceitful manner in which Sawsan was seized; he died in prison soon after.[38] This event gives us an impression of the political culture at court at this moment. Several interesting points emerge: the arrest of Sawsan was deliberately planned within the royal complex, but outside the palace itself, since Sawsan's staff/troops were likely concentrated inside; great care was taken to deceive Sawsan even inside the square: Ṣāfī feigned illness, and Takīn deviously pretended to lean on Sawsan when he was actually disarming him, presumably because Sawsan was a capable warrior; the caliph's most important commanders (excluding Muʾnis al-Khādim, but including Ṣāfī al-Ḥuramī) participated in this charade, again presumably because Sawsan possessed military skills and access to troops; and finally, Sawsan definitely commanded armed units whom al-Muqtadir took care to appease. In general, the emphasis in this account is the neutralization of Sawsan's military capabilities and supporters.

The selection of Sawsan's replacement as chamberlain is typically vague. One source states that Takīn had been groomed for the position, but another claims that Ibn al-Furāt promised Takīn the governorship of Egypt, and the latter indeed spent the next decades in Egypt. The sources all agree that Naṣr al-Qushūrī was appointed chamberlain, but no source presents this appointment in any detail.[39]

With the powerful and ambitious Sawsan now neutralized, Ṣāfī al-Ḥuramī was left to dominate the palace. He, along with Ibn al-Furāt, encouraged al-Muqtadir to send Muʾnis al-Khādim out of Baghdad; the impressionable caliph, probably acting on the advice of his mother, obliged by sending Muʾnis to the Byzantine front. Henceforth, until the time his death in 298/910–911, Ṣāfī controlled the palace.[40]

To summarize the fate of the armed commanders who protected al-Muqtadir during the failed coup of 296/908: Sawsan died in prison; Ṣāfī died (no cause mentioned); Muʾnis al-Khādim spent most of these years on military campaign, primarily against the Byzantines; Muʾnis al-Khāzin was head of the police in Baghdad (*ṣāḥib al-shurṭa*) until his death in 301/914, with few references to his influence at court; and Gharīb the uncle became an important commander, likely an advisor to his sister and nephew, but never reported to have taken independent action. I argue below that the deaths, absences and/or passiv-

37. Hilāl al-Ṣābī, *Wuzarāʾ*, 156.

38. ʿArīb, *Ṣilat*, 30.

39. ʿArīb, *Ṣilat*, 30.

40. Ibn al-Jawzī, *al-Muntaẓam*, 6:108. When Ṣāfī died in 298/910–911, he was replaced by one of his officers (*ghilmān*), about whom we never hear again.

ity of these various men left a power vacuum, filled for the next two decades by the new chamberlain, Naṣr.

A Dominant Chamberlain: Naṣr

Naṣr al-Qushūrī was apparently of Greek origin; he began his career as a military slave (*ghulām*) of the caliph al-Muʿtaḍid, most likely purchased at young age, trained in military arts, and manumitted.[41] He was dispatched along with other commanders in 282/895 to fight Ḥamdān b. Ḥamdūn, and was subsequently put in charge of tax collection in Mosul, which he delegated to his own men.[42] That same year he sent a threatening letter to a Khārijī rebel, but was apparently not in charge of the ensuing campaign.[43] Naṣr also appears on the long list of commanders who fought against the Qarmatians in 291/904.[44] By the year 296/908 Naṣr held high rank at court, and was possibly already a subchamberlain, for ʿArīb states that "Naṣr al-Ḥājib, known as al-Qushūrī, was appointed to the chamberlainship."[45] Thus, like his predecessors Khafīf and Sawsan, Naṣr was a soldier and commander with extensive military experience before becoming chamberlain.[46]

An anecdote from early in Naṣr's tenure describes his primary role at court: control over access to the imperial palace and the caliph. The setting for the following account is the arrest of the wazir Ibn al-Furāt in 299/912:

> The secretary of Naṣr al-Qushūrī reported: I was present with my boss on the day of Ibn al-Furāt's arrest. I saw that he [Naṣr] was terribly frightened, so I asked, "What is the news, Master?" He replied, "The eunuch whom I employ to observe the caliph's affairs just came and informed me that he saw [the caliph] had gathered a group of his special eunuchs; they stood around him armed, and he dropped the curtains of the chamber in which he was located. This is a serious matter, about which I know nothing." Only a short time passed before Abū al-Ḥasan Ibn al-Furāt arrived. Naṣr al-Ḥājib went out to greet him, as was his routine, and brought him into the chamber of the wazirs, which had been delegated to him. Naṣr then sent asking for permission for Ibn al-Furāt to come [to the caliph]. A note from the caliph arrived with the response: "I am in the

41. We know that Naṣr was Greek because his brother reportedly came from Byzantium (*Rūm*) and converted; in addition, Naṣr and Muʾnis both acted as interpreters for al-Muqtadir during the Byzantine visit in 305/917 (al-Khaṭīb *Tārīkh*, 1:104).

42. Ibn al-Athīr, *al-Kāmil*, 7:490.

43. Ibn al-Athīr, *al-Kāmil*, 7:490; al-Ṭabarī, *History*, 38:20n114.

44. al-Ṭabarī, *History*, 8:138. According to Massignon, Naṣr had been taken prisoner by the Samanids between 286/899 and 290/903 (*Passion*, 1:426).

45. ʿArīb, *Ṣilat*, 30. Of course, the attribution *al-ḥājib*, presented here as preceding Naṣr's appointment as chamberlain, might simply be the invocation of the name and title by which he is later known. Unfortunately, we have no information regarding the procedure for selecting chamberlains.

46. As noted earlier this is not a new phenomenon. See D. Sourdel, "Ḥadjib," *EI2*.

*Kennedy has also summarized Naṣr's career (in van Berkel et al, *Crisis and Continuity*, 129–34).

> private chambers, so tell him to enter with one of the eunuchs, and none of you [chamberlains] should accompany him. You should prevent or divert the military commanders, for today is not an audience day."
>
> So Ibn al-Furāt entered with the eunuchs. Nadhīr al-Ḥuramī, along with some of al-Sayyida's eunuchs, arrested him on the way [to the caliph], and conveyed him to where he was imprisoned. Naṣr al-Ḥājib found out about this situation, and feared his own arrest or dismissal, remaining frightened until sunset. I found out that these eunuchs were present because of al-Muqtadir's concern that the arrest of Ibn al-Furāt would not be successful, and that the army might riot and prevent it.

The man who transmitted this story from Naṣr's secretary explains one aspect of this sequence of events—the relationship between wazirs and the chamberlain—and provides the historical context for institutional change:

> It was customary—from previous times until [the wazirate] of the older al-Khāqānī [299/911–912]—that the wazir occupy a chamber within the royal palace, where he could sit and investigate matters, and where the court elite would attend him. When al-Khāqānī was appointed, after Ibn al-Furāt's [first] dismissal, he sat in the chamberlain's quarters, to be close to the latter and flatter him. ʿAlī b. ʿĪsā, who followed [al-Khāqānī] in office, did likewise. But when Abū al-Ḥasan Ibn al-Furāt was reappointed wazir, he returned to the original, separate quarters, which bothered the court retinue. When Ḥāmid was appointed [in 306/918] he sat in the chamberlain's quarters; then Ibn al-Furāt returned for his third wazirate [in 311/923] and went back to the original location. After him, sitting [in the wazir's quarters] was forbidden.[47]

This two-part anecdote is the most detailed account we possess for this era of Abbasid history regarding a chamberlain's role in the palace. Naṣr's most basic function, presumably like any chamberlain, is that to a certain extent he controlled movement within the royal palace, and access to the caliph.[48] Here we see that it was standard practice for the chamberlain to greet the wazir, either at the entrance of the palace or more likely at the wazir's suite within the palace. The chamberlain would then contact the caliph, asking permission for the wazir (normally accompanied by the chamberlain) to meet with the caliph. The chamberlain was entrusted with keeping out unwanted visitors—in this case the caliph told him to prevent access to military commanders—which suggests that the chamberlain had the means of denying entry; we might recall that the *maṣāffī* soldiers were reportedly attached to Naṣr, and possibly served this purpose. We also discover that Naṣr employed spies to monitor activity in the palace, including the actions of the caliph. We should also note that the spy in this particular case was a eunuch, which is

47. Hilāl al-Ṣābī, *Wuzarāʾ*, 290–91.
48. See Sourdel, "Hadjib," *EI2*, 45.

logical given that al-Muqtadir was located in his private chambers, which only women and eunuchs were allowed to enter.

Yet Naṣr obviously did not have total control over movement within the palace, or perfect information about internal machinations. First of all, even once he was informed that the caliph had gathered the special eunuchs, Naṣr had no idea what the caliph had planned. This was the first arrest of a wazir during al-Muqtadir's reign, and it took place inside the palace, yet the chamberlain was not involved in the planning or informed at all. In addition, we see that the caliph had access to an armed unit over which Naṣr had no control (the special eunuchs), and that Naṣr was not given advanced notice about their deployment. The caliph thus had multiple armed units within the palace, and the chamberlain supervised only part of them. Moreover, like many of his colleagues and subordinates, Naṣr was not a eunuch, and thus did not have access to the caliph in certain areas, while potential rival eunuchs did.

Finally, we see that Naṣr was afraid of arrest. This suggests that the chamberlain considered himself vulnerable, even in the palace, and that al-Muqtadir had access to enough military force within the palace (again, the eunuchs) that he could probably overcome Naṣr's own military support should he want to arrest the chamberlain. In general, we get the impression that while Naṣr served a crucial function and had both military assets and secret agents at his disposal, he by no means dominated the royal palace, and was even somewhat vulnerable. This event occurred only two years after Naṣr acquired his position, and we might assume that Naṣr would gradually consolidate power in the palace in the coming years. Nevertheless, certain of the themes highlighted above—the dispersion of armed units in the palace, the absence of transparency and subsequent paranoia—would recur for many years to come.

The second half of the anecdote contains two important themes. First, we see that palace protocol changed after Ibn al-Furāt was arrested, for subsequent wazirs (al-Khāqānī and ʿAlī b. ʿĪsā) convened their sessions at the palace in the chamberlain's quarters and not in the separate waziral suite.[49] This change was both symbolic and substantive: it reflects the growing power of the chamberlain, for his quarters were increasingly the focus of palace activity; and in a sense the wazirs had deferred to his authority, at least within the palace. Indeed, al-Khāqānī reportedly made the change in order to curry favor with Naṣr, from whose influence he could apparently benefit. Also, the wazirs were now under the direct observation of the chamberlain, which no doubt increased his influence, and certainly limited the potential for scheming against him or the caliph. Second, the repeated insistence of Ibn al-Furāt, upon reinstatement (in 304/917 and 311/923), to occupy the wazir's chambers in the palace and not Naṣr's, reflects an ongoing tension between these two men. Again, the implications had two levels: Ibn al-Furāt would not defer to the chamberlain; and he certainly did not want Naṣr monitoring his every action

49. Sourdel notes this in passing (*Vizirat*, 692).

in the palace. These issues—the occupancy of particular space in the palace, and the tensions between Ibn al-Furāt and Naṣr—would also recur during al-Muqtadir's reign.

Naṣr's Responsibilities

We hear very little of Naṣr for the first five years of his tenure as chamberlain, coinciding with the first years of al-Muqtadir's reign. During this period, Ṣāfī al-Ḥuramī (d. 298/910–911) and Mu'nis al-Khāzin (d. 301/914) dominated the palace; Naṣr would assert broader influence only when these two palace officials had died. By the year 301/913–914 Naṣr appears on a consistent basis. In court ceremonial, Naṣr takes his place within the powerful triumvirate at court: the wazir, the leading general, and the chamberlain. For example, in the procession celebrating the nominal appointment of the heir apparent (prince Abū al-ʿAbbās) over Egypt and Syria, Naṣr rode immediately in front of the prince, the wazir ʿAlī b. ʿĪsā rode on the prince's right, the general Mu'nis on his left.[50] Naṣr's position in front of the prince mirrors his function in the palace: of separating royalty from outsiders as the vanguard of protection. This triumvirate of leaders appeared again in the procession glorifying the capture of al-Ḥusayn b. Ḥamdān.[51] Naṣr's status as a leading functionary was consolidated ceremonially during the Byzantine ambassadorial visit in 305/917, for the envoys reportedly visited Naṣr's palace before visiting that of the wazir and the caliph, and were so impressed by its grandeur that they initially believed Naṣr was actually the caliph.[52] Naṣr also conducted the envoys' audience with the caliph, telling them where to stand, and acting as interpreter.

During the early years of the fourth/tenth century, Naṣr's emergence is apparent in additional honors and responsibilities. In 301/913–914 he was granted the governorship of Gundeshapur, and sent a eunuch to serve as his deputy.[53] Naṣr became the mentor of the second-ranking prince, Hārūn, whom he apparently trained and educated in the chamberlain's suites, and to whom he reportedly gifted expensive properties.[54] Administratively, Naṣr became involved in apportioning eastern governorships: first that of Fārs, nominally a post held by Prince Hārūn; this was followed by involvement in the appointments for Rayy, Qazwīn, Jurjān, and Ṭabaristān.[55]

50. ʿArīb, *Ṣilat*, 43.

51. ʿArīb, *Ṣilat*, 57 (in the latter half of the year 303/916); Bowen, *ʿAlī b. ʿĪsā*, 143.

52. This report comes from Hilāl al-Ṣābī (*Rusūm*, 17), repeated by al-Khaṭīb (*Tārīkh*, 1:100–101). Lassner points out that the chronology of this event is very confusing (*Topography*, 269n12).

53. ʿArīb, *Ṣilat*, 42. Naṣr acquired other unspecified honors. In 304/917 the wazir Ibn al-Furāt canceled some of these additional administrative appointments (Miskawayh, *Tajārib*, 52), as part of the ongoing feud between these two men.

54. ʿArīb, *Ṣilat*, 154–55.

55. ʿArīb, *Ṣilat*, 51; he remained involved in complex negotiations involving rival claimants to control over Rayy (see also Bowen, *ʿAlī b. ʿĪsā*, 155–58). Massignon argues that Naṣr "assumed responsibility for the eastern part [of the empire]," which might be slightly overstated (*Passion*, 1:426). Naṣr clearly had an

Naṣr's primary responsibility was ensuring the general security within the palace complex, particularly protecting the person of the caliph. Visitors to the palace were apparently taken immediately to the chamberlain: the tax farmer Ḥāmid, for example, appears outside the chamberlain's door after entering deeper within the palace; and a woman who wanted to report the hiding place of Ibn al-Furāt's son al-Muḥassin was also brought to Naṣr.[56] Indeed, the wazir Ibn al-Furāt tells Naṣr straightforwardly: "You are [the caliph's] chamberlain, the guardian of his palace."[57] Regarding the broader palace complex: Naṣr accompanied the caliph to the hippodrome; when troops initiated a riot, Naṣr advised him to return to the confines of the palace. At a later date Naṣr neutralized a more serious security threat: informed that disenchanted commanders were plotting to assassinate the caliph while riding from the Ḥasanī to the Thurayyā palaces, Naṣr posted large contingents of guards at the spot where the attack was supposed to take place, forcing the would-be assassins to abort their scheme. He then dispatched these men to provinces but chose not to incriminate them. This event demonstrates Naṣr's skill and political acumen: he had advanced knowledge of the plot and deployed troops to prevent the attack; but he avoided antagonizing elements in the military by quietly dispensing of the wayward commanders.[58]

Related to this responsibility for security, Naṣr was also partially responsible for state prisoners. A handful of incarcerated bureaucrats were held in his custody, though most were held by Zaydān.[59] The enigmatic al-Ḥallāj, executed in 309/922 for heresy, was held for years and treated very well by Naṣr, who had become an adherent of this controversial man and unsuccessfully tried to prevent his execution.[60] Naṣr was also sent by the caliph, along with Shafīʿ al-Muqtadirī, to arrest Ibn al-Furāt and his entourage at the wazir's home in 306/918, again confirming Naṣr's authority beyond the palace compound, as well as his command of armed units.[61]

---

interest and influence in these affairs, but I have seen no claims or consistent evidence in the sources that he had comprehensive control of policy.

56. Miskawayh, *Tajārib*, 96, 132.

57. Miskawayh, *Tajārib*, 118 (*Eclipse*, 132).

58. ʿArīb, *Ṣilat*, 124; Bowen notes Naṣr's reticence to antagonize the military (*ʿAlī b. ʿĪsā*, 248).

59. In 306/918–919, Ibn al-Furāt was held by Zaydān, while his son and close associates were in Naṣr's custody (Miskawayh, *Tajārib*, 57–58; Hilāl al-Ṣābī, *Wuzarāʾ*, 39). In 312/924, Ibn al-Furāt and al-Muḥassin were briefly imprisoned by Naṣr (Miskawayh, *Tajārib*, 126), and in 315/927 ʿAlī b. ʿĪsā's brother ʿAbd al-Raḥmān was held by Naṣr (Miskawayh, *Tajārib*, 185; Bowen, *ʿAlī b. ʿĪsā*, 275).

60. Massignon, *Passion*, 1:428.

61. Hilāl al-Ṣābī, *Wuzarāʾ*, 39; Miskawayh, *Tajārib*, 57–58; Sourdel, *Vizirat*, 412. ʿArīb, (*Ṣilat*, 73) states the exact date as the twenty-eighth of Rabi al-Thani (7 October 918). Sourdel claims that it was Naṣr's responsibility to arrest wazirs ("Hādjib," *EI2*, 45). This is the only example I can find, from among the eight arrests of wazirs during Naṣr's tenure, when he is explicitly involved in an arrest. We have already seen that in 299/911–912, Naṣr was not even aware that Ibn al-Furāt was going to be arrested in the palace.

Naṣr also attended the interrogations of dismissed wazirs.[62] The chamberlain's exact function at these interrogations is unclear. He was primarily an observer and representative on behalf of the caliph, who often did not attend, and by etiquette would certainly not participate. In one instance Naṣr asked Ibn al-Furāt a question at the specific behest of the caliph; yet al-Muqtadir also occasionally sent other officials to observe these interrogations, even when Naṣr was present, largely because Naṣr was known to be hostile to Ibn al-Furāt and could not be trusted to act solely in the caliph's interest.[63] Naṣr always occupied a position of honor, seated next to the wazir during these interrogations, he nevertheless deferred to the wazirs in the conduct of the questioning. In 306/918–919 he criticized Ḥāmid's handling of Ibn al-Furāt, but only after the session was over;[64] and in 311/923–924 he was appalled by al-Muḥassin's treatment of ʿAlī b. ʿĪsā, but left the room rather than witness the torture.[65] In both these cases Naṣr appears as an observer rather than participant, and cannot regulate the wazirs' behavior. Here again we receive an ambiguous picture of Naṣr's influence at court: he is recognized as a leading figure of state, and to an extent bears the authority of the caliph; yet he does not officiate in these proceedings, and the caliph can rather easily substitute him with other officials when the need arises.

Beyond the issues of security and prisoner incarceration and interrogation, Naṣr was involved in important strategic decisions. In 302/914–915 he deliberated with generals, the wazir, and other palace officials concerning the Fatimid threat in Egypt;[66] in 308/920–921 Naṣr was active in reducing the price of grain in Baghdad, and was apparently responsible for the selection of two police chiefs at about this same time.[67] He was also intricately involved in the defense of the state against the Qarmatians: in 312/924, al-Muqtadir consulted Naṣr about responding to the Qarmatian raid on pilgrims to Mecca;[68] in 315, Naṣr joined Muʾnis and ʿAlī. b. ʿĪsā in reporting to the caliph about another military defeat at the hands of the Qarmatians;[69] finally, later that year he led troops in a final effort to prevent the Qarmatians from assaulting Baghdad.

62. Three examples of such interrogations are: that of Ibn al-Furāt in 306/918–919, while al-Muqtadir listened behind a curtain (Miskawayh, *Tajārib*, 63; Hilāl al-Ṣābī, *Wuzarāʾ*, 110; al-Tanūkhī, *Nishwār*, 2:32; Ibn al-Athīr *al-Kāmil*, 8:112; Bowen, *ʿAlī b. ʿĪsā*, 165); that of of ʿAlī in 311/923 (Miskawayh, *Tajārib*, 110; Hilāl al-Ṣābī, *Wuzarāʾ*, 323); and that of lbn al-Furāt in 312/924 (Miskawayh, *Tajārib*, 132; Sourdel, *Vizirat*, 433). See also al-Tanūkhī, *Nishwār*, 2:32 for Naṣr's honorary status at these interrogations.

63. For example, when al-Muqtadir sent a eunuch to remove Ibn al-Furāt from interrogation (Miskawayh, *Tajārib*, 63).

64. Ibn al-Athīr, *al-Kāmil*, 8:112; Bowen, *ʿAlī b. ʿĪsā*, 171; Sourdel, *Vizirat*, 418.

65. Miskawayh, *Tajārib*, 110; Bowen, *ʿAlī b. ʿĪsā*, 217; Sourdel, *Vizirat*, 428.

66. Hilāl al-Ṣābī, *Wuzarāʾ*, 380. Sourdel mentions this in passing (*Vizirat*, 546n2).

67. ʿArīb, *Ṣilat*, 84,109.

68. Miskawayh, *Tajārib*, 121.

69. Miskawayh, *Tajārib*, 175.

With all of Naṣr's varied responsibilities, his most prominent activity at court involved the appointment, protection, and removal of wazirs, and bureaucratic personnel more generally. As early as 304/916–917, we hear that Naṣr and Gharīb were protecting the wazir ʿAlī b. ʿĪsā against intrigue.[70] We might note that ʿAlī was nevertheless arrested and, in general, none of the court elite—palace servants, generals, not even the caliph's mother—succeeded in stopping the constant, destabilizing turnover of wazirs. More generally, over the course of ten years Naṣr was active in the removal and appointment of four wazirs: in 306/918 he worked for the dismissal of Ibn al-Furāt, and the appointment of Ḥāmid; in 312/924 he again helped bring about the fall and execution of Ibn al-Furāt, and the appointment of al-Khāqānī; in 313/925 he schemed for al-Khaṣībī to replace al-Khāqānī; and in 316/928 he plotted against ʿAlī b. ʿĪsā, in favor of Ibn Muqla.

The Nature and Extent of Naṣr's Power

As a result of his position within the palace, Naṣr had considerable means of wielding power, which were especially effective against bureaucrats. We have seen that wazirs could only reach the caliph's presence by means of the chamberlain and usually had to wait in his chambers. Naṣr sometimes took advantage of this to detain bureaucrats. For example, in 312/924 the *ḥujarī* troops clamored for the arrest of Ibn al-Furāt; when the wazir visited the palace, Naṣr would not let him or his son leave, and made them wait while al-Muqtadir decided their fate.[71] A few years later, Naṣr had been asked by al-Muqtadir to suggest a new wazir; the chamberlain initially proposed a certain Muḥammad b. Khalaf, but when the caliph disapproved of this choice, Naṣr turned his support to Ibn Muqla. The latter was then brought to the palace, and detained in Naṣr's quarters, while the chamberlain's original candidate—Muḥammad b. Khalaf—continued to lobby for the wazirate.[72]

The most effective means by which Naṣr schemed for and against bureaucrats was by bringing information to the caliph that bureaucrats could not deliver by themselves. By 306/918 Naṣr had developed a dislike and fear of Ibn al-Furāt; so when Ibn Muqla, a former protégé of Ibn al Furāt, informed Naṣr that Ibn al-Furāt had previously lied about personal assets during an interrogation, Naṣr took the information straight to al-Muqtadir, resulting in the bureaucrat's arrest.[73] Indeed, Naṣr convinced lbn Muqla to divulge these secrets, by leading Ibn Muqla to believe that the chamberlain could make

70. Miskawayh, *Tajārib*, 44.

71. Miskawayh, *Tajārib*, 124–5, Hilāl al-Ṣābī, *Wuzarāʾ*, 59. Both sources state "He sat them down." Margoliouth/Amedroz misleadingly translate this phrase "Naṣr the chamberlain requested them to sit down" (*Eclipse*, 138); but no request or option was involved. As we shall see below, Ibn al-Furāt and son were eventually freed due to the intervention of Mufliḥ the senior eunuch.

72. Miskawayh, *Tajārib*, 185–86; Sourdel describes these events, but does not refer to Naṣr's participation (*Vizirat*, 448). On this occasion Naṣr was unsuccessful, and Ibn Muqla was appointed wazir.

73. Miskawayh, *Tajārib*, 52; Bowen, *ʿAlī b. ʿĪsā*, 157; Sourdel, *Vizirat*, 411. Similarly, in 316/928 Naṣr

him wazir. On this occasion, though, Naṣr decided to support the candidacy of Ḥāmid b. al-ʿAbbās, a tax farmer in Wāsiṭ; this Ḥāmid had garnered support from Naṣr and the caliph's mother, encouraging them, with bribes, to propose his candidacy for the wazirate to the caliph.[74] At a later date, Naṣr did assist Ibn Muqla. In 315/927, there was a lack of intelligence reports about Qarmatian troop movements; Ibn Muqla devised a way of procuring information with pigeons. He brought this innovation to Naṣr, who conveyed it to the caliph, later reminding the caliph of Ibn Muqla's efforts: "If this is [Ibn Muqla's] concern for your affairs when he is not in your employment, think of what it would be if you favored him!"[75] In general, Naṣr's access to the caliph made him well-placed to help aspiring bureaucrats, for he could forward information to the caliph and thereby enable plotters to circumvent the wazir; in return, he sometimes received bribes, or was granted additional administrative posts with commensurate stipends.

Naṣr's power vis-a-vis the bureaucrats—the ability to detain them, and his special connection to the caliph—were nevertheless limited. First of all, Naṣr could not detain wazirs frequently, for they were still the appointees of the caliph, and under the latter's authority. Naṣr could monitor bureaucrat activity and could sometimes manipulate access to the caliph, but not always. We have several examples of wazirs, especially Ibn al-Furāt and his son al-Muḥassin, obtaining audiences with the caliph and suggesting policies that Naṣr opposed.[76] In short, Naṣr could not consistently prevent contact between bureaucrats and the caliph. More importantly, when bureaucrats did need an intermediary with the caliph, they had several options other than Naṣr; we have already seen many instances in which individuals turned to the caliph's mother or her subordinates (Umm Mūsā, Zaydān, Thumal) as a means of reaching the caliph. As we shall now see, other male *mawlās* could also serve as intermediaries.

Palace Eunuchs

Mufliḥ

The best alternative of communicating with the caliph, and circumventing the authority of the chamberlain, was through senior palace eunuchs. As mentioned earlier, Ṣāfī al-Ḥuramī had been the dominant eunuch of his era but had been replaced in 298/910–911 by a *ghulām* we never hear of again, and nobody of prominence filled this role during the

---

passed along confidential information from another ambitious bureaucrat, regarding the disloyalty of a governor (Miskawayh, *Tajārib*, 166–68).

74. Ibn al-Athīr, *al-Kāmil*, 8:111, Miskawayh, *Tajārib*, 57; ʿArīb, *Ṣilat*, 73; Bowen, *ʿAlī b. ʿĪsā*, 160; Sourdel, *Vizirat*, 411. On this occasion, Naṣr was given credit for bringing about Ḥāmid's appointment.

*Osti also discusses the appointment of Ḥāmid ("ʿAbbāsid Intrigues" 10–14).

75. Miskawayh, *Tajārib*, 184–85 (parallel translation in *Eclipse*, 208); Bowen, *ʿAlī b. ʿĪsā*, 272–73.

76. Indeed, Ibn al-Furāt succeeded in meeting with the caliph while in the palace prison, under the supervision of Zaydān.

early years of al-Muqtadir's reign. We also have little information about the emergence of a certain Mufliḥ; but by 310/922–923 he was clearly the most powerful eunuch in the palace.[77] Like Naṣr the chamberlain, Mufliḥ had a variety of duties; his primary job was probably delivering messages from the caliph to dignitaries both within and outside the palace.[78] He appeared in public ceremonies, and supervised a prisoner exchange with the Byzantines; he also commanded armed palace troops.[79] Also similar to Naṣr, Mufliḥ frequently appears in the sources lobbying the caliph on behalf of specific bureaucrats, and against others; he differed from the chamberlain in his consistent support for Ibn al-Furāt. We are told of the origins of this alliance, from the time when Ḥāmid b. al-ʿAbbās was wazir and Ibn al-Furāt was in jail in the year 311/923–924:

> Mufliḥ al-Aswad (the Black) was close with al-Muqtadir and was dedicated to serving him. His position rose greatly, so that he was given land grants, and ownership of expensive properties. He happened to quarrel with [the wazir] Ḥāmid and referred to him in a crass way. Ḥāmid had responded, "I think I will buy one hundred black eunuchs and name each of them Mufliḥ, then give them to my pages." Mufliḥ harbored resentment from this [insult]. Al-Muḥassin [b. al-Furāt] took advantage of this and sent for Mufliḥ's secretary ... promising him administrative posts, money, and governorships if he would make an arrangement between himself [al-Muḥassin] and Mufliḥ. Al-Muḥassin then wrote a note to al-Muqtadir, which Mufliḥ delivered by hand, proposing that if [the wazir] Ḥāmid, [his deputy] ʿAlī b. ʿĪsā, Naṣr al-Ḥājib, Shafīʿ al-Luʾluʾī [the Chief of Police], Ibn al-Ḥawārī, Umm Mūsā and her brother, and the Mādhrāʾī [financiers] were turned over to him, he would extract from them seven million dinars.[80]

Hilāl al-Ṣābī adds more details to this story:

> [Al-Muḥassin] wrote a note to that effect, and gave it to Bishr b. ʿAbdallāh, Mufliḥ's secretary. They parted, and Bishr went to Mufliḥ and told him what had occurred, that al-Muḥassin had offered [Mufliḥ] a lot of money with which

77. Bowen states that Mufliḥ was chief of the black eunuchs and had risen in the caliph's esteem due to his able management of the eunuch corps, implying a hierarchy of eunuchs, over which Mufliḥ presided (*ʿAlī b. ʿĪsā*, 197). I have found no additional proof of such a hierarchy, nor any information regarding Mufliḥ's relations with other eunuchs.

78. On several occasions he delivered messages to Ibn al-Furāt (for example, Hilāl al-Ṣābī, *Wuzarāʾ*, 197), as well as to the bureaucrat al-Kalwādhī in 319/931 (Miskawayh, *Tajārib*, 212, 217), and to Muʾnis (in 320/932).

79. He commanded the troops when honoring the general Ibn Abī al-Sāj in 310/922–923 (Miskawayh, *Tajārib*, 82); when celebrating Muʾnis's return from victory over the Byzantines in 311/923–924 (Miskawayh, *Tajārib*, 115); and when honoring the second appointment of ʿAlī b. ʿĪsā in early 315/927 (Miskawayh, *Tajārib*, 151). In 311/923, al-Muqtadir ordered him to dispatch two hundred troops (one hundred *ḥujarīs* and one hundred *maṣāffīs*) to Wāsiṭ (Hilāl al-Ṣābī, *Wuzarāʾ*, 41).

80. Miskawayh, *Tajārib*, 87.

> to tempt al-Muqtadir. If this scheme succeeded and state finances were stabilized through his mediation, [Mufliḥ] would rise in standing, the ruler would praise him, and he would thrive under Ibn al-Furāt and al-Muḥassin. He therefore recommended that [Mufliḥ] speak with [al-Muqtadir] about this and show him the letter that al-Muḥassin had written. Mufliḥ agreed to do this.[81]

This complex intrigue came to successful fruition: al-Muqtadir received the note, asked Ibn al-Furāt for confirmation of the promises it contained, and then removed Ḥāmid and ʿAlī b. ʿĪsā from office.

This anecdote gives us a good idea of Mufliḥ's position in the palace. He had a close relationship with the caliph, as we might expect, given that he attended the caliph in the private chambers; and Mufliḥ was rewarded with outside sources of revenue, through land grants. We also see that Mufliḥ was not servile, for he had a dispute with the wazir, and even insulted him; in fact, Mufliḥ was offended by the suggestion of his servile status, which a hundred of his namesakes serving Ḥāmid's troops would have symbolized. Al-Muḥassin took advantage of this tension between the senior eunuch and the wazir and succeeded in convincing Mufliḥ to deliver a very tempting message to the caliph. For Mufliḥ, this intervention in bureaucratic affairs had several benefits: he could exact revenge for a slight: the insinuation that his origins as a slave and the realities of being a eunuch were shameful compared to supercilious bureaucrats; he received monetary compensation, in the form of bribes; and he gained prestige with the caliph and the broader court community, for involvement in governmental affairs. Like Naṣr, Mufliḥ took advantage of his access to the caliph in order to benefit from the turmoil within the bureaucracy. His support for the Banū al-Furāt, however, potentially put him at odds with Naṣr.

Mufliḥ's next reported intervention in bureaucratic affairs reiterates that he and Naṣr had opposing alliances, and distinctly different functions in the palace. The following anecdote is the only recorded interaction between Mufliḥ and Naṣr and thus allows unique insight into the relations and relative positions of the chamberlain and senior eunuch. The story takes place after Ḥāmid b. al-ʿAbbās had been dismissed in favor of Ibn al-Furāt in the year 312/924, but had been given permission to return to his home in Wāsiṭ and had not yet been arrested:

> [Ḥāmid] went to the *Dār al-Sulṭān* ... and up to the *Dār al-Ḥijaba*, where Naṣr the chamberlain was located.[82] Fāris b. Rundāq (Naṣr's subordinate) asked Naṣr to

81. Hilāl al-Ṣābī, *Wuzarāʾ*, 265–66; Sourdel (*Vizirat*, 243) and Bowen, (*ʿAlī b. ʿĪsā*, 197) note that Mufliḥ provided assistance to al-Muḥassin.

82. Margoliouth and Amedroz translate this as "where Naṣr lived," though the text only says "where Naṣr was located." This translation reflects an interesting quandary, namely what is meant by "*Dār al-Ḥijāba*?" It would seem that Naṣr occupied a residence very close to the caliphal (Ḥasanī) palace, within the greater royal palace complex; however, it is also possible, even likely, that the chamberlain had a suite of rooms within the Ḥasanī palace itself, where Naṣr presumably spent most of his working day,

> allow [Ḥāmid to enter], saying "Ḥāmid b. al-ʿAbbās is at the gate and requests permission to see the Ustadh (Naṣr)." Naṣr replied, "Tell him to come in." When he entered, Naṣr said to [Ḥāmid] before the latter could sit down, "What are you doing here?" Ḥāmid answered, "I came in accordance with your letter." Naṣr replied, "I wrote you to come here?" He would not stand up for [Ḥāmid], explaining that [Ḥāmid] was not in the caliph's favor. Naṣr then sent word to Mufliḥ, requesting his presence....[83] Mufliḥ arrived, and Naṣr spoke to him about Ḥāmid's condition, saying: "He is now in a state to be pitied, and it would appropriate to do him a good turn, and not take revenge on him for that earlier affair (Ḥāmid's insult of Mufliḥ)."

Ḥāmid then told Mufliḥ the conditions he wished to request from the caliph: incarceration in the palace, interrogation before state dignitaries, and under no circumstances to be handed over to the hostile and violent al-Muḥassin. The anecdote continues:

> Mufliḥ promised [to convey] that. He approached al-Muqtadir and spoke to him regarding Ḥāmid's conditions in exactly the opposite terms than he had promised. So al-Sayyida spoke up on behalf of Ḥāmid: "There is no harm in incarcerating him in the palace and interrogating him so that he can defend himself." Then Mufliḥ interjected: "If that is done, [the wazir] Ibn al-Furāt will not accomplish anything, for there are many rumors (that Ḥāmid will replace Ibn al-Furāt), while the world is being wrecked and finances ruined." Al-Muqtadir concurred with Mufliḥ: "You are right." He then ordered [Mufliḥ] to go out to Naṣr and order him to convey Ḥāmid to Ibn al-Furāt. So Mufliḥ went to Naṣr to execute this order.

The story concludes with Naṣr trying to calm Ḥāmid about being turned over to Ibn al-Furāt. Naṣr and Mufliḥ then disagreed over whether or not Ḥāmid could change clothes before leaving; "Naṣr continued to protest on his behalf until [Mufliḥ] gave permission for him to change clothes." Naṣr then sent Ḥāmid to Ibn al-Furāt (presumably in the wazir's palace, north of the royal palace complex), and Mufliḥ dispatched a messenger to the wazir informing him of the good news.[84]

This anecdote is fascinating, as it gives us a rare picture of the relative leverage of functionaries within the palace. We see that Mufliḥ, as senior eunuch, controlled access to the caliph when the latter was in the harem or visiting with his mother, which occurred

---

and where people came to ask for caliphal audiences. Did Naṣr indeed own a property separate from his rooms in the palace? If so, where did Ḥāmid arrive?

83. The exact wording is "to come out to Naṣr," possibly meaning to come out of the harem areas that were restricted space to Naṣr, as he was not a eunuch.

84. Miskawayh, *Tajārib*, 96–97. Versions of this account vary greatly: Ibn al-Athīr (*al-Kāmil*, 8:141) and Ibn al-Jawzī (*al-Muntaẓam*, 6:184) provide similar accounts, with different details; ʿArīb's version (*Ṣilat*, 112) is substantially different in that Naṣr himself goes personally talk to al-Muqtadir. Of course, in this case al-Sayyida is not present. (I have not yet seen any evidence that al-Sayyida and Naṣr were ever in the same room). In all versions, Mufliḥ convinces al-Muqtadir to send Ḥāmid to Ibn al-Furāt.

frequently. Mufliḥ used this control to influence policy decisions. Indeed, Mufliḥ's position was sufficiently secure that he could disagree with the caliph's powerful mother and even overcome her influence on her son. Finally, we see that Mufliḥ was squarely aligned with Ibn al-Furāt; and like his predecessor Khafīf, Mufliḥ made sure to inform Ibn al-Furāt of his deeds, presumably in order to reap the benefits.

Furthermore, this anecdote enables a comparison of the relative influence at court of Mufliḥ and Naṣr. Perhaps the most obvious point, and the most important, is that Naṣr had to call for Mufliḥ, because Naṣr could not enter the harem: in short, Mufliḥ had greater access to the caliph; and in this particular case, Mufliḥ's better access was decisive, as he influenced the caliph's final decision regarding Ḥāmid. We also witness the interaction between these two palace functionaries: Naṣr not only "requests" (rather than "orders") Mufliḥ to come, he also gently urges Mufliḥ to be kind to Ḥāmid and to represent him before the caliph. In no way does Naṣr give Mufliḥ a command. The point here is the absence of hierarchy: Mufliḥ is clearly not Naṣr's subordinate; and in general the two seem to have comparable status. In broader terms, we might say that Naṣr does not control the entire palace, but rather he is one of a number of personages (which includes women) who share control over the palace. This lack of a hierarchical relationship is also shown by Mufliḥ's deception of Naṣr with regard to the representation of Ḥāmid. Surely Naṣr would discover that Mufliḥ had lied, yet Mufliḥ impudently controverts Naṣr's intentions anyway. Finally, the dispute regarding Ḥāmid's fate serves to highlight the power relations even further: Naṣr protests, but ultimately Mufliḥ makes the final decision. In sum, the senior eunuch had special access to the caliph, he leveraged this access for political influence, and in no way was he subordinate to the chamberlain.[85]

Mufliḥ's alliance with the Banū al-Furāt continued to put him at odds with Naṣr. While Ibn al-Furāt was wazir, Mufliḥ acted as his intermediary with the caliph, and in particular helped Ibn al-Furāt's son al-Muḥassin gain control of prisoners.[86] At one point the Banū al-Furāt began to plot against Naṣr. One aspect of this plot was accusing Naṣr of supporting a rebellion in Azerbaijan; when the rebellion failed, "al-Muḥassin rode to al-Muqtadir. He asked Mufliḥ to conduct him to [the caliph] without Naṣr the chamberlain being present. Mufliḥ brought him; he informed [al-Muqtadir] of the victory and told him that Naṣr the chamberlain was disappointed ... and was now concealing news of the victory from the caliph."[87] In this instance Mufliḥ gave al-Muḥassin access to the

85. Sourdel's only comment on this event is that Naṣr and Mufliḥ did nothing to help Ḥāmid (*Vizirat*, 426). This obscures the different attitudes of these two men: Naṣr was wary but supportive, whereas Mufliḥ was hostile. This also obscures the underlying tension between the two officials, and their relative leverage. Bowen's view is more accurate: "Naṣr ... was willing to befriend [Ḥāmid]; but Mufliḥ, through whom alone [Ḥāmid] could get access to al-Muqtadir, took this chance of avenging Ḥāmid's unforgiven insult" (*ʿAlī b. ʿĪsā*, 224).

86. Sourdel (*Vizirat*, 426) and Bowen (*ʿAlī b. ʿĪsā*, 226) note the many examples of this phenomenon.

87. Miskawayh, *Tajārib*, 117; similar in Hilāl al-Ṣābī, *Wuzarāʾ*, 55. The "rebellion" is a convoluted narrative involving two regional military powers, one of whom enjoyed the official appointment of the ca-

caliph precisely in order to circumvent the chamberlain, so that al-Muḥassin could slander him.[88]

As the standing of the Banū al-Furāt declined, Mufliḥ still assisted his allies, against the wishes of Naṣr. We have already seen that Naṣr detained Ibn al-Furāt, while the *ḥujarī* troops urged the caliph to arrest the wazir. It was Mufliḥ who delivered the troops' demand, most likely because he was responsible for delivering sensitive messages to the caliph. When al-Muqtadir was about to accede to the troops' demand, Mufliḥ spoke up: "'The dismissal of the wazir at the urging of this unit would be a mistake in terms of authority, a temptation to the troops (*ghilmān*).' So [al-Muqtadir] ordered him to go out to Naṣr, order him to release [Ibn al-Furāt], and tell the troops: 'With regard to your request, we will do what is appropriate, and to your liking.'"[89] Here again Mufliḥ successfully worked against Naṣr's plans because he had better access to the caliph, and thus greater influence over policy.[90]

In sum, the eunuch Mufliḥ was a curb on Naṣr's power in the palace, an alternative means of contacting and influencing the caliph. He was particularly effective vis-à-vis Naṣr for one main reason: he served the caliph in the private quarters, where Naṣr could not enter. We should also note that Naṣr had no means, or at least made no attempt that we see, to undermine Mufliḥ's influence. Even after Mufliḥ's close allies, the Banū al-Furāt, fell from power, Mufliḥ remained in service, and retained influence. The relations between Mufliḥ and Naṣr serve as an example of the potential power of both eunuchs and chamberlains, and the limitations experienced particularly by the latter.

Naṣr vs. Ibn al-Furāt: The Final Showdown

By 311/923–924 Ibn al-Furāt—now in his third and final wazirate—was embittered by the vicissitudes of court intrigue, the constant cycle of incarceration and torture; he and his son al-Muḥassin lost all restraint, and attempted to systematically arrest, torture, and kill many state dignitaries. After avenging several personal grudges and convincing

liph. During the caliphate of al-Muqtadir we hear of many such conflicts in provinces; for our purposes, the details of the conflict are unimportant: we are trying to assess the relative influence of different members of the court elite, including the palace functionaries, not trying to untangle their alliances with various military commanders in the provinces.

88. Another explicit example of the alliance between Mufliḥ and the Banū Furāt is in Hilāl al-Ṣābī (*Wuzarāʾ*, 235), where the narrator states that Mufliḥ was very close with Ibn al-Furāt, and then reports that when Ibn al-Furāt arrested a bureaucrat, Mufliḥ sent his secretary to investigate. Ibn al-Furāt told the secretary that if he thought the arrest was unjust, Ibn al-Furāt would relent with no questions asked. Ibn al-Furāt then explained his reasons for arresting the man, and Mufliḥ's secretary concurred and the man was then executed.

89. Hilāl al-Ṣābī, *Wuzarāʾ*, 59; Miskawayh, *Tajārib*, 124–25. Sourdel (*Vizirat*, 432) and Bowen (*ʿAlī b. ʿĪsā*, 239) have slightly different interpretations, largely ignoring the tensions between Naṣr and Mufliḥ.

90. Mufliḥ would continue to perform this political role, long after both Ibn al-Furāt and Naṣr were dead.

the caliph to send the general Muʾnis off to Raqqa in semiexpulsion, they turned their sights on Naṣr the chamberlain. The means by which the Banū al-Furāt schemed against Naṣr, and the defenses he employed, shed light on the chamberlain's strengths and weaknesses.

The plot against Naṣr began when Ḥāmid was still wazir in 311/923–924, while Ibn al-Furāt was in prison. Al-Muḥassin wrote a note to the caliph, delivered by Mufliḥ (translated above), guaranteeing to extract a huge sum of money from several leading figures of state. Naṣr was on that list: he and Shafīʿ al-Luʾluʾī are the only men of military background mentioned, and Naṣr is the only dignitary who commanded troops.[91] Once returned to the wazirate, Ibn al-Furāt and al-Muḥassin enacted their plan and did, in fact, scheme against each of the people on their list, including Naṣr.

One report suggests that al-Muḥassin initially tried to assassinate Naṣr. According to ʿArīb:

> Naṣr the chamberlain used to flatter al-Muḥassin and his father, by sitting with them until the middle of the night, at which point he would leave.[92] [Naṣr] heard that al-Muḥassin had promised twenty thousand dinars to twenty soldiers to kill Naṣr when the latter [departed], in one of the corridors. Naṣr became wary of al-Muḥassin and would not ride without many soldiers armed and ready. [Al-Muḥassin] plotted for the fall of Naṣr in every possible way but did not succeed.[93]

This supposed attempt to kill Naṣr failed for a few reasons: the chamberlain employed spies and thereby discovered the plot; he also had armed troops available for his own personal defense. We might also note that assassination within the royal palace was extremely difficult to execute. Perhaps learning from the tragic example of his predecessor Sawsan some fifteen years earlier, Naṣr recognized that as chamberlain he was most vulnerable outside the palace; he would venture beyond the palace walls only with substantial protection. In general, though, the tone of this anecdote depicts Naṣr on the defensive; he reacts to al-Muḥassin's threat but does not retaliate.

The other sources depict the plot against Naṣr as developing in stages. The first stage played on the caliph's constant search for revenue:

---

91. Shafīʿ al-Luʾluʾī, head of imperial intelligence (*ṣāḥib al-barīd*) undoubtedly managed a staff, but we never hear of him commanding troops. The others on Ibn al-Furāt's list of targets were bureaucrats, and Hāshimīs (Umm Mūsā and her brother).

92. The locations involved here are not clear. It would seem that Naṣr visited the wazir in the latter's chambers within the royal palace.

93. ʿArīb, *Ṣilat*, 113; referred to briefly by Bowen (*ʿAlī b. ʿĪsā*, 236). ʿArīb too easily dismisses the other attempts made to destroy Naṣr, which are described in greater detail by other sources. This anecdote is somewhat perplexing in that the Banū al-Furāt coveted Naṣr's money, which would be easier to obtain via arrest and torture, as opposed to assassination. On the other hand, all our sources depict al-Muḥassin as drunk on violence by this point.

> [Ibn al-Furāt] described to al-Muqtadir what Naṣr possessed: cash, properties, the revenue from administrative positions he held, and secret profits. Al-Muqtadir agreed to turn [Naṣr] over to him. This information reached Naṣr; he turned to al-Sayyida and asked for help, so she spoke with her son, saying: "Ibn al-Furāt has already distanced Muʾnis from you, and he is your sword, the person you trust. Now he wants to ruin your chamberlain, to control and reciprocate for what you did to him (Ibn al-Furāt): withdrawing your favor and disgracing his harem.[94] I would like to know whom you would ask for help against him if he has evil intentions toward you, such as deposing you or controlling you, given the evil he has displayed and the exaggerated behavior of his son, beyond all limits." Naṣr had gone home, distributed his money in deposits, and had gone into hiding. Al-Sayyida wrote to him to return to the palace. He trusted [her], returned, and humbled himself before Ibn al-Furāt and his son.[95]

Here we see that Ibn al-Furāt swayed the caliph by simply tempting him with Naṣr's money, suggesting that al-Muqtadir's personal loyalty to Naṣr, as with so many other people, had waned due to the caliph's financial straits. Yet on this occasion al-Sayyida intervened, and argued that with Muʾnis already absent, Naṣr was crucial for the caliph's personal safety. This is the first explicit statement of the chamberlain's most important function for the caliph, and al-Sayyida convinced al-Muqtadir that Naṣr's contribution to security was more important than his money. But we should pay close attention to Naṣr's behavior: when threatened, he asks al-Sayyida for help, goes into hiding, and ultimately humbles himself before the clearly hostile wazir. In short, Naṣr does not employ an aggressive defense, despite commanding armed units; unlike Muʾnis, who would later mobilize troops when threatened with dismissal or arrest, Naṣr shows clear signs of weakness and deference.

The next stage of the plot against Naṣr involved criticism of his hostility toward the governor of Armenia and Azerbaijan, named Ibn Abī al-Sāj. Ibn al-Furāt told al-Muqtadir that Naṣr hated Ibn Abī al-Sāj, and was responsible for the loss of millions of dinars wasted in fighting the governor.[96] Somewhat later, al-Muḥassin came to al-Muqtadir, with Mufliḥ's help, and accused Naṣr of withholding information from the caliph due to his hostility toward Ibn Abī al-Sāj.[97] The argument underlying these accusations was that Naṣr was compromising the interests of the caliph for his own purposes.

Only days after al-Muḥassin leveled these accusations against Naṣr, Ibn al-Furāt intensified the plot. An intruder was found in the ceiling of one of al-Sayyida's chambers, where al-Muqtadir often visited; among other objects the intruder was carrying a knife. Ibn al-Furāt questioned the man about his origins and purpose; the stranger refused to

---

94. She is referring to events in 299/911–912, when al-Muqtadir fired Ibn al-Furāt and permitted incursions into the latter's harem, both to extract wealth and to dishonor the senior bureaucrat.

95. Miskawayh, *Tajārib*, 117; similar in Hilāl al-Ṣābī, *Wuzarāʾ*, 54.

96. Hilāl al-Ṣābī, *Wuzarāʾ*, 54.

97. Hilāl al-Ṣābī, *Wuzarāʾ*, 55; Miskawayh, *Tajārib*, 117.

answer, and during a beating mumbled incessantly in Persian. He was then tortured to death, and his body was burned. Hilāl al-Ṣābī informs us that "people said that Ibn al-Furāt inserted the man to deceive al-Muqtadir that Naṣr was plotting against him."[98] Ibn al-Furāt did in fact make this argument before the caliph:

> Ibn al-Furāt addressed Naṣr in the caliph's presence regarding this [intruder]: "I do not think you would like to happen in your palace what just took place in [the caliph's palace]. You are his chamberlain; you are the protector of his palace! Such a thing has never happened to any caliph, of old or recent!

Ibn al-Furāt then accused Naṣr of conspiring with other enemies of the caliph, by inserting this would-be assassin, in order to kill the caliph, in exchange for a bribe. Naṣr responded to this accusation by insinuating that Ibn al-Furāt had much more reason to want revenge against al-Muqtadir, given his previous falls from power. But al-Muqtadir was not impressed by this response and said to Naṣr: "If this [incursion] had happened even to a commoner, it would be an outrage."[99]

With this event, Ibn al-Furāt had sculpted his scheme to controvert Naṣr's best possible defense. Al-Sayyida had argued that Naṣr was indispensable for the caliph's safety, questioning the loyalty of the Banū al-Furāt. Now Ibn al-Furāt had turned the tables. With the capture of the supposed assassin, Ibn al-Furāt demonstrated that Naṣr was not in fact doing his job, was not ensuring the safety of the caliph. Indeed, Ibn al-Furāt went on to suggest quite the opposite: that Naṣr was planning to kill al-Muqtadir. Earlier, the temptation of seizing Naṣr's wealth had strained al-Muqtadir's commitment to his chamberlain; now, Ibn al-Furāt argued that Naṣr was at best incompetent, and quite possibly a traitor.

This attack on Naṣr was clearly effective, for the sources state that Naṣr's position became very weak, and al-Sayyida had to continually speak with al-Muqtadir in Naṣr's defense. Naṣr was probably on his way to being disgraced, when he was saved by the Qarmatian attack on the hajj. This traumatic event discredited lbn al-Furāt, widely known as a supporter of the Shiʿa, who was now labeled a Qarmatian; and Naṣr's role of providing security became crucial, so that the caliph probably dropped any intention of dismissing him. Al-Muqtadir consulted with his long-standing chamberlain regarding the Qarmatian threat, and Naṣr used this opportunity to severely criticize Ibn al-Furāt for poor policies and destructive scheming. Soon thereafter Ibn al-Furāt was arrested, and Naṣr, along with several other commanders, encouraged the military to riot if Ibn al-Furāt was not executed. Naṣr's greatest enemy was eliminated; yet Naṣr had only been saved by an external crisis. He had shown little ability to defend himself, and within palace politics appeared relatively weak.

98. Hilāl al-Ṣābī, *Wuzarāʾ*, 55.

99. Miskawayh, *Tajārib*, 118–19; similar in Hilāl al-Ṣābī, *Wuzarāʾ*, 56. Bowen (*ʿAlī b. ʿĪsā*, 236–37) and Sourdel (*Vizirat*, 430–31) report this incident.

Naṣr's Relations with Muʾnis

With Ibn al-Furāt dead in 312/924, Naṣr's position at court should have been secure. But later that same year, the new wazir al-Khāqānī provoked the caliph against Naṣr. Once again, al-Muqtadir seriously considered arresting his chamberlain; this time, however, al-Muqtadir recalled Muʾnis (who was not far off, in Wāsiṭ), as he wanted Muʾnis present at court to witness the proceedings and to give the caliph advice. Al-Khāqānī probably approved of this, for "he was under the mistaken impression that they [Muʾnis and Naṣr] had poor relations, and people thought the two were at odds. In reality, they were like one soul."[100] Muʾnis and Naṣr met outside Baghdad, and the general expressed support for the chamberlain. Thus, when Muʾnis reached the royal palace, he told the caliph, "Master, you have never had any substitute for [Naṣr]. If not for his role as your advisor and servant, I would never be willing to leave your palace or be absent from your affairs."[101] With this rationale, Muʾnis succeeded in preventing the chamberlain's dismissal. Naṣr himself put forward a similar argument. Aware of his own fragile position, Naṣr told the caliph: "How many plots have been hatched against the Commander of the Faithful ... and he was not aware of them! God save him from making the mistake of believing slander against me." Al-Muqtadir reacted defensively to his two *mawlās*: "[He] swore to them that he never considered either of them in a negative way, and would never harm either of them as long as he lived." The narrator concludes, "Thus Naṣr's position was strengthened and supported by Muʾnis."[102]

These events bring to mind themes that we have already seen. Al-Muqtadir was easily convinced by a wazir to arrest the chamberlain, though on this occasion no motives are stated. Here, as earlier, Naṣr's responsibility for the caliph's security (among other responsibilities) is invoked in the chamberlain's defense. As well, the chamberlain's potential military support is recognized by the caliph, for al-Muqtadir did not want to arrest Naṣr without the presence of Muʾnis, who could provide a military counterweight should Naṣr's dismissal provoke troop riots. More generally, Naṣr was able to escape the machinations of a wazir, and eventually turn the tables, getting the bureaucrat fired. We should note that Naṣr's escape, as before, depended upon the assistance of an outside party: this time, Muʾnis. Once again Naṣr does not seem to have the power to fend off such threats without help from allies.

Our source, ʿArīb, claims that Muʾnis and Naṣr were on excellent terms; but the view of al-Khāqānī and "people" in general suggests that a certain amount of tension existed in this relationship. In 315/927 this tension came out in the open. Naṣr worked for the dismissal of the wazir ʿAlī b. ʿĪsā, for he disliked the alliance between ʿAlī and Muʾnis, and wanted to weaken Muʾnis's influence within the palace. We have already seen that Naṣr

100. ʿArīb, *Ṣilat*, 123

101. ʿArīb, *Ṣilat*, 125.

102. This entire affair, reported by ʿArīb (*Ṣilat*, 123–25), is referred to by Sourdel (*Vizirat*, 436–37), but he does not relate that Muʾnis defended Naṣr.

promoted other waziral candidates in the past. Once ʿAlī was arrested, Naṣr contrived to have him accused of being a Qarmatian agent; only al-Sayyida's intervention with the caliph saved ʿAlī from being tortured.[103] These events again show the relative strengths and weaknesses of the chamberlain: with his proximity and regular access to the caliph, Naṣr managed to incriminate a wazir and contrive for his removal. Yet the chamberlain's true adversary at this late date was Muʾnis, and Naṣr could only damage Muʾnis by attacking a proxy: the wazir. Naṣr could not actually threaten Muʾnis himself. It is particularly striking that while this was basically a conflict between two military men, no troops are involved in the conflict, and rivalries are played out through bureaucratic proxies.

Naṣr's Final Responsibility: Commanding Troops

Naṣr's growing feud with Muʾnis was dwarfed by the Qarmatian approach to Baghdad in 315/927 and 316/928. Throughout Naṣr's tenure, there are fleeting indications of the chamberlain's control of troops: early on he led an army against rebellious bedouin; his secretary supposedly supervised the payments of certain troops; and Naṣr complained to al-Muqtadir that Ibn al-Furāt had cut the salaries of the *maṣāffī* troops under his control. The sources are more explicit about his leadership role during the defense of Baghdad. Naṣr led contingents of the *ḥujarīs*, *maṣāffīs*, and cavalry out of Baghdad, reportedly coordinating the movements of all the caliph's troops in confronting the Qarmatians as the latter approached the city. At a crucial moment Abū al-Hayjāʾ the Ḥamdānid advised Naṣr to cut a bridge, to hinder the Qarmatian advance; Naṣr hesitated but eventually agreed and gave the order. This brief account confirms that Naṣr was in charge of the defense of the imperial capital.[104] When the Qarmatians were forced to halt their advance, Naṣr planned a counteroffensive; but the attack was called off when Naṣr became sick. The army returned to Baghdad but had to come out to confront the Qarmatians again the following year (316/928). Naṣr again fell ill and this time he died. His corpse was carried back to Baghdad, where he was buried.[105]

Conclusion: Balance of Power within the Royal Palace

I set out to analyze the power structure within the royal palace: how different officials manipulated power, the limitations on their respective leverage, and the extent of a hierarchy. I also endeavored to test Pipes's dichotomy of government versus military slaves, the essential difference being possession of military force. While the material available in our sources is limited, the examination of palace officials enables some tentative hypotheses regarding power in the palace.

103. Miskawayh, *Tajārib*, 186–87.
104. Miskawayh, *Tajārib*, 176–77.
105. Miskawayh, *Tajārib*, 183.

The most prominent official of this era was Naṣr the chamberlain. Naṣr was entrusted with a variety of responsibilities, chief among them control over access to the caliph, which made him an intermediary link between the caliph and those outside the palace, particularly bureaucrats. Like his predecessor Khafīf, Naṣr used this status as intermediary to plot for or against various court officials. Yet the chamberlain's power could be circumvented, for he was not the only palace official with most reliable access to the caliph, and bureaucrats could employ other palace figures as means of communicating with the caliph. Palace women often served this function; but Naṣr's most consistent rival was Mufliḥ, the senior eunuch, who supported the chamberlain's enemies and successfully undermined his position on several occasions.

These observations lead to more general points. First, the palace did not have a single hierarchy of authority. Female officials were nominally under the control of the caliph's mother, yet they seem to have pursued independent policies and alliances. The chief eunuch also had an independent agenda. The chamberlain neither supervised nor dominated these officials. Second, the manipulation of power in the palace to a great extent involved spatial access. The chamberlain controlled access to the royal palace, and to some extent within the palace, in ceremonies and daily state business that might involve the caliph; this access to the interior of the palace was his source of power. This prerogative was undermined, to an extent, by women and eunuchs precisely because Naṣr could not prevent them from meeting with the caliph, and more importantly because they could attend the caliph precisely when and where the chamberlain could not: in his private quarters, and in the harem. To a great extent, power derived from the space people were allowed to enter, and the chamberlain could enter only so far.[106]

In this competition for influence within the palace, the chamberlain had one potential source of power others did not: he was a trained commander in charge of troops, and presumably had established relations of patronage and loyalty with these troops. According to Pipes's generalization, Naṣr should have been able to employ this military power base in order to dominate the palace.[107] The big surprise with Naṣr is that he never seems to have done this: he never openly used the troops at his disposal for political advantage. In his times of hardship—the execution of al-Ḥallāj, and more importantly the attacks on his position by Ibn al-Furāt and al-Khāqānī—Naṣr is frightened and goes into

106. We might recall that, in the letter he sent the caliph in 317/929, Muʾnis demanded that the women and eunuchs in the palace be banished. This demand confirms two points: these groups within the royal palace were powerful; and the best way of eliminating their influence was to remove them from within the palace. These groups did not have a powerful constituency, or command men at arms; but they had access to the caliph.

107. Here enters the big question regarding Mufliḥ. He was also supposedly in charge of troops, yet we know nothing of his background, nor do we see him in command. Was he basically a general in palace service, like Naṣr? Or a servant with control over small units of eunuchs? In any case, Mufliḥ certainly did not wield the same kind of military leadership as Naṣr, both before and during his official position within the royal palace.

hiding, seeks help from al-Sayyida and Muʾnis. Unlike Muʾnis, who would later mobilize troops and threaten rebellion (and ultimately make good on these threats) when faced with dismissal or imprisonment, Naṣr never mobilized troops to support his own position.

In general, we might say that Naṣr represented the juncture of palace service and military service. He was a military man whose position entailed a continued presence in the palace. Naṣr benefited from both aspects of his office: he enjoyed special access to the caliph, which he used for political influence, while his crucial role as defender of the palace, based upon military training, made him nearly indispensable to an otherwise disaffected caliph. But Naṣr only dominated these domains partially: unlike Mufliḥ he did not have total access to the caliph, and unlike Muʾnis he could not mobilize sufficient troops in order to reinforce his political position. With regard to the dichotomy established by Pipes, we see that the chamberlain was neither a true government slave nor a military slave, but rather an interesting combination of the two.

We should remember that Naṣr survived the continual political intriguing, and died of illness. In general, the most powerful figures in the palace—al-Sayyida, Mufliḥ, Zaydān, and Naṣr—maintained their positions even when protégés or allies were disgraced and/or executed.

This leaves us with a basic question: why did palace officials become so much more politically influential in this period? I believe that the increase in their influence is directly related to al-Muqtadir's style of rulership. Because al-Muqtadir, unlike his father, was a private rather than a public ruler, it was more difficult to acquire access to him. With the caliph passing most of his time in the royal palace, the only way to communicate with him was by way of an official in the palace. Moreover, as we shall see below, al-Muqtadir intensified the atmosphere of competition by constantly removing wazirs. The scheming that resulted provided palace officials with many occasions to either help or hurt bureaucrats, while they themselves were virtually immune to the effects of this scheming.[108]

108. *El Cheikh subsequently arrived at much the same conclusion: "The seclusion of the caliph ... accentuated the need of various power groups around the caliph for intermediaries"; and "The degree of power wielded by those in the palace corresponded not to the hierarchy of positions but, rather, to the frequency of access to the caliph" (van Berkel et al, *Crisis and Continuity*, 162, 163).

Chapter 4. The Military

In this chapter I analyze the Abbasid military of this era, with the goal of trying to understand its component parts, as well as the relations and tensions that characterize the institution. I begin by examining the revitalization of the army under al-Muwaffaq and al-Muʿtaḍid, and the ethic they instilled in their forces. This structure and ethic would carry over into the reign of al-Muqtadir, and would shape the way generals, troops, and the caliph responded to a period of financial and political chaos. I will argue that while the Abbasid military is generally seen as centralized and hierarchical, led by powerful commanders-in-chief (such as Badr and Muʾnis) and founded upon mutual loyalties and obligations, to a great extent the military was actually characterized by decentralization and chronic disloyalty. In the end, the decline of caliphal authority did not lead to a centralized military dictatorship, but to a complex of regional military competitors, the logical extension of a decentralized military. It was only with the later arrival of someone from outside this system, with different kinds of relations and distant sources of men and money—the Būyids—that military power was once again centralized.

The Policies of al-Muʿtaḍid and al-Muktafī

Since the caliphate of al-Muʿtaṣim (218–227/833–842), the Abbasid military had been dominated by slave soldiers. The theory behind importing these soldiers was presumably that they would be exceptional warriors, devoted to their Abbasid patrons/masters; yet during the Samarra period these soldiers usurped power from the Abbasid ruler, and initiated a period of political chaos.[1] Beginning in the 250s (mid-860s), the regent al-Muwaffaq (d. 278/891) and his son al-Muʿtaḍid—the real powers during the caliphate of al-Muʿtamid (256–279/870–892)—were determined to reassert caliphal authority over the military. The cornerstone of this revival was personal command of the army in battle, which facilitated closer relations with generals and troops, and prevented the empowerment of leading commanders. Through a series of policies instituted before and during his caliphate, al-Muʿtaḍid developed a system that curbed the power of individual generals, and concentrated military might in the hands of the caliph. Under capable rulers with plentiful funds, these policies forged a highly effective military and a supremely powerful caliph.

1. *For more on the military during this era of the Abbasid caliphate, see Gordon, *Breaking of a Thousand Swords*.

Al-Muʿtaḍid's Army: The Troops

Al-Muʿtaḍid's army likely included thousands of troops, about whom we know very little. These soldiers came from a variety of ethnic groups; presumably many of them were mercenaries, and others were the children of Abbasid soldiers from previous periods. The most important troops in al-Muʿtaḍid's army, as with previous Abbasids, were the numerous military slaves that he purchased, generally referred to as his *ghilmān*. We do not possess any statistics regarding the number of al-Muʿtaḍid's recruits; a generation later, under al-Muqtadir, most of the leading military figures (such as Muʾnis, Naṣr, and Nāzūk) were freedmen (*mawlās*) of al-Muʿtaḍid. This infusion of hand-picked foreigners was presumably intended, in accordance with standard Abbasid theory, to enhance military loyalty to the caliph; and in the hands of a capable and inspiring military leader such as the caliph al-Muʿtaḍid, this strategy was effective.[2]

Another means used by al-Muʿtaḍid for filling the military ranks was to attract soldiers from rival armies, and to absorb the surrendering soldiers of defeated armies. This policy was used on a large scale in the war with the Zanj (255–270/869–883), when al-Muwaffaq and al-Muʿtaḍid offered gifts and stipends to rebels who joined the caliphal army, and then displayed these turncoats before their former comrades to encourage further desertion.[3] Al-Muʿtaḍid continued this policy during his reign, on a variety of occasions: in 281/794 the commander al-Ḥasan b. ʿAlī Kūrah abandoned the rebel Rāfiʿ b. Harthama, and led one thousand troops to Baghdad;[4] the following year, when Ḥamdān b. Ḥamdūn had fled before the caliph's forces, his son al-Ḥusayn and many Kurdish troops received guarantees of safe conduct;[5] and in 287/900 al-Muʿtaḍid offered safety to the dispersed troops of the vanquished rebel Waṣīf al-Khādim.[6] In this last case al-Muʿtaḍid even forbade his own troops from looting the routed soldiers' camp, a gesture of generosity that succeeded in attracting the rebel's soldiers. This policy of offering amnesty, protection, and patronage to erstwhile opponents was effective in undermining opponent morale, swelling the caliph's military ranks, and creating a general reputation for al-Muʿtaḍid as a victorious and munificent ruler.

Yet the continual encouragement of desertion in return for benefits fostered a dangerous military ethic: that military service was granted only in exchange for benefits, and that soldiers had the right to switch patrons if that were beneficial for them. Under

2. For example, we have seen that at the death of al-Muktafī, al-Muʿtaḍid's *ghilmān* insisted that one of their patron's offspring should become caliph. Of course, this was in their best interest—and that was the point of bringing them into the military, that their best interest should coincide with that of the ruling caliph and his immediate family.

3. al-Ṭabarī, *History*, 37:43.

4. al-Ṭabarī, *History*, 38:15.

5. al-Ṭabarī, *History*, 38:21–22.

6. al-Ṭabarī, *History*, 38:90.

a well-funded and capable leader like al-Muʿtaḍid this ethic was advantageous; under a weaker and poorer caliph this ethic would bring disaster.

Al-Muʿtaḍid's army was divided into several large corps, about which Hilāl al-Ṣābī provides detailed, though somewhat confusing information.[7] The largest corps was the infantry, "*al-rajjāla*," comprising distinct "white" and "black" divisions. The white infantry included several units, the most prominent of which was the *maṣāffiyya* who were stationed at the *Bāb al-ʿĀmma* of the royal palace.[8] The black infantry consisted of slaves purchased by al-Muwaffaq from Egypt and Mecca, and the many Zanj soldiers who were given amnesty.[9] A second small corps, referred to as the "*ghilmān*," was divided into the *ghilmān al-khāṣṣa*, the corps that produced most of the chamberlains;[10] and the *ghilmān al-ḥujariyya*, comprised primarily of al-Muʿtaḍid's *mamlūks*, who were stationed inside the royal palace. As with the *maṣāffīs*, it is only the *ḥujarīs* that ever appear as an active, distinct unit among all the *ghilmān*.[11] In general, it is very important to note these groupings of the *rajjāla maṣāffiyya* and the *ghilmān al-ḥujariyya* never fight as a combined, unified corps; rather, it would seem that each corps was more a pool of soldiers, presumably made up of smaller units, and that these units were given temporary assignments under temporary commanders. Indeed, supporting this general hypothesis is the fact that we never hear of any commanders who are specifically attached to any corps; the generals who lead the *maṣāffīs* or *ḥujarīs* on campaign change with every report, and we most frequently hear that a group of *rajjāla* or *ghilmān al-ḥujariyya* were (temporarily) assigned to a particular general. In short, these corps do not seem to form a pyramidal structure, with a hierarchy of officers culminating in a fixed general; rather, the impression given is that these corps consisted of many small units that were assigned to leading commanders on an ad-hoc basis.

The organization of a third general corps, the cavalry (*fursān*) is somewhat clearer. Apparently the entire cavalry was inspected and tested by the caliph himself.[12] Outstanding warriors were set aside by al-Muʿtaḍid for his personal service (labeled *ʿaskar*

7. The information is confusing because it is presented in a budget that was updated several times over the course of decades, and the layers are difficult to distinguish (See Busse, "Hofbudget").

8. Hilāl al-Ṣābī, *Wuzarāʾ*, 15.

9. Hilāl al-Ṣābī, *Wuzarāʾ*, 15–16. We might note that the white infantry were paid more than the black infantry, and that the latter received food rations to supplement their income.

10. According to Hilāl al-Ṣābī, the *ghilmān al-khāṣṣa* included the freedmen of al-Muwaffaq, mixed in with the *quwwād* ("commanders") and *mawālī* (*Wuzarāʾ*, 16). I do not understand why *quwwād*, generally meaning commanders, are often referred to collectively as distinct from *ghilmān* and *mawālī*, when in other cases the *quwwād* clearly derive from these two and other groups. In general, the terminology in this budgetary report is difficult to decipher.

11. In other words, the *maṣāffīs* and *ḥujarīs* are the two important units in the palace complex. Apparently *maṣāffīs* were stationed at the *Bāb al-ʿāmma*, probably the outer part of the complex, while the *ḥujarīs* were inside the palace. It is impossible to know their functions for certain, and it is not clear if the *ḥujarīs* were trained as infantry or cavalry (though probably the latter).

12. This is described by Hilāl al-Ṣābī (*Wuzarāʾ*, 17), who provides all our details for this military unit.

al-khāṣṣa); mediocre horsemen were assigned to the standing army that defended the Khurāsān Road (called *ʿaskar al-khidma*) under the leading general Badr; and the least talented cavalrymen were sent to the provinces to assist in levying taxation and providing security. We should note, though, that despite this straightforward and apparently permanent distribution of cavalry, the *fursān* are later mentioned repeatedly in texts, but the commanders from within the *fursān* are never mentioned by name, and units from the corps are temporarily assigned to a variety of leading generals. As with the *rajjāla* and *ghilmān al-ḥujariyya*, the *fursān* undoubtedly had their own officers, but apparently no fixed higher command, and units from each of these corps were assigned to leading generals on a somewhat temporary basis.[13]

The Commanding Officers

With the generals who led al-Muʿtaḍid's army we are on firmer ground in the sources, and we derive a better idea of the flexibility and diffused hierarchy of the military. First, we can note that virtually every campaign not conducted by al-Muʿtaḍid himself was led by a different commander: for example, Waṣīf Mūshgīr and Naṣr al-Qushūrī were sent to capture a rebellious Ibn Ḥamdūn;[14] al-Ḥusayn b. Ḥamdān and Muʾnis al-Khāzin were dispatched on different occasions to confront Khārijites and rebellious bedouin;[15] and Badr was entrusted twice with recapturing Fārs.[16] In other words, responsibility was spread around, and military authority was not concentrated. Interestingly, roughly half of the most important commanders—al-Ḥusayn b. Ḥamdān, al-Ḥasan b. ʿAlī Kūrah, Khāqān al-Mufliḥī, Ibn Kundāj, Khumushjūr, and several others—defected to al-Muʿtaḍid from rivals or enemies, and each of them was given command of troops and sent on missions within a few years. Most of these commanders did not bring sizeable troop units with them; and the high proportion of such newly integrated officers meant that soldiers did not have long-standing loyalties to relatively new commanders, nor did commanders from different backgrounds have established alliances or bonds. The frequent infusion of new soldiers, especially officers, prevented the military from coalescing around certain interests or leaders.

The troops commanded by these numerous generals were probably of two types: first, each general undoubtedly had his own personal soldiers, probably military slaves that he had trained and freed, though we have remarkably little evidence of them for this period. These freedmen, perhaps in addition to relatives and sons, constituted a general's

---

13. In the description of the review of the *fursān*, Hilāl al-Ṣābī relates (*Wuzarāʾ*, 17) that every commander brought a list of his men and their salaries. The troops, however, were then redistributed.

*Kennedy also describes the different military regiments (in van Berkel et al, *Crisis and Continuity*, 114–19).

14. al-Ṭabarī, *History*, 38:20.

15. al-Ṭabarī, *History*, 38:27, 79.

16. al-Ṭabarī, *History*, 38:23, 95.

permanent force. These troops were substantially augmented, for specific campaigns or missions, by detachments of the *rajjāla*, *ghilmān al-ḥujariyya*, and/or *fursān*. As argued above, these detachments seem to have been entrusted to generals only on a temporary basis, which prevented them from creating large standing armies that could threaten the caliph.

The man with the highest rank in the army, and supposedly in control of the entire military, was Badr, the *mawlā* of al-Muᶜtaḍid. He is referred to as "*amīr*" while all other generals had the title "*qāʾid*;" he attended al-Muᶜtaḍid's inspection of the *fursān*, along with the wazir ᶜUbaydallāh b. Sulaymān;[17] and a popular saying from the era held that no administration benefited from such cooperation as when al-Muᶜtaḍid was caliph, ᶜUbaydallāh was wazir, Ibn al-Furāt was head of the chancellery (*dīwān*), and Badr was commander of the military (*amīr al-jaysh*).[18] This elite status and lofty praise encouraged al-Ṭabarī and later Ibn al-Jawzī to sum up the situation by saying that "Badr was the commander of al-Muᶜtaḍid's army and controlled his affairs."[19] Charles Pellat has gone one step further, arguing that "[Badr] played a political role of prime importance, for he became all powerful, with complete domination over the caliph, and exercising a veto over everything."[20]

While Badr was indisputably the official chief of the military, and participated in important political decisions, close scrutiny of his activities under al-Muᶜtaḍid indicates that he did not have real control over the entire military and certainly did not dominate the caliph. For the first three years of al-Muᶜtaḍid's reign, Badr was chief of police, presumably occupied with Baghdadi security and not with broader military affairs.[21] In 282/895, an ᶜAlid agitator distributing money in Iraq was arrested and brought to Badr's home, whereupon Badr asked the caliph what to do with the man; Badr's lack of initiative and deference to the caliph on this occasion are very obvious.[22] That same year (282/895), Badr was dispatched along with the wazir ᶜUbaydallāh to Rayy, to hunt down a rebel from the Dulaf family; the two remained in that region, as well as in Jibāl, through at least 285/898.[23] Stationed outside the capital for several years, and with no administrative duties (or financial opportunities) due to the presence of the wazir, Badr was obviously not in charge of either the armed forces, located in Baghdad, or the caliph's affairs in general. We first hear that Badr was back in Baghdad in 287/900, when he investigated the welfare of the populace and oversaw general security; but only one year later, Badr was again dispatched as governor of Fārs, where he was located when al-Muᶜtaḍid died in

17. Hilāl al-Ṣābī, *Wuzarāʾ*, 17.
18. Hilāl al-Ṣābī, *Wuzarāʾ*, 209.
19. al-Ṭabarī, *History*, 38:105; Ibn al-Jawzī, *al-Muntaẓam*, 5:34–35.
20. Pellat, "Badr," *EI2 Supplement*, 117.
21. al-Ṭabarī, *History*, 38:1.
22. al-Ṭabarī, *History*, 38:24–25.
23. al-Ṭabarī, *History*, 38:23, 70.

289/902.[24] Thus while Badr was the highest ranking officer in the military and certainly had some influence in governmental affairs, he could only have had limited involvement given that he was distant from Baghdad for most of al-Muʿtaḍid's reign. Indeed, we might hypothesize that the caliph intentionally removed his leading general from the capital, and kept him under the supervision of the wazir, in order to retain effective control of the military for himself.

Political machinations following the death of al-Muʿtaḍid in 289/902 reveal the limited control that Badr actually possessed over the military and are the best example we have of the flexible structure of the army. At some point while al-Muʿtaḍid was still alive, the new wazir al-Qāsim b. ʿUbaydallāh suggested to Badr that they arrange for the accession of an Abbasid from a different branch of the family. Badr refused to cooperate, citing loyalty to his master al-Muʿtaḍid; without the necessary support of the leading general, al-Qāsim gave up the plan. When al-Muʿtaḍid died and his son al-Muktafī became caliph, the wazir al-Qāsim feared that Badr might reveal his earlier proposal for an alternative caliph so al-Qāsim plotted against Badr (at the time in Fārs), and persuaded al-Muktafī to arrest the general. The caliph and wazir first tried to reduce the forces under Badr's command:

> Al-Muktafī reportedly sent Muḥammad b. Kumushjūr and a number of officers with messages and dispatches for the officers who were with Badr, ordering them to break away from Badr and come to him.... When al-Muktafī's dispatches reached the officers attached to Badr, a number of them left Badr and departed for [Baghdad], among them al-ʿAbbās b. ʿAmr al-Ghanawī, Khāqān al-Mufliḥī, Muḥammad b. Isḥāq b.Kundāj, Khafīf al-Adhkūtakīnī, and a number of others.[25]

All four of the officers who abandoned Badr were important generals, each of whom had previously led expeditions of his own. As well, Khāqān and Ibn Kundāj were fairly new in the Abbasid army, having defected from Ṭulūnid patronage six years earlier.[26] Thus a large part of Badr's forces in Fārs was commanded by men who did not have established ties with Badr, but had only been attached to his force for this particular mission. We should not be too surprised, therefore, that they heeded the recall from Baghdad, undermining Badr's military strength.

When Badr realized that there was a plot brewing against him, he set off for Iraq; al-Muktafī responded by arresting some of Badr's soldiers and officers who had remained in Baghdad. Badr reached Wāsiṭ and intended to approach the capital; but "when Badr left Wāsiṭ, he was deserted by his men and by most of his soldiers."[27] Al-Muktafī then duped Badr by offering him a guarantee of safe conduct; when Badr accepted, Ibn Kundāj (who

24. al-Ṭabarī, *History*, 38:82, 95.
25. al-Ṭabarī, *History*, 38:105–6; Ibn al-Athīr, *al-Kāmil*, 6:518.
26. al-Ṭabarī, *History*, 38:30.
27. al-Ṭabarī, *History*, 38:108.

had abandoned Badr in Fārs) brought the general into Baghdad, where he turned him over to an assassin named Luʾluʾ. This Luʾluʾ, himself a recent deserter from a rebel army, took Badr to an island and cut off his head.[28]

This episode demonstrates the diffuse nature of al-Muʿtaḍid's military, and the flimsy loyalties that the caliph's policies had intentionally produced. Much of the military consisted of autonomous commanders with their own troops, such as Khāqān al-Mufliḥī and Ibn Kundāj; and though these commanders might on occasion be individually or collectively placed under the command of Badr, they remained essentially independent units that quickly broke away from the supposed military chief. What's more, Badr could not even rely on the loyalty of his own troops, who also abandoned him and returned to Baghdad.

In summary, al-Muʿtaḍid had fashioned a military in which loyalty and power were focused on the caliph and which were prevented from concentrating in the hands of a premier general. The army was divided into a constellation of commanders, few of whom had grown up or trained in the same system: they thus had few or no bonds to one another, and only a common patron in the caliph. Al-Muʿtaḍid siphoned off the best soldiers for elite units that remained in the capital, who went on missions only with the caliph. By venturing out frequently on campaign, al-Muʿtaḍid filled the role of commander-in-chief himself; and under this energetic and charismatic caliph, the concentration of military power in the caliph's hands was very effective.

The Military under Al-Muktafī

Al-Muʿtaḍid's successor al-Muktafī, and his wazir al-Qāsim b. ʿUbaydallāh, followed a similar policy of diffused military hierarchy, albeit with slight modifications. In 290/903 the Qarmatians were ravaging Syria, and al-Muktafī and his wazir responded by dispatching a substantial part of the military to confront them. According to al-Ṭabarī,

> Al-Qāsim b. ʿUbaydallāh sent troops against [the Qarmatian leader], putting Muḥammad b. Sulaymān al-Kātib, who headed the Ministry of the Army, in charge of the campaign. Al-Qāsim attached all the officers to him and commanded them to obey him loyally. Muḥammad proceeded from al-Raqqah with a substantial army and wrote the officers in advance that they were to obey him loyally.[29]

Badr, the previous chief commander, had been assassinated the year before; therefore the wazir al-Qāsim appointed Muḥammad b. Sulaymān to lead the collection of armed forces, and coordinate this critical campaign. We should note a few features of Muḥammad's commission that are typical of the Abbasid military of the time: first, troops were at-

28. al-Ṭabarī, *History*, 38:109.
29. al-Ṭabarī, *History*, 38:133.

tached to Muḥammad b. Sulaymān specifically for this campaign; like all commanding officers (and in particular this Muḥammad, who seemingly held a bureaucratic post in the military ministry) he was not entrusted with a permanent force. In addition, the specific order that the officers obey Muḥammad b. Sulaymān is reiterated, for the officers were accustomed to independent command, and were not used to receiving orders, certainly not from this individual. At least twenty-one important generals are listed as participating in this campaign, most of whom led other campaigns in their own right.[30] Among these commanders were men who had abandoned Badr just the year before, so Muḥammad b. Sulaymān could hardly assume they would follow his command. Finally, since Muḥammad b. Sulaymān was apparently a bureaucrat, the caliph could endow him with central command and incur less of a threat that he might unify the military and rebel than if command had been given to a powerful general. In sum, the many branches of the Abbasid military were sent on the campaign, and the central authorities recognized (and partially intended) that Muḥammad b. Sulaymān would have a difficult time commanding the loyalties of these various generals.

One year later (in 291/904), Muḥammad b. Sulaymān was again sent on campaign in charge of several officers, this time against the faltering Ṭulūnids in Egypt. On this occasion the caliph himself apparently emphasized to the commanders that they were to obey Muḥammad b. Sulaymān.[31] This campaign was also typical in that Muḥammad b. Sulaymān achieved victory by luring the opponent's officers to change sides, in exchange for guarantees of safe conduct.[32] Badr al- Ḥammāmī, the leading Ṭulūnid general, abandoned the Ṭulūnids for Muḥammad b. Sulaymān, and was followed by much of the Ṭulūnid army. In accordance with standard practice, Badr al-Ḥammāmī was given a high rank and troops, and later that same year he returned to Egypt on behalf of the caliph to put down a rebellion—more evidence of the quickly shifting loyalties of the time.

But in keeping with Abbasid military policy, al-Muktafī and al-Qāsim b. ʿUbaydallāh did not want military force concentrated in one person's hands. Thus, immediately following the successful campaigns against the Qarmatians and the Ṭulūnids, Muḥammad b. Sulaymān was abruptly arrested, and the army was again left without even a nominal head.[33] For the remaining three years of al-Muktafī's brief reign, different commanders were put in charge of the various military campaigns, and on each occasion troops were temporarily attached to their command.[34] The Abbasid military remained intentionally decentralized.

30. al-Ṭabarī, *History*, 38:138–39.

31. al-Ṭabarī, *History*, 38:146.

32. al-Ṭabarī, *History*, 38:151.

33. al-Ṭabarī, *History*, 38:154 (in year 292/905). No explanation is given for this arrest in al-Ṭabarī.

34. Examples: Ibn Kundājīq (al-Ṭabarī, *History*, 38:160); Waṣīf b. Ṣawārtakīn (al-Ṭabarī *History*, 38:179); Badr al-Ḥammāmī (al-Ṭabarī, *History*, 38:183); Khāqān al-Mufliḥī (al-Ṭabarī, *History*, 38:184).

The Early Reign of al-Muqtadir

The first half of al-Muqtadir's reign was a period of gradual transition. As far as we can tell, the main features of the Abbasid military—decentralized authority and shifting loyalties—continued throughout the period. But one change that followed the accession of this young ruler was that unlike bureaucrats, who would be replaced with dizzying rapidity, military commanders enjoyed long tenures in office, certainly longer than under al-Muʿtaḍid and al-Muktafī. Decentralized authority was maintained, however, in that the large number of officers effectively balanced one another. Because these men retained command, we have a fair amount of information about them and can summarize the main activities for different official posts and analyze relations within the military elite. As the empire declined and external threats increased, military power began to be concentrated in the hands of one commander: Muʾnis. However, this consolidation of force was only remarkable in contrast to the limited authority of Muʾnis's predecessors (such as Badr), and he was still severely constrained by the diffuse structure of the Abbasid military.

The fractured nature of the Abbasid military at al-Muqtadir's accession, and the benefits therein for the Abbasid ruler, are demonstrated by the failed coup of 296/908. The sources agree that "commanders, bureaucrats, and judges" organized and led the coup attempt; yet while the bureaucrats and judges who participated are immediately listed by name, we have no such information regarding the military figures who participated in the coup. I would speculate that the important military officials at the time were so numerous, with no particular dominant figure, that even contemporary historians could not identify a military leadership.[35] Moreover, this group of military leaders was not cohesive. Al-Ḥusayn b. Ḥamdān, the one commander named as taking an active role, abandoned the coup amidst speculation that he had cut a deal with the caliph's loyalist supporters. The rest of the military scattered when attacked by loyalist troops, and completely abandoned the intended beneficiary of the coup, Ibn al-Muʿtazz, who was left alone to search for a place to hide. In short, the rebellious soldiers did not act as a unified group because Abbasid policy had discouraged cohesion and centralized leadership.

As for the loyalist troops, these were the elite *ghilmān* (probably the *ghilmān al-ḥujariyya*) whom al-Muʿtaḍid had selected and housed in his palace for just such an event. They had been kept separate from other military units to make them a bastion of loyalty

35. We should keep in mind that in 290/903, six years earlier, as many as twenty-one generals were listed as participating in the campaign against the Qarmatians. In both that campaign and the coup of 296/908, al-Ḥusayn b. Ḥamdān played a prominent role, yet he is never mentioned as leading either event, or as giving orders to other commanders. We also hear from a late source that Ibn ʿAmrawayh the police chief had gathered his men in support of the coup, but they scattered when attacked by a mob (Ibn al-Athīr, *al-Kāmil*, 8:17), again demonstrating the lack of military cohesion. However, we know that our sources focus more attention on individual bureaucrats and judges in general, so the absence of information about military personages is possibly, in part, the personal bias of the authors of our sources.

to the Abbasids, and this strategy worked. These men were also unified by their common status as *mawlās* purchased and trained by al-Muʿtaḍid, while many of the other commanders and troops had been absorbed into the Abbasid military from rivals and thus had less internal cohesion, less loyalty to the Abbasids in particular, and less of an ethic of loyalty in general. However, when we examine the loyalist officers, despite their loyalty and relative cohesiveness, they too do not seem to have a clear leadership. Five men—Ṣāfī, Sawsan, Gharīb, Muʾnis al-Khāzin, and Muʾnis al-Khādim—are mentioned as leading the defense of the palace, but none of them is said to predominate over the others, nor do we know which (if any) of them commanded the elite *ḥujarī* troops. Indeed, the figure who took the most decisive action, Muʾnis al-Khādim, in his counterattack and rout of the opposition forces was easily the lowest ranking member from that group of five men.[36] The impression we derive is that, probably by design, there was no clear hierarchy among the military figures located in the palace.

The Military Structure: Decentralized

For at least fifteen years following the failed coup, the Abbasid military structure remained for the most part unchanged. There were a number of leading officers, each one independent of the others; each possessed a loyal corps of *ghilmān* whom they had obtained (probably purchased) and trained; and each officer would be assigned a body of troops for a particular campaign.[37] As far as we can tell, the mass of troops was divided into the *rajjāla*, *fursān*, and *ghilmān al-ḥujariyya*, the latter corps being much smaller than the first two. The financial crises that plagued the government severely affected these corps, and we hear of many riots in these years, most of which were triggered by late salary payments.[38] While the riots do not provide much information about the soldiers themselves, they do give us an idea regarding military organization. First of all, no two corps are ever said to have rioted together, which suggests that they did not unite despite facing common problems. Perhaps the rationale behind paying these troops on different

---

36. Ṣāfī was the senior eunuch, Sawsan was chamberlain, Gharīb was the new caliph's uncle, and Muʾnis al-Khāzin was the treasurer, and formerly (and soon to be reappointed) chief of police. Muʾnis al-Khādim had no known post at this time.

37. For example: in 297/910, "al-Muqtadir sent al-Qāsim b. Simā on the summer raid of the Byzantine frontier, along with a large part of the army" (ʿArīb, *Ṣilat*, 33); or when Subkarā rebelled in Fārs, "Waṣīf Kāmah, the *ghulām* of al-Muwaffaq, was put in charge of fighting him. Along with him were sent leading generals, including al-Ḥusayn b. Ḥamdān, Badr the *ghulām* of al-Nūsharī, and Badr the elder, known as al-Ḥammāmī" (ʿArīb, *Ṣilat*, 34). These and other examples show that generals, when sent on campaign, were given temporary control of additional forces. We know these arrangements were temporary since the commanders sent with Waṣīf, lbn Ḥamdān and Badr al-Ḥammāmī, led other campaigns. In sum, these examples tell us that there was no centralized standing army, and hence no single powerful general.

38. Waines has reviewed the numerous riots ("Caliph and Amir," 69–70; 76–78).

schedules was precisely to prevent such a united front.[39] Also, no individuals are ever mentioned as leading these corps; and the simple fact that they resorted to riots indicates that they had no established link with any particular high-ranking commander who could act as their spokesman in the palace. In short, these riots support the earlier hypothesis of an organizational divide between the large corps of troops and the military commanders.

We get a glimpse of the decentralized nature of the military in the death notice, from the year 311/923–924, of Yānis al-Muwaffaqī. ʿArīb relates that Yānis held a high rank in government, commanded one thousand *fursān*, *ghilmān*, and eunuchs stationed near his home, and possessed great wealth and property. When Yānis died, Naṣr the chamberlain advised the caliph to send the heir apparent, prince Abū al-ʿAbbās, to seize Yānis's wealth and take control of his troops. Ibn al-Furāt, however, dissuaded the caliph from this course of action.[40] From this episode we see that Yānis was considered an important officer, with elite status, money, and men at arms. Yet Yānis was not among the handful of officers who led noteworthy campaigns, nor is he ever mentioned as influential in the capital. This suggests that beyond the commanders mentioned frequently in the sources, there were other officers of high rank who simply do not appear prominently in the historical records (we will encounter a few more below). More importantly, we see that Yānis was independent and did not fit into any clear chain of command. Naṣr eulogized his departed colleague, that "if something were to happen to the ruler (*Sulṭān*), and he gave out a yell, [Yānis] would arrive immediately [with his men] before anyone else would even know about it."[41] Clearly Yānis had personal command of his troops and was not under the immediate authority of anyone save the caliph. Indeed, the simple fact that the caliph, chamberlain, and wazir would discuss the fate of his troops reflects the absence of a chain of command, for otherwise these troops would automatically be redeployed by Yānis's commanding officer. From a different angle, the suggested transfer of these troops to the crown prince indicates that, in theory, soldiers would be expected to change loyalties or at least develop new loyalties. In sum, the case of Yānis shows that the Abbasid military included a number of important officers, some of whom are not even mentioned on a consistent basis; that these officers were independent of one another and did not belong to a clear military hierarchy; and that troops were intended to be transferred from one officer to another, as per momentary requirements.

39. The budget in Hilāl al-Ṣābī (*Wuzarā*ʾ, 15–27) demonstrates that different units were paid on different monthly schedules.

40. ʿArīb, *Ṣilat*, 115–16. Ibn al-Furāt and his son seized Yānis's wealth for themselves.

41. ʿArīb, *Ṣilat*, 115.

Composition of the Military

The composition of the military is difficult to assess, given the limited information available, yet it would seem that soldiers came from a wide variety of ethnic origins: we read of Africans, Berbers, Slavs, Khurāsānis, Daylamis, and Turks in the Abbasid forces. It is possible that men of common ethnic origin served together in units, which might simplify linguistic instruction and enhance unit cohesion; but this point seems impossible to prove, and given the ethnic diversity, it might not have been practical. We should note that even the military elite was diverse, and no ethnic group dominated: Naṣr the chamberlain, Gharīb the royal uncle, and possibly Muʾnis were of Greek origin;[42] Mufliḥ the eunuch was African; and Nāzūk the police chief, among others, was Turkish. Louis Massignon hints that these officers formed ethnic factions, but I see no evidence for this claim, and much evidence to the contrary;[43] in any case, the point here is that we cannot designate this a "Turkish" military, as no single ethnic group predominated.

The method of enlisting troops is also difficult to assess. Al-Muqtadir continued the policies of his predecessors in accepting deserters from rival armies: in 299/911–912, Qarmatian generals were welcomed into Baghdad;[44] and in 302/915, two hundred Fatimid cavalrymen followed their commander to the Abbasid capital, were honored with robes and were then dispatched to serve in Basra under Ibn Kundāj, himself originally a Ṭulūnid commander.[45] Al-Muqtadir also augmented his forces by pardoning previous rebels, and absorbing them and their followers into the state military.[46] Of course the widespread ethic of changeable loyalties could and did work the other way: when Hārūn b. Gharīb, the caliph's first cousin, murdered a Daylami soldier but went unpunished, one hundred of the victim's compatriots abandoned Baghdad en masse and joined the forces of Ibn Abī al-Sāj, who was rebelling in Azerbaijan at the time.[47]

In general, the policies of accepting deserters and pardoning rebels reflect the general ethic of shifting and changeable loyalties. While certain men were undoubtedly firmly loyal to their masters and/or commanders, large sections of the Abbasid army were coming and going, periodically reassessing the benefits of any given employer. From the reign of al-Muʿtaḍid through the first half of al-Muqtadir's rule, the Abbasids generally benefited from the fluid military loyalties of the time, that is, they enjoyed a net gain

---

42. Muʾnis's ethnicity is uncertain. The account of the Byzantine visit in al-Khaṭīb (*Tārīkh*, 1:104) states that Muʾnis translated, which suggests that he is Greek. Massignon follows this logic (*Passion*, 1:425). The editor of al-Tanūkhī's *al-Faraj*, however, refers to Muʾnis as "one of the leading Turkish commanders" (2:53n6). Perhaps this is simply a mistaken assumption that all commanders were Turks.

43. Massignon: "Leadership remained in the hands of a tightly-knit little group of Greeks, following the splitting up of the Turkish group" (*Passion*, 1:425).

44. ʿArīb, *Ṣilat*, 36. They appear later under the command of Muʾnis (ʿArīb, *Ṣilat*, 168).

45. ʿArīb, *Ṣilat*, 49.

46. Examples: Ibn Abī al-Sāj, the Ḥamdānid family, and a number of Ṣaffārids.

47. ʿArīb, *Ṣilat*, 56 (from the year 303/915–916).

in personnel, and successfully dispersed opposition at strategic moments. Later in al-Muqtadir's reign, however, the Abbasids would suffer severely from troop disloyalty.

The heart of the Abbasid military since the time of al-Muʿtaḍid had been purchased slaves, who were selected and trained for skill and loyalty. Most of the leading military figures of al-Muqtadir's reign—Naṣr, Muʾnis al-Khādim, Muʾnis al-Khāzin, Gharīb, Nāzūk—were first generation Abbasid soldiers trained under al-Muʿtaḍid. However, it is possible that this longstanding Abbasid practice began to change under al-Muqtadir. As first-generation Abbasid soldiers and defectors from other armies died, they were often replaced by their sons; thus Gharīb's posts were taken over by his son Hārūn;[48] Muʾnis al-Khāzin was briefly replaced by his son al-Ḥasan;[49] Naṣr's son was training to be chamberlain;[50] and the sons of other commanders—Ibn Kundāj, Warqa, Abū al-Agharr, Khafīf al-Samarqandī—succeeded their fathers in specific posts or became officers. This was not an entirely new development in the Abbasid military, and these second-generation soldiers acquired only a portion of the higher offices. Other posts were turned over to remaining *ghilmān* of al-Muʿtaḍid. Yet by the end of al-Muqtadir's reign, and through the period of the *amīr al-umarāʾ*, we should notice two trends: first, the most important generals are all second-generation, sons of al-Muʿtaḍid's recruits, such as Hārūn b. Gharīb, Muḥammad b. Yāqūt, Muḥammad b. Rāʾiq, and ʿAlī b. Yalbaq; and that we virtually never hear of commanders recruited under al-Muqtadir.[51]

This has a corollary among the troops: the *maṣāffī* infantry swelled in number during the latter part of al-Muqtadir's reign, reportedly due to the inclusion of offspring and relatives among their ranks.[52] The logical conclusion is that few recruits from outside the Abbasid domain were inducted into senior ranks of the military during al-Muqtadir's reign. There are various possible explanations: a lack of supply, due to the military chaos of the period, which might cut off trade routes; a caliph who did not seem to take an interest in military affairs, and hence did not actively recruit young warriors; and most likely, a deepening financial crisis which left little funding for very expensive military slaves. We cannot know how the adoption of heredity would influence the Abbasid military. We do know, though, that for generations the Abbasids had preferred first-generation troops as being more effective and loyal; and we can recognize that al-Muqtadir's army, especially in his later years when heredity took hold, was neither effective nor especially loyal.

---

48. ʿArīb, *Ṣilat*, 69, in year 305/917.

49. ʿArīb, *Ṣilat*, 45, in the year 301/914. In this instance, the second-generation commander al-Ḥasan was quickly dismissed; but his initial appointment still reflects a potential shift in policy.

50. ʿArīb, *Ṣilat*, 121. Naṣr's son died in the year 312/924, several years before his father.

51. Two exceptions are: Shafīʿ al-Muqtadirī; and Sarūr, "*mawlā* of al-Muqtadir" (ʿArīb, *Ṣilat*, 159).

52. Ibn al-Athīr, *al-Kāmil*, 8:216. In 310/922–923, the event that prompted a change in the chief of police was that "one of the sons of the *rajjāla*, with his compatriots" raped a bride before her wedding (ʿArīb, *Ṣilat*, 110).

The Commanding Officers of Decentralized Forces

The element of the military for which we have most detailed information is, as might be expected, those high-ranking officers who were stationed in Baghdad. As argued earlier, Abbasid policies created a decentralized military structure, whereby no single officer prevailed, as seen in the coup of 296/908. Thus, in the earliest part of al-Muqtadir's reign a number of officers directed state policy, along with the rotating wazirs and the caliph's mother, on behalf of the young ruler. We see this "rule by committee" in a report from 301/913–914, in which the wazir ʿAlī b. ʿĪsā consults with the two Muʾnises, Gharīb the uncle, Naṣr the chamberlain, and Shafīʿ, regarding the Abbasid response to the Fatimid invasion of Egypt. Each of these men belonged to the military, in that they were all trained as soldiers, and each was in command of troops.[53]

Ṣāḥib al-Shurṭa: The Chief of Police

This office was unusual for this period in that it changed hands frequently, whereas military commanders in other posts retained their positions for many years. Identifying the holders of this office is not simple, for despite the fact that this was one of the few official military positions with a title, the information regarding it in the sources is inconsistent, more so than with other positions such as the chamberlain. Indeed, while an author like Ibn al-Jawzī lists the wazirs and chamberlains of a given caliph, he does not list the police chiefs; and even ʿArīb, who reports the identity of the *ṣāḥib al-shurṭa* far more frequently than other sources, often neglects to report when and why the personnel changes took place, simply mentioning the new police chief in passing. The most prominent police chiefs were Ibn ʿAmrawayh (up to 296/908), Muʾnis al-Khāzin (296–301/908–914), Nizār b. Muḥammad (304–306/916–918), Muḥammad b. ʿAbd al-Samad (306–310/918–922), and Nāzūk (310–317/922–929).[54] The lack of interest in the sources regarding the identity of this official immediately gives the impression that this commission was not considered of primary importance, at least relative to other assignments held by military personnel.

One interesting aspect of the changes in this office is that police chiefs, once dismissed, were often sent to provincial governorships, that is, dismissal did not necessarily mean disfavor. The case of Ibn ʿAbd al-Ṣamad is instructive: he was reportedly one of Naṣr the chamberlain's commanders, and thus probably acquired the post of police chief due to Naṣr's influence; when his performance was found unsatisfactory, Naṣr contrived

53. Hilāl al-Ṣābī, *Wuzarāʾ*, 380. The second Muʾnis in the printed text is spelled "Mānis," though this is almost certainly the chief of police Muʾnis al-Khāzin. Shafīʿ is probably Shafīʿ al-Luʾluʾī, who at about this time was head of intelligence (*ṣāḥib al-barīd*). I cannot find any reference to his training. Gharīb held no official position that I know of but is frequently mentioned as an important officer. Naṣr has already been discussed, and I discuss Muʾnis al-Khādim below.

54. ʿArīb, *Ṣilat*, 45, 63, 76, 109–10. ʿArīb lists six deputy police chiefs for the period of 301–304/914–917, and other sources are silent.

the appointment of Nāzūk.[55] By the following year Ibn ʿAbd al-Ṣamad was in the service of Ibn Abī al-Sāj, a rival of Naṣr now back in the caliph's favor; apparently Ibn ʿAbd al-Ṣamad had changed patrons.[56] This is another example of the easily shifting positions and loyalties of the time.

The *ṣāḥib al-shurṭa* had a variety of responsibilities, most of which related to maintaining order in Baghdad. His most basic function was to patrol the city on horseback, though this was probably performed most of the time by deputies assigned to each of the two sides of Baghdad. At moments of unrest he was in charge of suppressing riots: for example, Nizār subdued a prison riot by capturing and beheading one escapee, and tossing the severed head to fellow inmates.[57] The *ṣāḥib al-shurṭa* was also responsible for making arrests and holding prisoners in custody, though we have seen that other officials also fulfilled this function.[58] Apparently the *ṣāḥib al-shurṭa*, like other officials, was expected to attend the interrogation of bureaucrats, for in 311/923 Nāzūk refused to witness al-Muḥassin's brutal questioning of ʿAlī b. ʿĪsā, whereupon al-Muḥassin responded indignantly: "You are the *ṣāḥib al-shurṭa*, you must do this, and if you don't do it and leave, my sitting here will have no meaning.... Stay here or I will leave, for I am not the *ṣāḥib al-shurṭa*."[59]

The police chief's most onerous task was the execution of prisoners. In 296/908–909, Muʾnis al-Khāzin executed some of the coup conspirators with no apparent hesitation or regret, though later officeholders expressed apprehension regarding executions, for both political and security reasons. Ibn ʿAbd al-Ṣamad was reluctant to take charge of the convicted heretic al-Ḥallāj, fearful that he and his men might be attacked by the prisoner's followers. Ibn ʿAbd al-Ṣamad eventually agreed to transfer al-Ḥallāj from the royal palace to the police headquarters, but only at night; he then surrounded al-Ḥallāj with his own men and a detachment of the wazir Ḥāmid's *ghilmān*, so as to disguise the fact that al-Ḥallāj was being transferred. The next day Ibn ʿAbd al-Ṣamad supervised the whipping, quartering, and burning of the convicted heretic.[60] In 312/924, al-Muqtadir ordered Nāzūk, by dispatch, to execute Ibn al-Furāt and his son al-Muḥassin. Nāzūk was likewise apprehensive about performing such a momentous act and insisted upon hearing the command from the caliph's own mouth before performing the execution.[61]

---

55. ʿArīb, *Ṣilat*, 76, 109–10.

56. Hilāl al-Ṣābī, *Wuzarāʾ*, 54–55. In 315/927 he was appointed governor of Kirmān (Ibn al-Athīr, *al-Kāmil*, 8:180).

57. Ibn al-Jawzī, *al-Muntaẓam*, 6:146. Another example is Ibn ʿAbd al-Ṣamad, who was apparently responsible for calming civilians during the price riots of 307–309/919–921.

58. Examples include: when Muʾnis al-Khāzin hunted down the conspirators of 296/908 (mentioned in many sources); when Nizār took the false Hāshimī to jail in the year 305/917–918 (ʿArīb, *Ṣilat*, 67); and when Nāzūk, along with Yalbaq, arrested Ibn al-Furāt (many sources).

59. Hilāl al-Ṣābī, *Wuzarāʾ*, 323–24. We might note here that like Naṣr the chamberlain, Nāzūk was not invested with the authority to change the nature of the interrogation; he could only leave.

60. Miskawayh, *Tajārib*, 90–91.

61. Hilāl al-Ṣābī, *Wuzarāʾ*, 71.

The effectiveness of the *ṣāḥib al-shurṭa*, and ultimately the strength of the position, depended upon the loyalty and steadfastness of the troops under his command. In order to perform such tasks as patrolling the city, riot control, and arrests, the police chief obviously required command of soldiers; one report states that he commanded fourteen thousand troops.[62] Presumably the police force consisted of a fixed number of troops allocated to the office, and the personal *ghilmān* in the service of any given commander. Yet this police force was not always reliable: Ibn ʿAmrawayh, al-Muqtadir's first *ṣāḥib al-shurṭa*, participated in the coup of 296/908, yet his troops scattered in the face of civilian attack, and Ibn ʿAmrawayh himself was subsequently arrested.[63] Similarly, for both the transfer of al-Ḥallāj and the pacification of popular rioting in 307–309/919–921, Ibn ʿAbd al-Ṣamad could not rely on his own forces alone, and needed the assistance of additional troops. On several occasions the police could not suppress military riots. We cannot know if the ineffectiveness of the police force was due to small numbers, relative to the needs of a given task, or due to questionable skill and/or determination. In any case, up to 310/922 the *ṣāḥib al-shurṭa* was weak relative to other military commanders, for the office lacked manpower.[64]

Ṣāḥib al-Barīd: The Chief of Intelligence

We have a great deal of proof that both Shafīʿ al-Luʾluʾī and Shafīʿ al-Muqtadirī, the two men named as chiefs of intelligence, were members of the military elite.[65] Yet Shafīʿ al-Luʾluʾī's official position as *ṣāḥib al-barīd* is mentioned only fleetingly in the sources. ʿArīb relates that after Muʾnis al-Khāzin died in 301/914, Shafīʿ al-Luʾluʾī was appointed over the *barīd*,[66] and Ibn al-Athīr reports that in 312/924–925 Shafīʿ al-Luʾluʾī, in charge of the *barīd* and other posts, died and was replaced by Shafīʿ al-Muqtadirī.[67] As with the

62. Hilāl al-Ṣābī, *Rusūm*, 14. We also know that Muʾnis al-Khāzin had troops attached to him when he died. According to al-Muʿtaḍid's budget, the sum allotted to the police is far smaller than to military forces (Hilāl al-Ṣābī, *Wuzarāʾ*, 20).

63. Ibn al-Athīr, *al-Kāmil*, 8:17.

64. *Kennedy has also summarized the activities of the various police commanders (in van Berkel et al, *Crisis and Continuity*, 134–40); he comes to a similar conclusion, that this position was weak relative to other military offices: "The chief of police was always an important figure, although he lacked the position at court and access to the caliph enjoyed by the *ḥājib* and his soldiers did not have either the status of the salaries of the elite *ghilmān*" (140). For more recent research on the police and criminal justice in the Abbasid period, see Allehbi, "It Is Permitted."

65. They had a rank equivalent to that of Mufliḥ, Hārūn, Nāzūk and others, one rung below Muʾnis and Naṣr (Hilāl al-Ṣābī, *Wuzarāʾ*, 173); Shafīʿ al-Luʾluʾī was involved in planning the counterattack against the Fatimids (Hilāl al-Ṣābī, *Wuzarāʾ*, 380); and both are included among the *ruʾasāʾ* (leaders) who convinced al-Muqtadir to remove Ibn al-Furāt from incarceration in the royal palace (ʿArīb, *Ṣilat*, 121).

66. ʿArīb, *Ṣilat*, 45 (also 113). We do not know who was *ṣāḥib al-barīd* before 301/914; Muʾnis al-Khāzin is never mentioned as holding this post, although he might have.

67. Ibn al-Athīr, *al-Kāmil*, 8:157.

chamberlain and the police chief, the sources generally show little or no interest in the personnel changes in this position, and moreover never refer to Shafīʿ with his title.

On a few occasions we get a glimpse of Shafīʿ al-Luʾluʾī's specifically intelligence-related activities: in 310/922–923 one of Shafīʿ's agents in Mecca uncovered and foiled a plot to kill ʿAlī b. ʿĪsā; and in 312/924 he warned the caliph, in writing, that the *ḥujarī*s would rebel and possibly remove the caliph if Ibn al-Furāt were allowed to remain imprisoned in the royal palace.[68] Most of the references to Shafīʿ, however, show him performing functions that other military leaders also engaged in: he made arrests, attended interrogations, protected bureaucrats' homes, and even distributed money to rioting troops. He is discussed most extensively with regard to the incarceration and protection of fallen wazirs, reflecting the trust with which he was regarded. In 309/921–922 the wazir Ibn al-Furāt did not want responsibility for an ailing ʿAlī b. ʿĪsā, so he sent the latter to Shafīʿ al-Luʾluʾī, who showed the pious bureaucrat respect and then offered to pay his fines; and in 312/924, when the Baghdadi elite unanimously wanted Ibn al-Furāt removed from the palace, everyone (including Ibn al-Furāt) agreed that he should be held by Shafīʿ al-Luʾluʾī. Ibn al-Furāt's trust in Shafīʿ is noteworthy, since Shafīʿ, like Naṣr and Muʾnis, consistently opposed Ibn al-Furāt.[69]

The official position of Shafīʿ al-Muqtadirī is even more difficult to ascertain. Ibn al-Athīr reports that he acquired the posts of Shafīʿ al-Luʾluʾī (primarily responsibility for the *barīd*) in 312/924–925;[70] yet the younger Shafīʿ had already been prominent for years, and there is no indication in the sources as to other specific offices he held. Another report informs us that in 320/932 the younger Shafīʿ was arrested, and his posts—control over the royal kitchen, the gardens, stables, and *barīd*—were divided up;[71] perhaps Shafīʿ had held control of the first three offices as early as 312/924. The point here is once again that official military positions are ignored by the sources, possibly because official positions were somewhat irrelevant.

Indeed, we see that Shafīʿ al-Muqtadirī's tasks were exactly the same as those of other colleagues with presumably different official positions. On the one hand he performed some relatively menial tasks: conveying messages from the caliph to wazirs,[72] and delivering presents from al-Sayyida to a newly appointed wazir.[73] On the other, he was also entrusted with more important responsibilities: he was in charge of the raid on the home of the jewelry merchant Ibn al-Jaṣṣāṣ in 302/914, even though the *ṣāḥib al-shurṭa* was also present (i.e., Shafīʿ had greater authority than the police chief, at least on this

68. ʿArīb, *Ṣilat*, 121.

69. Miskawayh, *Tajārib*, 127. Shafīʿ and Naṣr were suspected of plotting against Ibn al-Furāt in 305/917–918, so the latter removed Shafīʿ and Naṣr from some of their positions.

70. Ibn al-Athīr, *al-Kāmil*, 8:157.

71. ʿArīb, *Ṣilat*, 184.

72. A message to Ibn al-Furāt accompanied by Naṣr (*ʿUyūn*, 274, in the year 305/917–918); and to Ḥāmid b. al-ʿAbbās (ʿArīb, *Ṣilat*, 74).

73. To Ibn al-Furāt (*ʿUyūn*, 266).

occasion);[74] in 305/917–918 he was in charge of appointing the governor of Basra;[75] and in 306/918 he accompanied Naṣr at the arrest of Ibn al-Furāt and supporters.[76] Another indication of Shafīʿ's importance at court is that, in 311/923, Ibn al-Furāt encouraged the caliph to arrest Naṣr and Shafīʿ, citing the wealth, property, and income that both men enjoyed.[77] Interestingly, the caliph allowed Ibn al-Furāt to plot against Naṣr but not against Shafīʿ, reflecting Shafīʿ's importance to the caliph. When al-Muḥassin, according to a different source, did plot against both Naṣr and Shafīʿ, he tried to kill the former (and failed), but simply tried to bribe Shafīʿ to go into exile (and failed again). The difference in al-Muḥassin's tactics suggests that Shafīʿ was possibly less vulnerable than Naṣr.

Gharīb and Hārūn: The Royal Generals

Two other prominent military men in Baghdad were Gharīb, al-Sayyida's brother and hence the caliph's uncle, and Gharīb's son Hārūn. Typically, we do not know what posts these men held; in 305/917, when Gharīb died, "Hārūn b. Gharīb was appointed to the posts that his father had held," but these posts are not identified.[78] Gharīb was known to have access to the caliph, for the impostor who sought to deliver secret information to the caliph first came to the home of Gharīb and expected the general to obtain for him a royal audience, which in fact occurred.[79] The only military activity we hear of Gharīb engaging in, besides his defense of the palace during the coup of 296/908, is the suppression of popular looting.[80] He was also involved in politics, defending the wazir ʿAlī b. ʿĪsā (along with Muʾnis and Naṣr), against plotters,[81] and collaborating with Muʾnis on the ouster of Ibn al-Furāt.[82] His elite status at court is confirmed by the fact that all leading officials, including leading military commanders, attended his funeral and the funeral of one of his sons.[83]

Hārūn's role at court is predictably vague. The sources concur that he helped subdue the rioting of 307–309/919–921;[84] Ibn al-Athīr's remarks are particularly instructive:

74. ʿArīb, *Ṣilat*, 47. This is one instance in which Miskawayh is very imprecise with regard to military affairs, stating that "a group" was sent to arrest the jewelry merchant (*Tajārib*, 35).

75. ʿArīb, *Ṣilat*, 66.

76. Miskawayh, *Tajārib*, 57; Hilāl al-Ṣābī, *Wuzarāʾ*, 39.

77. Hilāl al-Ṣābī, *Wuzarāʾ*, 54; Miskawayh, *Tajārib*, 117.

78. ʿArīb, *Ṣilat*, 69. The other sources do not even mention that Gharīb died.

79. ʿArīb, *Ṣilat*, 49.

80. Hilāl al-Ṣābī, *Wuzarāʾ*, 34 (in 299/911–912). Ibn al-Athīr (*al-Kāmil*, 8:116) states that he helped suppress rioting in 307/919, but according to ʿArīb, Gharīb was already dead by then, so Ibn al-Athīr was probably referring to Hārūn b. Gharīb.

81. Hilāl al-Ṣābī, *Wuzarāʾ*, 36; Miskawayh, *Tajārib*, 44.

82. Hilāl al-Ṣābī, *Wuzarāʾ*, 36.

83. ʿArīb, *Ṣilat*, 68–69. The same honor was paid to Muʾnis al-Khāzin and other nonmilitary figures.

84. ʿArīb, *Ṣilat*, 85.

"Al-Muqtadir sent out a force with Gharīb the uncle,[85] who then attacked the commoners." Here we again see what seems like the standard practice of putting a body of troops under the command of an officer for one particular mission. Hārūn also witnessed and even conducted interrogations,[86] and participated in the conspiracy to have Ibn al-Furāt removed from custody in the palace.[87]

To summarize our knowledge of the military elite of Baghdad until roughly 311/923: the sources do not consistently report changes in personnel and tell us virtually nothing about individual posts. This might result from the overlap in the activities and responsibilities of military officials, regardless of the office they held; in other words, a person's specific office was largely irrelevant. All military officials raided the homes of civilians and made arrests, were responsible for prisoners, witnessed and/or participated in interrogations. They also all took part in subduing military or civil rioting. In effect, the caliph assigned any officer he wished to a given task, regardless of their official post; this overlap of functions is another aspect of the diffuse authority and hierarchy of the Abbasid military.

We might also note that we have no evidence of internal tension or rivalries during this period, and military officials united against a common enemy, the bureaucrat Ibn al-Furāt. As long as the empire remained relatively successful at defending its borders, the military elite were at least outwardly harmonious. In the later years of al-Muqtadir's reign, as military ineffectiveness became apparent and financial resources were extremely limited, these officers became open competitors.

Consolidated Military Command: The Ascendance of Muʾnis

The most prominent military commander in the first half of al-Muqtadir's reign was Muʾnis al-Khādim. We first hear of Muʾnis as one of al-Muʿtaḍid's many officers,[88] but he does not appear during the caliphate of al-Muktafī and was likely outside the capital. Muʾnis was definitely back in Baghdad by 296/908 and among the most important defenders of the new caliph, and his leadership of the counterattack against Ibn al-Muʿtazz's supporters likely solidified his leadership role going forward. Late in 296/909 Muʾnis was inexplicably at odds with Ṣāfī al-Ḥuramī, so the latter (apparently in conjunction with Ibn al-Furāt, the newly installed wazir) arranged for Muʾnis to be distanced from Baghdad, dispatched on a campaign to the Byzantine border with a large military attachment.[89] From 296/909 through 310/922, Muʾnis enjoyed a series of impressive mili-

85. I mentioned above that Gharīb had already died, so Ibn al-Athīr is likely referring to his son Hārūn (Ibn al-Athīr *al-Kāmil*, 8:116–17).

86. Miskawayh, *Tajārib*, 131–36; Hilāl al-Ṣābī, *Wuzarāʾ*, 65.

87. Miskawayh, *Tajārib*, 137.

88. al-Ṭabarī, *History*, 38:89, 160.

89. ʿArīb, *Ṣilat*, 31; al-Tabarī, *History*, 38:192. This is one typical case in which al-Ṭabarī's report is extremely brief, apparently avoiding any reference to the political tensions taking shape.

tary victories: in Fārs (298/910–911), Egypt (302/914), the Byzantine border and Mosul (303/915), Ardabīl (307/919), and again in Egypt (307–308/920–921). Muʾnis was put in charge of campaigns in all parts of the Abbasid Empire—from Egypt and the Byzantine border to Fārs and Azerbaijan—whereas Badr, the head of al-Muʿtaḍid's army a generation earlier, had been confined to Fārs and al-Jibāl.

We should make a few observations regarding Muʾnis's prominence in Abbasid military campaigns. First, it was not the caliph's original intention that Muʾnis should lead all of them. In this and other respects the campaign against Ibn Ḥamdān at Mosul in 303/915 is characteristic of the time. Al-Ḥusayn b. Ḥamdān, after receiving a pardon for participating in the coup of 296/908, rebelled once again. At first al-Muqtadir dispatched Rāʾiq, one of al-Muʿtaḍid's senior commanders, with other leading officers and *ghilmān*.[90] Rāʾiq was defeated by al-Ḥusayn's forces, so Muʾnis, at the time returning from the Byzantine border, was sent to capture the Ḥamdānid rebel. As Muʾnis's army approached, Ibn Ḥamdān's troops deserted; and following Ibn Ḥamdān's subsequent defeat in battle, his Kurdish supporters looted their own patron's camp, all of which again reflect the shaky loyalty typical of this era.[91] Thus Muʾnis only became involved in this campaign because Rāʾiq failed to subdue the rebel. Similarly, Muʾnis became involved in the campaign against Ibn Abī al-Sāj in 304/917 only after Khāqān al-Mufliḥī, whom the caliph dispatched, had been defeated.[92] In short, Muʾnis was not always al-Muqtadir's first option, as the caliph, in keeping with Abbasid policy, was probably wary of concentrating too much power in one commander, or of becoming too dependent upon him. Muʾnis came to dominate simply because he was consistently successful, perhaps largely due to individual tactical prowess.

Between the early and later years of al-Muqtadir's reign, there is a subtle but noteworthy change in ʿArīb's description of Muʾnis's campaigns. According to ʿArīb, Muʾnis set out for the Byzantine border in 296/909 with officers attached to him for this campaign;[93] similarly, in 297/910: "Muʾnis al-Khādim was sent to Fārs, and a group of five thousand troops were attached to him;"[94] and in 302/914, "al-Muqtadir sent Muʾnis al-Khādim, and assigned the army to him" for an attack on the Fatimids in Egypt.[95] In all these cases, ʿArīb is clear that Muʾnis did not already have command of enough troops for the mission in question, so the caliph added more men to his force. However, ʿArīb's descriptions subsequently change, for in all of Muʾnis's campaigns after 302/914, ʿArīb

90. This is a good example of a senior general who is mentioned only fleetingly in the sources, as well as of the ubiquitous practice of putting other officers and troops at a general's disposal for one specific campaign.

91. The accounts of Miskawayh (*Tajārib*, 36–38) and ʿArīb (*Ṣilat*, 56–57) differ drastically with regard to this battle. I am following Miskawayh, whose account is much more detailed.

92. Miskawayh, *Tajārib*, 46.

93. ʿArīb, *Ṣilat*, 31.

94. ʿArīb, *Ṣilat*, 32.

95. ʿArīb, *Ṣilat*, 52.

never again mentions that troops were assigned to Muʾnis. Thus, we might speculate that a series of units became permanently attached to Muʾnis's command, or in other words, that Muʾnis developed something approaching a standing or permanent army.

Parallel to his military victories, Muʾnis was honored, along with Naṣr, as the most important officers in the empire. In 301/913–914 the two eldest princes were put under the tutelage of Muʾnis and Naṣr, with Muʾnis becoming the mentor of the heir apparent, Abū al-ʿAbbās.[96] The heir apparent was then nominally appointed to oversee affairs in the western part of the empire; but we have seen that Muʾnis's campaigns took him far from the west, so this responsibility as mentor did not restrict the general's area of operations. In addition, we might recall that Muʾnis al-Khāzin (i.e., the other Muʾnis) commanded troops, who were transferred to prince Abū al-ʿAbbās in 301/913–914 (at four years of age); we might speculate that these troops in effect were transferred to Muʾnis al-Khādim, so that tutelage of the prince was actually a source of manpower. Beyond this honor, Muʾnis held a central role in Abbasid ceremonial, as he and Naṣr were the two officials who acted as intermediaries between the caliph and the Byzantine envoys.[97] In 309/921–922, following his second victory in Egypt, Muʾnis was named "al-Muẓaffar" ("The Victorious"), and became an official boon companion of the caliph.[98]

Like several members of the court elite, Muʾnis was repeatedly active in influencing the caliph's choice of wazir. Muʾnis followed a consistent policy of supporting ʿAlī b. ʿĪsā's fiscal conservativeness and opposing Ibn al-Furāt's heavy handedness and extravagance. In 301/913–914 he dissuaded the caliph from appointing Ibn al-Furāt, and successfully canvassed for ʿAlī b. ʿĪsā.[99] He protected ʿAlī during the latter's tenure as wazir, and later worked for the second removal of Ibn al-Furāt.[100] Muʾnis's good relations with ʿAlī, and his broader influence over multiple wazirs, perhaps gave him secure access to military funds, for it was almost always Muʾnis who calmed rioting troops with promises of payment.[101]

By 311/923, Muʾnis was clearly the most important military commander in the empire. This fact is attested to, ironically, by Muʾnis's colleague and rival Naṣr the chamberlain. Following the Qarmatian attack on the hajj, Naṣr rebuked the wazir Ibn al-Furāt for consigning Muʾnis to Raqqa: "You have shaken the foundations of the state, and exposed it to destruction by sending away Muʾnis, who has combated its enemies and defended the state. Now who will prevent [the Qarmatians] from seizing the throne!"[102] Naṣr was

96. ʿArīb, *Ṣilat*, 43, 154; Miskawayh, *Tajārib*, 32–33.

97. al-Khaṭīb, *Tārīkh*, 1:104.

98. Miskawayh, *Tajārib*, 76.

99. Miskawayh, *Tajārib*, 25–26; Ibn al-Athīr, *al-Kāmil*, 8:68.

100. He was also involved in the general conspiracy against Ibn al-Furāt in 312/924 and influenced the caliph to appoint al=Khāqānī (Hilāl al-Ṣābī, *Wuzarāʾ*, 36; Miskawayh, *Tajārib*, 127).

101. For example, ʿArīb, *Ṣilat*, 58.

102. Miskawayh, *Tajārib*, 121–22.

probably exaggerating the importance of Muʾnis's absence; yet his comments reflect the perception that Muʾnis was the leading commander of the Abbasid army.

Muʾnis's potential power was limited, however, by the decentralized structure of the Abbasid military. He was more the first among colleagues than the commanding officer for lower-ranking generals. Many commanders—Hārūn b. Gharīb, the various police chiefs, and even more obscure officers like Yānis al-Muwaffaqī and Rāʾiq al-Muʿtaḍidī—operated independently of Muʾnis, and their troops were not under his control. Moreover, the large units organized by al-Muʿtaḍid—the *maṣāffī* infantry, the *ḥujarī ghilmān*, the *fursān*—apparently remained independent of Muʾnis as well. In short, the military was not a unified whole, but a grouping of commanders and units among whom Muʾnis was clearly the most powerful and effective, but not a dominant commander in chief.[103]

Competition and Opportunism: 315–320/927–932

While the first half of al-Muqtadir's reign was characterized by military cooperation and stability, the latter half, particularly the years after 316/928, involved continuous military infighting. Partly with the encouragement of the caliph, high-ranking generals began competing for predominance. This competition, within the context of a decentralized military and fluid loyalties, had two main results: no single commander could triumph; and soldiers of all ranks, with no strong bonds to any particular commander, felt free to change allegiances frequently in search of the most beneficial patron. Gradually the multitude of loosely organized officers gave way to a number of regional strongmen, whose main preoccupation was acquiring cash to satisfy a soldiery with no permanent loyalties. By 324/936, with the further diffusion of authority and the dissolution of al-Muʿtaḍid's units, a coherent institution known as "the Abbasid army" ceases to exist.

The Competition

Through 315/927 Muʾnis was commonly recognized as the leading Abbasid commander, yet the diffuse nature of the military allowed for the emergence of competitors. Beginning around 315/927, the caliph seems to have encouraged the rise of challengers to Muʾnis's preeminent position. The first of these was Ibn Abī al-Sāj, the governor of Armenia and Azerbaijan. By 314/926 the Qarmatians were a continual threat to Iraqi cities, so al-Muqtadir ordered Ibn Abī al-Sāj to traverse Iraq from the north and confront the enemy in southern Iraq. Al-Muqtadir's decision to give Ibn Abī al-Sāj this task was not popular: Naṣr, Nāzūk, Shafīʿ al-Muqtadirī, and Hārūn all opposed his crossing of Iraq via

103. *Kennedy has written a lengthy description of Muʾnis's career, including both his military and political activities (in van Berkel et al, *Crisis and Continuity*, 120–28). Kennedy's analysis sees Muʾnis as a little more dominant, whereas I have emphasized the decentralized nature of the military, and a certain balance of opposing forces.

Baghdad, and Muʾnis wrote him to travel via Wāsiṭ and not the imperial capital.[104] Implied in this opposition is the fear that Ibn Abī al-Sāj might become the most powerful general in Baghdad. As Ibn Abī al-Sāj crossed Iraq, the wazir ʿAlī b. ʿĪsā calculated that this deployment would cost three million dinars, whereas local bedouin forces located closer to the Qarmatian threat would only cost one million;[105] moreover, the bedouin would be more effective, since Ibn Abī al-Sāj's troops were not accustomed to desert warfare.[106] ʿAlī further complained that Ibn Abī al-Sāj had been granted direct control over all eastern tax revenues, while Muʾnis received the money for his troops through the bureaucracy in Baghdad.[107] ʿAlī even wrote to Ibn Abī al-Sāj, directing him to remain in northern Iraq; but the general proceeded—and was subsequently defeated, captured, and executed by the Qarmatians. After his defeat, the generals in Baghdad led the local army and successfully halted the Qarmatian advance.

The deployment of Ibn Abī al-Sāj made little sense, and smacks of ulterior caliphal motives. Al-Muqtadir dragged an expensive, inappropriate army from northeastern to southwestem Iraq, when local troops were available, cheaper, and ultimately more effective. He ignored his generals' fears of Ibn Abī al-Sāj's proximity and even gave the governor unusual financial independence. All these factors suggest that al-Muqtadir was determined to limit his dependency on local generals, especially Muʾnis, and sought to bring a new force to central Iraq, creating a broader military balance of power. This attempt failed.

Another powerful general emerged from al-Muqtadir's apparent attempt to curtail Muʾnis's ascendance. As we have seen in an earlier chapter, the caliph reportedly schemed in 315/927 to assassinate Muʾnis in the royal palace; when the general learned of the scheme, he mobilized a mass of troops and intimidated the caliph. Al-Muqtadir must have learned from these events and resolved to curtail Muʾnis's power by building up a rival. There are indications that al-Muqtadir began to rely heavily upon his cousin Hārūn b. Gharīb: in 316/928, Hārūn was sent to Wāsiṭ and defeated a Qarmatian force; he was then sent to Qazwīn, but was turned back by a Daylami warlord; finally, he was appointed governor of al Jibal, and again "leading commanders were attached to him."[108] It would thus appear that Hārūn was being entrusted with important campaigns, and his

104. ʿArīb, *Ṣilat*, 128. Muʾnis appears here as the leading officer, and Ibn Abī al-Sāj follows Muʾnis's instructions. But Muʾnis obviously was not making decisions; he did not want Ibn Abī al-Sāj to traverse Iraq in the first place, but could not cancel the caliph's order.

105. ʿArīb, *Ṣilat*, 131.

106. Miskawayh, *Tajārib*, 153.

107. Miskawayh, *Tajārib*, 153.

108. ʿArīb, *Ṣilat*, 137–38. Other governors were also appointed at this time, but none are said to have received additional forces, and al-Jibāl was a particularly important province. At this time Muʾnis was at the Byzantine border.

forces were being augmented. By 317/929, rumors circulated in Baghdad that al-Muqtadir planned to replace Muʾnis with Hārūn as the military's highest-ranking officer.[109]

One additional commander who seems to have emerged was Nāzūk al-Muʿtaḍidī, who had been appointed police chief (*ṣāḥib al-shurṭa*) in 310/922–23. As we have seen, police chiefs were chronically weak, despite commanding a permanent armed unit, though presumable less skilled fighters than the forces ensconced in the royal palace complex. But with Nāzūk we see a dramatically new effectiveness, which we might attribute to several factors: he reportedly possessed three hundred of his own *mamlūks*, which gave him a reliable and well-trained foundation for his forces;[110] and he seems to have understood how to manipulate one military corps against another, a tactic that would become profoundly important due to the diffused nature of the military and declining resources.

Nāzūk immediately demonstrated his effectiveness upon being appointed. ʿArīb reports that "his severity was clear from the first day, and he took command as nobody had before, and subdued the *rajjāla*.... He fought them into submission.... They had approached his home to burn it ... but he asked for help from the *ghilmān* and thereby scattered [the *rajjāla*]."[111] Here we see that Nāzūk took firm action to suppress insurrection. His success, however, depended upon the *ghilmān*, and presaged a later tactic of employing one set of troops against another. In following years, Nāzūk was sent with a detachment of *ḥujarīs*, *fursān*, and *rajjāla* to capture Ḥāmid b. al-ʿAbbās's supporters in Wāsiṭ;[112] and in 315/927 Nāzūk prevented chaos in Baghdad by patrolling the city day and night, while the rest of the military was preoccupied with the Qarmatians.[113] Nāzūk's successes are in clear contrast with the failures of his predecessors, which suggests that he controlled an effective military force.

---

109. ʿArīb, *Ṣilat*, 139; Miskawayh (*Tajārib*, 188) and Ibn al-Athīr (*al-Kāmil*, 8:188) both use the term *amīr al-umarāʾ*, and it is difficult to know if this title was actually granted to Muʾnis, or if the sources are projecting backward a title that was first used in 324/936, seven years later. ʿArīb simply uses the term "the Amirate (*al-imāra*)," and since he generally pays more attention to military details than other sources, I follow his terminology and assume that the title *amīr al-umarāʾ* would only come later. In any case, as I have argued repeatedly, whatever Muʾnis's title, he was a leader among colleagues, not the commanding officer with authority over the entire military.

110. Ibn Taghrībirdī, *al-Nujūm*, 226.

111. ʿArīb, *Ṣilat*, 109–10. It is difficult to know if the *ghilmān* mentioned in the text refers to his personal slaves/freedmen, or the *ḥujarīs*; I suppose the latter, since he had to ask for their help, which he would not have done if they were already in his service, and there is no possessive pronoun to suggest that these were his own men. In addition, the *massāfīs* and *ḥujarīs* were frequently hostile to one another, and this is probably one instance.

112. Miskawayh, *Tajārib*, 95.

113. Miskawayh, *Tajārib*, 179.

Military Infighting: 316–317/928–929

The rising tension among competing forces first boiled over in 316/928, following a street fight between the stablemen of Nāzūk and Hārūn. Nāzūk, as police chief, arrested Hārūn's grooms; and Hārūn's men retaliated by attacking the jail and freeing their comrades. Nāzūk complained to the caliph, who refused to intervene; both sides mobilized, and the two forces battled outside Hārūn's home. Al-Muqtadir eventually sent Mufliḥ the eunuch and the wazir Ibn Muqla to broker a peace; but Nāzūk resented al-Muqtadir's failure to intervene earlier, which he interpreted as tacit support for Hārūn, "and for that reason he determined to replace al-Muqtadir [as caliph]."[114]

This event gives us some idea of the current military situation in Baghdad: rival generals commanded standing units in the capital; these rivals and their units were of comparable size and power; nobody was numerically or quantitatively dominant; the caliph did not, and probably could not, interfere in a military crisis; and the initial decision to remove al-Muqtadir was an outgrowth of internal military conflict.

The tensions within the military erupted in the short-lived coup of 317/929. I discussed it at length in chapter 1, so here I will review only the narrative elements specifically relevant to the military. The trouble began when Nāzūk and Abū al-Hayjāʾ b. Ḥamdūn told Muʾnis the rumor that Hārūn might replace Muʾnis as the leading general. Nāzūk, Abū al-Hayjāʾ, and Muʾnis mobilized outside the Shamsiyya Gate; other generals came out to join them, as did most of the troops stationed in the palace. Muʾnis then wrote a letter to al-Muqtadir, summarizing the army's criticism of the caliph's reliance upon women and eunuchs. Al-Muqtadir reassured the generals of his commitment to them and stressed their obligations to him; eventually the caliph and his generals agreed that Hārūn would be expelled from Baghdad.

For two days the crisis appeared to have been resolved. Then, according to some sources, Nāzūk remobilized with twelve thousand *fursān*, and Muʾnis joined him; Nāzūk and the *fursān* then invaded the palace, followed by Muʾnis, who managed to find al-Muqtadir and put him in protective custody outside the royal palace complex before Nāzūk could seize him. Nāzūk, Abū al-Hayjāʾ, and Muʾnis then chose a new caliph and gave him the oath of allegiance. Nāzūk, however, could not pay the *maṣāffi* units their accession bonus; what's more, the *maṣāffis* had remained hostile to Nāzūk ever since he had forced them into submission in 310/922–923. Muʾnis, unhappy with Nāzūk's domineering style of command, secretly made a deal with the disaffected *rajālla* to restore them to their positions if they would attack the palace and overturn Nāzūk. Three days after the new caliph had been installed, the *rajjāla* stormed the palace demanding their rightful pay; they pursued Nāzūk into the palace, and when he ran into barriers that had been set up to seal off certain passageways, they killed him. Abū al-Hayjāʾ was also killed in a brave attempt to protect the new caliph. With the support and probable encourage-

114. Ibn al-Athīr, *al-Kāmil*, 8:188; Miskawayh, *Tajārib*, 187–88.

ment of Muʾnis, the *rajjāla* moved al-Muqtadir back to the royal palace and restored him as caliph.[115]

The coup was primarily a battle for power within the military elite.[116] The initial goal for Nāzūk, Abū al-Hayjāʾ, and Muʾnis in mobilizing their troops was the removal of Hārūn from Baghdad to eliminate the threat he posed to their respective positions. Nāzūk sought a tactical and temporary alliance with Muʾnis in order to put pressure on the caliph to oust Hārūn and simultaneously prevent Muʾnis from defending the caliph. Nāzūk could not have done any of this alone. Muʾnis, for his part, initially collaborated with Nāzūk in order to get Hārūn banished; in other words, he could not have achieved this objective alone either. Yet Muʾnis underestimated Nāzūk's ambitions, and the strength of his forces, and thus was initially forced to participate in Nāzūk's broader program: not just removing Hārūn but deposing the caliph as well. According to Ibn al-Athīr, "it was said that Muʾnis al-Muẓaffar was not influential in the deposition of al-Muqtadir, but agreed with the group [of rebelling commanders] contrary to his own thinking, for he knew that if he opposed them he could not help al-Muqtadir; so he agreed with them to gain their trust, and then plotted with the *ghilmān al-maṣāffiyya*."[117] In other words, Muʾnis did not have the power to stop Nāzūk, and needed time and the rebel's trust, to execute an effective countercoup. In sum, the coup was not strictly a military action against the caliph, per se; it was a three-pronged competition between Hārūn, Nāzūk, and Muʾnis, in which the caliph was not much more than a pawn.

The decisive factor in this competition was the ability to attract, deploy, and satisfy previously unaffiliated troops. The weakness of the caliph, and of his protégé Hārūn, was immediately apparent when the *ḥujarī*s and *maṣāffī*s abandoned the palace to join Muʾnis.[118] Even those troops loyal to the caliph were weak, and fled from the palace upon attack.[119] Nāzūk's initial advantage, in addition to his police force and personal *mamlūks*, was that he apparently allied with the *fursān*, numbering some twelve thousand.[120] But Nāzūk made the fatal mistake of relying solely on one group and alienating the others. After seizing the palace, he ordered the *maṣāffī* infantry (and possibly also the *ḥujarī*s) to withdraw from the palace complex and had his own troops (probably augmented by the

115. Miskawayh, *Tajārib*, 189–200; ʿArīb, *Ṣilat*, 139–44.

116. Waines has argued that "this sudden reversal of events was not accomplished by a counter-coup of another army commander," but rather should be attributed solely to the disgruntled *maṣāffī*s ("Caliph and Amir," 79). He therefore sees the countercoup as an event in which the troops overwhelmed their own commanders. While this is possible, it overlooks the explicit comments in the sources that Muʾnis instigated the *maṣāffī*s to attack Nāzūk, and the very likely possibility that had Nāzūk and Muʾnis chosen to cooperate, the coup would have been successful.

117. Ibn al-Athīr, *al-Kāmil*, 8:207.

118. Ibn al-Athīr, *al-Kāmil*, 8:200.

119. Ibn al-Athīr, *al-Kāmil*, 8:201. For example, the chamberlain, his subordinates, eunuchs, and "others" abandoned the palace.

120. ʿArīb, *Ṣilat*, 141. This sounds like an exceedingly large number of cavalry within the city, so either this number is exaggerated, or perhaps the *fursān* were not all cavalry.

fursān) take their place.[121] Another account relates that he could not pay the *maṣāffīs* the accession bonus. Whether by intent or for lack of money, or both, Nāzūk alienated the *maṣāffīs* which may have left him lacking the manpower to defend the palace, since he was forced to put up barricades, possibly decreasing the number of guards needed. He tried to avoid a confrontation between his own troops and the *maṣāffīs* when the latter rioted. Muʾnis, on the other hand, knew how to manipulate the units in Baghdad. Recognizing his own relative weakness, Muʾnis waited for Nāzūk to commit to one unit and alienate others. Muʾnis then allied with these alienated troops and triumphed over his rival.

Another prominent aspect of these events is the prevalence of rapidly shifting loyalties. Al-Muqtadir had shifted his patronage from Muʾnis to Hārūn, but then abandoned Hārūn and expelled him; al-Muqtadir's elite forces left the palace and joined the rebellious forces; Nāzūk and his supporters initially accepted the compromise of Hārūn's dismissal, but then went on to attack the palace anyway; the *maṣāffīs* essentially fought for whoever promised to pay them; and Muʾnis undermined his supposed alliance with Nāzūk and Abū al-Hayjāʾ and brought about their deaths. The betrayal of Abū al-Hayjāʾ was particularly heinous, since the latter had expressed profound loyalty to Muʾnis, but was not warned about the countercoup. In general, the tentative loyalties that underlay the Abbasid military system were torn asunder. We get a sense of this rupture in the encounter between Abū al-Hayjāʾ and al-Muqtadir at the official deposal:

> [Abū al-Hayjāʾ] said to al-Muqtadir: "Master, it is awful for me to see you in this condition, which I feared for you, warned you about, and advised you to avoid. I warned you of the consequences of accepting [the views of] eunuchs and women, and giving their views prominence over mine, for I could see this coming. We are your slaves and servants." His eyes teared, as did those of al-Muqtadir. Then everyone witnessed the deposal.[122]

Here we see that even deeply felt loyalties were broken.[123]

The coup of 317/929 marks a turning point for the Abbasid military. Generals who previously cooperated within a loose military structure had become open rivals. These

121. Miskawayh, *Tajārib*, 194–95; Ibn al-Athīr, *al-Kāmil*, 8:202–3.

122. Ibn al-Athīr, *al-Kāmil*, 8:202.

123. Mottahedeh has used the letter written by al-Muqtadir, emphasizing his commitment to Muʾnis and expectation of loyalty for years of patronage, as an example of the importance of loyalty and patronage in this society (*Loyalty and Leadership*, 40–41). Mottahedeh is certainly correct that these were the means of conceptualizing social relations, and that loyalties were sometimes strong. In this particular instance, however, there is no doubt that al-Muqtadir was conspiring to subvert Muʾnis's position in the capital, his references to devotion and loyalty notwithstanding. Moreover, the caliph's letter was entirely ineffective: the rebellious generals removed him from the throne. "Loyalty" was merely rhetoric. The events of the next seven years, as described below, demonstrate that loyalty was not commonly practiced.

generals would now compete for the services of unaffiliated troops that, in the military structure conceived by al-Muʿtaḍid, had no permanent bonds to any particular commander, and generally weak loyalties. Even long-established relations were being broken. In short, the loosely structured military of al-Muʿtaḍid was unraveling.

Military Infighting: 318–320/930–932

The years following the failed coup of 317/929 involved constant military turmoil. With regard to the corps of troops, the *maṣāffīs* (*rajjāla maṣāffiyya*) used their restoration of al-Muqtadir as justification for monopolizing control of the palace and generally disruptive behavior. This quickly annoyed the caliph, so he encouraged the *fursān* (the cavalry who had deposed him!) to attack the *maṣāffīs;* with the help of leading commanders, the *fursān* chased the *maṣāffīs* out of Baghdad.[124]

As for competition at the higher political and military echelons, the tension between Muʾnis and al-Muqtadir continued unabated. Initially the two disputed over appointments to the offices of chamberlain and police chief. The caliph had appointed Yāqūt and his son Muḥammad b. Yāqūt to these posts, but Muʾnis feared this consolidation of power in one family, and mobilized his troops outside the city (as he had done in 315/927 and 317/929), implicitly threatening to again remove the caliph if Yāqūt and his son were not expelled.[125] The caliph relented, and when Muʾnis arranged for the appointment of the Banū Rāʾiq brothers, stability was temporarily restored. But jealousy and disloyalty ruled the day. In 320/932, when Muʾnis fell ill and appointed his deputy Yalbaq to fulfill his military duties, the Banū Rāʾiq were jealous of Yalbaq, fearing that he would replace them. They therefore turned on their patron and conspired with the caliph and wazir against Muʾnis.[126]

In the final confrontation between Muʾnis and al-Muqtadir, spanning the years 319–320/931–932, we already see the most important aspects of the dissolution of the Abbasid military. The following is a brief summary of events: Muʾnis heard that his main rivals, Hārūn b. Gharīb, Yāqūt, and lbn Yāqūt, had been recalled to Baghdad; in response, Muʾnis mobilized his troops outside the city, as on several previous occasions. This time, however, al-Muqtadir did not cave in: he summoned the *rajjāla* and *fursān* to the palace, offering them raises and granting pardons. Muʾnis tried to reconcile with the caliph, but his messenger was beaten; so the general distanced himself from the capital and moved north, whereupon many of his troops abandoned him and returned to the caliph. The wazir (al-Faḍl b. Jaʿfar) wrote to all provincial governors to oppose and capture Muʾnis.

124. Miskawayh, *Tajārib*, 202–3.

125. ʿArīb, *Ṣilat*, 159.

126. ʿArīb, *Ṣilat*, 166.

Hearing this, the general headed toward Mosul, home of the Ḥamdānid family, who owed him money as well as gratitude for years of patronage.[127]

The encounter at Mosul was the turning point in Muʾnis's showdown with al-Muqtadir. The Ḥamdānids decided they could not defy the caliph's directives, so they confronted Muʾnis with a much larger force but were defeated in battle. Muʾnis distributed the spoils of battle to his men, remaining in Mosul for nine months, collecting money and attracting a huge number of soldiers. Those troops that remained in Baghdad, nominally loyal to the caliph, demanded increased pay. Eventually Muʾnis became so strong that the new wazir, Jaʿfar b. al-Furāt, encouraged the general to return to Baghdad and restore order in the capital. Muʾnis agreed and headed south. At first the caliph concurred with this plan; but he was persuaded by a group of Muʾnis's enemies to face the general in battle outside the city. The two forces met, al-Muqtadir's troops were routed, and the caliph was killed in ignoble fashion.

The most striking feature of these events is the constantly shifting loyalties and total unreliability of the soldiers, and even officers, throughout the Abbasid army. During the buildup to the hostilities, Muʾnis suffered dramatic troop reduction. First the *rajjāla*, who had previously allied with Muʾnis, now settled long-standing grievances with the caliph and returned to service in the palace.[128] Then as Muʾnis headed north, "many of the men in his command left him for the palace," including a handful of commanders; indeed, ʿArīb repeats several times that soldiers continued to desert Muʾnis.[129] As a result, Muʾnis's forces, originally numbering 6000 cavalry and 7000 infantry, had reportedly shrunk to 100 white *ghilmān*, 400 blacks, and 1500 infantry.[130] Muʾnis concealed from his men that the caliph had ordered provincial governors to arrest him, presumably fearing that more of his men would defect.[131] By the time of his battle with the Ḥamdānids, Muʾnis could only field cavalry and 630 infantry.[132]

For high-ranking officers, the break between Muʾnis and al-Muqtadir created a dilemma of conflicting obligations and calculations. The confrontation with the Ḥamdānids demonstrates this conflict clearly: Muʾnis set out for Mosul, for "in thinking about his situation and where he should go, Muʾnis could not think of anyone more trustworthy and grateful to him than the Banū Ḥamdān, and whenever he referred to them he called them 'my children.'"[133] Despite presumed gratitude for years of patronage, the Ḥamdānids were wary of supporting Muʾnis blindly; Abū al-Hayjāʾ b. Ḥamdān had supported Muʾnis in

127. Miskawayh, *Tajārib*, 233.

128. ʿArīb, *Ṣilat*, 166.

129. ʿArīb, *Ṣilat*, 167–69.

130. ʿArīb *Ṣilat*, 159, 168.

131. ʿArīb, *Ṣilat*, 169.

132. These numbers are not necessarily precise, though the head count does sound reasonable; the important point is the dramatic decline in total troops: from 13,000 to 1500.

133. ʿArīb, *Ṣilat*, 169.

317/929, and ended up dead while disgracing his family. When Muʾnis approached Mosul, the Ḥamdānids sent him a message, summarized by the historian ʿArīb:

> They were grateful to him and recognized his claim, but they knew of no way out of the situation. If they obeyed their ruler (*Sulṭān*), they would be disavowing Muʾnis's munificence (*niʿma*); and if they obeyed Muʾnis and abandoned their ruler, they would be accused of rebellion. So they asked him to depart their region, to absolve them from confrontation and from being tested against him in battle.

Muʾnis responded disappointedly: "I expected something else from you. I came here only because I trusted you and your gratitude. If you do not have a change of heart, then there is no way out for you, since we are staying put, whatever happens."[134] The Ḥamdānids ostensibly chose loyalty to the caliph over loyalty to Muʾnis; underlying this choice was a political calculation: they had "rebelled" unsuccessfully several times before and did not want to fall into the same trap, especially given that their own forces far outnumbered those of Muʾnis. Simply put, a continued alliance with the general did not seem the wise option.

With Muʾnis's surprising victory in Mosul, the flow of unabashedly opportunistic soldiers changed direction. While he occupied Mosul, "many of the *ghilmān* of Ibn Ḥamdān joined his camp;" then "the news of Muʾnis's triumph and conquest reached the people of Baghdad, so all those who had abandoned him began returning to him.... Muʾnis remained in Mosul, his conquests continued and his prestige grew, so that the ruler's men in the palace started to escape, and claim devotion to him."[135] The absence of loyalty is astounding, as soldiers, even officers, switched sides back and forth, depending on who appeared stronger. When Muʾnis eventually approached Baghdad, "commanders and others came to him requesting safe-conduct."[136] Among the troops that remained with al-Muqtadir were the *ḥujarīs*, the supposed elite of the Abbasid military and bastion of loyalty to the caliph. Yet even they disappointed the caliph, for during the final battle "those who surrounded al-Muqtadir were disloyal ... the first of his men to flee were the *ḥujariyya*."[137] ʿArīb adds that al-Muqtadir "was left by himself, though none of his *ghilmān* or elite were killed in his presence, save one."[138] With the greater part of his troops, and especially the *ḥujarī* guard, having abandoned him, al-Muqtadir was left alone and became easy prey for Berber assassins.

Of course, the issue underlying the repeated defection of troops and officers was money. In short, whoever could pay would attract troops; money was military power, and

134. ʿArīb, *Ṣilat*, 170.
135. ʿArīb, *Ṣilat*, 171–72.
136. ʿArīb, *Ṣilat*, 175.
137. ʿArīb, *Ṣilat*, 177–78.
138. ʿArīb, *Ṣilat*, 178.

everyone knew it and spoke of it openly.[139] Al-Muqtadir recaptured services of the *rajjāla* by offering them bonuses; similarly, Muʾnis attracted soldiers to Mosul because he was now collecting regional tax revenues, and even intercepted revenues from other regions on their way to Baghdad.[140] The increasing "prestige" of Muʾnis's battlefield victories and territorial control simply boiled down to this: he gradually had more money to spend. By contrast, the ultimate source of al-Muqtadir's woes, and his weak grip on troop loyalty, was his lack of funds. Muʾnis, in a final attempt at reconciliation, wrote to the caliph: "if my *mawlā* [the caliph] would only give the troops in my possession their salaries, and pay them, they would come to him and be agreeable to him."[141] Al-Muqtadir was dissuaded from reconciliation; but in any case, he had no money. In desperation he turned to his mother for help, but the last of her liquid funds had been seized in 317/929.[142] She would later make the connection between money and military strength very clear, for when the next caliph al-Qāhir demanded that she divulge her assets, she cried, "If I had any money, I would not have let my son be killed!"[143]

The victory of Muʾnis signals the final shift in the relationship between regional and centralized power. Military might was based upon control of troops, in which loyalty had become trivial, and money was everything. In the events of 319–320/931–932, Muʾnis demonstrated that money, and hence the resources to attract troops and assert power, were located outside Baghdad. Muʾnis had instinctively left the capital, and by circumstance seized Mosul, where he could collect money and divert the flow of funds to Baghdad, only to return and effectively conquer the city. From now on the implementation of military power was inverted: for most of the Abbasid period, and certainly since Baghdad was reestablished as the capital by the caliph al-Muʿtaḍid some forty years earlier, Abbasid armies set out from Baghdad to impose submission on provinces. From now on, the regions around Baghdad, as the source of tax revenue, became centers of power that periodically dominated the imperial city. The victory of Muʾnis was the first concrete sign of the decentralization of power within Iraq itself.

---

139. Muḥammad b. Yāqūt told the caliph, "The soldiers only fight for money. If money is taken out [to Muʾnis's supporters], there will be no need to fight, for most of Muʾnis's men will ask for safe conduct" (Miskawayh, *Tajārib*, 235).

140. ʿArīb, *Ṣilat*, 172.

141. ʿArīb, *Ṣilat*, 175.

142. ʿArīb, *Ṣilat*, 183–84; Miskawayh, *Tajārib*, 235.

*Al-Sayyida did in fact retain valuable real estate assets, which I discuss in a forthcoming article (Marmer, "Asset Management"); but these assets were not liquid and could not be used in a crisis to pay military salaries.

143. Miskawayh, *Tajārib*, 243.

Postscript: The Dissolution of the Abbasid Military, 320–324/932–936

The years 320–324/932–936 saw the final dissolution of the Abbasid military that had been revitalized by al-Muʿtaḍid. The decentralization and fluid loyalties of this military system had, by 320/932, developed into infighting and opportunism. In the following years troops and officers would change allegiances rapidly, fighting against one commander after another, until all high-ranking generals were eliminated. The resulting absence of military leadership, and inability to control, or pay, troops forced the caliph to accept the domination of regional strongmen (the *amīr al-umarāʾ*) and then a foreign dynasty (the Būyids).

The disarray of the Abbasid army is already obvious in 321/933. Al-Muqtadir's leading supporters—Hārūn b. Gharīb, Muḥammad b. Yāqūt, the Banū Rāʾiq, and Mufliḥ—had fled Baghdad, and Muʾnis sent Yalbaq with a large army to retrieve them. Yalbaq's army, however, was not unified. According to Miskawayh,

> Deserters were leaving the ranks; Yalbaq was growing weary, his troops were out of control, and he was thinking of retreating. He was steadied by Abū ʿAbdallāh al-Barīdī[144] who went from commander to commander, flattering and bribing them [to stay].[145]

Al-Barīdī was so struck by the military disunity and Yalbaq's incompetence that he resolved to become a powerful general himself; within a few years he was an important contender for control of Iraq. During this campaign, he urged Yalbaq to employ a basic strategy of divide and conquer, for not surprisingly, the opposition forces lacked cohesion.[146] Early on, Hārūn b. Gharīb requested and received a guarantee of safe conduct from the new government, so he abandoned his allies and received a governorship, thus reconciling with the murderers of his cousin al-Muqtadir.[147] Once Hārūn abandoned the opposition, "Muḥammad b. Yāqūt took command of affairs, thereby alienating those officers and troops who were with him;" likewise, "he became unpopular and the others decided to oppose him."[148] Here we see that military officers were not accustomed to centralized command, and thus the authoritarian behavior of Muḥammad b. Yāqūt antagonized them, further dividing their ranks. The Banū Rāʾiq accepted an offer to become

144. Al-Barīdī was in charge of the army's finances. For more on this man and his family, see D. Sourdel, "al-Barīdī," *EI2*.

145. Miskawayh, *Tajārib*, 256. This anecdote, like many others, shows that commanders felt free to abandon a campaign if they chose.

146. Al-Barīdī, with a strong financial sense, urged Yalbaq to hurry in defeating the opposition, lest they gain strength from the wealth of Ahwāz. Here is the explicit realization that the provinces were the source of funds, and hence military power. Al-Barīdī would later make Ahwāz his base for a bid at controlling Iraq.

147. Miskawayh, *Tajārib*, 253–54; Ibn al-Athīr, *al-Kāmil*, 8:248.

148. Miskawayh, *Tajārib*, 254–55; Ibn al-Athīr, *al-Kāmil*, 8:248.

the governors of Basra and abandoned their allies with no advanced warning. Mufliḥ followed their example and took the prince ʿAbd al-Wāḥid (son of al-Muqtadir) with him back to Baghdad. Without his most important allies, "Muḥammad b. Yāqūt was left alone, weakened."[149] He communicated with Yalbaq, and a deal was arranged whereby Ibn Yāqūt was also granted safe conduct.[150] Yalbaq's army, while far from cohesive, overcame the disunited opposition without even engaging in battle.

At this time Muʾnis dominated Baghdad. He soon forced his rival Muḥammad b. Yāqūt back into exile and made sure his own deputy Yalbaq assumed control of the palace. But Muʾnis's dominance was short-lived. ʿAlī b. Yalbaq conspired to replace the new caliph al-Qāhir. Yet al-Qāhir was able to foil this plot, and arrest the powerful faction of Muʾnis, Yalbaq, and ʿAlī b. Yalbaq by manipulating military divisiveness and jealousies. He knew that two of Muʾnis's officers, named Ṭarīf and Bushrā, were jealous of the ascendancy of Yalbaq and ʿAlī; he also knew that the Sājī troops,[151] now attached to Muʾnis, were disappointed that Muʾnis's promises to them were unfulfilled, and disliked the favor shown to the *ḥujarīs*. Al-Qāhir initiated communication with Muʾnis's disgruntled officers and troops and promised to raise their statuses. Thus, when ʿAlī b. Yalbaq moved to seize al-Qāhir, Tarif betrayed the plan to the caliph, who assembled the Sājī troops inside the palace. The Sājīs confronted ʿAlī b. Yalbaq, who went into hiding, later to be found in a baker's oven; and before al-Qāhir's new allies could stop the caliph, he had Yalbaq and Muʾnis arrested.[152] When the whole Baghdadi army rioted in order to have Muʾnis released, the caliph simply executed him, along with Yalbaq and ʿAlī.[153] The great general Muʾnis had finally been bested, only because al-Qāhir was able, if only temporarily, to turn Muʾnis's own officers and troops against him. Not long after this event, the Sājīs and *ḥujarīs* allied and exacted revenge against the caliph, removing him from the throne and appointing al-Muqtadir's oldest son, al-Rāḍī, as the new caliph.[154]

The military infighting did not end with the deaths of Muʾnis and his leading generals. The new caliph al-Rāḍī appointed Muḥammad b. Yāqūt as chamberlain, and the latter again returned to Baghdad and dominated state affairs. But Hārūn b. Gharīb, out in the eastern provinces, believed that military leadership should belong to him; he marched on the capital, and Ibn Yāqūt set out to confront him. Here the common features of Abbasid military campaigns reappear: Ibn Yāqūt's men deserted in droves to Hārūn, and the various units under his control dispersed in battle. However, a fateful accident changed the course of events: Hārūn was thrown from his horse, and inexplicably his own slave

149. Ibn al-Athīr, *al-Kāmil*, 8:249.

150. Miskawayh, *Tajārib*, 256–57; Ibn al-Athīr, *al-Kāmil*, 8:249.

151. These were the troops who formerly belonged to Ibn Abī al-Sāj. They became an important faction in Baghdad until their dissolution is 324/936.

152. Miskawayh, *Tajārib*, 261–64: Ibn al-Athīr, *al-Kāmil*, 8:250–56. Ibn al-Athīr relates an interesting report about how al-Qāhir duped Ṭarīf into betraying Muʾnis.

153. Miskawayh, *Tajārib*, 261–64; Ibn al-Athīr, *al-Kāmil*, 8:260–61.

154. Miskawayh, *Tajārib*, 286–89.

pulled out a sword and cut off his head. Hārūn's forces immediately disbanded and returned to Baghdad; Ibn Yāqūt emerged victorious by default. This battle is reminiscent of the campaign in 321/933, in that neither side could command the loyalty of its troops. On this occasion, the Abbasid military lost another of its commanding officers.[155]

The purge of high-ranking officers continued. Ibn Yāqūt still dominated state administration, which irked al-Rāḍī and the wazir Ibn Muqla. In 323/935 they lured Ibn Yāqūt to the palace and arrested him; the next year he was found dead in prison.[156] His father Yāqūt remained in a military encampment outside Ahwāz, and for some reason accepted the caliph's arrest of his sons. Yet he soon encountered trouble. Abū ʿAbdallāh al-Barīdī, Yāqūt's financial officer stationed in Ahwāz, was amassing wealth through the revenues of this rich province. Through a variety of clever schemes, al-Barīdī siphoned off Yāqūt's best troops, attracting them to Ahwāz by offering them more money than Yāqūt. The latter's advisors suggested that he either attack al-Barīdī or return to Baghdad as the commander with seniority and take control of the *ḥujarīs*. Yalbaq remained undecided and stalled; his troops continued to desert, until even Yāqūt's son al-Muẓaffar abandoned his father for the wealthy tax collector. Al-Barīdī, unsure that his new troops would remain bound to him, forced a showdown with Yāqūt; and while the latter's troops were valiant in battle, they were outnumbered and routed. Yāqūt tried to conceal himself as a pauper in a monastery, but he was found by Berber soldiers and executed.[157]

The state's most important generals—Muʾnis, Yalbaq, Ibn Yalbaq, Hārūn, Yāqūt, and Ibn Yāqūt—were now dead; the troops in Baghdad rioted incessantly for lack of pay; and the government had no funds, since even the revenues of Basra, Wāsiṭ, Ahwāz, and Mosul had been diverted. With no money and his army in chaos, the caliph al-Rāḍī accepted Ibn Rāʾiq's offer to control both the military and civil administration as *amīr al-umarā'* (general of generals), using funds from his regional base in Wāsiṭ. In essence al-Rāḍī was trying to recentralize state institutions that had become chaotically decentralized. Waines notes that the appointment of Ibn Rāʾiq as *amīr al-umarāʾ* was not all that revolutionary: both Muʾnis and Ibn Yāqūt had essentially combined military and administrative authority in preceding years, though this might be the first time a caliph openly acknowledged such joint delegation of authority. Waines rightly points out that the appointment of Ibn Rāʾiq represents the triumph of a governor with regional resources over the capital, and

155. Miskawayh, *Tajārib*, 306–9; Ibn al-Athīr, *al-Kāmil*, 8:288–89.

156. Miskawayh, *Tajārib*, 318, 330; Ibn al-Athīr, *al-Kāmil*, 8:305. Ibn Yāqūt's brother al-Muẓaffar was also arrested and later released. There is no indication how Ibn Yāqūt's troops responded to his arrest. This seems to be another example of the troops stationed in the palace acting as a counterbalance to troops attached to leading generals. (It is remarkable that the leading commander of the day could be arrested in the palace. This was only possible because leading commanders did not have control over the entire military; power was divided).

157. Miskawayh, *Tajārib*, 341–47; Ibn al-Athīr, *al-Kāmil*, 8:315–21. Berbers are always attributed with these executions (for example: Abū al-Hayjāʾ, al-Muqtadir, Yāqūt).

that the caliph retained limited power by playing regional powers against one another.[158] I would only add that the attempt at centralization failed. The decentralized military established fifty years earlier had unraveled into a system of competing regional powers (in Mosul, Basra, Wāsiṭ and Ahwāz); and the period of the *amīr al-umarāʾ* saw innumerable regional competitions and alliances, in which the military chief of Baghdad was only one among many competitors. Only with the arrival of the Būyids, wielding new kinds of loyalty over Daylami and Turkish troops, was military and administrative authority again centralized.

158. Waines, "Caliph and Amir," 134; Waines, "Pre-Buyid Amirate," 346–47.

Chapter 5. The Bureaucracy

In this chapter I analyze the internal sociopolitical dynamics of the Abbasid bureaucracy. We have far more source material for this social group than for any other, so on the one hand examples are more plentiful and detailed, and on the other every generalization has its exceptions. Nevertheless, I will try to demonstrate that bureaucratic relations, especially at the highest levels, were characterized by instability and divisiveness. These conditions contributed to an atmosphere of constant competition, which involved distinct strategies and patterns of behavior. I argue that these patterns of competition were designed to maximize bureaucratic divisiveness, so that bureaucrats directed their political energies inward rather than outward. The end result was that bureaucrats had less control than other groups (the caliph and military in particular) over court politics.

The most prominent feature of bureaucratic life, especially at its pinnacle, the wazirate, was instability. The extent of this instability, and the issues which emanated from it, are emphasized by al-Tanūkhī at the very beginning of the *Nishwār*. The author opens his work with an anecdote that praises the generosity of the Barmakids, the bureaucratic family that acquired tremendous power under the caliphs al-Mahdī and al-Rashīd toward the beginning of the Abbasid dynasty, who were swiftly removed from power by the latter caliph, and subsequently mythologized and revered by generations of bureaucrats. Al-Tanūkhī's second anecdote presents a later interpretation of the Barmakid experience, as indicative of bureaucratic life in general. In this report, Ibn al-Zayyāt (d. 232/847), a wazir of many years, had just fallen into disfavor, and had the following conversation with one of his eunuchs:

> Eunuch: "It was for just such an occasion that we advised you to do kindnesses for people, put obligation to you upon their necks, and take on clients during a time of strength, so that you could be repaid now in time of need."
>
> Ibn al-Zayyāt: "If I had done that, it would not have done me any good, given the weakness of brotherhood in people's souls. So much betrayal, so little loyalty. Do you think I could have done more than the Barmakids? Did it help them when they reached a situation similar to mine, with the passing of time and the tyranny of the ruler (*Sulṭān*)?"
>
> Eunuch: "If it benefited them no more than to have you refer to them in such a situation as you are in, there could be no greater benefit."[1]

In this conversation, juxtaposed to the first anecdote about the Barmakids, al-Tanūkhī introduces the reader to the most important themes in bureaucratic life. The reference to the Barmakids immediately brings to mind that the most glorious of bureaucrats end-

1. al-Tanūkhī, *Nishwār*, 1:17; also translated by Margoliouth, *Table-talk*, 12.

ed their careers in disfavor, one of their members (Jaʿfar b. Yaḥyā) subject to a traumatic and infamous execution; if the reader missed this hint at first, Ibn al-Zayyāt makes it explicit. The initial comment of the eunuch in the second anecdote has two messages: first, that every bureaucrat, especially those in power, must acknowledge and address the likelihood of falling into disfavor: such a fall is to be expected. This realization is the foundation of all bureaucratic strategy. Second, a wazir can address this inevitability by cultivating clients, endowing benefits in exchange for future support. To some extent, a network of patronage is envisioned as mediating the impact of inevitable disfavor. Ibn al-Zayyāt's response, however, emphasizes the futility of opposing the fall from power; after all, even the model Abbasid bureaucrats, the Barmakids, had ended in disgrace. This futility has two main reasons: first, patronage is ineffective, because bureaucrats are simply not trustworthy; and second, and more decisive, no amount of bureaucratic unity can overcome caliphal tyranny. In short, wazirs and bureaucrats in general are doomed to instability, since they lack unity, and in any case the ruler has despotic power. The final remark by the eunuch is a sad commentary on a bureaucrat's fate: that the ultimate goal for bureaucrats is fame and prestige through posterity. This is a virtual admission that achieving lasting power during one's lifetime is nearly impossible, and that disgrace is merely to be expected.

Chronic Instability: Standard Abbasid Policy

The vicissitudes of bureaucratic life, and the inevitability of disfavor, are prevalent themes throughout the Abbasid era. Accounts from a variety of periods demonstrate that both bureaucrats and caliphs believed that any wazir's appointment was ultimately temporary, and that dismissal, asset seizure, and/or incarceration were inevitable. Already in the caliphate of al-Manṣūr, the wazir al-Mawaryānī (d. 154/771) expressed sorrow upon obtaining a large agricultural profit, for "if this is the extent of prosperity, then what will adversity be like!" The narrator continues that within a short time al-Manṣūr arrested al-Mawaryānī, confiscated his money and killed him.[2] The same sentiment was expressed by a high-ranking official during al-Mahdī's reign, who wept after receiving a special honor from the caliph, for "I have achieved the height of success; nothing remains but to descend." Though al-Mahdī reassured the official, the caliph later found the need to dismiss him.[3] In each of these cases, leading bureaucrats assumed that favor would naturally be followed by disfavor, and their fears came to pass.

Generations later, the caliph al-Muʿtamid articulated what had become standard caliphal practice: dismissing bureaucrats in order to seize their wealth. He told his wazir Sulaymān b. Wahb (d. 272/885): "You have held a variety of positions from the days of al-Muʿtazz until now, including the wazirate ... and you have never been in disfavor, nor

2. al-Tanūkhī, *Nishwār*, 8:131–33.
3. al-Tanūkhī, *Nishwār*, 8:136–38.

been fined. I want half a million dinars from you." On this occasion Sulaymān was temporarily held and released, but before long he was dismissed, arrested, and fined.[4] Like Sulaymān b. Wahb, officials with long tenures had to expect a reversal of fortune. The wazir al-Faḍl b. Marwān (d. 250/864) was known for holding bureaucratic posts from youth through death, enjoying a longer tenure than any other Abbasid official. Yet perhaps precisely because of this extended tenure, and the riches that accompanied it, the caliph al-Muʿtaṣim was tempted by al-Faḍl's vast resources, so he arrested and fined al-Faḍl forty million dirhems.[5]

In fact, the vicissitudes endured by leading bureaucrats were so common, they became proverbial. This theme was expressed on several occasions by the poet Ibn Bassām. He recited to the wazir al-Qāsim b. ʿUbaydallāh:

> Tell he who governs the ruler's state: it is at time of fullness to anticipate decline
>
> How many lofty wazirs have I seen, who have fallen to humiliation and disgrace![6]

Ibn Bassām reiterated the ups and downs of the wazirate in two poems dedicated to al-ʿAbbās b. al-Ḥasan:

> Don't you see the [fate] of those who preceded you, and how the whirlwind has carried them off in misfortune?
>
> You are building along the Tigris a palace to rival those of earlier men.
>
> But do not rejoice! For how many such as this have we seen uncompleted when their owner met his end.[7]

The perception that misfortune was inevitable for bureaucrats led Sulaymān b. Wahb to teach his son ʿUbaydallāh a submissive attitude: "A person should bow his head before ordeals, humble himself when they occur, and not oppose them."[8]

The stories and mindset of bureaucratic suffering were transmitted from one generation to the next. The anecdote of al-Mawaryānī's fall during the caliphate of al-Manṣūr was related to Ibn al-Furāt and ʿAlī b. ʿĪsā, the most prominent wazirs of al-Muqtadir's reign; the moral of the story made such a strong impression on them that they both wrote it down.[9] Similarly, a reflective comment by one of al-Maʾmūn's ministers was

4. al-Tanūkhī, *Nishwār*, 8:96–97.
5. al-Tanūkhī, *Nishwār*, 8:48.
6. al-Masʿūdī, *Murūj*, 264. Al-Qāsim died young (in 291/904) and therefore experienced no downfall.
7. al-Masʿūdī, *Murūj*, 265–66. Al-ʿAbbās was murdered by a general during the coup of 296/908.
8. al-Tanūkhī, *Nishwār*, 8:103.
9. al-Tanūkhī, *Nishwār*, 8:133.

transmitted by four different wazirs, all of whom no doubt sympathized with the man's bitterness that "only unlucky men enter this office."[10]

All these anecdotes and poems support one of Ibn al-Zayyāt's basic assertions, as presented in the beginning of the *Nishwār*: that the ultimate source of bureaucratic misfortune was the caliphs. It was obviously the caliphs who maintained their wazirs in a precarious position, and seemingly few caliphs had serious misgivings about replacing bureaucrats. The simple yet important conclusion we must draw is that caliphs did not have strong sentiments of obligation to their ministers, at least not strong enough to prevent dismissal. What's more, the caliphs used this instability to incite hostility and suspicion among bureaucrats. For example, the regent al-Muwaffaq[11] had replaced Sulaymān b. Wahb with Saʿīd b. Makhlad (d. 276/889); he repeatedly urged his new wazir to interrogate Sulaymān, but Saʿīd refused, explaining that Sulaymān had been his patron. Al-Muwaffaq then encouraged Sulaymān and his son ʿUbaydallāh (both incarcerated) to plot against Saʿīd: the regent planned to use evidence of this plotting to provoke Saʿīd into harming his former associates. Sulaymān saw through this scheme, but ʿUbaydallāh did not, and obliged al-Muwaffaq by slandering the new minister and asking for his position. Al-Muwaffaq, as planned, informed Saʿīd of ʿUbaydallāh's deeds, which, as expected, induced Saʿīd to extract a great deal of money from his former patron.[12] Here we see precisely what Ibn al-Zayyāt had described: with Abbasid encouragement, bureaucrats inevitably betrayed their colleagues, so that bonds of patronage could not effectively curb the chronic instability.

Instability under al-Muʿtaḍid

The uncertainty and turmoil of bureaucratic life continued in the reign of al-Muʿtaḍid, although at a somewhat lesser intensity. Hilāl al-Ṣābī begins his work on the wazirs of this period (*Kitāb al-Wuzarāʾ*) with an anecdote that demonstrates bureaucratic vicissitudes and immediately conditions the reader to the realities of bureaucratic life that will appear repeatedly throughout the book. ʿUbaydallāh b. Sulaymān, al-Muʿtaḍid's new wazir, had been incarcerated during the previous reign and was no longer familiar with state affairs; he therefore turned for help to the Banū al-Furāt (Abū al-ʿAbbās and Abū al-Ḥasan), who had served under the previous wazir, but were now in disfavor.[13] The report continues:

> [ʿUbaydallāh] summoned Abū al-Ḥasan ʿAlī b. Muḥammad b. al-Furāt, who at the time was imprisoned with his brother Abū al-ʿAbbās Aḥmad. They had been

10. al-Tanūkhī, *Nishwār*, 8:197.

11. He was not officially caliph (his brother al-Muʿtamid was); but he had effective control over the state.

12. al-Tanūkhī, *Nishwār*, 8:101–2.

13. Their patron, the wazir Ismāʿīl b. Bulbul, had been executed in 279/892.

> exposed to rough treatment: Abū al-ʿAbbās had been hung from a rope tied to his hands, which left a scar for the rest of his life; he had been required to pay 120,000 dinars, of which he paid 60,000. [Abū al-Ḥasan] was brought from his cell shackled in chains, wearing a filthy coat, his hair unkempt. When he was standing before [ʿUbaydallāh] he said: "God bless the wazir." He began to complain about the harshness that befell him and his brother Abū al-ʿAbbās. His body was trembling. ʿUbaydallāh b. Sulaymān calmed him and brought him close, sat him down and spoke in a manner that soothed his fear and dismay.[14]

When Abū al-Ḥasan demonstrated detailed financial expertise, ʿUbaydallāh was convinced that he needed the assistance of the Banū al-Furāt; the wazir ordered that the brothers' shackles be removed, and that they receive better conditions.

This first anecdote of Hilāl al-Ṣābī's work establishes the vicissitudes of bureaucratic life. ʿUbaydallāh b. Sulaymān, once the deputy wazir, had been in prison but was now promoted to the wazirate. The Banū al-Furāt, previously deputies to a different wazir, had also fallen into disfavor and had been tortured. When ʿUbaydallāh found them indispensable, however, their fate changed again, and they were appointed to important posts. We therefore see that it was common for the highest of bureaucrats to fall and even be tortured; their circumstances could change with great frequency and rapidity.

The next anecdote in Hilāl al-Ṣābī's book shows ʿUbaydallāh in consultation with the caliph al-Muʿtaḍid, requesting that the Banū al-Furāt be removed from jail and appointed to ministries. The conversation continued:

> Al-Muʿtadid: "How can their intentions toward us be good, when we have treated them poorly, harmed them and fined them?"
>
> ʿUbaydallāh: "If you wish to employ them and engender good will...."
>
> Al-Muʿtaḍid: "Perhaps they will gang up on you and estrange you and me from one another. But the decision whether to hold or release them is yours."

In need of their financial expertise, ʿUbaydallāh released the Banū al-Furāt and gave them appointments.[15]

The caliph's remarks in this conversation contain several implications. First, the Banū al-Furāt cannot be completely trusted, since they have experienced the harshness of disfavor. However, this was a fate common to most bureaucrats, meaning that—in the caliph's mind—no lasting trust could develop between caliph and wazir. Second, al-Muʿtaḍid subtly hints at the precariousness of ʿUbaydallāh's position. By suggesting that the Banū al Furat could theoretically alienate the caliph from his wazir, al-Muʿtaḍid implied that his own bond with ʿUbaydallāh was tentative and vulnerable to rupture. Fi-

14. Hilāl al-Ṣābī, *Wuzarāʾ*, 12. Note the symbolism endowing favor: bringing him close, allowing him to sit—reminiscent of spatial relations as discussed in the introduction.

15. Hilāl al-Ṣābī, *Wuzarāʾ*, 14.

nally, al-Muʿtaḍid embeds a kernel of distrust among the bureaucrats by suggesting that the Banū al-Furāt might plot against their superior, ʿUbaydallāh. In short, al-Muʿtaḍid reiterates the transitory nature of the wazir's ties to both his patron and his clients and colleagues.

As the interpretation of the above passage suggests, al-Muʿtaḍid was a brilliant manipulator of court politics, and he kept his wazir defensive and nervous without damaging state affairs by actually removing him. At one point al-Muʿtaḍid considered dismissing ʿUbaydallāh but concluded that "changing wazirs only hurts the state."[16] The public awareness of the caliph's ambivalence toward his wazir, and the hint of tenuous personal commitment, weighed on ʿUbaydallāh; as a result, like most wazirs before and after, ʿUbaydallāh was perpetually paranoid. For example, when he was once summoned to the royal palace in the middle of the night, he was afraid that he would be dismissed.[17] The tension between caliph and wazir also contributed to the typical court atmosphere of uncertainty; thus, when ʿUbaydallāh publicly honored a friend, the merchant Ibn Abī ʿAwf, and al-Muʿtaḍid criticized the wazir for neglecting etiquette, ʿUbaydallāh advised Ibn Abī ʿAwf to save money in case they both fell upon hard times.[18]

Al-Muʿtaḍid further emphasized ʿUbaydallāh's precarious position by undermining his administrative authority. The caliph frequently empowered the Banū al-Furāt at the wazir's expense. For example, while ʿUbaydallāh was away in Fārs and had deputized his son al-Qāsim, the caliph established a new protocol that no important financial document would be acted upon without the approval of Abū al-ʿAbbās b. al-Furāt.[19] Such a subversion of waziral authority occurred often enough that ʿUbaydallāh's subordination to the Banū al-Furāt was noted, and criticized, by many people at court.[20]

Al-Muʿtaḍid curbed the power of the wazir by keeping him in a constant state of uncertainty and by undermining his authority among leading bureaucrats. But this caliph wisely recognized that constant change brought financial turmoil, so he never dismissed his wazir; nor did his son al-Muktafī in the latter's brief reign.[21] The tumultuous na-

16. al-Tanūkhī, *Nishwār*, 8:92.

17. al-Tanūkhī, *Nishwār*, 8:14. There are many similar examples of ʿUbaydallāh's fear of al-Muʿtaḍid, and the risk of dismissal.

18. al-Tanūkhī, *Nishwār*, 1:78–80. Another example of this engrained assumption of bureaucratic vicissitudes appears in a poem sent to ʿUbaydallāh by a colleague: "Take advantage of the unique opportunity while you are in power, because who knows when things will change" (Hilāl al-Ṣābī, *Rusūm*, 54).

*For a lengthier analysis of the relationship between the wazir and the merchant, and a broader view of Ibn Abī ʿAwf's mercantile career, see my recent article: Marmer, "Greed Is Good."

19. Hilāl al-Ṣābī, *Wuzarāʾ*, 208.

20. Criticisms include those by ʿUbaydallāh b. ʿAbdallāh b. Ṭāhir (Hilāl al-Ṣābī, *Wuzarāʾ*, 241); the bureaucrat Ibn Thawāba (Hilāl al-Ṣābī, *Wuzarāʾ*, 278); and the financial expert al-Mādhrāʾī (al-Tanūkhī, *Nishwār*, 8:112). Here I differ from Mottahedeh who argues that under al-Muʿtaḍid the wazir monopolized administrative powers ("Bureaucracy and the Patrimonial State").

21. ʿUbaydallāh died in office year 287/900, and was succeeded by his son al-Qāsim, who also died in office in 291/904.

ture of the bureaucracy was in full force, however, under the caliph al-Muqtadir, as this impressionable and financially strapped caliph appointed fifteen wazirs in twenty-five years. These continual changes stoked the atmosphere of bureaucratic instability, and the assumption that any given wazir was vulnerable to dismissal. For example, when a dejected Ibn al-Furāt returned home from the palace, his associates all assumed that he had been dismissed;[22] a judge visiting ʿAlī b. ʿĪsā found the wazir distressed, and surmised that ʿAlī was having troubles with the caliph;[23] and the wazir Ibn Muqla told a subordinate to cash a promissory note as soon as possible, for who knew how long he would remain wazir, whence the document would lose validity.[24] This atmosphere of instability was further intensified by the rumors that circulated about the fall of virtually every wazir. It is in this period that the strategies of bureaucratic competition are most evident.

The Reign of al-Muqtadir: Networks of Patronage and Alliance

Establishing Relations

We have seen that caliphs frequently removed wazirs, which encouraged other bureaucrats to plot against the wazir and seek the highest administrative post for themselves.[25] In this atmosphere of instability and competition, one fundamental means of creating a measure of stability and loyalty was by establishing networks of patron-client relations.[26] Such relations developed in a variety of ways; presumably the most basic method of establishing a personal relationship was to hire a subordinate for administrative or scribal skills. This kind of working relationship could develop into a personal bond for two reasons: an employee generally worked for his boss, not for the state; and an employee also attended his patron in social and leisure activities. Both these facts reflect a blurring of the private and public aspects of court life. The other basic source of patronage relations was inheritance and family tradition, namely adopting the patrons, clients, and allies of one's parents and ancestors. We have countless examples, from all social groups—but especially the bureaucrats—of men employing the sons of protégés, mentors, and distant

22. Hilāl al-Ṣābī, *Wuzarāʾ*, 134.

23. al-Tanūkhī, *Nishwār*, 1:19.

24. al-Tanūkhī, *Nishwār*, 2:26.

25. The subject of relations has been discussed extensively by Mottahedeh, particularly with reference to a somewhat later period (the mid-fourth/tenth century). Below I outline the basic principles that guided bureaucratic relations, often parallel to Mottahedeh's elucidation, using examples from this slightly earlier period.

*M. van Berkel has also discussed the importance of bureaucratic alliances and networks, especially within extended families (van Berkel et al, *Crisis and Continuity*, ch. 3, esp. 77–82; "The successes of al-Muqtadir's viziers were dependent upon their ability to build networks of allies and supporters" [81]).

26. This is what Ibn al-Zayyāt's eunuch had argued at the beginning of the *Nishwār* (1:17). I will avoid the chicken-and-the-egg question of whether patronage or instability existed first; for now, we will focus on relations of patronage as one counterbalance to the inescapable reality of instability.

relatives. In many cases the principles of technical skill and inherited relations overlapped, for a patron could assume that a protégé's son was properly trained.

Another common impetus for establishing or deepening relations was to repay someone for a favor. On several occasions Ibn al-Furāt rewarded the kindness of commoners, that is, individuals with no established administrative skills or experience, with money or an official post.[27] Bureaucrats and other people at court helped disgraced officials pay fines, which also created a mutual obligation.[28] The most obligating favor was that of hiding someone in disgrace, who faced reprisal and/or asset confiscation. For example, the merchant Ibn Abī ʿAwf housed ʿUbaydallāh b. Sulaymān while the latter was in disfavor; upon appointment to the wazirate, ʿUbaydallāh summoned his erstwhile protector to a public gathering, showed him various honors, and arranged for him to receive a great deal of money.[29]

Relations could also be initiated by a client. It was not uncommon to woo a prospective patron, by giving him presents and bribing intermediaries for recommendations. On one such occasion, a prospective client thanked the regional official Ibn Abī al-Baghl for being exceedingly rude and eliminating any possibility of employment, since this saved the man months of effort and all kinds of expenditures intended to win over the patron.[30]

Alliances were formed in response to a common enemy. One example of the formation of alliances embodies many of the elements of bureaucratic intrigue. In the early 290s/900s, two high-level ministers, Muḥammad b. Dāwud and Ibn ʿAbdūn, unified against their colleague, Abū al-Ḥasan b. al-Furāt, and encouraged the wazir al-ʿAbbās b. al-Ḥasan to arrest him. The wazir first tried to convince the caliph al-Muktafī to dismiss Ibn al-Furāt but failed. Sometime thereafter, the leading bureaucrats assembled for a routine meeting. The scene was described by Ibn al-Furāt's secretary Zanjī:

> I entered al-ʿAbbās's palace with Abū al-Ḥasan [Ibn al-Furāt]; we found the wazir sitting in his reception room, with the whole group [of leading bureaucrats] before him. [The wazir] rose [and departed], and the bureaucrats remained

---

27. In one entertaining example, Ibn al-Furāt is said to have been traversing Baghdad one day, when his clothes were soiled; he was given refuge by a conscientious tailor. In gratitude, Ibn al-Furāt repaid the tailor (whom he managed to remember some years later) by paying him one thousand dinars and granting him a minor governmental post (al-Tanūkhī, *Nishwār*, 1:66–67; translated by Margoliouth, *Table-talk*, 41–42).

28. For example, the financier al-Mādhrāʾī offered to help Ibn al-Furāt pay a fine; in return, the latter was accommodating to al-Mādhrāʾī's son a few years later (Hilāl al-Ṣābī, *Wuzarāʾ*, 110).

29. Al-Muʿtaḍid was angry at ʿUbaydallāh for this breach of etiquette—a grandiose display of respect for a mere merchant—but forgave him once ʿUbaydallāh explained that the man had housed him (al-Tanūkhī, *Nishwār*, 1:80–81). Parallel examples include: Ibn al-Furāt appointing one of his protectors to be a judge, though the man was not qualified (al-Tanūkhī, *Nishwār*, 1:233); Ibn al-Furāt being angry at a client who had neglected to repay the man who had hidden him (Hilāl al-Ṣābī, *Wuzarāʾ*, 228).

30. al-Tanūkhī, *Nishwār*, 2:153–54.

> waiting for him. His secretary appeared and summoned Ibn al-Furāt, who entered [to see the wazir]. Everyone present had no doubt that he would be arrested.... I (Zanjī) was overcome with fear, which increased since [Ibn al-Furāt] was with him a long time, and people were anxious for news of what had happened to him. Then al-ʿAbbās emerged with Ibn al-Furāt, sat down, and seated [Ibn al-Furāt] to his right, kissed his face, and demonstrated intimacy with him. Those present looked at one another, surprised to see the opposite of what they had expected.

When Ibn al-Furāt later returned to his chambers, he explained to Zanjī what had transpired. The wazir al-ʿAbbās had told his chamberlain to keep everyone out so that the two could speak in private. Alone, al-ʿAbbās told Ibn al-Furāt: "If you have any desire for [the wazirate], I will surrender it to you and resign it on your behalf, if in return you will safeguard myself, my harem, my money and my children." Ibn al-Furāt declined, claiming satisfaction with his current status; al-ʿAbbās insisted that he would make Ibn al-Furāt his successor to the wazirate in return for safeguarding al-ʿAbbās's family. According to Ibn al-Furāt, "[al-ʿAbbās] was not satisfied until he made me swear. Then he grasped me with his hand, hugged me and said, 'Our affairs are now one, our power (hand) is one. Don't pay attention to those bureaucrats and the things they say, don't think about their slander. Be confident of your standing with me.'"[31]

Here we see the basic scenario of court competition. Instability is everywhere: everyone assumes that Ibn al-Furāt will be dismissed; his secretary Zanjī is frightened by this likelihood and the implications for himself. More surprisingly, even the wazir al-ʿAbbās feels insecure; indeed, he is so concerned about his own safety and that of his family, that he is willing trade his position for protection.[32] To partially alleviate this uncertainty, alliances were formed: just as two men had joined forces against Ibn al-Furāt, the wazir now courts Ibn al-Furāt in a mutually beneficial security pact.

Another aspect of this event was typical: most relations, both patron/client and alliance, were formally displayed in public. On this occasion, al-ʿAbbās demonstrated his alliance with Ibn al-Furāt by honoring him (with a seat, a kiss, and other signs of intimacy) before the assemblage of bureaucrats. In an earlier example of ʿUbaydallāh b. Sulaymān and his friend the merchant, the wazir expressed his gratitude to Ibn Abī ʿAwf by standing in his honor in the wazir's assembly, which had enraged the caliph al-Muʿtaḍid. Such public demonstrations enabled bureaucrats and their allies to present a united front vis-a-vis competitors; this reflects the enmeshed quality of court relations, for a bond was most valuable in the context of other social relations.

---

31. Hilāl al-Ṣābī, *Wuzarāʾ*, 252–53.

32. Unlike many wazirs, al-ʿAbbās was not dismissed or executed: he was murdered by a general (at the outset of the failed coup of 296/908).

Maintaining Relations

Patrons and clients were expected to fulfill basic obligations. The primary responsibility of a patron, aside from providing clients with official posts, was munificence. For example, when Ibn al-Furāt was appointed wazir he distributed money to each of his protégés; we should not be surprised that the largest of these gifts were publicized.[33] We most often hear of clients being given the right to bring petitions to their patrons, a service for which they took sizable fees. When ʿAlī b. ʿĪsā once complained that a protégé had brought too many petitions, the man replied, "Wazir, if it is our fate to be beaten by your enemies during your disfavor, and denied [favors] during your appointment, when, I would like to know, are we to benefit?"[34] Patrons were also expected to be protective of clients. This was a responsibility that the Banū al-Furāt took particularly seriously, as on several occasions they shielded subordinates,[35] refused to take money from them,[36] and even forgave them for plotting.[37]

Clients, aside from being skilled administrators, were expected to be loyal to their patrons. Such loyalty was not taken for granted in a setting of constant competition and was often tested. For example, Zanjī demonstrated his loyalty to Ibn al-Furāt, and was praised for it, by rejecting a bribe to spy on his boss,[38] and by defending Ibn al-Furāt before the caliph al-Muʿtaḍid.[39] Loyalty was especially important when a patron had fallen on hard times. Three of Ibn al-Furāt's staff are singled out for staying with their boss when it was rumored that he would be arrested, though it was standard practice for such men to hide lest they be arrested as well.[40] Bureaucrats, and friends or colleagues from other professions, were thanked or rewarded for helping a disgraced patron in some manner. Of course, clients were expected to be trustworthy, and a reputation for discretion and keeping secrets was highly cultivated. Thus, one secretary was ashamed of himself and concerned about his reputation when he revealed secret news that a friendly bureaucrat had imparted to him.[41] Finally, clients were not supposed to criticize or con-

33. Ibn Muqla and Zanjī received the largest gifts (Hilāl al-Ṣābī, *Wuzarāʾ*, 197–99).

34. al-Tanūkhī, *Nishwār*, 1:84.

35. Hilāl al-Ṣābī, *Wuzarāʾ*, 226.

36. Hilāl al-Ṣābī, *Wuzarāʾ*, 113, 235–36. There was a general ethic of not taking back gifts or loans from one's protégés. This principle is stated twice by the caliph al-Muqtadir (Hilāl al-Ṣābī, *Wuzarāʾ*, 97–98; al-Tanūkhī, *Nishwār*, 4:70).

37. Hilāl al-Ṣābī, *Wuzarāʾ*, 83–84.

38. Hilāl al-Ṣābī, *Wuzarāʾ*, 192.

39. Hilāl al-Ṣābī, *Wuzarāʾ*, 204–6. This is a fascinating story. The caliph was actually disguised as a soldier and complained to Zanjī about the failures of different government officials. Zanjī defended each one, and supposedly only later found out that he had been talking to the caliph.

40. The three men were Ibn Farjawayh, Zanjī, and Ibn Jubayr (Hilāl al-Ṣābī, *Wuzarāʾ*, 181, 250).

41. al-Tanūkhī, *Nishwār*, 2:22. Also, Ibn Jubayr acknowledged that ʿAlī b. ʿĪsā had an advantage over Ibn al-Furāt, in that ʿAlī was an accomplished scribe and therefore did not need to dictate letters to a subordinate, which enabled him to better conceal state secrets (Hilāl al-Ṣābī, *Wuzarāʾ*, 272).

tradict their patrons in public. When men were asked for their opinions, and these contradicted those of their superiors, they first asked for permission and guarantee of safety before speaking their minds.[42]

As patrons accumulated clients, they developed something approaching factions. Each of these factions presumably had a common goal: keeping the patron in power, which would result in appointments, prestige, and wealth for his supporters. By extension, each faction would suffer decline as a unit. The benefit of such a system was unity among a group of bureaucrats; the disadvantage was inevitable competition between factions. However, as Mottahedeh has pointed out, a common interest among bureaucrats sometimes overcame factional differences, and those in power often assisted their colleagues (and rivals) who were in disfavor.[43] The entire system provided a measure of predictability in a setting of continual change, and enabled the bureaucrats to order their own relations, and even develop camaraderie and (occasionally) reciprocal safeguards, in the face of caliphal tyranny.

Enmity and Betrayal

Yet the unity derived from patronage and alliance, and even from group identity, only tempered in a minor way the more important phenomenon of internal bureaucratic competition. The most basic point we must recognize here, which is often overlooked, is that bureaucrats often had multiple patrons. Examples of this abound: Zanjī, Ibn al-Furāt's trusted confidant, worked for Ḥāmid b. al-ʿAbbās while Ibn al-Furāt was in jail;[44] so did ʿUbaydallāh b. Muḥammad al-Kalwādhī and Ṣaqr b. Muḥammad.[45] Al-Khāqānī employed the staffs of previous wazirs;[46] and one of his employees, named Abū ʿĪsā, continued working for the next wazir.[47] A certain Abu Aḥmad al-Shirāzī worked for the wazir Ibn Muqla, but still visited his former patron al-Khaṣībī, at the time under house arrest.[48] There were several reasons for these multiple loyalties: with wazirs changing so rapidly, particularly under al-Muqtadir, it would have been foolish for a bureaucrat to tie his career to only one patron; as well, the large number of wazirs meant there were many different patrons available. Moreover, the state administration could hardly function if every single official was replaced every few years, so bureaucrats became somewhat more attached to their jobs than to their patrons.[49]

42. Hilāl al-Ṣābī, *Wuzarāʾ*, 72.

43. The best example is Ibn al-Furāt, who at various critical moments helped ʿAlī b. ʿĪsā, Sulaymān b. al-Ḥasan, and Muḥammad b. Dāwud, all of whom were his rivals.

44. Miskawayh, *Tajārib*, 59.

45. Miskawayh, *Tajārib*, 71.

46. Hilāl al-Ṣābī, *Wuzarāʾ*, 293.

47. al-Tanūkhī, *Nishwār*, 1:42.

48. al-Tanūkhī, *Nishwār*, 2:60–66.

49. We have already seen that the Banū al-Furāt, who originally worked for Ibn Bulbul, agreed to

This multiplicity of loyalties meant that a client could betray one patron in favor of another. Ironically, this happened most often with the most conscientious patrons, the Banū al-Furāt. A certain Ibn Māshāllāh was originally promoted and favored by Abū al-Ḥasan b al-Furāt, and went on to work for ʿAlī b. ʿĪsā and Ḥāmid; Ibn Māshāllāh then produced false testimony at Ibn al-Furāt's interrogation, for which he was later murdered by his former patron.[50] Ibn al-Furāt was particularly shocked by the betrayal of two highly favored protégés, Ibn Muqla and Sulaymān b. al-Ḥasan, both of whom plotted against their patron while still working for him.[51] Nor did such men become social outcasts, as both Ibn Muqla and Sulaymān b. al-Ḥasan later became wazirs. The fluidity of loyalties is particularly evident in the wazirate of al-Khāqānī (the younger), for he hired the officials of previous wazirs, but then complained to the caliph that these men had betrayed him to yet another prospective patron.[52] These high-profile cases in fact reflect a very widespread phenomenon of changing loyalties. Even back in the caliphate of al-Muʿtaḍid, the Banū al-Furāt were given a chest full of letters written by supporters who were plotting against them;[53] and when Zanjī refused to spy on Ibn al-Furāt, he discovered that most of his colleagues had not refused.[54] It is difficult to generalize, given the multiplicity of instances, as to why so many bureaucrats betrayed their patrons; we can simply point out that the availability of alternative patrons made such betrayal possible, and often financially attractive.

In addition to worrying about betrayal, virtually every bureaucrat had to be concerned about enemies. Many high-ranking officials—Ibn al-Furāt, al-Khāqānī, Ḥāmid b. al-ʿAbbās, Zanjī, and even the judge Abū ʿUmar—refer to their "enemies." They probably had no specific people in mind but simply assumed that such enemies existed. This endemic hostility, along with betrayal of patrons and allies, were products of an atmosphere of constant competition. Since wazirs could be changed fairly frequently, high-level bureaucrats became locked in a struggle to knock down the current wazir and fend off foes to maintain the wazirate upon obtaining it; logically, such competition was more intense in periods with rapid change in the wazirate. Moreover, this competition for the wazirate filtered down among the bureaucrats, all of whom sought to take advantage of the instability to obtain higher positions. All this competition was self-reinforcing: as bureaucrats schemed for higher rank, they provoked jealousies and made enemies, who

work for the latter's rival ʿUbaydallāh b. Sulaymān, who needed their financial expertise.

50. Hilāl al-Ṣābī, *Wuzarāʾ*, 234–37.

51. Ibn Muqla told Naṣr about Ibn al-Furāt's monetary deposits, the existence of which the latter had denied under oath (Hilāl al-Ṣābī, *Wuzarāʾ*, 81–82); Sulaymān b. al-Ḥasan wrote a note to the caliph, suggesting that Ibn al-Furāt should be replaced by Ibn Abi al-Baghl (Hilāl al-Ṣābī, *Wuzarāʾ*, 33, 117; al-Tanūkhī, *Nishwār*, 8:191–93; *al-Faraj*, 129).

52. Hilāl al-Ṣābī, *Wuzarāʾ*, 291–94.

53. Hilāl al-Ṣābī, *Wuzarāʾ*, 83.

54. Hilāl al-Ṣābī, *Wuzarāʾ*, 83.

in turn sought revenge and a return to power, thereby continuing the cycle of competition in perpetuity.[55]

Competition and Hostility

The prevalence of shifting loyalties, competition for official posts, betrayal, and revenge created an atmosphere of continuous plotting. We see this best in cases when people assumed the existence of a plot that did not actually exist. We have already seen that Zanjī returned a bribe, fearful that his enemies would leak this transgression to his patron.[56] Similarly, Ibn Muqla (at the time the wazir's assistant) feared that an anonymous letter brought to the wazir contained accusations against him, when actually the accusations were directed at the wazir himself.[57] Constant plotting fostered distrust and skepticism about people's intentions. Thus, after the failed coup of 296/908, when Ibn al-Furāt encouraged Muḥammad b. Dāwud to stay in hiding, the disgraced bureaucrat suspected Ibn al-Furāt's intentions, came to the royal palace, was seized by the chamberlain and executed.[58] Much later (315/927), ʿAlī b. ʿĪsā declared that he had forgiven all long-standing rivals, including a certain Hishām b. ʿAbdallāh; yet Hishām quickly became afraid that other enemies would urge ʿAlī to arrest him, so he remained in hiding.[59]

Preemptive Measures

Because plotting was ubiquitous, bureaucrats and others at court took preemptive and precautionary measures. One important strategy was to appease one's enemies. This often took the form of helping rivals pay their fines, such as when the financial officer al-Mādhrāʾī, terrified of Ibn al-Furāt, offered to assist the latter with a payment and thereby reduce future enmity.[60] Another man allowed a rival to escape from prison, assuming that this favor would eventually be repaid.[61] Some wazirs even granted wholesale pardons to subdue hostility: for example, Ibn al-Furāt burned the list of men who had participated in the coup of 296/908, explaining: "If I had read [the list of names], I would have ruined people's intentions toward me, since they would have feared me," and hence plotted against him.[62] Years earlier, the Banū al-Furāt had thrown away conspiratorial letters

55. *M. van Berkel has come to a similar conclusion: that despite a shared bureaucratic ethos, "many narrative sources relate how scribes constantly tried to outdo their colleagues and how they plotted against each other" (van Berkel et al, *Crisis and Continuity*, 106).
56. Hilāl al-Ṣābī, *Wuzarāʾ*, 218–19.
57. Hilāl al-Ṣābī, *Wuzarāʾ*, 123.
58. Hilāl al-Ṣābī, *Wuzarāʾ*, 29–30.
59. Hilāl al-Ṣābī, *Wuzarāʾ*, 338–39.
60. Hilāl al-Ṣābī, *Wuzarāʾ*, 110.
61. al-Tanūkhī, *Nishwār*, 8:65–66.
62. Hilāl al-Ṣābī, *Wuzarāʾ*, 136.

without reading them, to avoid further alienating the authors of these letters.[63] We have also seen that ʿAlī b. ʿĪsā publicly announced that he did not bear a grudge against those who had plotted against him.[64] All these actions were taken with the assumption that plotting was endemic to court life, but could be curbed through appeasement and forgiveness.

Other preemptive measures were also championed. The judge Abū ʿUmar intentionally spoke in a vague fashion, so that he could protect himself from any particular interpretation of anything he said; this cautiousness was considered shrewd on his part.[65] Similarly, the jewelry merchant Ibn al-Jaṣṣāṣ pretended to be stupid, so that bureaucrats would not be threatened by his wealth.[66] Ḥāmid b. al-ʿAbbās encouraged an entirely different approach: he urged bureaucrats to publicize their hostile relations with enemies, so that people would disregard an enemy's slanderous remarks.[67]

All these strategies were intended to delay or prevent enemy plotting. Additional strategies were employed as preparation for dismissal. Most wazirs embezzled large sums of money, both for themselves and for supporters, knowing that their tenure was short and would certainly be followed by fines.[68] The trick, however, was to leave no trace of the cash flow, since documentary evidence was bound to fall into the hands of successors and inquisitors.

Having amassed wealth, the court elite sought methods of concealment. One means of protection was through diversification: dividing one's wealth into revenue-producing property, *waqfs*, jewelry, and cash (coins). A hostile successor was somewhat restricted by legalities from liquidating property and *waqfs*, and jewelry was easy to hide and transport.[69] The more difficult challenge was to hide cash. Ḥāmid b. al-ʿAbbās, for one, hid hundreds of thousands of dinars in wells and toilets.[70] The standard practice, however, was to scatter one's holdings by depositing them with various members of the court elite. This practice was very common and involved nearly everyone, as bureaucrats deposited money with one another, with judges and with merchants.[71] In fact, deposits were so

63. Hilāl al-Ṣābī, *Wuzarāʾ*, 83.

64. Hilāl al-Ṣābī, *Wuzarāʾ*, 337.

65. al-Tanūkhī, *Nishwār*, 1:61.

66. al-Tanūkhī, *Nishwār*, 1:30.

*For more examples of the tactics employed by Ibn al-Jaṣṣāṣ, see Marmer, "Asset Management" (forthcoming).

67. al-Tanūkhī, *Nishwār*, 8:63.

68. For example, one official was persuaded to take a bribe, since he was probably going to be dismissed soon anyway (al-Tanūkhī, *Nishwār*, 8:270–71).

69. *For more on the diversification of assets, see Marmer, "Asset Management" (forthcoming).

70. Hilāl al-Ṣābī, *Wuzarāʾ*, 327; al-Tanūkhī, *Nishwār*, 1:24.

71. Judges: Ibn al-Buhlūl held money for Ibn al-Furāt (Hilāl al-Ṣābī, *Wuzarāʾ*, 114; al-Tanūkhī, *Nishwār*, 4:12); Abū ʿUmar concealed funds for Ibn al Furat (Hilāl al-Ṣābī, *Wuzarāʾ*, 114) and for al-ʿAbbās b. al-Ḥasan (Miskawayh, *Tajārib*, 14); merchants assisted Ibn al-Furāt (Miskawayh, *Tajārib*, 44; Hilāl al-Ṣābī, *Wuzarāʾ*, 85; al-Tanūkhī, *Nishwār*, 7:136).

diffusely held that they were impossible to track down, and inquisitors generally had no idea where deposits were located or how large they were. These deposits were neither morally questionable, since judges and pious men held them; nor were they politically dangerous, as people were rarely criticized or resented for concealing the wealth of a man in disfavor.[72] This widespread dispersal of deposits was another practice that unified the court elite, and solidified cross-professional friendships.

If fall from favor seemed imminent—based upon rumors or warnings from informants—bureaucrats took final steps to safeguard themselves, their families, and supporters. When ʿAlī b. ʿĪsā surmised that he would soon be dismissed and arrested, he turned his property into *waqfs*, freed his slaves, and offered his resignation (which was rejected).[73] By these actions, ʿAlī protected his wealth, prevented the resale of his slaves, and tried to preempt dismissal by actually quitting first, giving his successor less justification for interrogation. Interestingly, the caliph would not grant ʿAlī this tactical advantage. Bureaucrats also made provisions for the protection of their harem, their children, and even their homes, all of which became subject to abuse during the caliphate of al-Muqtadir.

Most importantly, when a wazir's client or network of supporters anticipated disfavor, they went into hiding. Wazirs themselves never hid and they performed administrative duties until dismissal; but their subordinates usually disappeared days in advance. This was facilitated by the custom whereby the caliph arrested wazirs at the royal palace on audience days, which enabled bureaucrats to gauge when they should go into hiding.[74] As with deposits, it would seem that bureaucrats hid with diverse members of the court elite, particularly merchants and judges, who were relatively immune from reprisals. But the most surprising aspect of hiding was that hidden bureaucrats were rarely found. This was partially due to the fact that Baghdad, and the court elite within the city, was so geographically spread out. One might be tempted to think that the intelligence services were incompetent. However, the success of hiding was primarily by design: as noted above, the caliph usually gave the wazir's supporters advance warning by spreading rumors, then waiting until audience days to make the arrest. What's more, there seemed to be a taboo against searching the homes of the court elite, which made it virtually impossible to find

72. One exception: Mūsā b. Khalaf was tortured for not divulging the deposits of Ibn al-Furāt. But this was very much an aberration—the torture was carried out under Ḥāmid b. al-ʿAbbās, who exceeded commonly accepted limits involving interrogation and punishment.

73. Hilāl al-Ṣābī, *Wuzarāʾ*, 307–8.

74. For example, in 306/918 Ibn al-Furāt's supporters habitually hid when he went to the palace (assuming that he would be arrested there), and came out of hiding on days when he worked in the waziral palace. On this occasion, al-Muqtadir departed from tradition and arrested Ibn al-Furāt at his home, precisely in order to capture his associates as well (Hilāl al-Ṣābī, *Wuzarāʾ*, 38).

fugitives.[75] Lastly, people who hid fallen bureaucrats were never punished, even though their identities became known once their guests returned to favor.

In fact, I believe that the caliphs instituted these customs and frequently turned a blind eye because they generally did not want fugitives to be found. From the caliph's perspective, hidden bureaucrats meant uncertainty for the current wazir, as they were a source of plotting. In general, the caliph wished to keep wazirs perpetually off balance, and tried to strengthen the internal rivalries of the bureaucracy; the existence of hidden bureaucrats furthered both these goals. In support of this argument is the fact that caliphs always captured hidden bureaucrats when they expressed determination. For example, al-Muqtadir took the unusual step of announcing that anyone who hid Ibn al-Furāt's son al-Muḥassin would be severely punished; as a result, al-Muḥassin resorted to disguising himself as a woman, and was nevertheless quickly discovered.[76] Other important officials, such as the conspirators of 296/908 (Ibn al-Muʿtazz and Muḥammad b. Dāwud), were found by a combination of intelligence work, troop patrols, and popular assistance. My sense is that had the caliph wanted to find more hidden bureaucrats, he would have.

Open Hostility

Short of actually plotting for someone's arrest, bureaucrats could be openly hostile to a rival in order to diminish his standing and power. An excellent example of this open hostility, which reflects the basic mechanisms of political competition, was the conflict between the wazir Ibn al-Furāt, and the jewelry merchant Ibn al-Jaṣṣāṣ.[77] For some unspecified reason the wazir disliked Ibn al-Jaṣṣāṣ, and was treating him poorly: he canceled some of the merchant's contracts, slandered and humiliated him in public meetings, and avoided eye contact when the merchant entered the wazir's assembly. Ibn al-Jaṣṣāṣ tried to appease the wazir through intermediaries, but to no avail. Then one day Ibn al-Jaṣṣāṣ heard the wazir's chamberlain refer to him as a walking treasure chest and concluded that he would soon be incarcerated. So that night the jewelry merchant went to the wazir's palace; because of the unusual hour the wazir initially feared that Ibn al-Jaṣṣāṣ had come on behalf of the caliph. After being reassured of the personal nature of this visit, the wazir removed all servants and guards from his bedchamber, and the two men had a tête-à-tête. Ibn al-Jaṣṣāṣ said that he had failed, after much effort, to conciliate the wazir, and now he insisted on reaching a rapprochement. Otherwise, continued the merchant,

75. Hilāl al-Ṣābī, *Wuzarāʾ*, 178–80. Ibn al-Furāt criticized his son al-Muḥassin for searching someone's home and reading the owner's correspondence.

76. Hilāl al-Ṣābī, *Wuzarāʾ*, 63–64; Miskawayh, *Tajārib*, 131–32.

77. For more information on Ibn al-Jaṣṣāṣ, see Ch. Pellat, "Ibn al-Djassās," *EI2*.

*For in-depth analysis of the career of Ibn al-Jaṣṣāṣ, see Marmer, "Asset Management" (forthcoming).

> I will go straight to the caliph and promise him one million dinars in gold and silver from my treasury, to be delivered by morning—and you know that I have that kind of money. I will say to him: 'Take this money, and turn Ibn al-Furāt over to so and so whom you will appoint as wazir' and I will suggest someone who I think he will agree to appoint.... I would choose one of your secretaries, for the [caliph] will not distinguish between you and them if money is at stake. He will turn you over to that person. The appointee will consider me the person who elevated him from a low status to wazir, having paid a huge sum on his behalf. He will consider me his patron, the source of his benefit, and will serve me, and see to my affairs in everything he does. I will turn you over to him, so that he can torture you, until you give him one million dinars. You know that your wealth will cover that, but you will become poor, and the money will return to me, such that I will not have spent anything. I will have destroyed my enemy, vented my anger, received back my money, maintained my position of favor, and increased my stature by removing one wazir and appointing another.

Ibn al-Furāt was dumbstruck by this threat; but he agreed to a compromise, recognizing that "al-Muqtadir, with money at stake, would not differentiate between me—with my abilities, wealth and standing—and the lowliest of my secretaries, just as you said." The two swore a mutual nonaggression oath. The next day Ibn al-Furāt honored the merchant in his *majlis*, praised him, and ordered that various properties be returned to him. Eventually Ibn al-Jaṣṣāṣ left the assembly with an impressive armed escort. The jewelry merchant concludes his report: "The attendees saw all of this and were surprised by it; my honor was restored, and nobody knew the reason for our reconciliation."[78]

The dynamics of this confrontation, somewhat reminiscent of the alliance between Ibn al-Furāt and al-ʿAbbās b. al-Ḥasan, are typical of political competition among the Baghdadi elite. First of all, there is a slow build-up in tension: Ibn al-Furāt wants to seize the merchant's money but is cautious, gradually wearing down Ibn al-Jaṣṣāṣ's reputation in public. We get the impression that the wazir is constrained, probably by the caliph, from simply arresting the merchant. Ibn al-Jaṣṣāṣ for his part wants to avoid a climactic confrontation and tries to appease the wazir through intermediaries. In general, the relations between these two men are filled with anxiety, but both are hesitant to make a decisive move.

More importantly, Ibn al-Jaṣṣāṣ is victorious in this confrontation because of the inherent weaknesses of the wazirate, and the merchant's ability to exploit these weaknesses. The wazir's status is unstable: Ibn al-Furāt was frightened by the merchant's appearance in the middle of the night; he is surrounded by armed guards while he sleeps; and both men clearly state that the caliph has no personal attachment to the wazir. Moreover, relations within Ibn al-Furāt's staff are not cohesive, since both men also recognize the fact that one of the wazir's protégés will no doubt agree to replace him. Indeed, this

78. al-Tanūkhī, *Nishwār*, 1:30–33; also translated by Margoliouth, *Table-talk*, 18–23.

replacement would quickly shift his loyalty to Ibn al-Jaṣṣāṣ, the source of his promotion. The factor that puts these two unstable sets of relationships in motion, working against the wazir, is money: money will persuade the caliph to change ministers, and money will prompt a subordinate bureaucrat to switch patrons. As in the case of ʿAlī and Abū ʿĪsā, the precarious nature of the wazirate, and the subsequent ease of threatening the wazir, severely limited his authority over the rest of the court elite.

The Strategies of Plotting

As argued above, the traditional instability of the wazirate continually stoked the belief that the position was always theoretically available, which led competitors to plot against the current wazir. Plotting was especially prevalent under al-Muqtadir, for the financial crises engulfing the state made the wazir particularly vulnerable, and within a short time the caliph had developed a reputation for changing wazirs frequently, all of which invited further conspiracies. However, al-Muqtadir rarely dismissed a wazir or selected a replacement without external prompting; he usually switched wazirs only when presented with a convincing argument for doing so. It was therefore the responsibility of an aspiring wazir to present an attractive, convincing, and unsolicited bid to the caliph.

Because al-Muqtadir's disillusionment with virtually every wazir originated in lack of funds, most plots began with a promise to provide the state with more money. For example, Ibn al-Furāt's second and third appointments were brought about by guarantees to pay the caliph and the royal family higher stipends.[79] Such offers usually included a promise to extract a specified amount of money from other bureaucrats or even nonbureaucratic members of the court, if the caliph granted permission for this extraction. The offer to pay money also involved an implicit attack on the actions of current officials. For example, when Ḥāmid b. al-ʿAbbās plotted against Ibn al-Furāt, he emphasized to the caliph that he (Ḥāmid) was generous; this was meant to contrast with the widespread conjecture that Ibn al-Furāt had stored away millions of dinars for himself, but refused to assist the caliph in paying military salaries.[80] On another occasion al-Muḥassin offered to extract money from Ḥāmid, ʿAlī b. ʿĪsā, Naṣr, Shafīʿ al-Luʾluʾī, Ibn al-Ḥawārī, Umm Mūsā, and al-Mādhrāʾī. The implication behind these offers, and generally the promise to extract money from state officials, was that it was disloyal of state employees to amass wealth when the caliph and the state were nearly bankrupt.[81] In effect, a promise to pay more money was also an accusation of financial mismanagement and embezzlement.

79. Hilāl al-Ṣābī, *Wuzarāʾ*, 36, 265–66; Miskawayh, *Tajārib*, 43–44, 87.

80. Hilāl al-Ṣābī, *Wuzarāʾ*, 38.

81. Another example of this is when Ibn al-Furāt showed the caliph a pile of fifteen thousand dinars—the sight of which obviously impressed the caliph—and then informed him that Ibn al-Ḥawārī embezzled that amount every month. The caliph became hostile to Ibn al-Ḥawārī, and soon after ordered that he be killed (Hilāl al-Ṣābī, *Wuzarāʾ*, 97–98).

Sometimes the promise of more money was not enough to sway the caliph into replacing wazirs, so claimants had to fortify their offers with an explicit attack on the loyalty of the current wazir. In 299/911–912, al-Muqtadir had been considering the dismissal of Ibn al-Furāt for some time but hesitated; this was only the beginning of his caliphate, not long after the failed coup of 296/908, and government finances were still relatively stable. The bureaucrat al-Khāqānī had already been negotiating for the wazirate, but seeing the caliph's reticence, he concluded that "nothing would bring it about except for executing a plot." Hatching a complicated scheme, al-Khāqānī wrote the caliph, accusing Ibn al-Furāt of planning to turn the empire over to the Qarmatians. After a perfunctory check of the facts, al-Muqtadir was convinced of Ibn al-Furāt's treason, arrested him and appointed al-Khāqānī.[82] This escalation from an offer of money to an accusation of treason was later used by Ibn al-Furāt against Naṣr the chamberlain, as he first promised to extract Naṣr's wealth, and then arranged a complex scheme that was meant to demonstrate Naṣr's betrayal of the caliph.[83]

Since only certain royalty and palace staff had consistent access to the caliph, bureaucrats plotting for the wazirate had to find a way of transmitting their messages to the caliph. The most frequent method was to write a letter, outlining one's promises and accusations, and send it via influential contacts in the palace. For example, al-Khāqānī communicated with the caliph through Umm Mūsā and Dastanbūya, while Ibn al-Furāt used Zaydān, Ḥāmid used Naṣr, and al-Muḥassin used Mufliḥ. These palace officials forwarded such letters in return for a bribe (Umm Mūsā, Dastanbūya, and Mufliḥ), for the prospect of improved standing (Mufliḥ), or for revenge against the current wazir (Naṣr). But this service, even if performed a number of times, did not necessarily evolve into a lasting alliance: Umm Mūsā helped al-Khāqānī acquire the wazirate, but later assisted Ibn Abī al-Baghl in his plot against al-Khāqānī.[84] Palace officials were never considered the patrons of particular bureaucrats, nor were they held responsible for the later failures of the men they had helped.[85] The whole system smacks of both corruption and collusion; the caliph generally encouraged plotting, which kept his wazirs defensive and continually brought him attractive promises, while palace officials received bribes but were not held responsible for the messages they transmitted.

Counterplotting

Before wazirs could respond to a plot, they first had to know that it was taking place. It was generally easy to know that something was amiss, since there were usually wide-

82. Hilāl al-Ṣābī, *Wuzarāʾ*, 288–90.

83. As discussed in ch. 3.

84. Hilāl al-Ṣābī, *Wuzarāʾ*, 292.

85. For example, Mufliḥ was not held accountable for having helped al-Muḥassin come to power, despite the latter's egregious violence; and Mufliḥ retained his position even when al-Muḥassin was executed.

spread rumors of an imminent change. But in addition to these rumors, wazirs seem to have built excellent intelligence networks, and often found out the precise details of plots against them. For example, Ibn al-Furāt found out that Sawsan was plotting for the wazir's removal; and al-Khāqānī discovered that Ibn Abī al-Baghl was negotiating for his job. In fact, on at least one occasion the caliph had to bring a new appointee to the capital under the guise of appointing him to a lower post, so that when the wazir found out about it he would not take action.[86]

Wazirs responded to rumors or plots in different ways. The safest response, employed by ʿAlī b. ʿĪsā on several occasions, was to resign, which, if accepted by the caliph, would spare the wazir the evils that accompany dismissal. In general, al-Muqtadir did not want anyone else dictating when, and under what conditions a wazir would be replaced, so he rejected these resignations. ʿAlī and lbn al-Furāt also tried writing letters to the caliph, and his mother, in which they defended their record as wazir and addressed criticisms. In a letter to al-Sayyida in 304/916–917, ʿAlī refers to the two important themes of financial competence and loyalty to the caliph. He argues that he has saved the resources of the caliph's treasury, unlike his predecessors, and adds that "I patiently endure misfortune in the service of my master, the Commander of the Faithful."[87] In general these defensive measures had little influence on the caliph: he did not want explanations of complicated circumstances; he wanted promises of money.

The most successful means of fighting off a plot was to counterattack: to accuse the competition of something worse than had been alleged against oneself. The initial attack was usually a charge of incompetence and embezzlement, which hinted at disloyalty; the counterattack generally escalated to treason. A very simple example of this is the plotting between the chamberlain Sawsan and Ibn al-Furāt in late 296/909. Sawsan had previously been integrally involved in state administration but had been pushed aside by this wazir; he therefore plotted to replace (and probably kill) Ibn al-Furāt, and offered to extract money from him in return for the caliph's approval of this plan. Apparently the caliph agreed, and Sawsan sent a military officer to fetch a bureaucratic replacement from Ahwāz. Sawsan tried to conceal the plot from Ibn al-Furāt, but the latter found out anyway; he then convinced the caliph that Sawsan planned to kill both the wazir and the caliph and revealed that Sawsan had initially supported the coup of earlier that same year. Al-Muqtadir, convinced of the chamberlain's treachery, permitted Ibn al-Furāt to seize Sawsan and have him executed.[88] This example demonstrates the three important elements of a counterplot: discovery; access to the caliph; and discrediting the opponent with an accusation of treason.

We get a more detailed look at counterplotting and bureaucratic intrigue in general from al-Khāqānī's self-defense in the year 301/913–914. Like other wazirs, al-Khāqānī

86. Miskawayh, *Tajārib*, 26.

87. Hilāl al-Ṣābī, *Wuzarāʾ*, 308–9.

88. Miskawayh, *Tajārib*, 12; Hilāl al-Ṣābī, *Wuzarāʾ*, 31–32.

was the subject of popular rumors; the caliph was considering reappointing Ibn al-Furāt, and other court officials were plotting on behalf of a certain Ibn Abī al-Baghl. Al-Khāqānī found out about these threats to his position and decided to counteract them. He arranged for the court elite to gather at the royal palace on a Friday (not an official reception day) and then had Naṣr ask the caliph for an audience, claiming to have pressing news that needed to be discussed immediately. Once al-Khāqānī was brought to the caliph, he asked that all attendants (including Naṣr) be removed, so that he and the caliph could speak privately. This accomplished, al-Khāqānī began a long speech justifying his own actions and vilifying his competitors:

> You have raised me, Commander of the Faithful, and have given me wealth after poverty. I have not been negligent in serving you, nor refrained from anything that would promote the state, as seen in my efforts to seize roughly one million dinars from Ibn al-Furāt, not including vast properties. I do not deny that I am not as competent as [Ibn al-Furāt], given my lengthy unemployment and his experience, my being out of office and him in office. Yet I am loyal to you, I believe in your caliphate, while these people (Ibn al-Furāt and supporters) are all *Rāfiḍīs*[89] and your enemies. They support the Talibids, not your ancestors. God has given you the properties of lbn al-Furāt with revenues worth one million yearly. The harm caused by my supposed inadequate administration is not nearly equivalent to that much money.

Al-Khāqānī then responds to accusations of nepotism, claiming that he has actually hired officials who worked for previous wazirs, in order to maintain administrative continuity. Those of his relatives who have received money have acquired it by legitimate means, after suffering years of poverty. He continues his lengthy defense and counterattack:

> Ibn Abī al-Baghl is more an enemy to my master [the caliph] than Ibn al-Furāt, for he is an apostate, denies Islam and prophecy, renounces the Qur'an and claims that it has errors and defects about which he has written a book. How can such a man be trusted in service? Yet a group of my tax officials have helped him in his quest, anticipating their share of money when his day comes. Today I heard that one of his confidants said: 'The Commander of the Faithful has sent his signet ring via Faraj the Christian, (a female) employee of Umm Mūsā,' as proof of his appointment on the next reception day. If that is true, then I come to the royal palace having gathered my children, relatives, secretaries, and supporters, without informing them of my situation; if our master wishes, and intends to arrest them, then we are all in his hands. He can order that someone be sent to take the whole group, after granting us protection.... But if our *mawlā* terminates his patronage of [lbn Abi al-Baghl] and gives me control of that apostate—whom previous wazirs banished due to his evilness, and ex-

89. The term *Rāfiḍī* refers to a supporter of the Shi'a, often in a pejorative sense (see E. Kohlberg, "al-Rāfiḍa," *EI2*).

> pelled from the [royal] presence due to his evil deeds (which others know better than I), then I will extract from him and his brother a great deal of money, for his brother received some of Ibn al-Furāt's wealth, which was huge in extent.[90]

Al-Muqtadir was impressed by this speech and therefore canceled the appointment of Ibn Abī al-Baghl. He also agreed to turn the latter over to al-Khāqānī; when the wazir complained about the intervention of Umm Mūsā, the caliph promised that she and al-Sayyida would not interfere in this matter. Ibn Abī al-Baghl was summoned to the palace; ironically, he arrived thinking that al-Khāqānī had been duped, but in reality it was Ibn Abī al-Baghl who had been duped, and he was arrested. This complex tale ended when Umm Mūsā and al-Sayyida complained about the arrest to al-Muqtadir, and the caliph backed down, ordering that Ibn Abī al-Baghl should be appointed to a provincial post.[91]

The complex intrigue surrounding al-Khāqānī encompasses many of the elements of court politics. First, we see endemic instability, as the caliph is considering two alternatives to al-Khāqānī—Ibn Abī al-Baghl and Ibn al-Furāt—the latter of whom had been dismissed only one year before. Al-Khāqānī also mentions that much of his staff comes from earlier administrations, some of whom have already arranged deals with Ibn Abī al-Baghl, reflecting the shifting loyalties and rampant opportunism resulting from waziral change. None of this scheming is well hidden: rumors abound; al-Khāqānī knows the identity of his competitors; he knows that his own subordinates have betrayed him; he also somehow knows about conversations among the supporters of a rival.

We also see the role of other actors at court. Umm Mūsā, who helped al-Khāqānī attain the wazirate, is now working on behalf of Ibn Abī al-Baghl. Her influence, primarily due to contact with al-Sayyida, is so great that al-Khāqānī specifically asks the caliph for protection from her; even once this is granted the caliph backtracks in the face of protests from his female relatives. Naṣr also has an important role: he partially controls access to the caliph and normally attends caliphal audiences. Al-Khāqānī tries to eliminate both publicity and intervention by Umm Mūsā and Naṣr by insisting on secrecy and coming to the palace on a nonceremonial day. Al-Khāqānī's initial achievement, then, is that he arranges for a private meeting with the caliph, where his arguments cannot be rebutted.

Al-Khāqānī's speech intertwines self-defense and counterattack, presented in strategic rhetoric. His opening comment invokes the caliph's status as his patron, which immediately puts the caliph on the defensive, since rupturing the bonds of patronage was theoretically taboo and rarely admitted publicly. Al-Khāqānī then sets out in his own defense. First, he has served both the caliph and the state energetically, and here he makes the first passing reference to his rival's faults (Ibn al-Furāt's incredible wealth). He then addresses the two criticisms that have been directed at him, incompetence and nepo-

90. Hilāl al-Ṣābī, *Wuzarāʾ*, 291–94; also referred to by Miskawayh, *Tajārib*, 21.

91. Ibn Abī al-Baghl retained his position under several wazirs, until Umm Mūsā was arrested in 310/922–923, whereupon Ibn Abī al-Baghl was promptly fired.

tism. Al-Khāqānī concedes that he is not exceedingly competent, mostly due to unemployment (hinting this is the caliph's fault). Yet he is very loyal (unlike Ibn al-Furāt), and his incompetence is not all that damaging (unlike Ibn al-Furāt's embezzlement). As for nepotism, al-Khāqānī argues that his first priority was maintaining administrative stability by employing other people's clerks, and his family and supporters who deserve some wealth after extended poverty (again hinting at the caliph's responsibility). Through this entire defense al-Khāqānī has taken on the key accusations and turned them on their head, either by focusing the blame elsewhere, such as on the caliph himself, or by making favorable comparisons with his predecessor Ibn al-Furāt.

Al-Khāqānī is vociferous in his counterattack, which escalates from the typical offer of wealth to accusations of embezzlement and treason. He begins with the subtle rhetorical ploy of attacking his rival by insinuation, as a contrast to himself, which gives him the initial appearance of distributing guilt without particular intention. He reminds the caliph of the vast sums of money which he extracted from Ibn al-Furāt; and if the caliph missed this insinuation, al-Khāqānī soon argues that this vast wealth—from embezzlement—is worse than any incompetence. Another unstated implication is that, should al-Muqtadir reappoint Ibn al-Furāt all this lucrative property will revert to the bureaucrat (which it did in 304/917, just a few years later). The intention is to provoke the caliph's anger at Ibn al-Furāt for acquiring wealth, and his distaste at the thought of returning it to him. Al-Khāqānī then intensifies the counterattack: he accuses Ibn al-Furāt of being an ʿAlid supporter, and an enemy of the caliph. This accusation of treason is extended to Ibn Abī al-Baghl, who is not even a practicing Muslim, and is a danger to Islam. Rhetorically it is clever and convenient to attack Ibn Abī al-Baghl second and more strongly, for on the one hand he is the leading challenger as he has the support of Umm Mūsā, and on the other hand, Ibn al-Furāt has already served as wazir, so that accusations against him are implicitly a criticism of the caliph's past judgment. Al-Khāqānī finishes with a swipe at both rivals: he offers to extract money from Ibn Abī al-Baghl's brother, which tempts the caliph to arrest him, incriminates Ibn Abī al-Baghl by suggesting that he has already embezzled money that belongs to the caliph, and is yet another reference to the vast wealth obtained by Ibn al-Furāt.

The brilliant aspect of al-Khāqānī's counterplot, however, is that he has staged the whole scene. By coming to the palace on a nonceremonial day al-Khāqānī can override normal etiquette and arrange a private conversation with the caliph, who was irresolute in personal confrontations. Al-Khāqānī has, however, assembled the court elite and his supporters at the palace complex, which gives the proceedings an official air, that is, while al-Khāqānī has the advantage of adjusting etiquette, the outcome of this meeting will be made public and hence be recognized as official policy. Al-Khāqānī then forces the caliph to make a snap decision about whether or not to arrest the wazir and his faction, who are waiting obediently in the palace complex. This appears to be a bold demonstration of submission to the caliph's will; in reality, however, this is a brilliant manipulation of etiquette, for by the nature and timing of this event al-Muqtadir cannot arrest al-Khāqānī at this time. First of all, it was customary to arrest the wazir on a formal reception day, which this was not (though al-Muqtadir would deviate from this custom in later years). More importantly, it was taboo to arrest the wazir on a day in which he had already seen the caliph; indeed, in firing thirteen wazirs during his reign, al-Muqtadir never broke this rule. In other words, al-Khāqānī has challenged the caliph to arrest him, knowing full well that al-Muqtadir is constrained by convention from doing so. Nor is it in al-Muqtadir's nature to take up such a challenge and make a rapid decision. Moreover, the presence of the court elite at the palace serves to make this an official event, witnessed by all. So, by not arresting al-Khāqānī, the caliph has essentially, though unwillingly, given the wazir a public vote of confidence.

We should nevertheless not be surprised to learn that al-Khāqānī was dismissed within a year and replaced by a third candidate, ʿAlī b. ʿĪsā, who had the support of the general Muʾnis. Thus, while al-Khāqānī succeeded in delaying removal and dissuaded al-Muqtadir from appointing Ibn Abī al-Baghl and Ibn al-Furāt, his days in office were still numbered. The lesson we learn from his and other experiences is that there were specific ways in which to tempt or anger the caliph, usually beginning with money and ending with treason. Yet in the final analysis, these were only methods for delaying the inevitable: wazirs would be replaced on a regular basis and held responsible for all setbacks in the empire. We should note that while all bureaucrats generally suffered similar fates, they were encouraged to spend most of their political energy incriminating one another, rather than somehow working to change the system that kept them in constant turmoil.

Gradations of Punishment

For bureaucrats and everyone else at court, there was a hierarchy of levels of punishment. Each level involved its own rules. As with competitive strategies, most of the forms of punishment were enacted upon bureaucrats, and hence constitute our primary examples. In general, factions of bureaucrats suffered disfavor and punishment at the same time. But this generalization has two qualifications: first, men of the same faction experienced different levels of punishment based upon status and acquired enemies; and second, as argued earlier, factions were not as cohesive as we generally assume, and many supporters of a given wazir were spared punishment and retained in subsequent administrations.

Disgrace and Dismissal

The most basic form of punishment was blemishing a person's reputation. Everyone from the secretary Zanjī to the jewelry merchant Ibn al-Jaṣṣāṣ was concerned about reputation: in court society commanding respect was intricately linked to status and power. Honor could be damaged both before and after dismissal and/or arrest. We have seen that ʿAlī b. ʿĪsā could not fire Ibn Muqla, so he intentionally embarrassed this administrator in public; Ibn al-Furāt did likewise with Ibn al-Jaṣṣāṣ. These insults were conveyed either by demonstrating the rival's incompetence or by lowering their status through manipulation of etiquette. However, it was not acceptable to verbally assault an adversary; verbal abuse brought dishonor more upon the speaker than upon the target.

Disgrace after dismissal took two forms: bureaucrats were subjected to public interrogations, where the court community witnessed their disgrace through altered forms of etiquette and speech; and generals were publicly disgraced in processions that wound through Baghdad. The disgrace of generals was paraded before the broader public, probably because these men had more openly challenged the authority of the caliph, and their submission was therefore important propaganda.

The next level of punishment was dismissal from office. As noted above, this most often occurred in groups, based on faction. We saw earlier that dismissals of wazirs usually took place on reception days, while the wazir was on the way to the royal palace, or already inside, but before he had met with the caliph. Al-Muqtadir gradually abandoned this set schedule for dismissals, probably to give the rest of the falling faction less warning so that they could be more easily captured.[92] Some of a fallen wazir's supporters were dismissed immediately, while others were replaced by the new wazir; still others were retained in office. The impact of unemployment differed widely: some men, like ʿAlī b. ʿĪsā, seem to have lived comfortably on accumulated savings and donations. But it was not unusual for both high- and low-ranking bureaucrats to suffer from poverty during unemployment. We hear that ʿUbaydallāh b. Sulaymān, after removal from his position as deputy wazir, was incarcerated for owing a debt of three hundred dinars; while other important officials, whose reputations were irreparably scarred and were never again employed, resorted to begging.[93] These tales of poverty were probably the exception rather than the norm; they were transmitted among bureaucrats as a means of encouraging adherence to social and professional norms, and likely as warnings to save money for uncertain times.

Incarceration

Dismissed officials were subject to different forms of incarceration. Some were ordered to "remain at home," under house arrest; others were expelled from Baghdad; and many were imprisoned. Each of these fates had advantages and disadvantages. House arrest was the mildest form, and usually meant no interrogation or torture and leaving the victim to worry only about sustenance. Expulsion was clearly unpleasant in that people were forced to leave behind family and possessions, but at least this did not involve strict physical confinement. Removal from Baghdad was also a form of protection, alleviating

92. For example, Ibn al-Furāt's arrest after his second tenure in office occurred at his home, precisely because his supporters hid while he was at the royal palace.

93. al-Tanūkhī, *Nishwār*, 2:111.

exposure to plotting and torture, and was generally a vacation from the bureaucratic cycle of intrigue.[94]

Imprisonment was far more common for the highest officials, such as wazirs, and is therefore the form of incarceration for which we have most information. Such men could be imprisoned in a variety of locations. Most prisoners were held in the royal palace. Here there seem to have been two alternatives: the dungeon underneath the Ḥasanī palace, to which most people seem to have disappeared; or custody in the care of either Zaydān or Naṣr.[95] Of this latter option, being held by Zaydān was preferable, since she had direct communication with al-Sayyida and al-Muqtadir, and her chambers were close enough to the caliph's that he made regular visits; in general, the most important prisoners were held by Zaydān, all others by Naṣr. Incarceration in the palace implied a measure of safety, as violence was taboo in the palace. Prisoners were also held by the chief of police, which could be unnerving since he was also in charge of executions, and less frequently by the chief of intelligence (*ṣāḥib al-barīd*). The worst place to be held seems to have been in the official waziral palace, for the wazir was often a bitter rival of a dismissed official, and more importantly was responsible for extracting money from such officers. If the royal palace meant safety, the waziral palace meant being in the sole custody of an enemy.

The conditions of imprisonment could also vary and were not necessarily related to location. Some prisoners were subjected to neglect; others were tortured. Many prisoners were actually treated well and granted comforts, which reflected both the benevolence and wisdom of their hosts or jailers, given political vicissitudes. For example, when Ḥāmid b. al-ʿAbbās was turned over to Ibn al-Furāt, the latter ordered "that Ḥāmid should be given spacious and well-furnished quarters, and be provided with the food, drink, and perfume to which he was accustomed as wazir, as well as be given splendid clothing."[96] Hosts also wanted to ensure that prisoners did not perish in their custody, which would immediately be assumed to be murder.[97] Among the most important issues for prison-

94. On two occasions ʿAlī b. ʿĪsā asked to be sent away from Baghdad, thinking this would ensure his own safety.

95. I cannot be completely sure that there was a dungeon beneath the Ḥasanī palace in this period. Al-Muʿtaḍid is said to have built one, but there are no explicit references to it in the period of al-Muqtadir. However, we do hear of many prisoners held in the palace, most of whom were disconnected from the rest of court; for example, Ibn al-Furāt was out of contact for a handful of years, and people speculated whether he was still alive or dead.

96. Miskawayh, *Tajārib*, 98; Hilāl al-Ṣābī, *Wuzarāʾ*, 195–96. The sources differ somewhat, Hilāl al-Ṣābī reporting a very long story about the clothes that were made especially for Ḥāmid. At first Ḥāmid did not trust Ibn al-Furāt's gestures and only agreed to wear these new clothes once Zanjī, who had worked for both men, put the clothes on first. We also have the reverse example, when Ḥāmid treated Ibn al-Furāt with respect (*Wuzarāʾ*, 62).

97. In 311/923–924, Ibn al-Furāt was eager to transfer a sick ʿAlī b. ʿĪsā away from the waziral palace. He was turned over to Shafīʿ al-Luʾluʾī (Miskawayh, *Tajārib*, 111); Miskawayh also states that Ibn al-Furāt sent ʿAlī somewhere safe, where he would not be harmed (*Tajārib*, 109).

ers were access to writing utensils, and visitation rights. These provisions would allow a prisoner to maintain contact with the outside world, seek a pardon, or perhaps engage in plotting. Not surprisingly, such privileges were often withheld. At desperate moments a prisoner might ask his host to send a message for him, but this generally failed.[98]

The fall of an official also left his home and family vulnerable. A residence was generally understood as an outward manifestation of a person's honor and status; violating a residence was therefore a public symbol of humiliation. It was common for the private dwellings of high-ranking officials to be pillaged and/or destroyed. This happened, for example, to the homes of al-ʿAbbās b. al-Ḥasan and Ibn al-Muʿtazz (in 296/908), Ibn al-Furāt (299/911–12), and ʿAlī b. ʿĪsā (318/930);[99] when other wazirs were arrested, special provisions had to be made in order to protect their homes from vandalism.[100] Even the military was subject to this practice: the homes of the *rajjāla* were razed when they fell out of favor.[101] This violence also extended to the family of the disgraced official; in the most dramatic cases the official's harem was violated, so that the protection of female relatives also became a concern. Here we again see the blurring of distinctions between public and private, as both the residence and family of the court elite were part and parcel of their public status.

Fines

The most ubiquitous and impactful aspect of personal decline was the fine. For newly appointed officials, the amount of money they could extract from those in disfavor was a sign of effectiveness in office. They had usually been appointed after promising to extract a certain amount of money from particular individuals and failure to fulfill this promise meant quicker dismissal for them. Collecting fines was also a source of enrichment. For a disgraced official, a fine meant a drain on savings that would be needed to survive unemployment. It also entailed a serious obligation: once someone had agreed to a fine, they were expected to pay a large fraction of the agreed amount, or else face the threat of torture.

Negotiations for the amount of a fine were like a game of cat and mouse: the inquisitor—sometimes the wazir, but often an official specifically delegated this responsibility—had a numerical target which had usually been promised (sometimes on oath) to the caliph; but due to the widespread use of secret deposits, he usually had no idea how much the person in disfavor could actually pay. The person being fined, for his part, knew that he would have to pay some amount of money in order to satisfy the inquisitor, wazir, and

98. Ibn al-Furāt tried to send messages with Shafīʿ al-Luʾluʾī, and then with Nāzūk. Both men refused (Miskawayh, *Tajārib*, 138).

99. Hilāl al-Ṣābī, *Wuzarāʾ*, 28, 34; Miskawayh, *Tajārib*, 20; ʿArīb, *Ṣilat*, 151.

100. For example, Ḥāmid's home (Hilāl al-Ṣābī, *Wuzarāʾ*, 46).

101. Miskawayh, *Tajārib*, 203.

caliph, but if he agreed too quickly or to too low a sum, he would invite a larger fine. The objective was to agree to a large enough sum, but not too much. The inquisitor arrived at a numerical value either by computing the previous income (partially embezzled) of the person in question, or by fixing an arbitrary amount that would be whittled down in further negotiation. His leverage was the threat of continued disfavor, and torture: that is, if a person did not pay willingly, he would be forced to pay. The person being fined tried to argue that his income had been less that what was calculated, his expenses had been great, or simply that he did not possess the money to pay. His tactical advantage was that only he really knew how much he could afford. Of course, this meant that people resisting a fine often had to lie. Such lying was later held against them: one of the reasons why Ibn al-Furāt was dismissed for a second time was that following his first arrest he had lied about the extent of his deposits. ʿAlī b. ʿĪsā, too, was criticized for substantially undervaluing some property he owned.

Two other factors complicated the system of fines. First of all, people only paid, and were only expected to pay, a fraction of the agreed upon fine. One part of the fine, commonly one quarter, was paid immediately, another part was to be paid in the future, and a large chunk, as much as half, was allowed to lapse. Stranger still, people often refused to pay fines until they were tortured, whereupon they conceded and paid. Why would people endure physical punishment, only to pay a fine that they refused to pay before torture? Why not agree from the start? The answer seems to be related to the cat and mouse game: if a person agreed too easily, this usually meant that the fine was too low, and a fresh one would be imposed. But once a person had agreed under duress, then the fine was probably accurate. There seems to have been a common understanding that a minimum amount of torture was necessary to demonstrate the limits of financial capability and to demonstrate veracity.

Violence/Torture

Torture was an integral part of the bureaucratic cycle, and virtually everyone experienced it at some point. People were tortured as punishment for administrative abuse, in order to extract fines, or simply out of hatred and revenge.

There were certain standard forms of torture: being forced to wear heavy chains, an iron collar, and/or a wool coat smeared with various unpleasant substances; and direct physical abuse in the form of beating or whipping. These were applied in stages, as we can see from al-Muqtadir's orders regarding ʿAlī b. ʿĪsā: "Make him confess about his deposits, and if he does not, then shackle him; if he still does not submit, then in addition to the shackles make him wear a wool coat; and if he continues to refuse, beat his body in front of the commanders as punishment for refusing obedience."[102] It seems that there was a conceptual difference between devices that inflicted pain (such as chains or

102. Hilāl al-Ṣābī, *Wuzarāʾ*, 322–23.

a wool coat) and direct human abuse (beating); the latter was more grave. There were interesting variations in the forms of torture: for example, al-Muḥassin had been subjected to heavy chains, a wool coat dipped in olive oil buttoned up to his neck, his head immersed in a toilet.[103] There were also less common forms of torture: we have seen that Ibn al-Furāt was hung from a rope tied to his hands, a form of punishment which reappears;[104] and the bureaucrat ʿAbdallāh b. Jubayr, one of Ibn al-Furāt's loyalists, had his head shaved and tarred until he agreed to pay a fine.[105]

There was general consensus that such torture had to be regulated. Limitations were necessary for obvious reasons: first of all, most periods of disfavor were followed by reappointment, so bureaucrats had to be left in condition to function. The caliph al-Muʿtaḍid insisted on a reasonable condition for officials he himself dismissed, since in his words "they are the pillars of the state ... if they are not protected, it will detract from state interests."[106] Just as important, because of endemic instability, the person being tortured could soon be the torturer, which necessitated prudence. We hear of one man who counted the number of lashes he received out loud; when asked by the responsible party to explain the counting, he replied that he wanted to know how many times to whip his adversary when their roles were reversed: the whipping was promptly halted.[107]

We get a clear sense of how torture was expected to be measured and limited from an anecdote involving Ibn al-Furāt in 299/911–912. He had been dismissed from the wazirate and was being held for money. To soften him up, the inquisitor turned to torture, which Ibn al-Furāt later described:

> I was locked outside, exposed to the sun with no shade. [The inquisitor] shackled me with heavy chains, made me wear a wool coat soaked in ox urine, and an iron collar. He locked the door and left; I was close to collapsing. I began to recall what I had done to people and realized that I had inflicted all these forms of punishment: interrogation, plundering, seizure of property, imprisonment, oppression, the wearing of wool coats, and turning people over to enemies for a beating. Yet I could not remember collaring anyone, so I yelled: "Hey people, this is excessive!"

Ibn al-Furāt then remembered that he had indeed ordered the collaring of two separate men, each for two hours. When four hours had passed, Ibn al-Furāt called to a passing eunuch, and asked him to plead his case before the royal women who dominated the state at that time; soon thereafter Ibn al-Furāt's torture was terminated and he was granted better conditions.[108] The point of this story is that lbn al-Furāt wore the iron collar only

103. Hilāl al-Ṣābī, *Wuzarāʾ*, 264.
104. Hilāl al-Ṣābī, *Wuzarāʾ*, 11, 138.
105. al-Tanūkhī, *Nishwār*, 8:93–94.
106. al-Tanūkhī, *Nishwār*, 8:92.
107. al-Tanūkhī, *Nishwār*, 8:60.
108. Hilāl al-Ṣābī, *Wuzarāʾ*, 118–20; similar in al-Tanūkhī, *al-Faraj*, 2:43–49.

for the precise amount of time for which he had imposed it on others: a parable for the court elite, that torture is to be precisely measured, and excessiveness and innovation are discouraged.

Beyond an abstract expectation of appropriate limits to torture, there also seem to have been explicit rules to curb abuses. We have seen that al-Muʿtaḍid did not want his officials overly abused; thus when the Banū al-Furāt tried to force one official to pay a fine, they could only shackle him and give him seven lashes, for no further torture was allowed at that time.[109] Special consideration was also to be given to the children of wazirs, who were not supposed to be tortured; and if punishment was indeed employed, it was not to take place in the presence of their father.[110]

During the caliphates of al-Muʿtaḍid and al-Muktafī these rules were generally followed, if for no other reason than few functionaries were dismissed and tortured. Under al-Muqtadir, however, the norms for torture were exceeded. The initiator of this excess was Ḥāmid b. al-ʿAbbās, who had served for decades as a provincial tax farmer and was generally unfamiliar with court etiquette, including the limits of torture. He insulted, beat, and tortured Ibn al-Furāt's son al-Muḥassin beyond acceptable limits; al-Muḥassin warned him: "Wazir, do not introduce this practice among the children of wazirs!"[111]

Once the barriers were broken, a cycle of violence set in that was difficult for anyone to control. Al-Muḥassin, intensely vengeful after his harsh experience, was given control of prisoners in 311–312/923–924 and implemented torture of unprecedented proportions.[112] When he beat the pious ʿAlī b. ʿĪsā, al-Sayyida and Zaydān were incensed, saying: "We protected Ibn al-Furāt and prevented his enemies from getting hold of him, since wazirs are to be protected, and their rights are well known. Now this crazy man, his son [al-Muḥassin], takes pleasure in defying tradition and causing evil and harm!"[113]

The gradual increase in violence culminated in the execution of Ibn al-Furāt and al-Muḥassin. After the arrest of Ibn al-Furāt in 312/924, military leaders decided that this former wazir could no longer be trusted (for a whole variety of reasons); to prevent his reappointment, he had to be killed. They threatened the caliph that if Ibn al-Furāt were not executed, the military would rebel. Interestingly, the new wazir al-Khāqānī (the younger) argued against execution, for "once you make it easy for kings to kill, they get tempted by it and are not discriminating in applying it."[114] Al-Khāqānī was calling for a halt in the escalation of violence, but he could not save his colleague. Ibn al-Furāt became the only wazir during al-Muqtadir's reign to be executed, and the first Abbasid wazir executed since the return to Baghdad over thirty years before. After this execution, the lim-

---

109. al-Tanūkhī, *Nishwār*, 8:27. The Banū al-Furāt eventually extorted money by threatening the official with permanent unemployment, which he considered worse than the fine.

110. Hilāl al-Ṣābī, *Wuzarāʾ*, 264; al-Tanūkhī, *Nishwār*, 8:104–5.

111. Hilāl al-Ṣābī, *Wuzarāʾ*, 268.

112. Many examples; see Hilāl al-Ṣābī, *Wuzarāʾ*, 120.

113. Hilāl al-Ṣābī, *Wuzarāʾ*, 324.

114. Hilāl al-Ṣābī, *Wuzarāʾ*, 70.

its of torture and violence seem to have been reasserted, once everyone had witnessed the result of escalating violence.[115]

Publicly Stated Conflict: Interrogations

The most dramatic and complex events in court life were the semipublic interrogations of dismissed officials. These interrogations incorporated many of the important aspects of court life: ceremonial, betrayal, fear, accusations and counteraccusations, fining, and torture. The most important interrogations took place at the wazir's assembly within the royal palace and were generally convoked by the caliph. They were usually attended by the most important members of the court: the caliph, sitting off to the side, behind a curtain, unseen; the wazir, his supporters, and his predecessor in office; eunuchs and commanding officers; and judges. On such occasions each of these people played their characteristic roles in court intrigue. This gathering of the various forces at court in a hostile setting gives us a composite view of court intrigue.

The ostensible purpose of these interrogations was to prove, for all to witness, the guilt of a dismissed official, and sometimes to set an appropriate fine. We get an immediate inkling of the staged nature of this event by the fact that evidence against the accused was usually presented first to the caliph in private; he would then give the order for a public interrogation, rather than simply taking action himself. The interrogation, usually conducted by the wazir with assistance from associates, began with investigation of the subject's wealth, and escalated to accusations of mismanagement, embezzlement, and occasionally treason. In this escalation the interrogations closely resembled plotting. But there are big differences: the interrogator was under a greater obligation to produce proof; the accused had the right to respond to any and all accusations; and the entire debate took place in public, where every comment could have reverberations on court politics.

The accused was brought to the wazir's *majlis*, where the court elite had assembled. The caliph, in a nearby chamber, could hear the proceedings but not be seen; he was represented by a eunuch, chamberlain, or military officer, who would bring him information, relay questions or convey orders. Within the *majlis* itself sat commanding officers who rarely played an active part; in fact, the reason for their presence is not immediately apparent. Judges were also for the most part silent, but on occasion were asked to pass judgment on the most serious allegations. Significantly, most of the action took place between leading bureaucrats currently in office and those under investigation.

115. The escalation of torture in this period was paralleled by increasing violence toward women, though few specific details are recorded. In 299/911–912, Ibn al-Furāt's harem was violated, which became a concern for subsequent wazirs. In 306/918–919, al-Muḥassin's wife was arrested and beaten. Four years later, Umm Mūsā was arrested for treason, and millions of dinars were extracted from her under duress. Finally, following the death of al-Muqtadir, his mother al-Sayyida was imprisoned, beaten, and hung upside down, so that urine flowed down her chest to her face.

The interrogation consisted primarily of accusations directed at the dismissed official, and his responses. Each party employed specific tactics for establishing guilt or innocence. The inquisitor tried to present as much evidence as possible, including statistical data from financial documents, and witnesses, who were frequently reluctant to give testimony due to the unstable nature of the wazirate.[116] The inquisitor also resorted to threats: if the accused did not confess or pay a fine, he would be tortured. A sure sign of defeat, however, were insults and curses, which were forbidden in the palace and demonstrated both frustration and vulgarity. The accused, for his part, could answer accusations straightforwardly, arguing that they were inaccurate or not his responsibility. For accusations of treason the accused was sometimes defended by a judge, who would not consent to severe punishment without establishing the truth as best he could. Most importantly, as with plotting, the accused could counterattack with insinuations and accusations of his own. These were particularly devastating, given the public nature of the interrogation, and often succeeded in displacing attention from the accused to the men currently in power.

The interplay of these tactics can be seen in the interrogation of Ibn al-Furāt in the year 306/918–919.[117] The wazir Ḥāmid b. al-ʿAbbās first announced that Ibn al-Furāt's initial fine of 1.6 million dinars was insufficient; he then surveyed Ibn al-Furāt's possessions and revenues, including 500,000 dinars in deposits that Ibn al-Furāt had disavowed under oath five years earlier.[118] Ibn al-Furāt explained away each of Ḥāmid's claims. The latter responded: "We know that you are clever during interrogation ... but this is a situation that calls for paying money, and you will not mislead [us] into protecting you from torture. I made a guarantee to the Commander of the Faithful, God exalt him, so that you would be turned over to me. Save yourself while you are still under his protection, before I give you such abuse that you cannot withstand." Ibn al-Furāt responded to this threat with a counteraccusation, alleging that it was Ḥāmid who had stolen money from the caliph, that Ḥāmid had only sought the wazirate in order to protect himself from investigation, and in the process was ruining the state. This accusation evoked an insult from Ḥāmid, which was tantamount to a confession.

116. For example, al-Mādhrāʾī testified against Ibn al-Furāt in 306/918–919, and was ineffective. As a result, he refused to testify again in 312/924. Ibn Muqla had betrayed Ibn al-Furāt by revealing the latter's financial secrets to Naṣr; he was willing to write down allegations for the subsequent interrogation of Ibn al-Furāt, but refused to confront his former patron and testify in public (Miskawayh, *Tajārib*, 52–53).

117. In addition to the wazir (Ḥāmid) and his assistant (ʿAlī b. ʿĪsā), Naṣr, commanders, and judges were present. The interrogation took place in the wazir's assembly within the royal palace.

*The interrogation of Ibn al-Furāt in 306/918–919 has subsequently been described in great detail by van Berkel, "Vizier and the Harem Stewardess."

118. The only reason these deposits ever became public, was that Ibn Muqla told Naṣr about them. This was the extent of Ibn Muqla's betrayal of Ibn al-Furāt, and one reason why the latter was dismissed a second time.

Ibn al-Furāt scolded Ḥāmid for cursing in the royal palace, at which point ʿAlī b. ʿĪsā took over the interrogation. He introduced the financial governor of Egypt and Syria, Abū Zanbūr al-Mādhrāʾī, who proceeded to accuse Ibn al-Furāt of receiving bribes from him during the course of four years. Ibn al-Furāt presented a multifaceted defense: first he demanded proof of this assertion, either a document or a witness, which al-Mādhrāʾī could not produce. He also argued that he had already paid a huge fine, which surely covered these relatively small bribes. Then he counterattacked: he accused al-Mādhrāʾī of owing money to the central treasury and accused ʿAlī b. ʿĪsā of being lax in collecting revenues from Egypt. These counteraccusations were relayed by Shafīʿ al-Luʾluʾī (chief of intelligence) to the caliph, who demanded that al-Mādhrāʾī and ʿAlī pay one hundred sixty thousand dinars. ʿAlī noted with irony the turn of events: "We came to interrogate [Ibn al-Furāt], and he interrogated us." The remainder of the interrogation was conducted in the same manner: Ḥāmid, ʿAlī, and al-Mādhrāʾī made accusations, while Ibn al-Furāt responded with stinging attacks of his own. In recognition of Ibn al-Furāt's success during the interrogation, al-Mādhrāʾī eventually tried to appease the fallen wazir by offering to help him pay his fine.[119]

We get a better glimpse of the roles of the court elite, and the escalation of accusations and violence, in a series of three interrogations conducted against ʿAlī b. ʿĪsā in 311/923–924.[120] Ibn al-Furāt, in his third and final wazirate, had brought incriminating evidence to the caliph, who called for the initial interrogation. Ibn al-Furāt first accused ʿAlī of mismanagement, to which ʿAlī responded methodically (and unconvincingly). The next accusation was that ʿAlī had lied about the extent of his personal wealth, which was proven with a witness. Finally, Ibn al-Furāt criticized ʿAlī for cutting court stipends—a sensitive issue for the caliph—and argued that the funds were either lost due to neglect or embezzled by ʿAlī. This amounted to contempt for the caliph; and in the face of such an accusation ʿAlī shed his noncombatant attitude and counterattacked. He argued that Ibn al-Furāt had appropriated much of the caliph's properties and allowed subordinates to take bribes, neither of which ʿAlī had condoned. Moreover, Ibn al-Furāt had maintained high salaries by taking money from the caliph's private treasury, so that within five years the treasury was drained of nearly seventeen million dinars. All of this put Ibn al-Furāt on the defensive; he tried to justify his own behavior, but damage had clearly been done, and ʿAlī's fine was not increased.

The second round of the interrogation, at a later date, brought more severe accusations. Ibn al-Furāt now presented a witness and documentation that, in correspondence with the Qarmatians, ʿAlī had not denounced the enemy as heretics, and had even sent them presents. ʿAlī responded that, in the best interest of the Muslim community, he had

119. Hilāl al-Ṣābī, *Wuzarāʾ*, 103–10; al-Tanūkhī, *Nishwār*, 2:32–35. Al-Mādhrāʾī was criticized by ʿAlī and Naṣr for conciliating Ibn al-Furāt. It was a smart maneuver: upon reappointment, Ibn al-Furāt was more lenient on al-Mādhrāʾī than on other foes.

120. Miskawayh, *Tajārib*, 104–13.

engaged the Qarmatians in a diplomatic manner. Ibn al-Furāt then turned to Baghdad's two senior judges, Abū ʿUmar and Ibn al-Buhlūl, for verification that ʿAlī had committed a grave sin. Abū ʿUmar chastised ʿAlī but was reluctant to sign a formal condemnation; Ibn al-Buhlūl actually defended ʿAlī, arguing that by sparing Muslim lives ʿAlī had taken the right course, and in any case the Qarmatians were not heretics simply because they rejected the legitimacy of the Abbasid caliph. Ibn al-Buhlūl was highly respected at court, and his ruling ended any further legal action. Nevertheless, Naṣr took ʿAlī aside and warned him that the caliph would be enraged at ʿAlī's contact with the Qarmatians: he should agree to pay a large fine to save himself from physical punishment. ʿAlī assented and agreed to increase his fine from three thousand to three hundred thousand dinars. It turned out that Naṣr was right: the caliph remained hostile to ʿAlī for years to come.

The third and final round of interrogation was prompted by the caliph's lingering suspicion of ʿAlī's treason. Proclaiming that "this man is a Qarmatian! His blood and money are licit," the caliph ordered al-Muḥassin to bring ʿAlī before the assembled court, and demand that his remaining cash deposits be divulged; if ʿAlī refused, al-Muḥassin should torture him in increasing stages of severity. Al-Muḥassin carried out these orders and convened a public interrogation; ʿAlī refused to surrender any money until he was incarcerated somewhere safe, with access to his associates. Upon this refusal, al-Muḥassin called for initiation of torture. At this point the military figures spoke out: Naṣr the chamberlain refused to watch the torture of ʿAlī, so he left the chamber; when the shackles were first applied, Nāzūk rose and departed, also refusing to watch; then the general Yāqūt implored al-Muḥassin not to make ʿAlī wear a wool coat soaked in urine, but when ʿAlī again refused to pay, the coat was put on, and ʿAlī was beaten. The former wazir soon began to moan. The caliph, seated off to the side, heard this moaning and sent Mufliḥ the eunuch to intervene in the proceedings and take ʿAlī back to his cell. Al-Sayyida and Zaydān also hear of ʿAlī's torment and were angered by the excessive violence perpetrated against a former wazir.[121]

This series of interrogations encompasses most of the features of court intrigue. First, we see the gradual escalation of accusations: ʿAlī is accused of mismanagement, lying, and embezzling, whereupon he counteraccuses Ibn al-Furāt of embezzling. ʿAlī is then prosecuted for treason. In the final session, guilt is no longer even relevant, and ʿAlī must either pay or suffer. The level of violence also escalates: first ʿAlī is dishonored verbally and threatened; later he is subjected to devices of torture; finally, he is beaten.

In essence these interrogations are subtle demonstrations of autocratic power orchestrated by the caliph. He insists on their public nature and convenes the court elite for what turns into a communal display of powerlessness. Generals are always present; but as seen in ʿAlī's third interrogation, they cannot influence the course of affairs. In other words, they are present precisely to demonstrate that the military cannot intervene in the unstable relations of the bureaucrats. Judges are also present and are sup-

121. The torture inflicted upon ʿAlī b. ʿĪsā appears in Miskawayh, *Tajārib*, 110–11.

posedly asked to determine guilt in serious matters; but even after Ibn al-Buhlūl bravely defended ʿAlī b. ʿĪsā, the caliph resolved to torture ʿAlī regardless of legal niceties such as judicial approval. This confirms that the caliph had the power to disregard the legal process.

The main objects of this caliphal power play are the bureaucrats. These men were pitted against one another and encouraged to engage in volleys of accusations and recriminations that damaged the reputations of everyone involved. Here the right of the accused for self-defense, and the emphasis on counterattacking are crucial: these customs forced the bureaucrats to reveal secrets and publicly vent their hostilities. These interrogations thus intensified the disunity of the bureaucracy, brought to light previously hidden misconduct, and generally provided public evidence that justified the dismissal of any and all bureaucrats. Figuratively speaking, the bureaucrats were forced to battle one another in a public arena; the rest of the court elite were helpless spectators; and the caliph manipulated the systematic humiliation of the bureaucracy—indeed the entire court elite—from a safe distance.

Violent Death: Execution and Murder

Though our sources do not use distinct terminology, people at the Abbasid court generally distinguished between two forms of violent death: executions and murder. Execution was usually by order of the caliph, following confessions or trials that established guilt; they often involved dismemberment of the body, and included some public ceremony. Stories about the caliph al-Muʿtaḍid follow a clear pattern in this regard: every time this caliph apprehended a criminal, he forced the transgressor to confess, and then mutilated the corpse in some public setting.[122] For the period of al-Muqtadir's reign we have fewer details of executions, partly because this caliph was less violent—or sadistic—than his father. Aside from the conspirators killed after the coup of 296/908, about whom we hear remarkably little, al-Muqtadir ordered two famous executions: of the pseudo-mystic al-Ḥallāj, and of the thrice-wazir Ibn al-Furāt. Both these executions were preceded by lengthy interrogations that established the guilt of each party; on both occasions the caliph procrastinated and was pressured into giving the order; and on both occasions the victims were beheaded and dismembered, and some of their limbs hung from the city bridges for public display.[123]

Murder, by contrast, was secretive, was not necessarily preceded by the establishment of guilt, and left the victim's body intact. Once again, al-Muʿtaḍid serves as model. On his deathbed this caliph wanted certain men eliminated; aware that he had no le-

122. *For several examples of al-Muʿtaḍid's gruesome forms of punishment and execution, see F. Malti-Douglas, "Texts and Tortures."

123. For the respective executions of al-Ḥallāj and Ibn al-Furāt (along with the latter's son), see Miskawayh, *Tajārib*, 82, 138; ʿArīb, *Ṣilat*, 86–108, 120–21; L. Massignon, "al- Ḥallādj," *EI2*, 101.

gal justification, the caliph ordered that these men be poisoned, to leave no perceptible traces of wrongdoing.[124] Indeed, in al-Muqtadir's reign, with its heightened level of feuding and recrimination, murder became more common. One interesting example is the death of Ibn al-Muᶜtazz. In 296/908 he was the nominal figurehead for the coup against al-Muqtadir and had been captured. Ibn al-Muᶜtazz was, however, a member of the Abbasid family and it had long been taboo for Abbasids to harm each other publicly.[125] Ibn al-Muᶜtazz was therefore not publicly executed; instead, he was murdered in some mysterious way in the royal palace, and his body returned to his family, unblemished and therefore not dishonored.[126] Similarly, in 311–312/923–924, Ibn al-Furāt and his son al-Muḥassin set out on a binge of violence, with the tacit approval of the caliph, but not with his explicit public support. Their victims, Ḥāmid, Ibrāhīm b. ᶜĪsā (ᶜAlī's brother), and Ibn al-Ḥawārī, were either poisoned or drowned, which left less evidence of harm, and made no claims about guilt.[127]

Summary: The Senior Bureaucracy and Alternative Strategies

In this world of constant competition and intrigue, there were two general strategies for political behavior. The first, which al-Tanūkhī describes in opening the *Nishwār*, was based on the model of the Barmakids. As those anecdotes show, the Barmakids practiced partisan politics: they sought out clients and developed a reputation for munificence. These policies were part of a larger package. On the administrative level, the Barmakids dominated government and filled most positions with their clients; and on a symbolic level, they built a palace to rival that of the caliphs and carried themselves like kings. These attempts to unify the government under their control, combined with a tendency toward splendor—in short, the assertion of effective and symbolic power—constituted a challenge to the authority of the caliph. This was why Hārūn al-Rashīd destroyed them.

The second and alternative strategy was embodied by ᶜUbaydallāh b. Sulaymān, the wazir of al-Muᶜtaḍid. Though not prominent in historical chronicles, ᶜUbaydallāh is an important figure in the works of al-Tanūkhī and Hilāl al-Ṣābī that focus on bureaucrats; he was also the primary patron of the generation of bureaucrats who later served under al-Muqtadir. In contrast to the Barmakids, ᶜUbaydallāh espoused humility, discretion, and cooperation. He did not insist on centralized bureaucratic power and delegated sig-

124. al-Tanūkhī, *Nishwār*, 165–66. In a separate anecdote from al-Ṭabarī, an already incapacitated al-Muᶜtaḍid ordered his trusted servant Ṣāfī al-Ḥuramī, via hand gestures, to murder a member of the Ṣaffārid family; Ṣāfī was unwilling to perform this act without justification (*History*, 38:103–4).

125. See Lassner (*Shaping*, 43 regarding "the excruciating difficulty that confronted the caliph when dealing with an important member of the ᶜAbbāsid house."

126. Miskawayh, *Tajārib*, 8. A similar instance: the caliph al-Muᶜtazz's brother al-Muʾayyad was murdered by suffocation, so that his body revealed no obvious incriminating marks (al-Ṭabarī, *History*, 35:132).

127. Miskawayh, *Tajārib*, 103–4, 113.

nificant authority to the Banū al-Furāt. When informed that he was commonly thought of as dependent upon them, he responded: "Take note: I am a prisoner in the hands of any capable person."[128] We might note that despite, or perhaps because of this nonhierarchical attitude, nobody ever plotted against him. ʿUbaydallāh was also considerate of nonbureaucratic colleagues: for example, he showed concern that the military chief Badr not fall into disfavor with al-Muʿtaḍid. Most importantly, ʿUbaydallāh was respectful of the authority of the caliph. He was always submissive in the caliph's presence and took care not to anger him. An interesting anecdote shows how ʿUbaydallāh intentionally cultivated this attitude. When a wild animal supposedly ran amok in the royal palace, ʿUbaydallāh scampered away in fear, whereupon al-Muʿtaḍid promptly killed the animal. ʿUbaydallāh was criticized for his cowardice; but he informed a colleague that he intentionally demonstrated weakness before the caliph, as a way of communicating that he had no pretensions to power.[129] These strategies resulted in harmony among the various branches of the state, which was captured in a popular saying:

> At no time has there ever been a combination of caliph, wazir, chief of the *dīwān*, and chief of the military like al-Muʿtaḍid billāh, Abū al-Qāsim ʿUbaydallāh b. Sulaymān, Abū al-ʿAbbās b. al-Furāt, and Badr. Under them, control of affairs was stable, government orderly, prosperity abundant, and wealth free-flowing.[130]

In the reign of al-Muqtadir, these differing ways of approaching court politics were embodied by Ibn al-Furāt and ʿAlī b. ʿĪsā. Contemporaries already saw these two men as a pair of opposites and compared them.[131] Ibn al-Furāt, in the tradition of the Barmakids, was a champion of partisan politics. He strove for unity among a faction of bureaucrats by being fiercely loyal to his clients. He indulged loyalists with positions and grants of money; when he (or more accurately the caliph) needed cash, he vehemently refused to take money back from his clients, stating "what could be worse ... than to appoint associates ... then remove their benefits and positions with my own hand, during my tenure? Death would be easier than that."[132] When protégés betrayed him, he was quick to forgive. Yet, after decades of such policies, Ibn al-Furāt was continually betrayed, and in the glory years of 296–312/908–924 he spent more time in prison than in office. As a result, he became bitter. In his third and final wazirate he remarked: "In considering all the bad things that have happened to me, all of them were perpetrated by people I

128. Hilāl al-Ṣābī, *Wuzarāʾ*, 278. For a different version with a similar message, see al-Tanūkhī, *Nishwār*, 8:262.

129. Hilāl al-Ṣābī, *Rusūm*, 43–44.

130. Hilāl al-Ṣābī, *Wuzarāʾ*, 209.

131. In Hilāl al-Ṣābī's *Wuzarāʾ*, 72; the first section on Ibn al-Furāt begins with a contrast between this bureaucrat and ʿAlī b. ʿĪsā.

132. Hilāl al-Ṣābī, *Wuzarāʾ*, 113.

favored."[133] Disillusioned, Ibn al-Furāt allowed his son al-Muḥassin to abuse and kill several bureaucrats, and justified the violence by saying: "I have treated people well in two tenures; they were not grateful to me, but rather plotted for my blood. By God I will now follow the opposite course!"[134] In the end, this once indulgent and forgiving patron left a trail of blood.

Beyond adhering to a particular faction, Ibn al-Furāt also saw the entire bureaucratic class as natural allies, particularly vis-à-vis the military. On a number of occasions he tried to protect rival bureaucrats, for he believed in professional solidarity. As the quotations above indicate, he was disappointed with the fruits of his labor. In his view, bureaucrats were meant to oppose and dominate the military, which we see in his statement that "the sword is a follower, the pen is a leader; it is rare that the sword dominates the pen without bringing destruction."[135] This attitude of inherent opposition translated into his personal relations, as we frequently hear that Ibn al-Furāt was the enemy of Sawsan, Shafīᶜ al-Luʾluʾī, Shafīᶜal-Muqtadirī, Naṣr, and Muʾnis. This policy also backfired, as it was a unified military, led by all the prominent generals, who demanded the execution of Ibn al-Furāt in 312/924. In short, Ibn al-Furāt's intentional hostility to the military brought about his own demise.

Finally, Ibn al-Furāt had an ambiguous relationship with the caliph. On the one hand he portrayed himself as a loyal client of the caliph: ensuring al-Muqtadir's succession, reconquering provinces, and providing the caliph with as much spending money as possible. Ibn al-Furāt was therefore genuinely bitter that the caliph repeatedly dismissed him.[136] Yet to judge strictly by his actions, it is more accurate to see Ibn al-Furāt as competing with the caliph for authority. In the governmental sphere, he encouraged the appointment of a young caliph precisely in order to dominate state administration himself and is even said to have governed "in the style of the caliph."[137] He was the patron par excellence, distributing largesse on unheard of scales for bureaucrats of this era. More symbolically, Ibn al-Furāt was extravagant, expending large sums of money on delicacies such as ice. As a counter to the caliph's authority, Ibn al-Furāt insisted on living in the official waziral palace and spent a huge amount of money to refurbish it. These various aspects of his play for authority came together during the visit of the Byzantine envoys. Not only did Ibn al-Furāt plan the whole event, giving directions to the entire court elite and even instructing the caliph how to speak, he also hosted the envoys at his official residence in an elaborate ceremony that was a nearly identical precursor to the ceremony at the royal palace. In short, Ibn al-Furāt styled himself as a ruler, in everything but title. Eventually neither the caliph nor the military tolerated such pretensions.

133. al-Tanūkhī, *Nishwār*, 2:253.

134. Hilāl al-Ṣābī, *Wuzarāʾ*, 121.

135. Hilāl al-Ṣābī, *Wuzarāʾ*, 83.

136. He ridiculed the caliph's pliability and indecision (Hilāl al-Ṣābī, *Wuzarāʾ*, 134).

137. Miskawayh, *Tajārib*, 13.

In other words, Ibn al-Furāt saw court life strictly as a series of competitions: his faction against other factions, his profession against other professions, himself against the caliph. His obsession with factionalism and hostility is clear in a dialogue with Ibn al-Buhlūl. When this judge disproved allegations that ʿAlī b. ʿĪsā was a Qarmatian, Ibn al-Furāt accused the judge of being partial to ʿAlī. The qāḍī then reminded Ibn al-Furāt that he was a nonpartisan observer, and had defended Ibn al-Furāt in similar circumstances only a few years earlier.[138] Ibn al-Furāt refused to see court life as anything but mutual opposition; he perceived a system with built-in competition, and could think in no other terms—in effect, he followed one set of rules to its logical conclusion. But by seeing his world as "us against them," he incited opposition in a system that already encouraged it. He failed to realize that the best way to survive such a system was not through vehement partisanship, but through broad relationships that defied and actually undermined competition. This is related to Ibn al-Furāt's second failure: he did not realize that the competition instilled within court politics could not be won, least of all by a bureaucrat; he confused administrative responsibility, which the bureaucrats possessed, with the real power of military might, majesty, and legitimacy. Ultimately, it was the caliph who dominated court society, and the military who could destroy it; the bureaucrats were simply pawns.

ʿAlī b. ʿĪsā, by contrast, was more in the mold of ʿUbaydallāh b. Sulaymān. First of all, he was not nearly as partisan or faction-oriented as Ibn al-Furāt; he would not grant his employees widespread powers, and even thought it unethical to appoint his sons. More important was his attitude to the military: like ʿUbaydallāh, ʿAlī saw governance as a collaborative endeavor that required cooperation, rather than a prize to be fought over in competition with the military. He therefore nurtured close relations with several generals; he was protected by Gharīb and Naṣr and was particularly close with Abū al-Hayjāʾ and Muʾnis. In several instances we get the impression that ʿAlī and Muʾnis worked together for the benefit of the state, with little concern for competition between professions. In short, while ʿAlī recognized that competition was an integral part of court life, he was never consumed by it as Ibn al-Furāt was and was therefore rarely disillusioned or bitter.

Even more striking is ʿAlī's attitude towards the caliph. Unlike Ibn al-Furāt, who competed for authority, ʿAlī was submissive to caliphal authority. When Ibn al-Furāt argued for a weak caliph, ʿAlī argued for a competent ruler. When important decisions were to be made, ʿAlī always sought the caliph's approval; and when he was appointed wazir, he maintained a modest retinue and lived in his private home, leaving extravagance and majesty to the caliph. ʿAlī also recognized that periodic dismissal was an expression of the caliph's authority and could not be contested. Thus, he usually tried to resign, rather than plot to retain his job. Through a combination of alliance with military figures, and

138. Hilāl al-Ṣābī, *Wuzarāʾ*, 319.

personal submission to the caliph, ʿAlī remained safe over a long period of violent court turmoil.

This brings us to the question of power. It has been asserted that the early years of al-Muqtadir's reign saw the apex of bureaucratic power for this era of the Abbasid Empire, certainly since the downfall of the Barmakids; and the man who wielded this power most was Ibn al-Furāt. I believe that this is a misconception of power. Ibn al-Furāt and his colleagues certainly controlled state administration; but this was not power, at least not power relative to other members of the court elite. The simplest proof of the bureaucrats' lack of power is the continual removal of wazirs; Ibn al-Furāt alone was dismissed three times in twelve years. In short, bureaucrats could not retain possession of their own positions.

Instead, we should understand power as the ability to regulate, manipulate, and benefit from court politics. According to this conception, the caliph, and to a certain extent the military, possessed power; the bureaucrats did not. This was what Ibn al-Furāt refused to accept, and what ʿAlī b. ʿĪsā very willingly acknowledged. The lesson we learn from Ibn al-Furāt is that the Abbasid court was designed in such a way that bureaucrats could not seize power; the lesson we learn from ʿAlī b. ʿĪsā is that, in this world of imposed competition and instability, the main goal is, perhaps, survival.[139]

---

139. *Kennedy and van Berkel (in van Berkel et al, *Crisis and Continuity*) have arrived at similar conclusions, at least in regard to bureaucratic influence vis-à-vis the military. Van Berkel notes that, while this era is often considered the "heyday" of the vizier, "one cannot escape the impression that it is the military, rather than the bureaucrats, who dictate court politics" (66, reiterated at 77, 86); and Kennedy asserts: "Although many sources for this period ... put great emphasis on the influence and activities of civil administrators, it is clear that the military increasingly controlled the political life of the caliphate" (111).

Conclusion

Having examined the social and political dynamics that typify various groups, we can now make more general remarks about the system of relations and power at the Abbasid court. The center and guiding force behind the system was the caliph, who held virtually absolute power. In theory, this power was limited by divine law, justice, and obligations of patronage; in practice, the caliph could remove any official with little need for justification. The practical limitation of the caliph's power was that he needed specialized assistance in governing the state and needed to delegate authority. Over the course of Abbasid history, the caliphs developed standard strategies for manipulating their subordinates and undermining the latter's ability to accumulate or seize power. These policies in turn shaped the internal dynamics of each social group, and court relations in general. The goal of this study has been to elucidate caliphal policy, the resulting patterns of relations, and how officials responded to or opposed these policies for their own benefit.

Social Groups: Manipulated and Undermined

The group whose standing at the court changed the most during the Abbasid period was the extended royal family. Under the early Abbasid caliphs, royalty held some of the most important posts in the state; by the late third/ninth century, they were relegated to religious and ritual posts that forced them to legitimize the caliph and exposed them to popular abuse. More than any other individuals at court, members of the royal family were completely dependent upon the caliph for their well-being. They had no practical means of challenging his authority, no indispensable skill to offer; their sole leverage was that they enjoyed a degree of respect from court officials and the general populace. However, the caliphs further undermined the status of the extended royal family by emphasizing the importance of their own particular branch of the Abbasid family. This was the primary role of the princes; their prominence emphasized dynastic succession, which legitimized the reigning caliph and simultaneously distanced the larger royal family from power.

The most complex and important set of relations for the caliph to balance were those with his military clients. The caliph needed these men for the defense of the state and for his own personal protection. They were also very expensive to acquire or replace. These warriors, however, posed a tremendous threat to the caliph in that they could forcibly remove him from the throne, as witnessed, repeatedly, in previous Abbasid history. The caliphs responded to this dilemma with various policies. Regarding his officials in the palace, the caliph divided authority between the eunuchs and the chamberlain. The former had jurisdiction over the inner palace—the caliph's personal space—and the latter controlled outer areas of the palace and the entire royal complex. The potential power of the eunuchs was also diluted by the caliph's reliance on several eunuchs for any given period. The caliph thereby discouraged the development of a hierarchy in the palace, which prevented the consolidation of power in the hands of any particular official.

This principle of divide and rule was also applied to the army. The caliph usually had one main general who supervised military policy and cultivated a very personal relationship with him. However, the caliph limited the power of this general by dividing the armed forces into independent units, some of which were attached to prominent commanders who were not under the direct command of the senior general, while other units seem to have had no fixed commanding officers. As with palace officials, the army had no clear hierarchy at the highest ranks; responsibilities were divided, and central military command was retained only by the caliph.

The same policy of fragmenting the power of subordinates was applied most severely to the bureaucrats. These officials were replaced at frequent intervals and were encouraged to form factions and scheme against one another. The caliphs fostered this pervasive atmosphere of instability among bureaucrats more aggressively than among the military for several reasons. Bureaucrats were more plentiful and cheaper to acquire: they reproduced themselves, which much of the military elite did not. Their skills seem to have been less appreciated by the caliphs, who, after all, were generally trained in the martial arts but not in accounting and penmanship; and the caliphs seem to have developed deeper personal attachments to military clients than to bureaucrats.

What's more, it seems that court rivalries and politicking were channeled through bureaucratic rather than military infighting. The most dramatic public events at court were interrogations of bureaucrats, which forced these men to incriminate one another for the benefit of the caliph. In addition, the military and even court women competed for power via bureaucratic proxies: Naṣr and Mufliḥ dueled over the status of Ibn al-Furāt, and Naṣr and Muʾnis did the same concerning ʿAlī b. ʿĪsā. In such cases, military patrons and/or allies retained their own positions regardless of the outcome of these competitions, and only the bureaucrats suffered consequences. With little respect from the caliph, and serving as the pawns for the rest of the court elite, the bureaucrats occupied the most vulnerable position at court.

The one member of the court elite who was not perceived as a competitor of the caliph, and whose influence was not systematically undermined, was the royal mother. The caliph's bond with his mother was probably the only relationship he experienced that was not overwhelmingly influenced by political interests; indeed, the only time the sources truly depict the caliph as an ordinary human being—his strictly human, non-symbolic side—is when he is with his mother. She could be trusted, since her interests were entirely linked to those of her son; what was good for him was good for her. She also benefited from her status as a woman: she was not accessible to most men, which created the illusion that she was outside the system of intrigue; and she was protected by the taboo against hurting women. Eventually her sanctified status crumbled due to repeated involvement in the political arena; and when her son perished, so did her access to power. Until that point, however, she had more latitude in her political behavior, and met with less opposition, than anyone else at court.

Such were the basic patterns along which court society was organized. Yet within this framework, the manipulation of the court community varied with different caliphs. Al-Muʿtaḍid recognized that constant change damaged the administration of the state, so he employed methods of maintaining control without changing personnel. He developed strong ties with the military by participating in campaigns and acquiring many military clients, but at the same time reinforced the diversity and fragmentation of the army by inducting new units and keeping them separated. His manipulation of the bureaucracy was especially effective, as he instilled fear in the wazir and undermined the latter's authority, yet maintained administrative stability by not replacing him. Al-Muʿtaḍid thus established a stable regime in which no important official could threaten the caliph.

Al-Muqtadir, less astute and experienced than his father, was not as successful at manipulating subordinates while maintaining stability. In all fairness, he reigned during a period of severe economic decline that had possibly taken root before his accession. Nevertheless, his policies exacerbated the decline of the state. Instead of intimidating bureaucrats, as his father had done, al-Muqtadir replaced them on a regular basis. In the very short term this seemed attractive: the caliph was promised ever increasing stipends and fines, and the only men who really suffered were the bureaucrats. Within about ten years, however, this policy brought about administrative abuse and corruption, which could never be corrected. Al-Muqtadir's failures with regard to the military were equally dire: at first he failed to distribute power among his generals, relying too heavily on Muʾnis; and then he abandoned his relations with Muʾnis and fell back upon his supposedly divinely sanctioned status as caliph, which proved entirely ineffective on the battlefield.

In response to the policies of the caliphs, members of the military and bureaucracy developed strategies of their own for maximizing power. Fearful of internal military opposition, the Abbasid caliphs had come to rely upon personal clients to command the army; these clients understood that their own fate was tied to that of their patrons and generally remained loyal. Gratitude and self interest coincided in creating strong bonds between client and caliph, certainly much stronger than existed for bureaucrats. To strengthen their position within a fragmented army, generals had to maintain good relations with independent units and opportunistic soldiers. This generally meant acquiring enough money to keep the troops satisfied, and to attract unaffiliated soldiers when necessary. Generals tried to achieve this by establishing alliances with wazirs and by scheming to promote friendly bureaucrats to important positions that entailed access to funds. As state finances declined, this strategy unraveled, as soldiers continually changed allegiances in search of pay. Eventually Muʾnis stumbled upon an effective alternative: occupy a province, collect local taxes, attract troops, and then make a play for power in the capital.

The bureaucrats responded to the instability and vulnerability of their positions in divergent ways. One strategy was embodied by Ibn al-Furāt: seek a factional power base, compete vigorously with rival bureaucrats and generals, and try to usurp authority from the caliph. A similar set of policies had ended in tragedy for the Barmakids; Ibn al-Furāt repeated their failure, not recognizing the inherent weakness of the bureaucrats relative to the caliph and the military. ʿAlī b. ʿĪsā espoused a different approach: accept caliphal disenchantment and betrayal by colleagues and seek out alliances and protection with members of other groups. ʿAlī did not manage to impose his fiscal policies; but he did succeed in retaining an honored and influential position at court for decades.

The Mechanisms of Power

We can now try to consolidate the trends discussed above into a compact understanding of how power was acquired and manipulated. In general, power was based upon personal relations, historical precedent, and practical skills, in that order. The caliph dominated the court, for he had a network of relations with military clients, and an inherited and continually cultivated image of majesty; the extent to which he was a skilled ruler had serious consequences for the state but had little bearing on the caliph's appointment to or retention of his post. The powerful members of the court possessed one or both of the two important elements of power: the caliph's mother enjoyed the closest of relations with the caliph, and was endowed with respect and protection as a woman; military clients developed close bonds with the caliph; and even the royal family retained a degree of influence due to their historical status as relatives of the caliph and the Prophet. The bureaucrats, however, had the weakest relations with the caliph, and commanded little respect among the court elite, which meant they had limited influence over court politics. Like the military, the bureaucrats were needed at court because they possessed necessary skills; but for the most part the caliph could find replacements to supply such skills.

Competition at court thus involved undermining a rival's hold on these basic forms of power. Small-scale plotting usually entailed attacks on someone's competence which was often enough to topple the unstable bureaucrats who had no stronger base of power than their skills. From here plotting escalated to attacks on the honor and prestige of a rival and undermining his image; and ultimately to elaborate schemes designed to upset personal relations—usually with the caliph—with allegations of treason. The most powerful members of the court—Muʾnis, Naṣr, Umm Mūsā—could only be threatened by destroying their bonds to the caliph, which was the basis of their power.

These forms of power were systematized through spatial relations. The caliph's mother and select military clients, whom the caliph trusted most at court, had permanent positions in the palace and hence had access to the ultimate center of authority. By contrast, members of the extended royal family were distanced from the palace—and the caliph—as punishment, and bureaucrats could generally get access to the caliph only through intermediaries. This system of spatial relations and access was not simply a symbolic representation of power, it was the main mechanism by which power was manipulated on a daily basis.

As the state declined, the power of personal relations and sanctified images waned. Between 317/929 and 320/932, the caliph al-Muqtadir could no longer dominate court politics, for his network of relations and image of majesty had become damaged. The murder of the caliph in 320/932 put an end to these two pillars of power: personal bonds were broken in the worst possible way, as a client brought about the gruesome death of his patron, in public; simultaneously, the caliph's majestic image was systematically stripped and destroyed. This signaled a broader change in court politics: personal relations, particularly within the military, became very weak as soldiers embraced opportunism; and the caliph, his mother, and the extended royal family all lost their sanctified status at court. With personal relations and traditional myths shattered, the importance of practical skills increased, particularly the ability to raise money. As a result, in the next era of Abbasid politics, the military and bureaucracy survive as important groups, due to the skills they provided, while the caliph and his family fade from power.

The Individual and Society

All the issues discussed above involve the relative power of different groups. We can now turn our attention to the place of the individual. First, we should examine the assumption that affiliation with a particular social group shaped an individual's participation at court. Social groups were very strictly defined: there was absolutely no mobility between groups; and there was little overlap of functions, as royalty, soldiers, secretaries, and judges generally performed distinct roles throughout their lifetimes, and did not intrude on the jurisdiction of others. More importantly, members of a given group enjoyed the same opportunities and confronted similar problems: royalty suffered systematic removal from power; bureaucrats endured instability, competition, and cycles of violence; generals enjoyed relatively long tenures and closer relations with the caliph; and judges were forced to balance deference, prudence, and justice. In short, it seems that people had permanent membership in a particular social group, and this membership defined the social and political framework of their lives.

The fundamental importance of affiliation with a group did not, however, necessarily lead to group solidarity. In fact, quite the opposite was true: the caliphs deliberately encouraged divisiveness within social groups at court and were largely successful in this endeavor. The bureaucrats constantly schemed against one another with caliphal provocation; the eunuch and chamberlain in the palace supported different bureaucratic candidates and remained rivals rather than partners; and the military was kept divided and balanced so that at crucial moments, such as the coups of 296/908 or 317/929, one group could be played against another. Indeed, the most effective strategy for countering caliphal tyranny and endemic competition was the development of cross-group alliances.

The most successful members of the court—Muʾnis, Naṣr, ʿAlī b. ʿĪsā, and al-Sayyida—consistently pursued alliances with members of other groups. Each person at court had advantages and disadvantages; in combination they could maximize their positions of influence and minimize vulnerability.

Given the importance of social position, how much latitude did individuals have within the structure of their particular positions? The binary oppositions set up by authors such as Hilāl al-Ṣābī and al-Tanūkhī indicate that individuals could vary tremendously within the limits of a given social position. In the bureaucracy, Ibn al-Furāt was competitive, extravagant, and power hungry; ʿAlī b. ʿĪsā, on the other hand, was noncombative, practical, and relatively humble. The judges Abū ʿUmar and Ibn al-Buhlūl are depicted as near opposites: the former was gullible and unscrupulous, the latter wise and principled. The position with the greatest flexibility for personality was that of the caliph. On the one hand caliphs inherited standard policies and systems of etiquette that encouraged society to see them as a figure, "The Caliph," and not as a unique individual. On the other hand, the caliphate was a hereditary position, based entirely on familial identity, irrespective of merit or qualifications. This meant that divergent characters could obtain the office, and with virtually absolute powers were not subject to supervision and selection to the same extent as everyone else.

Such latitude is relevant, however, only if individuals could have a serious impact on court politics. Here we might note that the personal divergences among bureaucrats and judges were ultimately inconsequential. Bureaucrats had differing personalities and strategies, but in the long run none of them established lasting government policy and certainly could not alter the structure of power at court. Similarly, judges had different understandings of justice, but in any case, their rulings went unheeded. Both these groups were dominated by the caliph, who determined state policy, guilt and punishment, and the fate of nearly everyone at court by his own will. It is therefore divergences among the caliphs that are truly important in shaping court life. Indeed, the personality and policies of one caliph—al-Muʿtaḍid—determined the patterns of court politics for one generation, while his drastically different son al-Muqtadir pushed court politics in an altogether different direction.

The only other individuals with the power to fundamentally change the court were generals. With control over military force, these men could bring down virtually anyone, including the caliph, and could even alter the despotic nature of the court. Consequently, the most important relationship at court was between the caliph and his generals, who were the only social actors capable of hurting one another. The goal for the caliph was to convince military clients that his rule was beneficial for them. When al-Muqtadir emphasized his divinely sanctioned dynastic right to rule, and broke the bonds with his main client, he destroyed this partnership and made the military realize as they had realized generations earlier—that the caliph was essentially weak and replaceable. The myth of legitimate caliphal authority was shattered, and the Abbasid caliphs would lose all power.

Finally, we might ask whether individuals could retain independence of the court, develop a "personal life" insulated from their professional lives, or even retire to another social world. Earlier we saw that to a great extent professional and personal, public and private aspects of life overlapped at the court. This was particularly true of the caliph: his entire person was a public image, his every action had potential political implications; he could have no identity outside of the court. The same is more or less true for military clients, who were imported specifically to fulfill a state function, necessitating participation at court; accordingly, these men seemingly developed few connections to local society. Thus, when the state declined and violence set in, the caliph and his military elite had no way to escape, and generally suffered violent deaths. This is where bureaucrats and judges had a distinct advantage: as local residents with wide cultural connections and possible noncourtly interests, these individuals had the option of retiring from court life and becoming civilians. Their weak personal bonds with other members of the court ironically meant that they could sever relations with court society altogether. In the long run this provided bureaucrats and judges with a potential escape from the hostilities of a collapsing state, while the caliph and his military elite, their identities entirely enmeshed with their court functions, were doomed to endure the decline.

Bibliography

Primary Sources

Anonymous. *Kitāb al-ʿUyūn wa-l-ḥadāiq fī akhbār al-ḥaqāiq*. Edited by M. J. de Goeje and P. de Jong. Brill, 1869.

ʿArīb b. Sʿad al-Qurṭubī. *Ṣilat tārīkh al-Ṭabarī*. Edited by M. J. de Goeje. Leiden, 1897.

al-Hamadhānī, Muḥammad b. ʿAbd al-Malik. *Takmilat Tārīkh al-Ṭabarī*. Edited by A. Y. Kanʿān. Beirut, 1961.

Ibn al-Athīr, ʿAlī b. Muḥammad. *al-Kāmil fī al-tārīkh*, vols. 7 and 8. Beirut, 1979.

Ibn al-Jawzī, ʿAbd al-Raḥmān. *al-Muntaẓam fī tārīkh al-mulūk wa-l-umam*, vols. 5, 6, 7. Beirut, 1968.

Ibn Kathīr. *al-Bidāya wa-l-nihāya*. Beirut, 1966.

Ibn Khallikān, Aḥmad b. Muḥammad. *Kitāb Wafayāt al-aʿyān*. Translated by M. G. de Slane as *Ibn Khallikān's Biographical Dictionary*. 5 vols. Paris, 1843–1871.

Ibn Taghrībirdī, Yūsuf. *al-Nujūm al-zāhira fī mulūk Miṣr wa-l-Qāhira*, vol. 3. Cairo, 1932.

Ibn Abī Usaybiʿa, Aḥmad b. al-Qāsim. *ʿUyūn al-anbā fī ṭabaqāt al-aṭibbāʾ*. Edited by A. Müller. 2 vols. Cairo, 1882.

Ibn al-Zubayr, al-Qāḍī al-Rashīd. *Kitāb al-Dhakhāʾir wa-l-tuḥaf*. Edited by M. Ḥamīd-Allāh and S. al-Munajjid. Kuwait, 1959. Translated by G. al-Hijjawi al-Qaddumi as *Book of Gifts and Rarities*. Harvard, 1996.

al-Khaṭīb al-Baghdādī, Aḥmad b. Thābit. *Tārīkh Baghdād*. 14 vols. Beirut, 1968.

al-Masʿūdī, ʿAlī b. al-Ḥusayn. *Murūj al-dhahab wa maʿādin al-jawhar*. Edited and translated by C. Barbier de Meynard. 8 vols. Paris, 1861–1917.

——. *Kitāb al-Tanbīh wa-l-Ashrāf*. Beirut, 1965

al-Māwardī, Abū al-Ḥasan ʿAlī b. Muḥammad. *al-Aḥkām al-sulṭānīyya wa-l-wilāyāt al-dīnīyya*. Cairo, 1966.

Miskawayh. *Tajārib al-umam*. Edited by H. F. Amedroz and D. S. Margoliouth. Vol. 1. Oxford, 1921.

——. *The Eclipse of the Abbasid Caliphate: Original Chronicles of the Fourth Islamic Century*. Translated by H. F. Amedroz and D. S. Margoliouth. Oxford, 1921.

al-Ṣābī, Hilāl b. al-Muḥassin. *Tuḥfat al-umarāʾ fī tārīkh al-wuzarāʾ*. Edited by ʿA. A. Farrāj. Cairo, 1958.

——. *Rusūm dār al-khilāfa*. Translated by E. Salem as *The Rules and Regulations of the ʿAbbāsid Court*. Beirut, 1977.

al-Shābushtī, Abū al-Ḥasan. *Kitāb al-Diyārāt*. Edited by G. Awad. Baghdad, 1951.

al-Ṭabarī, Muḥammad b. Jarīr. *Tārīkh al-rusul wa-l-mulūk*. Edited by M. J. de Goeje et al. Leiden, 1879–1901.

——. *The History of al-Ṭabarī*, vol. 30: *The ʿAbbāsid Caliphate in Equilibrium*. Translated by C. E. Bosworth. Albany: State University of New York Press, 1989.

——. *The History of al-Ṭabarī*, vol. 34: *Incipient Decline*. Translated by J. Kraemer. Albany: State University of New York Press, 1989.

——. *The History of al-Ṭabarī*, vol. 35: *The Crisis of the ʿAbbāsid Caliphate*. Translated by G. Saliba. Albany: State University of New York Press, 1985.

——. *The History of al-Ṭabarī*, vol. 36: *The Revolt of the Zanj*. Translated by D. Waines. Albany: State University of New York Press, 1992.

——. *The History of al-Ṭabarī*, vol. 37: *The ʿAbbāsid Recovery*. Translated by P. Fields. Albany: State University of New York Press, 1987.

——. *The History of al-Ṭabarī*, vol. 38: *The Return of the Caliphate to Baghdad*. Translated by F. Rosenthal. Albany: State University of New York Press, 1985.

al-Tanūkhī, al-Muḥassin b. ʿAlī. *Nishwār al-muḥāḍara wa-akhbār al-mudhākara*. Edited by ʿA. Shāljī. 8 vols. Beirut, 1971–1973.

——. *Kitāb al-Faraj baʿd al-shidda*. Edited by ʿA Shāljī. 5 vols. Cairo, 1978. Partial translation by J. Bray as *Stories of Piety and Prayer, Deliverance Follows Adversity*. New York: New York University Press, 2019.

Yāqūt b. ʿAbdallāh al-Ḥamawī. *Muʿjam al-buldān*. Edited by F. Wüstenfeld. 6 vols. Göttingen, 1866–1873.

——. *Irshād al-arīb ilā maʿrifat al-adīb* (*Muʿjam al-udabāʾ*). Edited by D. S. Margoliouth. 7 vols. Leiden, 1907–1927.

Secondary Sources

(An asterisk * indicates publications that postdate the original research undertaken for this text as a dissertation in 1994).

Abbott, N. *Two Queens of Baghdad*. Chicago: University of Chicago Press, 1946.

Ahmed, L. *Women and Gender in Islam: Historical Roots of a Modern Debate*. New Haven: Yale University Press, 1992.

Ahsan, M. *Social Life Under the Abbasids*. London: Longman, 1979.

Ali, Y. *The Holy Quran: Text Translation and Commentary*. 3rd ed. Lahore: Shaikh Muhammad Ashraf Publishers, 1938.

*Allehbi, M. "'It Is Permitted for the Amīr but not the Qāḍī': The Military-Administrative Genealogy of Coercion in Abbasid Criminal Justice." *Islamic Law and Society* 30 (2022): 65–95. https://doi.org/10.1163/15685195-bja10030.

Ayalon, D. *The Mamluk Military Society*. London: Variorum Reprints, 1979.

——. "On the Eunuchs in Islam." *Jerusalem Studies in Arabic and Islam* 1 (1979): 67–124.

*van Berkel, M. "Politics of Access at the Court of the Caliph." In *New Perspectives on Power and Political Representation from Ancient History to the Present Day: Repertoires of Representation*, edited by H. Kaal and D. Slootjes, 26–36. Leiden: Brill, 2019.

*van Berkel, M. "The Young Caliph and His Wicked Advisors: Women and Power Politics under Caliph al-Muqtadir (r. 295–320/908–932)." *Al-Masaq* 19 (2007): 3–15. https://doi.org/10.1080/09503110601068414.

*——. "The Vizier and the Harem Stewardess: Mediation in a Discharge Case at the Court of Caliph al-Muqtadir." In *Abbasid Studies II: Occasional Papers of the School of ʿAbbasid Studies Leuven 28 June–1 July 2004*, edited by J. Nawas, 303–18. Leuven: Peeters, 2010.

*van Berkel, M., N. M. El-Cheikh, H. Kennedy, and L. Osti. *Crisis and Continuity at the Abbasid Court: Formal and Informal Politics in the Caliphate of al-Muqtadir (295–320/908–32)*. Leiden: Brill, 2013.

Bonebakker, S. A. "*Adab* and the Concept of *belles-lettres*." In *ʿAbbasid Belles-Lettres*, edited by J. Bray,

T. M. Johnstone, J. D. Lathan, and R. B. Serjeant, 16–30. Cambridge: Cambridge University Press, 1990. https://doi.org/10.1017/CHOL9780521240161.003.
Bowen, H. *The Life and Times of ʿAlī b. ʿĪsā, "the Good Vizier."* Cambridge: Cambridge University Press, 1928.
*Bray, J. "A Caliph and His Public Relations." *Middle Eastern Literatures* 7 (2004): 159–70. https://doi.org/10.1080/1366616042000236851.
*——. "Ibn al-Muʿtazz and Politics: The Question of the *Fuṣūl Qiṣār*." *Oriens* 38 (2010): 107–43. https://doi.org/10.1163/187783710X536680.
*——. "Place and Self-Image: The Buhlūlids and Tanūḫids and Their Family Traditions." *Quaderni di Studi Arabi* NS 3 (2008): 39–66.
Busse, H. "Das Hofbudget des Chalifen al-Muʿtaḍid billāh (279/892–289/902)." *Der Islam* (1967): 11–36.
Canard, M. *Histoire de la dynastie des H'amdanides de Jazîra et de Syrie*. Paris: Presses universitaires de France, 1953.
Chejne, A. *Succession to the Rule in Islam*. Lahore: Ashraf, 1960.
Dozy, R. P. A. *Dictionnaire détailleé des noms des vêtements chez les Arabes*. Amsterdam: Müller, 1845.
Elias, N. *The Court Society*. New York: Pantheon, 1983.
*El Cheikh, N. "An Abbasid Caliphal Family." In *Approaches to the Byzantine Family*, edited by L Brubaker and S. Tougher, 327–44. Ashgate, 2013.
*——. "The Qahramâna in the Abbasid Court: Position and Functions." *Studia Islamica* 97 (2003): 41–55.
*——. "Revisiting the Abbasid Harems." *Journal of Middle East Women's Studies* 1 (2005): 1–19.
*——. "To Be a Prince in the Fourth/Tenth-Century Abbasid Court." In *Royal Courts in Dynastic States and Empires: A Global Perspective*, edited by J. Duindam, T. Artan, and M. Kunt, 199–216. Leiden: Brill, 2011. https://doi.org/10.1163/ej.9789004206229.i-444.49.
Fakkar, R. *At-Tanûhi et son livre: La déliverance après l'angoisse*. Cairo: L'Institut français d'archéologie orientale, 1955.
Fischel, W. *Jews in the Economic and Political Life of Medieval Islam*. New York: Ktav, 1969.
Forand, P. G. "The Development of Military Slavery under the Abbasid Caliphs of the Ninth Century A.D. (Third Century A.H.)." PhD diss., Princeton University, 1962.
——. "Relation of the Slave and the Client." *International Journal of Middle East Studies* 2 (1971): 59–66. https://doi.org/10.1017/S0020743800000878.
Geertz, C. "Centers, Kings, and Charisma: Reflections on the Symbolics of Power." In *Local Knowledge: Further Essays in Interpretive Anthropology*, 121–46. New York: Basic Books, 1983.
Glagow, R. *Das Kalifat des al-Muʿtaḍid billāh*. Bonn, 1968.
*Gordon, M. *The Breaking of a Thousand Swords: A History of the Turkish Military of Samarra (200–275 Ah/815–889 CE)*. Albany: State University of New York Press, 2000.
*Hamori, A., "Rising to Greet You: Some Comedies of Manners." *Middle Eastern Literatures* 11 (2008): 205–10. https://doi.org/10.1080/14752620802223806.
*al-Hasan, A. "The Financial Reforms of the Caliph al-Muʿtaḍid (279–89/892–901)." *Journal of Islamic Studies* 18 (2007): 1–13. https://doi.org/10.1093/jis/etl045.
*Kennedy, H. "Caliphs and Their Chroniclers." In *Texts, Documents and Artefacts: Islamic Studies in Honour of D. S. Richards*," edited by C. Robinson, 17–35. Leiden: Brill, 2003. https://doi.org/10.1163/9789047401797_005.
——. *The Prophet and the Age of the Caliphates*. London: Longman, 1986.

al-Kubaysī, A. *ʿAṣr al-khalīfa al-Muqtadir b'illāh, 295–320*. Najaf, 1974.
von Kremer, A. *The Orient under the Caliphs*. Translated by S. Khuda Bukhsh. Calcutta: University of Calcutta, 1920.
Lane-Poole, S. *A History of Egypt in the Middle Ages*. 4th ed. London: Cass, 1968.
Lassner, J. *The Shaping of ʿAbbāsid Rule*. Princeton: Princeton University Press, 1980.
——. *The Topography of Baghdad in the Early Middle Ages*. Detroit: Wayne State University Press, 1970.
Le Strange, G. *Baghdad during the Abbasid Caliphate*. Oxford, 1900.
Lewis, B. *The Political Language of Islam*. Chicago: University of Chicago Press, 1988.
Malti-Douglas, F. "The Classical Arabic Detective." *Arabica* 35 (1988): 59–91.
*——. "Texts and Tortures: The Reign of al-Muʿtaḍid and the Construction of Historical Meaning." *Arabica* 46 (1999): 313–36.
Margoliouth, D. S. *The Table-talk of a Mesopotamian Judge*. London: Royal Asiatic Society, 1922.
——. "The Table-talk of a Mesopotamian Judge." *Islamic Culture* 5 (1931): 352–71.
*Marmer, D. "Asset Management and Wealth Preservation in 3rd/9th Century Baghdad: The Case of Ibn al-Jaṣṣāṣ, the Jewelry Merchant." *Journal of Abbasid Studies* (forthcoming)
*——. "Greed Is Good: A Look at the Mercantile World of 3rd/9th Century Baghdad." *Journal of Abbasid Studies* 11 (2024): 1–26. https://doi.org/10.1163/22142371-00802020.
——. "The Political Culture of the Abbasid Court, 279–324 (A.H.)." PhD diss., Princeton, 1994.
Massignon, L. "Cadis et Naqibs." In *Opera Minora*, edited by Y. Moubarac. Beirut, 1963.
——. *The Passion of al-Hallaj: Mystic and Martyr of Islam*, vol. 1: *The Life of al-Hallaj*. Translated by H. Mason. Princeton: Princeton University Press, 1982.
Mez, A. *The Renaissance of Islam*. Translated by S. Khuda-Bukhsh and D. S. Margoliouth. New York: AMS Press, 1975.
Mottahedeh, R. "Bureaucracy and the Patrimonial State in Early Islamic Iran and Iraq." *al-Abhath* 29 (1981): 25–36. https://doi.org/10.1163/2589997X-02901007.
——. *Loyalty and Leadership in an Early Islamic Society*. Princeton: Princeton University Press, 1980.
*Osti, L. "ʿAbbāsid Intrigues: Competing for Influence at the Caliph's Court." *Al-Masāq* 20 (2008): 5–15.
*——. *History and Memory in the Abbasid Caliphate: Writing the Past in Medieval Arabic Literature*. London: Taurus, 2022.
*——. "The Remuneration of a Court Companion in Theory and Practice: A Case Study." *Journal of Abbasid Studies* 1 (2014): 85–107.
*——. "The Wisdom of Youth: Legitimising the Caliph Al-Muqtadir." *Al-Masāq* 19 (2007): 17–27. https://doi.org/10.1080/09503110601068430.
Peirce, L. *The Imperial Harem: Women and Sovereignty in the Ottoman Empire*. Oxford: Oxford University Press, 1993.
Pipes, D. *Slave Soldiers and Islam: The Genesis of a Military System*. New Haven: Yale University Press, 1978.
Sanders, P. *Ritual, Politics, and the City in Fatimid Cairo*. Albany: State University of New York Press, 1994.
Sourdel, D. *Le vizirat ʿabbāside de 749 à 936 (132 à 324 l'hégire)*. Damascus: Institut français, 1959.
——. "Questions de cérémonial abbaside." *Revue d'études islamiques* 28 (1960): 121–48.
Tyan, E. *Institutions du droit public musulman*, vol. 1, *"Le Califat."* Paris: Sirey, 1954.
Waines, D. "Caliph and Amir: A Study of the Socio-Economic Background of Medieval Political Power." PhD diss., McGill University, 1973.

——. "The Pre-Buyid Amirate: Two Views from the Past." *International Journal of Middle East Studies* 8 (1977): 339–48. https://doi.org/10.1017/S002074380002585X.

——. "The Third Century Internal Crisis of the Abbasids." *Journal of the Economic and Social History of the Orient* 20 (1977): 282–306. https://doi.org/10.2307/3631960.

Walther, W. *Woman in Islam*. London: Prior, 1981.

Walzer, R. *Regicide and Revolution: Speeches at the Trial of Louis XVI*. Cambridge: Cambridge University Press, 1974.

*Wickham, C. "Administrators' Time: The Social Memory of the Early Medieval State, East and West." In *Islamic Cultures, Islamic Contexts: Essays in Honor of Professor Patricia Crone*, edited by A. Ahmed, B. Sadeghi, R. G. Hoyland, and A. Silverstein, 430–67. Leiden: Brill, 2015. https://doi.org/10.1163/9789004281714_017.

Index

(Note: for individuals or themes that appear throughout the text, only the most important references are cited)

9781957454566.